TODAY'S TECHNICIAN

Classroom Manual for

Automotive Electricity and Electronics

TODAY'S TECHNICIAN

Classroom Manual for

Automotive Electricity and Electronics

Barry Hollembeak

Technical Training Inc.
Rochester Hills, Michigan

Jack Erjavec, Series Advisor

Columbus State Community College
Columbus, Ohio

030292

Delmar Publishers Inc.™

I(T)P™

NOTICE TO THE READER

Publisher does not warrant or guarantee any of the products described herein or perform any independent analysis in connection with any of the product information contained herein. Publisher does not assume, and expressly disclaims, any obligation to obtain and include information other than that provided to it by the manufacturer.

The reader is expressly warned to consider and adopt all safety precautions that might be indicated by the activities described herein and to avoid all potential hazards. By following the instructions contained herein, the reader willingly assumes all risks in connection with such instructions.

The publisher makes no representations or warranties of any kind, including but not limited to, the warranties of fitness for particular purpose or merchantability, nor are any such representations implied with respect to the material set forth herein, and the publisher takes no responsibility with respect to such material. The publisher shall not be liable for any special, consequential or exemplary damages resulting, in whole or in part, from the readers' use of, or reliance upon, this material.

Portions of materials contained herein have been reprinted with permission of General Motors Corporation, Service Technology Group.

COVER PHOTO: Courtesy of Ford Motor Company

DELMAR STAFF

    Senior Administrative Editor: Vernon Anthony
    Developmental Editor: Catherine Eads
    Project Editor: Eleanor Isenhart
    Production Coordinator: Karen Smith
    Art/Design Coordinator: Heather Brown

For information address Delmar Publishers Inc.
3 Columbia Circle, Box 15015
Albany, New York 12212-5015

COPYRIGHT © 1994
BY DELMAR PUBLISHERS INC.

The trademark ITP is used under license.

Printed in the United States of America
Published simultaneously in Canada
by Nelson Canada
a division of the Thomson Corporation

10 9 8 7 6 5 4 3 2 1 XXX 00 99 98 97 96 95 94

Library of Congress Catalog Card Number: 93-073929

ISBN: 0-8273-6182-3 (set)

CONTENTS

PREFACE

Unlike yesterday's mechanic, the technician of today and for the future must know the underlying theory of all automotive systems and be able to service and maintain those systems. Today's technician must also know how these individual systems interact with each other. Standards and expectations have been set for today's technician, and these must be met in order to keep the world's automobiles running efficiently and safely.

The *Today's Technician* series, by Delmar Publishers, features textbooks that cover all mechanical and electrical systems of automobiles and light trucks. Principal titles correspond with the eight major areas of ASE (National Institute for Automotive Service Excellence) certification. Additional titles include remedial skills and theories common to all of the certification areas and advanced or specialized subject areas that reflect the latest technological trends.

Each title is divided into two manuals: a Classroom Manual and a Shop Manual. Dividing the material into two manuals provides the reader with the information needed to begin a successful career as an automotive technician without interrupting the learning process by mixing cognitive and performance-based learning objectives.

Each Classroom Manual contains the principles of operation for each system and subsystem. It also discusses the design variations used by different manufacturers. The Classroom Manual is organized to build upon basic facts and theories. The primary objective of this manual is to allow the reader to gain an understanding of how each system and subsystem operates. This understanding is necessary to diagnose the complex automobile systems.

The understanding acquired by using the Classroom Manual is required for competence in the skill areas covered in the Shop Manual. All of the high priority skills, as identified by ASE, are explained in the Shop Manual. The Shop Manual also includes step-by-step instructions for diagnostic and repair procedures. Photo Sequences are used to illustrate many of the common service procedures. Other common procedures are listed and are accompanied with fine-line drawings and photographs that allow the reader to visualize and conceptualize the finest details of the procedure. The Shop Manual also contains the reasons for performing the procedures, as well as when that particular service is appropriate.

The two manuals are designed to be used together and are arranged in corresponding chapters. Not only are the chapters in the manuals linked together, the contents of the chapters are also linked. Both manuals contain clear and thoughtfully selected illustrations. Many of the illustrations are original drawings or photos prepared for inclusion in this series. This means that the art is a vital part of each manual.

The page layout is designed to include information that would otherwise break up the flow of information presented to the reader. The main body of the text includes all of the "need-to-know" information and illustrations. In the side margins are many of the special features of the series. Items such as definitions of new terms, common trade jargon, tools lists, and cross-references are placed in the margin, out of the normal flow of information so as not to interrupt the thought process of the reader. Each manual in this series is organized in a like manner and contains the same features.

Jack Erjavec, Series Advisor

Classroom Manual

To stress the importance of safe work habits, the Classroom Manual dedicates one full chapter to safety. Included in this chapter are common safety practices, safety equipment, and safe handling of hazardous materials and wastes. This includes information on MSDS sheets and OSHA regulations. Other features of this manual include:

Cognitive Objectives

These objectives define the contents of the chapter and define what the student should have learned upon completion of the chapter.
Each topic is divided into small units to promote easier understanding and learning.

Marginal Notes

Page numbers for cross-referencing appear in the margin. Some of the common terms used for components, and other bits of information, also appear in the margin. This provides an understanding of the language of the trade and helps when conversing with an experienced technician.

Cautions and Warnings

Throughout the text, cautions are given to alert the reader of potentially hazardous materials or unsafe conditions. Warnings are also given to advise the student of things that can go wrong if instructions are not followed or if a nonacceptable part or tool is used.

References to the Shop Manual

Reference to the appropriate page in the Shop Manual is given whenever necessary. Although the chapters of the two manuals are synchronized, material covered in other chapters of the Shop Manual may be fundamental to the topic discussed in the Classroom Manual.

A Bit of History

This feature gives the student a sense of the evolution of the automobile. This feature not only contains nice-to-know information, but also should spark some interest in the subject matter.

Summaries

Each chapter concludes with summary statements that contain the important topics of the chapter. These are designed to help the reader review the contents.

Terms to Know

A list of new terms appears next to the Summary. Definitions for these terms can be found in the Glossary at the end of the manual.

Review Questions

Short answer essay, fill-in-the-blank, and multiple-choice type questions follow each chapter. These questions are designed to accurately assess the student's competence in the stated objectives at the beginning of the chapter.

To stress the importance of safe work habits, the Shop Manual also dedicates one full chapter to safety. Other important features of this manual include:

Performance Objectives

These objectives define the contents of the chapter and define what the student should have learned upon completion of the chapter. These objectives also correspond with the list of required tasks for ASE certification. *Each ASE task is addressed.*

Although this textbook is not designed to simply prepare someone for the certification exams, it is organized around the ASE task list. These tasks are defined generically when the procedure is commonly followed and specifically when the procedure is unique for specific vehicle models. Imported and domestic model automobiles and light trucks are included in the procedures.

Photo Sequences

Many procedures are illustrated in detailed photo sequences. These detailed photographs show the students what to expect when they perform particular procedures. They also can provide a student a familiarity with a system or type of equipment, which the school may not have.

Marginal Notes

New terms are pulled out and defined. Common trade jargon also appears in the margin and gives some of the common terms used for components. This allows the reader to speak and understand the language of the trade, especially when conversing with an experienced technician.

Cautions and Warnings

Throughout the text, cautions are given to alert the reader of potentially hazardous materials or unsafe conditions. Warnings are also given to advise the student of things that can go wrong if instructions are not followed or if a nonacceptable part or tool is used.

References to the Classroom Manual

Reference to the appropriate page in the Classroom Manual is given whenever necessary. Although the chapters of the two manuals are synchronized, material covered in other chapters of the Classroom Manual may be fundamental to the topic discussed in the Shop Manual.

Customer Care

This feature highlights those little things a technician can do or say to enhance customer relations.

Tools Lists

Each chapter begins with a list of the Basic Tools needed to perform the tasks included in the chapter. Whenever a Special Tool is required to complete a task, it is listed in the margin next to the procedure.

Service Tips

Whenever a special procedure is appropriate, these are described in the text. These tips are generally those things commonly done by experienced technicians.

Case Studies

Case Studies concentrate on the ability to properly diagnose the systems. Each chapter ends with a case study in which a vehicle has a problem, and the logic used by a technician to solve the problem is explained.

Terms to Know

Terms in this list can be found in the Glossary at the end of the manual.

Diagnostic Chart

Chapters include detailed diagnostic charts linked with the appropriate ASE task. These charts list common problems and most probable causes. They also list a page reference in the Classroom Manual for better understanding of the system's operation and a page reference in the Shop Manual for details on the procedure necessary for correcting the problem.

ASE Style Review Questions

Each chapter contains ASE style review questions that reflect the performance objectives listed at the beginning of the chapter. These questions can be used to review the chapter as well as to prepare for the ASE certification exam.

Instructor's Guide

The Instructor's Guide is provided free of charge as part of the Today's Technician Series of automotive technology textbooks. It contains Lecture Outlines, Answers to Review Questions, Pretest and Test Bank including ASE style questions.

Classroom Manager

This complete ancillary package is designed to aid the instructor with classroom preparation and provide tools to measure student performance. For an affordable price, this comprehensive package contains:

Instructor's Guide
200 Transparency Masters
Answers to Review Questions

Lecture Outlines and Lecture Notes
Printed and Computerized Test Bank
Laboratory Worksheets and Practicals

Reviewers

Special thanks to the following instructors for reviewing this material:

Steve V. Hatch, Denver Automotive and Diesel College

Roger E. Adams, Pittsburgh State University

David W. Gilbert, Neo A & M College

Neal Clark, Erie Community College

Ken Kruse, Southwestern Technical College

Safety

Upon completion and review of this chapter, you should be able to:

- Explain how safety is a part of professionalism.
- Describe the basic safety rules of servicing electrical systems.
- Properly lift objects.
- Properly work around batteries.
- Explain the safety precautions associated with charging and starting system service.
- List and describe personal safety responsibilities.

- Classify fires and fire extinguishers.
- Describe the proper use of floor jacks and safety stands.
- Explain the safe use of hoists.
- Properly run the engine in the shop.
- List the safety precautions associated with servicing the air bag system.
- Explain the safety precautions that are necessary when servicing the antilock brake system.

Introduction

Being a professional technician requires more than knowledge of the vehicle systems; a technician should have an understanding of all the hazards in the work area. Your professionalism is expressed through your safe work habits. Safety is everyone's job. However, never assume the person working next to you is as cautious as you are. Be aware of what is going on around you.

As a professional technician, you should work to protect yourself and the people around you. In this chapter you will learn about the safety concerns associated with working on the vehicle's electrical system, and how to prevent injury through proper work procedures. In addition to basic shop safety, working on the electrical systems presents special concerns. A review of some of the basic shop safety practices is included, and how these practices relate to electrical service is discussed.

Personal Safety

Personal safety encompasses things that you do concerning dress and actions to prevent injury. Technicians must be aware of their responsibility to prevent injuries in the shop, and that their actions and attitudes reflect how seriously they accept that responsibility.

Dress and Appearance

Nothing displays professional pride and a positive attitude more than the way you dress. Customers are demanding a professional atmosphere in the service shop. Your appearance instills customer confidence, as well as expresses your attitude toward safety. The wearing of proper and clean clothes prevents injuries. Clothing that hangs out or fits loose can cause serious injury.

Long sleeve shirts should have their cuffs buttoned or rolled up tightly. Shirt tails should be tucked in at all times. If a necktie is to be worn in the shop area, tuck it inside your shirt. The clip-on type is recommended if you must wear a tie. Shop coats provide for safe clothing and a professional appearance (Figure 1-1).

Long hair is a serious safety concern. Very serious injury can result if the hair becomes caught in rotating machinery, fan belts, or fans. If your hair is long enough to touch the bottom of the collar, it should be tied and tucked under a hat.

Shop Manual
Chapter 1, page 1

Figure 1-1 Shop coats are professional and safe clothing.

Jewelry has no place in the automotive shop, especially when working on the electrical systems. Rings, watches, bracelets, necklaces, earrings, and so forth, can cause serious injury. The gold, silver, and other metals used in jewelry are excellent conductors of electricity. Your body is also an excellent conductor. Electrical current that flows through a conductor generates heat. The heat generated as the jewelry shorts the circuit can cause severe burns. In addition, jewelry can get caught in moving parts and result in the severing of fingers and hands. Necklaces can cause serious injury or even death if they become caught in moving equipment.

Because your body is a conductor of electricity, wear shoes that will insulate you. In addition, choose shoes or boots that will protect your feet if objects fall onto them and that have oil resistant soles. Tennis or sport shoes are not satisfactory footwear in the automotive shop.

Eye Protection

The importance of wearing proper eye protection cannot be overemphasized. Every working day there are over 1,000 eye injuries, many resulting in blindness. Almost all of these are preventable. The safest and surest method of protecting your eyes is to wear proper eye protection anytime you enter the shop. At the least, wear eye protection when performing any grinding, using power tools, hammering, cutting, chiseling, or performing under the car service. In addition, wear eye protection when doing any work that can cause sparks, dirt, or rust to enter your eyes, and when working around chemicals. Remember, just because you are not doing the work yourself does not mean you are immune from eye injury. Many injuries are the result of a co-worker doing something to cause objects to be airborne.

The key to protecting your eyes is in the use of *proper* eye protection. Ordinary dress glasses do not provide adequate protection. Dress glasses are designed to impact standards that are far below that required in the workplace. A flying object may be stopped by the lens, but the frame may allow the lens to break free and cause injury. In addition, dress glasses do not provide protection from the side.

There is a variety of popular eye protection devices (Figure 1-2). One of the best ways to protect your eyes is to wear occupational safety glasses. These glasses are light and comfortable. They are constructed of tempered glass or safety plastic lens, and have frames that prevent the

A **conductor** is capable of supporting the flow of electricity through it.

A **short** allows for electrical current to bypass its normal path.

An **insulator** is not capable of supporting the flow of electricity.

Occupational safety glasses are designed with special high impact lens and frames, and provide for side protection.

Figure 1-2 Most popular types of eye protection used in the automotive service industry: (A) occupational safety glasses; (B) safety goggles; (C) full face shield. (Courtesy of Goodson Shop Supplies)

lens from being pushed out during impact. They have side shields to prevent entry of objects from the side. Occupational safety glasses are available in prescription lens so they can be worn instead of regular corrective lens dress glasses.

Safety goggles fit snugly around the eye area to prevent entry of objects and to provide protection in the event of liquid splashes. The force of impact to the lens is distributed throughout the entire area that the safety goggles are in contact with the face and forehead. In addition, goggles are designed to fit over dress glasses.

Face shields are used when there is potential for sparks, flying objects, or splashed liquids to cause facial and eye injuries. The plastic is not as strong or impact resistant as occupational safety glasses or safety goggles. If there is a danger of high impact objects hitting the face shield, wear additional eye protection with the face shield.

> **CAUTION:** Before removing the eye protection device, close your eyes. Pieces of metal, dirt, or other foreign material may have accumulated on the outside. These could fall into your eyes when you remove the glasses or shield.

Rotating Belts and Pulleys

Many times the technician must work around rotating components such as alternators, power steering pumps, air pumps, water pumps, and air conditioner (A/C) compressors. Always think before acting. Be aware of where you are placing your hands and fingers at all times. Do not place rags, tools, or test equipment near the moving parts. In addition, make sure you are not wearing any loose clothing or jewelry.

Be very cautious around electric cooling fans. Many of these fans will operate even if the ignition switch is turned off. They are controlled by a temperature sensing unit in the engine block or radiator and will turn on anytime the coolant temperature reaches a certain point. Before working on or around the electric cooling fan, disconnect the wire connector to the fan motor or the negative battery terminal.

> **WARNING:** Reconnect the fan connector before returning the vehicle to service or engine damage may result.

Safety goggles provide eye protection from all sides because they fit against the face and forehead to seal off the eyes from outside elements.

A **face shield** is a clear plastic shield that protects the entire face.

Other rotating equipment or components of concern include tire changers, spin balancers, drills, bench grinders, and drive shafts.

Lifting

Back injuries are one of the most crippling injuries in industry, yet most of them are preventable. Most occupational back injuries are caused by improper lifting practices. These injuries can be avoided by following a few simple lifting guidelines:

1. Do not lift a heavy object by yourself. Recruit assistance from someone else to share the load.

2. Do not lift more than you can handle. If the object is too heavy, use the proper equipment to lift it.

3. Do not attempt to lift an object if there is no secure means of holding onto it. Study the object to determine balance and grip points.

4. Do not lift with your back. Your legs have some of the strongest muscles in the body. Use them.

5. Place your body close to the object. Keep your back and elbows straight (Figure 1-3).

Figure 1-3 Keep your back straight and lift with the legs.

6. Make sure you have a good grip on the object. Do not attempt to readjust the load once you have lifted it. If you are not comfortable with the balance and grip, lower the object and reposition yourself.

7. When lifting, keep the object as close to your body as possible. Keep your back straight and lift with your legs.

8. While carrying the object, do not twist your body to change directions. Turn your whole body into the new direction.

9. To set the load down, keep the object close to your body. Bend at the knees and keep your back straight. Do not bend forward or twist.

10. If you need to place the object onto a shelf or bench top, place the edge of the object on the surface and slide it into place. Do not lean forward.

Tool and Equipment Safety

A technician would not be able to perform vehicle service without using tools and equipment. Most injuries caused by tools and equipment are the result of improper use, improper maintenance, and carelessness.

Hand Tools

There are some very simple steps that the technician can take to help assure safe hand tool use:

1. Do not use tools that are worn out or broken.
2. Do not use a tool to perform a function that it was not designed for. Use the proper tool for the job.
3. Keep the tools clean and in good condition.
4. Point sharp edges of tools away from yourself.
5. Do not attempt to hold small components in your hands while using tools such as screwdrivers. The tool may slip and cause injury to your hand.
6. Examine the work area for hazards that can cause injury if the tool slips or the fastener breaks loose quickly.
7. Do not put sharp tools into your pockets.

Power Tool Safety

Many times the technician will be required to use power tools when performing electrical service. Drills and hole saws will be used to install new accessories onto the vehicle or to drill holes for wiring to pass through. Grinders, drill presses, and hydraulic presses may be used to help fabricate or modify components. Pneumatic tools are used to remove or fasten components. All of these tools can cause injury if not used properly. Use the following guidelines when working with power tools:

1. Ask your supervisor if you are not sure of the correct operation of a tool.
2. Always wear proper eye protection when using power tools.
3. Check that all safety guards and equipment are installed onto the tool.
4. If using an electrical tool, check the condition of the plug and cord. The plug should be a three-prong plug. Never cut off the grounding prong. Do not use the tool if the wires are frayed or broken. Plug the tool into a grounded receptacle.
5. If using an air tool, check the condition of the air hose. Do not use it if the hose shows signs of weakness such as bulges or fraying. Also the tool should be properly oiled.
6. If using a hydraulic tool, check the condition of all hoses and the gauge. Do not use the tool if any of these is defective.
7. Make sure other people are not in the area when you turn the tool on.
8. Do not leave the area with the tool still operating. Stay with the tool until it stops. Then unplug it.
9. Make all adjustments to the tool before turning it on.
10. If the tool is defective or does not pass your safety inspection, put a sign on it and report it to your supervisor.

Compressed Air Safety

Compressed air is used in the automotive shop to perform many functions; however, cleaning off your clothes is not one of them. Dirt and other objects blown off of your clothes can cause serious injury to yourself and others. There may be dirt in the nozzle or hose that will be ejected at a high rate of speed and can be forced into the skin or eyes. In addition, most compressed air systems used in automotive shops are equipped with automatic oilers. Under the right circumstances oil and air bubbles can be injected into the blood stream.

Use only approved safety nozzles when using compressed air to dry parts that have been cleaned. Safety nozzles have a relief passage that prevents high pressures from being expelled directly out the front. It is best not to use compressed air to dry parts. However, there are

---

Hand tools use only the force generated from the body to operate. They multiply the force received through leverage to accomplish the work.

Shop Manual
Chapter 1, page 2

Power tools use forces other than those generated by the body. They can use compressed air, electricity, or hydraulic pressure to generate and multiply force.

Pneumatic tools are powered by compressed air.

instances where it must be used to dry small passages. In these cases, use air pressure regulated between 25 and 30 psi.

Check the air hoses for signs of wear. Do not use them if they are bulging, frayed, or if the couplers are damaged.

Lifting the Vehicle Safely

There will be times when it will be necessary to raise the vehicle off the floor to perform a service operation. The vehicle can be lifted by use of floor jacks or a hoist. Each method has its own safety precautions and rules that must be followed.

Jack and Jack Stand Safety

Shop Manual
Chapter 1, page 2

A **floor jack** is a portable hydraulic tool used to raise and lower a vehicle.

Floor jacks are used to lift the vehicle a short distance off the floor or when only a portion of the vehicle needs to be raised (Figure 1-4). Before using the floor jack, check it for signs of hydraulic fluid leaks and for damage that would compromise its safe use. Before lifting the vehicle, place wheel blocks in front of and behind one of the tires.

CAUTION: Place the wheel blocks around a tire that is going to be lifted last. If the front of the vehicle is being lifted, place the wheel blocks around one of the rear tires. When the vehicle is being lowered, place blocks around one of the tires on the floor before lowering the other end of the vehicle.

Some shops may have an end lift to raise one half of the vehicle at a time. These lifts are used on older vehicles and light duty trucks. When using an end lift, do not block the wheels until the vehicle is raised. If the wheels are blocked, the lift will tip toward the vehicle. Be careful to lift the vehicle only on a level surface.

Figure 1-4 Floor jacks are used to raise the vehicle a short distance off the floor. (Courtesy of Blackhawk Automotive, Inc.)

Many jack manufacturer's and service manuals provide illustrations of proper lift locations on the vehicle (Figure 1-5). If this information is not available, always place the floor jack on major strength parts. These areas include the frame, cross member, or differential. If you are in doubt about the proper lift point, ask your supervisor. Never lift on sheet metal or plastic parts.

The floor jack is to be used only to lift the vehicle off of the floor. It is not intended to support the vehicle while someone is under it. Use jack stands to support the vehicle (Figure 1-6). Use one jack stand for each quarter of the vehicle that is lifted (Figure 1-7). Place the jack stand under the frame or major support component of the vehicle. When the vehicle is lowered onto the stands, make sure that they do not tilt.

□ Drive-on hoist ▨ Frame-contact hoist ◩ Twin-post hoist

▨ Drive-on hoist ■ Twin-post suspension hoist ■ Frame-engaging hoist

Do not lift or support on track bar

Figure 1-5 Examples of lift point illustrations.

Jack stands, or safety stands, are support devices used to hold the vehicle off of the floor after it has been raised by the floor jack.

Figure 1-6 Jack stands are used to support the vehicle after it has been raised by the floor jack. (Courtesy of Lincoln, St. Louis)

Figure 1-7 Do not trust the floor jack to support the vehicle. Never go under a vehicle that is not supported by jack stands.

The **hoist** is a lift used to raise the entire vehicle.

Hoist Safety

Hoists are used when the entire vehicle needs to be raised, usually high enough for the technician to stand underneath the vehicle (Figure 1-8). When a vehicle is placed on the hoist, it must be centered over it. The balance of the vehicle must be taken into consideration, as well as the effects on balance if a heavy component is removed from the vehicle.

Place the hoist pads under proper lift points of the vehicle. It may be necessary to adjust the pad height in order to lift the vehicle level. Stop raising the vehicle when it is a few inches off the floor to confirm good pad contact. Once the vehicle is raised to the desired height, use the hoist's locking mechanism to prevent accidental lowering of the vehicle.

If the vehicle is not level on the pads, or the pads are not in the proper position, lower the vehicle and readjust as needed. Never get under a vehicle that is not properly situated on the hoist.

Figure 1-8 One type of hoist that can be found in the automotive shop. The hoist is used to lift the entire vehicle.

Operating the Vehicle Inside the Shop

Shop Manual
Chapter 1, page 6

Before leaving the shop to get a vehicle, make sure the aisle is clear and wide enough for the vehicle to pass. Check your bay area to make sure it is clean and there is nothing lying on the floor. Before moving the vehicle, test the brakes for proper operation. Turn off the radio and roll down the driver's window so you can hear if someone calls out to you.

There will be instances when the engine will have to run while the vehicle is in the shop. Follow this list of safety rules when the engine needs to be started in the shop:

1. Place wheel blocks in front of and behind one of the tires.

2. Make sure the transmission is in neutral or park.

3. Set the parking brake.

4. Engine exhaust contains carbon monoxide. Connect the vehicle exhaust system to the shop ventilation system *before* starting the engine (Figure 1-9). The signs of carbon monoxide poisoning include headaches, drowsiness, incoherentness, and lack of coordination. Be aware of these symptoms in yourself and others and get outside to fresh air if poisoning is suspected. Prolonged inhalation of carbon monoxide will result in coma or death. Some shops use carbon monoxide monitors that will sound an alarm if the level is dangerously high.

Carbon monoxide is an odorless, colorless, and toxic gas that is produced as a result of the combustion process.

Figure 1-9 Do not start the engine unless the shop's ventilation system is connected to the exhaust pipe(s).

Fires and Fire Extinguishers

Shop Manual
Chapter 1, page 7

Fires are classified by the types of materials that are involved (Figure 1-10). Technicians should be able to locate the correct fire extinguisher to control the fire types that they are likely to experience. Technicians must also be able to fight a fire in an emergency.

CAUTION: Do not risk your life in fighting a fire. If it is evident that the fire is out of control, get out. Always be aware of where you are and the location of the closest exit. Do not open the garage doors in the event of a fire.

Labels on the fire extinguisher will indicate the types of fires that it will put out. Become familiar with the use of the fire extinguisher.

Figure 1-10 GUIDE TO EXTINGUISHER SELECTION

	Class of Fire	Typical Fuel Involved	Type of Extinguisher
Class **A** Fires (green)	**For Ordinary Combustibles** Put out a class A fire by lowering its temperature or by coating the burning combustibles.	Wood Paper Cloth Rubber Plastics Rubbish Upholstery	Water[*1] Foam[*] Multipurpose dry chemical[4]
Class **B** Fires (red)	**For Flammable Liquids** Put out a class B fire by smothering it. Use an extinguisher that gives a blanketing, flame-interrupting effect; cover whole flaming liquid surface.	Gasoline Oil Grease Paint Lighter fluid	Foam[*] Carbon dioxide[5] Halogenated agent[6] Standard dry chemical[2] Purpole K dry chemical[3] Multipurpose dry chemical[4]
Class **C** Fires (blue)	**For Electrical Equipment** Put out a class C fire by shutting off power as quickly as possible and by always using a nonconducting extinguishing agent to prevent electric shock.	Motors Appliances Wiring Fuse boxes Switchboards	Carbon dioxide[5] Halogenated agent[6] Standard dry chemical[2] Purple K dry chemical[3] Multipurpose dry chemical[4]
Class **D** Fires (yellow)	**For Combustible Metals** Put out a class D fire of metal chips, turnings, or shaving by smothering or coating with a specially designed extinguishing agent.	Aluminum Magnesium Potassium Sodium Titanium Zirconium	Dry powder extinguishers and agents only

[*]Cartridge-operated water, foam, and soda-acid types of extinguishers are no longer manufactured. These extinguishers should be removed from service when they become due for their next hydrostatic pressure test.

Notes:

(1) Freeze in low temperatures unless treated with antifreeze solution, usually weighs over 20 pounds, and is heavier than any other extinguisher mentioned.

(2) Also called ordinary or regular dry chemical. (solution bicarbonate)

(3) Has the greatest initial fire-stopping power of the extinguishers mentioned for class B fires. Be sure to clean residue immediately after using the extinguisher so sprayed surfaces will not be damaged. (potassium bicarbonate)

(4) The only extinguishers that fight A, B, and C classes of fires. However, they should not be used on fires in liquefied fat or oil of appreciable depth. Be sure to clean residue immediately after using the extinguisher so sprayed surfaces will not be damaged. (ammonium phosphates)

(5) Use with caution in unventilated, confined spaces.

(6) May cause injury to the operator if the extinguishing agent (a gas) or the gases produced when the agent is applied to a fire is inhaled.

Electrical System Safety

There are many safety requirements that must be followed when working on the vehicle's electrical system. In addition to personal safety, there is the concern of damaging the electrical system with improper service techniques. The following are a few of the safety rules. Throughout the text there will be cautions and warnings to alert you to potential hazards associated with working on a particular electrical system or component.

Battery Safety

Before attempting to do any type of work on or around the battery, the technician must be aware of certain precautions. To avoid personal injury or property damage, follow these precautions:

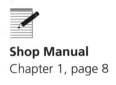

Shop Manual
Chapter 1, page 8

1. Battery acid is very corrosive. Do not allow it to come into contact with skin, eyes,or clothing. If battery acid should get into your eyes, rinse them thoroughly with clean water and seek immediate medical attention. If battery acid comes into contact with skin, wash with clean water. Baking soda added to the water will neutralize the acid. If the acid is swallowed, drink large quantities of water or milk followed by milk of magnesia and a beaten egg or vegetable oil.

2. When making connections to a battery be careful to observe polarity, positive to positive and negative to negative.

3. When disconnecting battery cables, always disconnect the negative (ground) cable first.

4. When connecting battery cables, always connect the negative cable last.

5. Avoid any arcing or open flames near a battery. The vapors produced by the battery cycling are very explosive. Do not smoke around a battery.

6. Follow manufacturers' instructions when charging a battery. Charge the battery in a well-ventilated area. Do not connect or disconnect the charger leads while the charger is turned on.

7. Do not add additional electrolyte to the battery if it is low. Add only distilled water.

8. Do not wear any jewelry or watches while servicing the battery. These items are excellent conductors of electricity. Severe burns may occur if current flows through them by accidental contact with the battery positive terminal and ground.

9. Never lay tools across the battery. They may come into contact with both terminals, shorting out the battery and causing it to explode.

10. Wear safety glasses or a face shield when servicing the battery.

Starting System Service Safety

Before testing or servicing the starter system, become familiar with these precautions that should be observed:

1. Refer to the manufacturer's manuals for correct procedures for disconnecting a battery. Some vehicles with on-board computers must be supplied with an auxiliary power source.

2. Disconnect the battery ground cable before disconnecting any of the starter circuit's wires or removing the starter motor.

3. Be sure the vehicle is properly positioned on the hoist or on safety jack stands.

4. Before performing any cranking test, be sure the vehicle transmission is in park or neutral and the parking brakes are applied. Put wheel blocks in front of and behind one tire.

5. Follow manufacturer's directions for disabling the ignition system.

6. Be sure the test leads are clear of any moving engine components.

7. Never clean any electrical components in solvent or gasoline. Clean with compressed air, denatured alcohol, or wipe with clean rags only.

Charging System Service Safety

The following are some general rules for servicing the charging system:

1. Do not run the vehicle with the battery disconnected. The battery acts as a buffer and stabilizes any voltage spikes that may cause damage to the vehicle's electronics.

2. When performing charging system tests, do not allow output voltage to increase over 16 volts.

3. If the battery needs to be recharged, disconnect the cables while charging.

4. Do not attempt to remove electrical components from the vehicle with the battery connected.

5. Before connecting or disconnecting any electrical connections, the ignition switch must be in the "off" position.

6. Avoid contact with the BAT terminal of the AC generator while the battery is connected. Battery voltage is always present at this terminal.

Air Bag Safety

The air bag system demands that the technician pay close attention to safety warnings and precautions when working on or around it. Most air bags are deployed by an explosive charge. Accidental deployment of the air bag can result in serious injury. When working on or around the steering wheel or air bag module, be aware of your hands and arms. Do not place your arm over the module. If the air bag deploys, injury can result.

> **CAUTION:** Obey the warnings in the service manual when working on the air bag system. Failure to follow these warnings may result in air bag deployment and injury.

Air bag systems contain a means of deploying the bag even if the battery is disconnected. This system is needed in the event that the battery is damaged or disconnected during an accident. The reserve energy can be stored for over 10 minutes after the battery is disconnected. Follow the service manual procedures for disabling the system.

When carrying the air bag module, carry it so that the bag and trim are facing away from your body (Figure 1-11). In the event of accidental deployment, the charge will be away from you. Do not face the module toward any other people.

Figure 1-11 Carry the module so that the bag and trim are away from your body. (Courtesy of General Motors Corporation)

BAT is the terminal identifier for the conductor from the AC generator to the battery positive terminal.

Shop Manual
Chapter 1, page 9

The air bag system is designed as a supplemental restraint that in the case of an accident will deploy a bag out of the steering wheel or passenger side dash panel to provide additional protection against head and face injuries.

The **air bag module** is the air bag and inflator assembly together in a single package.

Always place inflator module on workbench with trim cover up, away from loose objects.

Figure 1-12 Place the module on the bench with the bag and trim facing up. (Courtesy of General Motors Corporation)

When you place the module on the bench, face the bag and trim up (Figure 1-12). This provides a free space for the bag to expand if it deploys..

While troubleshooting the air bag system, do not use electrical testers such as battery-powered or AC-powered voltmeters, ohmmeters, and so on, or any other equipment except those specified in the service manual. Do not use a test light to troubleshoot the system.

When it is necessary to make a repair or replace a component in the air bag system, always disconnect the negative battery cable before making the repair. It is a good practice to insulate the clamp terminal with tape or a rubber hose to prevent it from coming into contact with the battery post.

Antilock Brake Service Safety

Antilock brakes (ABS) have become very popular on today's vehicles. There are many different systems used and each has it own safety requirements regarding servicing the system. Become familiar with the warnings and cautions associated with the system you are working on by studying the service manual before performing any service.

Certain components of the ABS are not intended to be serviced individually. Do not attempt to remove or disconnect these components. Only those components with approved removal and installation procedures in the service manual should be serviced.

Some operations require that the tubes, hoses, and fittings be disconnected. The ABS uses hydraulic pressures as high as 2,800 psi and an accumulator to store this pressurized fluid. Before disconnecting any lines or fittings, the accumulator must be fully depressurized. Follow the service manual procedures for depressurizing the system.

Summary

❑ Being a professional technician encompasses more than knowledge of the vehicle systems. It also requires an understanding of all the hazards in the work area.

❑ As a professional technician, you should work responsibly to protect yourself and the people around you.

Shop Manual,
Chapter 1, page 10

Antilock brake systems (ABS) automatically pulsate the brakes to prevent wheel lock-up under panic stop and poor traction conditions.

Terms to Know
Air bag module
Antilock brake system (ABS)

❑ Technicians must be aware that it is their responsibility to prevent injuries in the shop, and their actions and attitudes reflect how seriously they accept that responsibility.

❑ Long sleeve shirts should have their cuffs buttoned or rolled up tightly, and shirt tails should be tucked in at all times. Neckties should be tucked inside your shirt.

❑ Long hair should be tied and tucked under a hat.

❑ Jewelry has no place in the automotive shop.

❑ The safest and surest method of protecting your eyes is to wear proper eye protection anytime you enter the shop.

❑ When working around rotating pulleys and belts, be aware of where you are placing your hands and fingers at all times.

❑ Most occupational back injuries are caused by improper lifting practices.

❑ Most injuries caused by tools and equipment are the result of improper use, improper maintenance, and carelessness.

❑ Never use compressed air for cleaning off your clothes.

❑ The floor jack is to be used only to lift the vehicle off the floor. Use jack stands to support the vehicle after it is lifted.

❑ Carbon monoxide is an odorless, colorless, and toxic gas that is produced as a result of the combustion process.

❑ Fires are classified by the types of materials involved. Fire extinguishers are classified by the type of fire they will extinguish.

❑ Batteries can cause serious injury if all safety rules are not followed when working on or around them.

❑ The air bag system demands that the technician pay close attention to safety warnings and precautions when working on or around it.

❑ Air bag systems contain a means of deploying the bag even if the battery is disconnected. The reserve energy can be stored for over 10 minutes after the battery is disconnected.

❑ Carry the air bag module so that the bag and trim are away from your body and place the module on the bench with the bag and trim facing up.

❑ Do not use a test light to troubleshoot the air bag system.

❑ Become familiar with the warnings and cautions associated with the antilock brake system that you are working on by studying the service manual before performing any service.

Review Questions

Short Answer Essays

1. Explain how safety is a part of professionalism.

2. List the basic safety rules of proper lifting.

3. List three safety rules that should be followed when working around the battery.

4. What type of materials are involved in a Class B fire?

5. Describe the proper use of floor jacks and safety stands.

6. Why must a shop ventilation system be connected to the exhaust when running an engine in the shop?

7. What type of tool is never to be used in troubleshooting the air bag system?

8. What must be done before tubes, hoses, and fittings are disconnected on an ABS?

9. What are the safety regulations that should be followed when lifting a vehicle on a hoist?

10. What must be done before disconnecting any of the wires to the starter or alternator?

Fill-in-the-Blanks

1. Carbon monoxide is an odorless, colorless, and _____ gas produced as a result of the combustion process.

2. As a professional technician, you should work in such a manner as to protect _____ and the people around you.

3. The safest and surest method of protecting your eyes is to wear proper eye protection _____ you enter the shop.

4. Most occupational back injuries are caused by _____ lifting practices.

5. Never use _____ _____ for cleaning off your clothes.

6. Carry the air bag module so that the bag and trim are facing _____ from your body.

7. Do not use a _____ _____ to troubleshoot the air bag system.

8. Become familiar with the warnings and cautions associated with the anti-lock brake system that you are working on by studying the _____ _____ before performing any service.

9. Long hair should be _____ and _____ under a hat.

10. Most injuries that are caused by tools and equipment are the result of improper _____ , improper _____, and _____ .

ASE Style Review Questions

1. The use of power equipment and tools is being discussed:
   Technician A says eye protection should be worn.
   Technician B says to check the condition of the tool before using it.
   Who is correct?
   A. A only
   B. B only
   C. Both A and B
   D. Neither A nor B

2. The battery is going to be removed from the vehicle:
   Technician A says to disconnect the positive cable first.
   Technician B says not to lay tools across the top of the battery.
   Who is correct?
   A. A only
   B. B only
   C. Both A and B
   D. Neither A nor B

3. The engine is running while in the shop:
   Technician A says to connect the exhaust pipe to the shop's ventilation system.
   Technician B says new vehicles run with such low emissions that shop ventilation is not needed.
   Who is correct?
   A. A only
   B. B only
   C. Both A and B
   D. Neither A nor B

4. Fire extinguisher use is being discussed:
   Technician A says electrical fires are extinguished with Class A fire extinguishers.
   Technician B says gasoline is extinguished with Class B fire extinguishers.
   Who is correct?
   A. A only
   B. B only
   C. Both A and B
   D. Neither A nor B

5. Service of the air bag system is being discussed:
   Technician A says to use a test light to check for applied voltage.
   Technician B says to disconnect the battery negative cable before repairing the system.
   Who is correct?
   A. A only
   B. B only
   C. Both A and B
   D. Neither A nor B

6. Servicing the antilock brake system is being discussed:
   Technician A says the system must be depressurized before disconnecting lines and fittings.
   Technician B says the system may have accumulated pressures as high as 2,800 psi.
   Who is correct?
   A. A only
   B. B only
   C. Both A and B
   D. Neither A nor B

7. Carbon monoxide is being discussed:
   Technician A says it puts out a very distinct odor.
   Technician B says one of the first signs of carbon monoxide poisoning is a headache.
   Who is correct?
   A. A only
   B. B only
   C. Both A and B
   D. Neither A nor B

8. Proper dress in the shop is being discussed:
   Technician A says the way a person dresses reflects little about their attitude on safety.
   Technician B says jewelry can be worn in the shop, just be careful.
   Who is correct?
   A. A only
   B. B only
   C. Both A and B
   D. Neither A nor B

9. The vehicle is being raised by a floor jack:
Technician A says the floor jack will support the vehicle safely.
Technician B says to use jack stands at each corner of the vehicle that is lifted.
Who is correct?
A. A only
B. B only
C. Both A and B
D. Neither A nor B

10. Battery service is being discussed:
Technician A says to charge the battery in a well-ventilated area.
Technician B says do not add additional electrolyte to the battery if its level is low.
Who is correct?
A. A only
B. B only
C. Both A and B
D. Neither A nor B

Basic Theories

Upon completion and review of this chapter, you should be able to:

❑ Explain the theories and laws of electricity.

❑ Describe the difference between insulators, conductors, and semiconductors.

❑ Define voltage, current, and resistance.

❑ Define and use Ohm's law correctly.

❑ Explain the basic concepts of capacitance.

❑ Explain the difference between AC and DC currents.

❑ Define and illustrate series, parallel, and series-parallel circuits and the electrical laws that govern them.

❑ Explain the basic theory of semiconductors.

❑ Explain the theory of electromagnetism.

❑ Explain the principles of induction.

Introduction

The electrical systems used in today's vehicles can be very complicated. However, through an understanding of the principles and laws that govern electrical circuits, technicians can simplify their job of diagnosing electrical problems. In this chapter you will learn the laws that dictate electrical behavior, how circuits operate, the difference between circuits, and how to apply Ohm's law to each type of circuit. You will also learn the basic theories of semiconductor construction. Because magnetism and electricity are closely related, a study of electromagnetism and induction is included in this chapter.

Basics of Electron Flow

Because electricity is an energy form that cannot be seen, some technicians regard the vehicle's electrical system as being more complicated than it is. These technicians approach the vehicle's electrical system with some reluctance. It is important for today's technician to understand that electrical behavior is confined to definite laws that produce predictable results and effects. To facilitate the understanding of the laws of electricity, a short study of atoms is presented.

Atomic Structure

An atom is constructed of a complex arrangement of electrons in orbit around a nucleus—much like planets orbiting the sun (Figure 2-1). The two types of particles that make up the nucleus are

An **atom** is the smallest part of a chemical element that still has all the characteristics of that element.

Electrons are negatively charged particles. The **nucleus** contains positively charged particles called **protons** and the particles that have no charge are called **neutrons**.

Electron

Proton

Neutron

Figure 2-1 The basic construction of an atom.

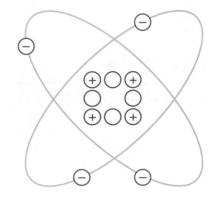

Figure 2-2 If the number of electrons and protons are equal, the atom is balanced.

tightly bound together. The electrons are free to move within their orbits at fixed distances around the nucleus. The attraction between the negative electrons and the positive protons causes the electrons to orbit the nucleus. All of the electrons surrounding the nucleus are negatively charged, so they repel each other if they approach another electron. The electrons attempt to stay as far away from each other as possible without leaving their orbits.

The number of electrons and the number of protons in the atom structure will attempt to be equal. To remain balanced, an atom will shed or attract electrons with neighboring atoms. There may be several different orbits of electrons around the nucleus and each shell will contain a specific amount of electrons (Figure 2-3). In studying the laws of electricity, the only concern is with the electrons that are in the valence ring.

Atoms seek to be balanced, thus atoms that have several electrons missing in their valence ring will attempt to gain other electrons from neighboring atoms. Also, if an atom has an excess amount of electrons in its valence ring it will try to pass them on to neighboring atoms.

Conductors and Insulators

Some substances can readily shed or attract electrons. How easily the atom accomplishes this depends on the number of electrons needed in the valence ring to balance the atom. An atom is a good conductor if it sheds electrons easily; on the contrary, it is a good insulator if it does not shed its electrons easily.

The difference between the atomic structures of conductors and insulators is how tight the electrons in the valence ring are held together by the nucleus. The outermost electrons in a conductor's atoms are loosely held together by the nucleus and the electrons in an insulator are tightly held together. For example, a copper atom has 29 electrons and 29 protons arranged as shown in Figure 2-3A. Notice that there is only one electron in the valence ring. For the valence ring to be completely filled it would require 32 electrons. The one electron is loosely tied to the

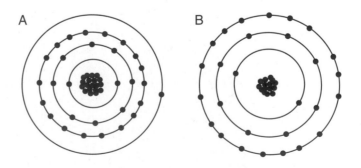

Figure 2-3 Basic structure of an atom. Atom A is copper and atom B is nickel.

atom and can be easily removed, making it a good conductor. In comparison, the nickel atom shown in Figure 2-3B has 28 electrons and 28 protons. The valence ring of the nickel atom can only contain 18 electrons, thus it is completely full. These electrons are tightly held to the atom and are not removed easily, thus making a good insulator. The number of electrons in the valence ring determines whether an element is an insulator or conductor.

1. three or less electrons—conductor
2. five or more electrons—insulator
3. four electrons—semiconductor

The electrons in the atoms of a conductor can be freed from their outer orbits by forces such as heat, friction, light, pressure, chemical reaction, and magnetism. When electrons are moved out of their orbit, they form an electrical current under proper conditions. Insulators are required to control the routing of the flow of electricity.

▲ **WARNING:** Any broken, frayed or damaged insulation material requires replacement or repair to the conductor. Exposed conductors can result in a safety hazard and circuit component damage.

■ **CAUTION:** The human body is a conductor of electricity. When performing service on electrical systems, be aware that electrical shock is possible. Although the shock is usually harmless, the reaction to the shock can cause injury. Observe all safety rules associated with electricity. Never wear jewelry when servicing or testing the electrical system.

Electricity Defined

Electricity is the movement of electrons from atom to atom (Figure 2-4). If there is an excess amount of positive charges (protons) placed on the left, one of the positive ions will pull the outer electron away from the atom on the far left. For the electrons to move in the same direction, there must be an electromotive force (EMF) applied. When electrons in the atoms of a conductor are affected by the EMF, an unbalanced condition will occur in the atom between the negative charges of the electrons and the positive charges of the nucleus. The EMF attempts to push the electron from its orbit. If an electron is freed from its orbit, the atom acquires a positive charge because it now has one more proton than it has electrons. This action will cause the far left atom to be slightly positively charged. The unbalanced atom attempts to return to its balanced state so it will attract electrons from the orbit of other balanced atoms to the right. This starts a chain reaction as one atom captures an electron and another releases an electron. As this action continues to occur, electrons will flow from right to left. A stream of free electrons forms and an electrical current is started. This does not mean a single electron travels the length of the insulator; it means that the electrons bump each other out of their orbits. All this happens at the speed of light. The strength of the electron flow is dependant on the strength of the affecting force.

Conductor

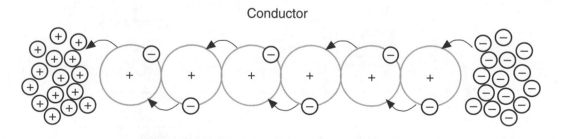

Figure 2-4 As electrons flow from one atom to another, an electrical current is developed.

Semiconductors are neither conductors nor insulators.

The term **circuit** means a circle and is the path of electron flow consisting of the voltage source, conductors, load component, and return path to the voltage source.

The electrical term **open** is used to mean that current flow is stopped. The path for electron flow is broken by opening the circuit. **Closed circuit** means there are no breaks in the path and current will flow.

An **ion** is an atom or group of atoms that has an electrical charge.

Electromotive force (EMF) is referred to as voltage.

Random movement of electrons is not electric current; the electrons must move in the same direction.

The speed of light is 186,000 miles per second (299,000 kilometers per second).

In Figure 2-4 the electrons are flowing from a negative point to a positive point. If the flow of electrons is used to describe the direction of current flow, the direction of current flow is based on the electron theory. However, while negative charges are flowing from negative to positive, a positive charge is also flowing in the opposite direction. Using the flow of the positive charges to describe the direction of current flow is called the conventional theory. The conventional theory is used in this textbook and most manufacturers' service manuals to define the direction of current flow.

An electrical current will continue to flow through a conductor as long as the electromotive force is acting on the conductor's atoms and electrons. If a potential exists in the conductor, with a buildup of excess electrons at the end of the conductor the farthest from the EMF, and there is a lack of electrons at the EMF side, current will flow. The effect is called *electron drift* and accounts for the method in which electrons flow through a conductor.

An electrical current can be formed by the following forces: friction, chemical, heat, pressure, and magnetism. An electrical current is formed whenever electrons flow or drift in mass. There are eight laws that regulate this electrical behavior:

1. Electrons repel each other.
2. Like charges repel each other.
3. Unlike charges attract each other.
4. Electrons flow in a conductor only when affected by an electromotive force.
5. A voltage difference is created in the conductor when an EMF is acting on the conductor.
6. Electrons flow only when a voltage difference exists between the two points in a conductor.
7. Current tends to flow to ground in an electrical circuit.
8. Ground is defined as the area of lowest voltage.

The three elements of electricity are voltage, current, and resistance. How these three elements interrelate governs the behavior of electricity. Once the technician comprehends the laws that govern electricity, understanding the function and operation of the various automotive electrical systems is an easier task. This knowledge will assist the technician in diagnosis and repair of automotive electrical systems.

Voltage

Voltage can be defined as an electrical pressure (Figure 2-5) and is the electromotive force (EMF) that causes the movement of the electrons in a conductor. In Figure 2-4, voltage is the difference between the positive and negative charges. An electrical pressure difference is created when there is a mass of electrons at one point in the circuit, and a lack of electrons at another point in the circuit. In the automobile, the battery or alternator is used to apply the electrical pressure.

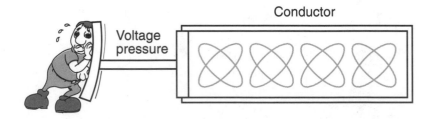

Figure 2-5 Voltage is the pressure that causes the electrons to move.

Figure 2-6 A simplified light circuit illustrating voltage potential.

The amount of pressure applied to a circuit is stated in the number of volts. If a voltmeter is connected across the terminals of an automobile battery it may indicate 12.6 volts. This is actually indicating that there is a difference in potential of 12.6 volts. There is 12.6 volts of electrical pressure at one battery terminal compared to 0 volts pressure at the other terminal.

In a circuit that has current flowing, voltage will exist between any two points in that circuit (Figure 2-6). The only time voltage does not exist is when the potential drops to zero. In Figure 2-6 the voltage potential between points A and C and B and C is 12 volts. However, between points A and B the pressure difference is zero and the voltmeter will indicate 0 volts.

Current

Current can be defined as the rate of electron flow (Figure 2-7) and is measured in amperes. Current is a measurement of the electrons passing any given point in the circuit in one second. Because the flow of electrons is at the speed of light, it would be impossible to physically see electron flow. However, the rate of electron flow can be measured. Current will increase as pressure or voltage is increased—provided circuit resistance remains constant.

Resistance

The third component in electricity is resistance. The size, type, length, and temperature of he material used as a conductor will determine the resistance of the conductor. Devices that use electricity to operate (motors and lights) have a greater amount of resistance than the conductor.

Conductor

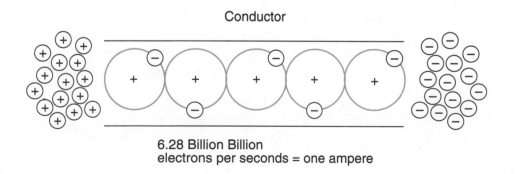

6.28 Billion Billion
electrons per seconds = one ampere

Figure 2-7 The rate of electron flow is called current.

A complete electrical circuit consists of the following: (1) a power source, (2) a load or resistance unit, and (3) conductors. Resistance (load) is required to change electrical energy to light, heat, or movement. This type of resistance is found in the working device of the circuit, such as the lamp, motor, relay, or other load component.

There are five basic characteristics that determine the amount of resistance in any part of a circuit:

1. The atomic structure of the material: The fewer the number of free electrons, the higher the resistance of the conductor.

2. The length of the conductor: The longer the conductor, the higher the resistance.

3. The diameter of the conductor: The smaller the cross-sectional area of the conductor, the higher the resistance.

4. Temperature: The higher the temperature of the conductor, the greater the resistance.

5. Physical condition of the conductor: If the conductor is damaged by nicks or cuts, the resistance will increase.

There may be unwanted resistance in a circuit. This could be in the form of a corroded connection or a broken conductor. In these instances the resistance may cause the load component to operate at reduced efficiency or to not operate at all.

It does not matter if the resistance is from the load component or from unwanted resistance. There are certain principles that dictate its impact in the circuit:

1. Voltage always drops as current flows through the resistance.

2. The current flow through the resistance does not change.

3. All resistances change the electrical energy into heat energy to some extent.

Ohm's Law

Ohm's law is a mathematical formula that shows how current, voltage, and resistance work together to produce electricity. The formula for Ohm's law can be expressed in the form of a triangle (Figure 2-8). If any two electrical values are known, the third can be found.

Ohm's law is the basic law of electricity. It states that the amount of current in an electric circuit is inversely proportional to the resistance of the circuit, and is directly proportional to the voltage in the circuit. For example, if the resistance decreases and the voltage remains constant, the current will increase. If the resistance stays the same and the voltage increases, the current will also increase.

Using Figure 2-8, if resistance (R) and voltage (V) are known, cover the unknown (I) to see the formula. Current equals voltage divided by resistance ($I = V \div R$). The illustration (Figure 2-9) shows a simplified 12-volt light circuit where the unknown value is current (I). The lamp is designed to have 3-Ω resistance. Cover the I in the triangle.

$$I = V \div R = 12\,\text{V} \div 3\,\Omega = 4\,\text{A}$$

A starter motor circuit uses a 12-volt battery and a motor that draws 150 amperes. To determine the amount of resistance, cover the R in the triangle.

$$R = V \div I = 12\,\text{V} \div 150\,\text{A} = 0.08\,\Omega$$

Figure 2-8 The mathematical formula for Ohm's law using a triangle. To determine the formula to find the unknown value, cover the unknown value.

Figure 2-9 Simplified light circuit with 3 ohms of resistance in the lamp.

Watt's Law

Power is another term used in analyzing electrical circuits. Power is found by using Watt's law, which defines the relationship between current, voltage, and power (Figure 2-10). Cover the unknown value on the triangle and find the formula. The power used can be determined by using the previous example of a 12-volt starter motor that draws 150 amperes. Cover the unknown value (P) on the triangle.

$$P = V \times I = 12 \text{ V} \times 150 \text{ A} = 1800 \text{ W}$$

Another example of the use of Watt's law would be if additional accessories are added to the vehicle. If the accessory is rated at 75 watts, the current draw is

$$I = P \div V = 75 \div 12 = 6.25 \text{ A}$$

Power (P) is a measure of the total electrical work being performed per unit of time.

It is possible to convert horsepower ratings to electrical power rating using the conversion factor: 1 horsepower equals 746 watts.

Figure 2-10 The mathematical formula for Watt's law using a triangle.

Figure 2-11 Capacitors that can be used in automotive electrical systems.

Capacitance

Capacitance (*C*) is the ability of two conducting surfaces to store voltage. The two surfaces must be separated by an insulator.

Capacitors are rated in units called **farads.** Capacitors are rated in terms of their maximum safe voltage levels, as well as their capacitance.

Some automotive electrical systems will utilize a capacitor or condenser to store electrical charges (Figure 2-11). A capacitor does not consume any power. All of the voltage stored in the capacitor is returned to the circuit when discharged. Because the capacitor stores voltage, it will also absorb voltage changes in the circuit. By providing for this storage of voltage, damaging voltage spikes can be controlled.

Most capacitors are connected in parallel across the circuit (Figure 2-12). Capacitors operate on the principle that opposite charges attract each other, and that there is a potential voltage

Figure 2-12 A capacitor connected to a circuit.

Figure 2-13 The positive plate sheds its electrons.

26

Figure 2-14 The electrons will be stored on the negative plate.

Figure 2-15 Capacitor when fully charged.

between any two oppositely charged points. When the switch is closed, the protons at the positive battery terminal will attract some of the electrons in one plate of the capacitor away from the area near the dielectric. As a result, the atoms of the positive plate are unbalanced because there are more protons than electrons in the atom. This plate now has a positive charge because of the shortage of electrons (Figure 2-13). The positive charge of this plate will attract electrons on the other plate. The dielectric keeps the electrons from the negative plate from crossing over to the positive plate, resulting in a storage of electrons on the negative plate (Figure 2-14). The movement of electrons to the negative plate and away from the positive plate is an electrical current.

Current will flow "through" the capacitor until the voltage charges across the capacitor and across the battery are equalized. Current flow through a capacitor is only the effect of the electron movement onto the negative plate and away from the positive plate. Electrons do not actually pass through the capacitor from one plate to another. The charges on the plates do not move through the electrostatic field. They are stored on the plates as static electricity. When the charges across the capacitor and battery are equalized, there is no potential difference and no more current will flow "through" the capacitor (Figure 2-15). Current will now flow through the load components in the circuit (Figure 2-16).

When the switch is opened, current flow from the battery through the resistor is stopped. However, the capacitor has a storage of electrons on its negative plate. Because the negative plate of the capacitor is connected to the positive plate through the resistor, the capacitor acts as a battery. The capacitor will discharge the electrons through the resistor until the atoms of the positive plate and negative plate return to a balanced state (Figure 2-17).

The plate connected to the positive battery terminal is the **positive plate.**

An atom that has less electrons than protons is said to be a **positive ion.**

The insulator in a capacitor is called a **dielectric.** The dielectric can be made of some insulator material such as ceramic, glass, paper, plastic, or even the air between the two plates.

The field that is between the two oppositely charged plates is called the **electrostatic field.**

Static electricity is electricity that is not in motion.

Figure 2-16 Current flow with capacitor fully charged.

Figure 2-17 Current flow with the switch open and the capacitor discharging.

In the event that a high voltage spike occurs in the circuit, the capacitor will absorb the additional voltage before it is able to damage the circuit components. A capacitor can also be used to stop current flow quickly when a circuit is opened (such as in the ignition system). It can also store a high voltage charge and then discharge it when a circuit needs the voltage (such as in some air bag systems).

Types of Current

There are two classifications of electrical current flow; direct current (DC) and alternating current (AC). The type of current flow is determined by the direction it flows and by the type of voltage that drives them.

Direct Current

DC current is the type of current that is created and stored in the automotive battery.

Direct current (DC current) results from a source voltage and current that remain constant and flow in the same direction (Figure 2-18). Voltage and current are constant if the switch is turned on or off. Most of the electrically controlled units in the automobile require DC current.

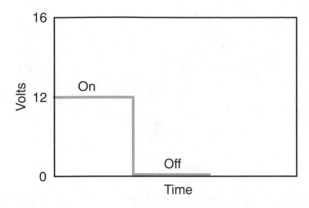

Figure 2-18 Direct current flows in the same direction and remains constant throughout the circuit.

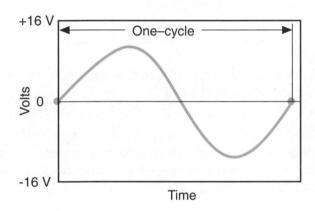

Figure 2-19 Alternating current does not remain constant.

Alternating Current

In an alternating current (AC current) circuit, voltage and current do not remain constant AC current changes directions from positive to negative. The voltage in an AC circuit starts at zero and rises to a positive value. Then it falls back to zero and goes to a negative value. Finally it returns to zero (Figure 2-19). Each cycle of AC current occurs in an equal amount of time.

Electrical Circuits

The electrical term continuity refers to the circuit being continuous. For current to flow, the electrons must have a circular path from the source voltage to the load component and back to the source. A simple automotive circuit is made up of four parts:

1. Battery (power source).
2. Wires (conductors).
3. Load (light, motor, etc.).
4. Ground (return back to battery).

The unrectified current produced within an alternator is the most common example of alternating current found in the automobile. Automobile circuits convert AC current to DC current.

The AC voltage shown in Figure 2-19 is called a **sine wave.**

Each time the voltage returns to zero one **cycle** has been completed.

Figure 2-20 A basic electrical circuit including (A) a switch, (B) a fuse, and (C) a lamp.

The portion of the circuit from the positive side of the source to the load component is called the **insulated side** of the circuit. The portion of the circuit that is from the load component to the negative side of the source is called the **ground side** of the circuit.

Shop Manual
Chapter 2, page 13

The **series circuit** provides a single path for current flow from the electrical source through all the circuit's components, and back to the source.

The basic circuit shown (Figure 2-20) includes a switch to turn the circuit on and off, a protection device (fuse), and a load. In this instance, with the switch closed, current flows from the positive terminal of the battery through the light and returns to the negative terminal of the battery. To have a complete circuit the switch must be closed or turned on. The effect of opening and closing the switch to control electrical flow would be the same if the switch was installed on the ground side of the light.

There are basically three different types of electrical circuits: (1) the series circuit, (2) the parallel circuit, and (3) the series-parallel circuit.

Series Circuit

A series circuit consists of one or more resistors (or loads) with only one path for current to flow (Figure 2-21). If any of the components in the circuit fails, the entire circuit will not function. All of the current that comes from the positive side of the battery must pass through each resistor, then back to ground.

Total resistance in a series circuit is figured by simply adding together all of the resistances in the circuit. For example, a series circuit that has two light bulbs with a resistance of 2 Ω each and a third bulb with 1 Ω of resistance would have a total resistance of 5 Ω (Figure 2-22).

$$R = 2\,\Omega + 2\,\Omega + 1\,\Omega = 5\,\Omega$$

The characteristics of a series circuit are:

1. The total resistance is the sum of all resistances.

2. The current through each resistor is the same.

Figure 2-21 A simplified series circuit.

Figure 2-22 The total resistance in a series circuit is the sum of all resistances in the circuit.

3. The current is the same at every point in the circuit.
4. The voltage drop across each resistor will be different if the resistor values are different.
5. The sum of the voltage drop of each resistor equals the source voltage.

Parallel Circuit

In a parallel circuit each path of current flow has separate resistances that operate either independently or in conjunction with each other (depending on circuit design). In a parallel circuit, current can flow through more than one resistor at a time (Figure 2-23). In this type of circuit, failure of a component in one shunt does not affect the components in other shunts of the circuit.

The resistance in a parallel circuit is calculated by using the following formula:

$$R = \frac{1}{\frac{1}{R_1} + \frac{1}{R_2} + \frac{1}{R_3}} \quad \text{or} \quad \frac{1}{R} = \frac{1}{R_1} + \frac{1}{R_2} + \frac{1}{R_3}$$

However, if there are only two resistors in parallel it is easier to use the following formula:

$$R = \frac{R_1 \times R_2}{R_1 + R_2}$$

If the values of R_1, R_2, and R_3 are 4 Ω, 6 Ω, and 8 Ω respectively, the total resistance is as follows:

$$R = \frac{1}{\frac{1}{4} + \frac{1}{6} + \frac{1}{8}} = 1.85 \ \Omega$$

Figure 2-23 A parallel circuit with different resistances in each branch.

Shop Manual
Chapter 2, page 14

A **parallel circuit** provides two or more paths for electricity to flow.

The parallel branches of the circuit are called **shunt circuits.**

Total resistance in a parallel circuit is always less than the lowest individual resistance because current has more than one path to follow. If more resistors are added, more conductors are added, and the total resistance will decrease.

If all resistances in the parallel circuit are equal, use the following formula:

$$R_T = \frac{\text{Value of one resistor}}{\text{Total number of resistors}}$$

To calculate current in a parallel circuit, each shunt branch is treated as an individual circuit. Applied voltage is the same to all branches. To determine the branch current simply divide the source voltage by the shunt branch resistance:

$$I = V \div R$$

Using the branch resistance shown in Figure 2-23, the current in each branch is found:

$$12 \ V \div 4 \ \Omega = 3 \ A$$
$$12 \ V \div 6 \ \Omega = 2 \ A$$
$$12 \ V \div 8 \ \Omega = 1.5 \ A$$

Total current is the sum of the amperes of the branches:

$$I = 3 \ A + 2 \ A + 1.5 \ A = 6.5 \ A$$

The characteristics of a parallel circuit are:

1. The voltage applied to each parallel branch is the same.
2. The total resistance is less than the lowest resistor.
3. The current flowing through each resistor is different if the resistor values are different.
4. The voltage drop across each resistor is the same.
5. The sum of the separate currents in each branch equals the total current in the circuit.

Shop Manual
Chapter 2, page 15

A **series-parallel circuit** is a combination of the series and parallel circuits.

Series-Parallel Circuits

The series-parallel circuit has some loads that are in series with each other and some that are in parallel (Figure 2-24). To calculate the total resistance in this type of circuit, calculate the equivalent series loads of the parallel branches first. Next, calculate the series resistance and add it to the equivalent series load. For example, if the parallel portion of the circuit has two branches with 4 ÷ resistance each, and the series portion has a single load of 3 ÷ (Figure 2-25), use the following method to calculate the equivalent resistance:

$$V \div I = R$$
$$12 \ V \div 6 \ A = 2 \ \Omega \text{ (equivalent resistance)}$$

Then add the equivalent resistance to the actual series resistance to determine the total circuit resistance:

$$2 \ \Omega + 3 \ \Omega = 5 \ \Omega$$

Figure 2-24 A series-parallel circuit.

Figure 2-25 A series-parallel circuit with known resistance values.

The **equivalent series load,** or **equivalent resistance,** is the total resistance of a parallel circuit and is equivalent to the resistance of a single load in series with the voltage source.

The total current through the two branches of the parallel portion of the circuit is 6 amperes. (12 V ÷ 4 Ω = 3 A; 3 A + 3 A = 6 A).

With the total resistance being known, total current draw can now be calculated. Because the source voltage is 12 volts, divide 12 volts by 5 ohms to find the current.

$$12 \text{ V} \div 5 \text{ }\Omega = 2.4 \text{ A}$$

Total current flow will be determined by the total resistance and the total source voltage.

Voltage Drop

Voltage drop occurs when current flows through a load component (resistance). There must be a voltage drop present for current to flow through a resistor. Kirchhoff's voltage law states that the total voltage drop in an electrical circuit will always equal available voltage at the source. All of the voltage from the source must be dropped in the circuit before it returns to the source.

If resistance is excessive at any point, it will result in an excessive voltage drop across that portion of the circuit. By using Ohm's law, the amount of voltage drop across any resistor can be calculated. When performing the calculation, use only the voltage, current, and resistance at that particular resistor. Voltage drop is shown by the formula:

$$\text{Voltage drop} = \text{Resistance} \times \text{current}$$

Shop Manual
Chapter 2, page 16

Voltage drop is a resistance in the circuit that reduces the electrical pressure available after the resistance.

Figure 2-26 Using Ohm's law on a series circuit to find the amount of voltage drop.

A resistance can be either the load component, the conductors, any connections, or unwanted resistance.

Using the figure shown (Figure 2-26) as an example, voltage drop over R_1 can be determined by using Ohm's law. This is a series circuit, so total resistance is the sum of all resistances. Total resistance is 4 ohms. Using Ohm's law, current is

$$12 \text{ V} \div 4 \text{ }\Omega = 3 \text{ A.}$$

The voltage drop through R_1, is

$$2 \text{ }\Omega \times 3 \text{ A} = 6 \text{ V}$$

This means that 6 volts are dropped through R_1 and is the amount of voltage available to R_2. The voltage drop through R_2 is:

$$2 \text{ }\Omega \times 3 \text{ A} = 6 \text{ V}$$

The total voltage drop in the circuit is 12 volts.

Voltage drop can also be measured by using a voltmeter. With current flowing through a circuit, the voltmeter may be connected in parallel over the resistor, wire, or component to measure voltage drop. As previously stated, the voltmeter indicates the amount of voltage potential between two points in the circuit. The voltmeter reading indicates the difference between the amount of voltage available to the resistor and the amount of voltage after the resistor. Using a voltmeter to measure voltage drop is shown in Figure 2-27.

Figure 2-27 Using a voltmeter to determine the amount of voltage drop over a resistance.

Figure 2-28 A series circuit with known resistance values.

Using Ohm's Law

If additional components, branches, or excessive resistances are placed in a circuit, the technician must understand their effect. The following examples will assist you in understanding how to use Ohm's law in different types of circuits.

As stated earlier, when two factors are known the third can be calculated using Ohm's law. The following are examples of using Ohm's law on various types of electrical circuits:

1. To determine the amount of current flow (Figure 2-28), first find the total resistance in the circuit.

$$R_T = R_1 + R_2 + R_3 = 12\ \Omega + 8\ \Omega + 4\ \Omega = 24\ \Omega$$

Once total resistance is figured, then current flow can be determined as follows:

$$I = V \div R = 12\ V \div 24\ \Omega = 0.5\ A$$

2. To determine the voltage drop across each resistance in Figure 2-28:

For the 12-Ω resistance: $I \times R = 0.5\ A \times 12\ \Omega = 6\ V$
For the 8-Ω resistance: $I \times R = 0.5\ A \times 8\ \Omega = 4\ V$
For the 4-Ω resistance: $I \times R = 0.5\ A \times 4\ \Omega = 2\ V$

Figure 2-28 is a series circuit, so the total of all the voltage drops over all resistors must equal source voltage:

$$6\ V + 4\ V + 2\ V = 12\ V$$

3. To determine the current in each resistor and the total current draw on the battery of the parallel circuit shown (Figure 2-29) follow these procedures:

Current for the 12-Ω resistor: $12\ V \div 12\ \Omega = 1\ A$
Current for the 10-Ω resistor: $12\ V \div 10\ \Omega = 1.2\ A$
Current for the 14-Ω resistor: $12\ V \div 14\ \Omega = 0.86\ A$

To determine the total current draw on the battery, add the individual circuits:

Total current: $1\ A + 1.2\ A + 0.86\ A = 3.06\ A$

Because 12 V is dropped across each resistor in this parallel circuit, the voltage is a constant value when determining current flow.

Figure 2-29 A parallel circuit with known resistor values.

Figure 2-30 A conventional point-type ignition system.

4. The illustation (Figure 2-30) shows a point-type ignition system that requires 6 A flowing through the primary winding of the coil. If the resistance of the primary winding is 1.4 Ω, and there is no resistance through the points, the value of the ignition resistor can be determined.

First figure the total resistance that there should be in the circuit:

$$R = V \div I = 12 \text{ V} \div 6 \text{ A} = 2.0 \text{ } \Omega$$

The difference between the required resistance and the known resistance will give the resistance needed through the ignition resistor:

$$2.0 \text{ } \Omega - 1.4 \text{ } \Omega = 0.6 \text{ } \Omega$$

5. The illustration (Figure 2-31) shows a series-parallel circuit. To determine the current flowing through each resistor and the voltage drop across each resistor, the equivalent resistance in the parallel branch must be found.

$$R = \frac{R_1 \times R_2}{R_1 + R_2} = \frac{3 \text{ } \Omega \times 12 \text{ } \Omega}{3 \text{ } \Omega + 12 \text{ } \Omega} = 2.4 \text{ } \Omega$$

Figure 2-31 A series-parallel circuit with known resistance values.

Total resistance in the circuit is:

$$2.4 \ \Omega + 2.0 \ \Omega = 4.4 \ \Omega$$

Next determine the amount of current flowing in the circuit by dividing voltage by the resistance:

$$I = V \div R = 12 \ V \div 4.4 \ \Omega = 2.73 \ A$$

The voltage drop across the 2.0-Ω resistor can be determined by multiplying current by resistance:

$$V = I \times R = 2.73 \ A \times 2.0 \ \Omega = 5.46 \ V$$

The voltage drop across the parallel branches of the circuit is:

$$12 \ V - 5.46 \ V = 6.54 \ V$$

Therefore, the current through each resistance is:

$$3\text{-}\Omega \text{ resistor: } V \div R = 6.54 \ V \div 3 \ \Omega = 2.18 \ A$$
$$12\text{-}\Omega \text{ resistor: } V \div R = 6.54 \ V \div 12 \ \Omega = 0.55 \ A$$

Tabulations of the currents and voltages are shown (Figure 2-32).

Resistor	Current	Voltage
2.0 Ω	2.73 A	5.46 V
3.0 Ω	2.18 A	6.54 V
12.0 Ω	0.55 A	6.54 V

Figure 2-32 Table indicating the determined amount of current and voltage at each resistor.

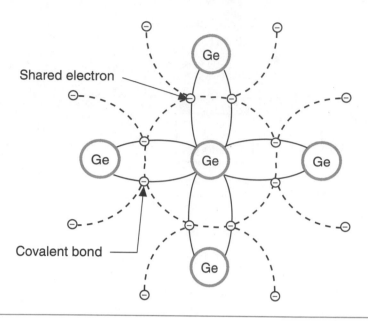

Figure 2-33 Crystal structure of germanium.

Semiconductors

Classroom Manual Chapter 3, page 60

As discussed earlier, electrical materials are classified as conductors, insulators, or semiconductors. Semiconductors include diodes, transistors, and silicon-controlled rectifiers. These semiconductors are often called solid-state devices because they are constructed of a solid material. The most common materials used in the construction of semiconductors are silicon or germanium. Both of these materials are classified as crystals.

Silicon and germanium have four electrons in their outer orbits. Because of their crystal-type structure, each atom shares an electron with four other atoms (Figure 2-33). As a result of this covalent bonding, each atom will have eight electrons in its outer orbit. All the orbits are filled and there are no free electrons, thus the material (as a category of matter) falls somewhere between conductor and insulator.

Semiconductors are materials that conduct electric current under certain conditions, yet will not conduct under other conditions.

A **crystal** is the term used to describe a material that has a definite atom structure.

When atoms share electrons with other atoms it is called **covalent bonding.**

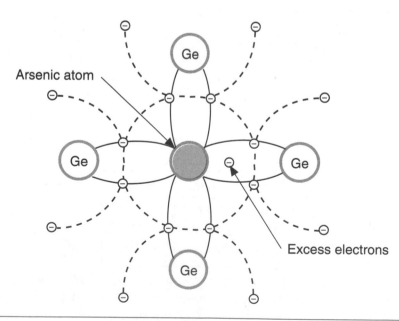

Figure 2-34 Germanium crystal doped with an arsenic atom to produce a N-type material.

Perfect crystals are not used for manufacturing semiconductors. They are doped with impurity atoms. This doping adds a small percentage of another element to the crystal. The doping element can be arsenic, antimony, phosphorous, boron, aluminum, or gallium.

If the crystal is doped by using arsenic, antimony, or phosphorous the result is a material with free electrons (Figure 2-34). Materials such as arsenic have five electrons, which leaves one electron left over. Under the influence of an EMF, it will support current flow.

If boron, aluminum, or gallium are added to the crystal, a P-type material is produced. Materials like boron have three electrons in their outermost orbit. Because there is one fewer electron, there is an absence of an electron that produces a hole (Figure 2-35).

By putting N-type and P-type materials together in a certain order, solid-state components are built that can be used for switching devices, voltage regulators, electrical control, and so on.

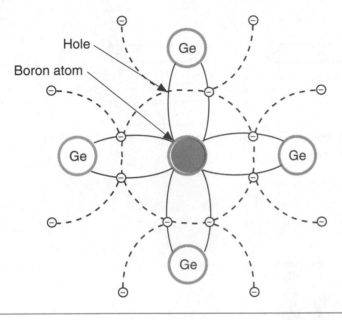

Figure 2-35 Germanium crystal doped with a boron atom to produce a P-type material.

Magnetism Principles

Magnetism is used in the automobile to produce the electrical current to run electrical systems. It is also used in the starter motor to cause it to turn. A magnet is a material that will attract iron, steel, and a few other materials. Because magnetism is closely related to electricity, many of the laws that govern electricity also govern magnetism.

Magnets

All magnets have polarity. A magnet that is allowed to hang free will align itself north and south. The end facing north is called the north pole, and the end facing south is called the south pole. Like poles will repel each other, and unlike poles will attract each other. These principles are shown (Figure 2-36). The magnetic attraction is the strongest at the poles.

A strong magnet produces many lines of force, and a weak magnet produces fewer lines of force. Invisible lines of force leave the magnet at the north pole and enter again at the south pole. While inside the magnet, the lines of force travel from the south pole to the north pole (Figure 2-38).

The field of force (or magnetic field) is all the space, outside the magnet, that contains lines of magnetic force. Magnetic lines of force penetrate all substances; there is no known insulation against magnetic lines of force. The lines of force may be deflected only by other magnetic materials or by another magnetic field.

Figure 2-36 Magnetic principles: (A) All magnets have poles, (B) unlike poles attract each other, and (C) like poles repel.

Figure 2-37 Iron filings indicate the lines of magnetic flux.

Figure 2-38 Lines of force through the magnet.

Figure 2-39 A magnetic field surrounds a conductor that has current flowing through it.

Figure 2-40 Right-hand rule to determine direction of magnetic lines of force.

Figure 2-41 Looping the conductor increases the magnetic field.

Electromagnetism

Whenever an electrical current flows through a conductor, a magnetic field is formed around the conductor (Figure 2-39). The number of lines of force, and the strength of the magnetic field produced, increases in direct proportion to increases in current flow.

The direction of the lines of force is determined by the right-hand rule. Using the conventional theory of current flow being from positive to negative, the right hand is used to grasp the wire with the thumb pointing in the direction of current flow. The fingers will point in the direction of the magnetic lines of force (Figure 2-40).

Andre Marie Ampére noted that current flowing in the same direction through two nearby wires will cause the wires to be attracted to one another. Also, he observed that if current flow in one of the wires is reversed, the wires will repel one another. In addition, he found that if a wire is coiled with current flowing through the wire, the same magnetic field that surrounds a straight wire combines to form one larger magnetic field. This magnetic field has true north and south poles (Figure 2-41). Looping the wire doubles the flux density where the wire is running parallel to itself. The illustration (Figure 2-42) shows how these lines of force will join and attract each other.

Electromagnetism is a form of magnetism that occurs when current flows through a conductor.

Figure 2-42 Lines of force join together and attract each other.

The north pole can be determined in the coil by use of the right-hand rule. Grasp the coil with the fingers pointing in the direction of current flow (+ to -) and the thumb will point toward the north pole (Figure 2-43).

As more loops are added, the fields from each loop will join and increase the flux density (Figure 2-44). To make the magnetic field even stronger, an iron core can be placed in the center of the coil (Figure 2-45). The soft iron core is a material that has high permeability and provides an excellent conductor for the magnetic field that travels through the center of the wire coil.

The strength of an electromagnetic coil is affected by the following factors:

1. The amount of current flowing through the wire.

2. The number of conductors.

Figure 2-43 Right-hand rule to determine magnetic poles.

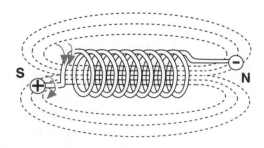

Figure 2-44 Adding more loops of wire increases the magnetic flux density.

Figure 2-45 The addition of an iron core concentrates the flux density.

1 ampere $^+$ 10 amperes $^+$

=

1000 turns   100 turns

Figure 2-46 Magnetic field strength is determined by the amount of amperage and the number of coils.

3. The size, length, and type of core material.

4. The angle at which the lines of force are cut.

The strength of the magnetic field is measured in ampere-turns:

$$\text{ampere} - \text{turns} = \text{amperes} \times \text{number of turns}$$

The magnetic field strength is measured by multiplying the current flow in amperes through a coil by the number of complete turns of wire in the coil. For example, in the illustration (Figure 2-46), a 1,000 turn coil with 1 ampere of current would have a field strength of 1,000 ampere-turns. This coil would have the same field strength as a coil with 100 turns and 10 amperes of current.

Theory of Induction

Electricity can be produced by magnetic induction. Magnetic induction occurs when a conductor is moved through the magnetic lines of force (Figure 2-47). A difference of potential is set up between the ends of the conductor and a voltage is induced. This voltage exists only when the magnetic field or the conductor is in motion.

The induced voltage can be increased by either increasing the speed in which the magnetic lines of force cut the conductor, or by increasing the number of conductors that are cut. It is this principle that is behind the operation of all ignition systems, starter motors, charging systems, and relays.

Induction is the magnetic process of producing a current flow in a wire without any actual contact to the wire.

To induce 1 volt, 100 million magnetic lines of force must be cut per second.

Conductor movement

Voltmeter
reads voltage

Figure 2-47 Moving a conductor through a magnetic field induces an electrical current.

An example of an inducer is the ignition coil. As the current increases, the coil will reach a point of saturation. The magnetic lines of force represent stored energy, which will collapse when the applied voltage is removed. When the lines of force collapse, the energy is returned back to the wire.

If an electrical current is generated in the wires of a coil itself when a current is first connected or disconnected, it is called self-induction. This induced current is in the opposite direction of the applied current and tends to reduce the magnetizing force. Self-induction is governed by Lentz's law, which states:

An induced current is in such direction that its magnetic effect opposes the change by which the current is induced.

Self-induction is generally undesirable because any automotive circuit contains an inductor that is switched. Self-induction tends to continue to supply current in the same direction as the original current. This can cause an electrical arc to occur in the switch. Self-induction is commonly found in any electrical components that contain a coil or an electric motor. To help reduce the high-voltage arc, a capacitor or clamping diode may be connected in the circuit. The capacitor will absorb the high voltage that is created by turning inductive circuits on and off.

Mutual induction is used in ignition coils where a rapidly changing magnetic field in the primary windings creates a voltage in the secondary winding (Figure 2-48).

Contact points

Coil 1

Coil 2

Battery

Figure 2-48 A mutual induction is used to create an electrical current in coil 2 if the current flow in coil 1 is turned on and off.

EMI Suppression

As manufacturers began to increase the number of electronic components and systems in their vehicles, the problem of EMI had to be controlled. The low power integrated circuits used on modern vehicles are sensitive to the signals produced as a result of EMI. EMI is produced as current in a conductor is turned on and off. EMI is also caused by static electricity that is created by friction. The friction is a result of the tires and their contact with the road, or from fan belts contacting the pulleys.

EMI can disrupt the vehicle's computer systems by inducing false messages to the computer. The computer requires messages to be sent over circuits in order to communicate with other computers, sensors, and actuators. If any of these signals are disrupted, the engine and/or accessories may turn off.

EMI can be suppressed by any one of the following methods:

1. Adding a resistance to the conductors. This is usually done to high-voltage systems such as the secondary portion of the ignition system.

2. Connecting a capacitor with a chock coil in parallel to the circuit.

3. Shield the conductor or load components with a metal or metal impregnated plastic.

4. Increase the number of paths to ground by using designated ground circuits. This provides a clear path ground that is very low in resistance.

Electromagnetic Interference (EMI) is an undesirable creation of electromagnetism whenever current is switched on and off.

Summary

- An atom is constructed of a complex arrangement of electrons in orbit around a nucleus. If the number of electrons and protons are equal, the atom is balanced or neutral.
- A conductor is capable of supporting the flow of electricity through it.
- An insulator is not capable of supporting the flow of electricity.
- Electricity is the movement of electrons from atom to atom. For the electrons to move in the same direction, there must be an electromotive force (EMF) applied.
- The electron theory defines current flow as motion from negative to positive.
- The conventional theory of current flow states that current flows from a positive point to a less positive point.
- Voltage is defined as an electrical pressure and is the difference between the positive and negative charges.
- Current is defined as the rate of electron flow and is measured in amperes. Amperage is the amount of electrons passing any given point in the circuit in one second.
- Resistance is defined as opposition to current flow and is measured in ohms (Ω).
- Ohm's law defines the relationship between current, voltage, and resistance. It is the basic aw of electricity and states that the amount of current in an electric circuit is inversely proportional to the resistance of the circuit, and is directly proportional to the voltage in the circuit.
- Wattage represents the measure of power (P) used in a circuit. Wattage is measured by using Watt's law, which defines the relationship between amperage, voltage, and wattage.
- Capacitance is the ability of two conducting surfaces to store voltage.

Terms to Know

Capacitance

Circuit

Conductor

Electromagnetism

Electromotive force (emf)

Equivalent series load

Induction

Insulator

Parallel circuit

Potential

Semiconductors

Series circuit

Series-parallel circuit

Valence ring

❑ Direct current is produced from a voltage and current that remains constant and flows in the same direction.

❑ In an alternating current circuit, voltage and current do not remain constant. AC current changes direction from positive to negative.

❑ For current to flow, the electrons must have a circular path from the source voltage to the load component and back to the source.

❑ The series circuit provides a single path for current flow from the electrical source through all the circuit's components, and back to the source.

❑ A parallel circuit provides two or more paths for electricity to flow.

❑ A series-parallel circuit is a combination of the series and parallel circuits.

❑ The equivalent series load, or equivalent resistance, is the total resistance of a parallel circuit and is equivalent to the resistance of a single load in series with the voltage source.

❑ Voltage drop is a resistance in the circuit that reduces the electrical pressure available after the resistance.

❑ Kirchhoff's voltage law states that the total voltage drop in an electrical circuit will always equal available voltage at the source.

Review Questions

Short Answer Essays

1. List and define the three elements of electricity.

2. Describe the use of Ohm's law.

3. List and describe the three types of circuits.

4. Explain the principle of electromagnetism.

5. Describe the principle of induction.

6. Describe the basics of electron flow.

7. Define the two types of electrical current.

8. Describe the difference between insulators, conductors, and semiconductors.

9. Explain the basic concepts of capacitance.

10. What does the measurement of "Watt" represent?

Fill-in-the-Blanks

1. _____ are negatively charged particles. The nucleus contains positively charged particles called _____ and particles that have no charge called _____ .

2. A _____ is capable of supporting the flow of electricity through it. An _____ is not capable of supporting the flow of electricity.

3. For the electrons to move in the same direction, there must be an _____ applied.

4. The _____ _____ of current flow states that current flows from a positive point to a less positive point.

5. Resistance is defined as _____ to current flow and is measured in _____ .

6. _____ is the ability of two conducting surfaces to store voltage.

7. Kirchhoff's voltage law states that the _____ _____ _____ in an electrical circuit will always _____ available voltage at the source.

8. The _____ series load is the total resistance of a parallel circuit.

9. _____ is defined as an electrical pressure.

10. _____ is defined as the rate of electron flow.

ASE Style Review Questions

1. The methods that can be used to form an electrical current are being discussed:
   Technician A says electricity can be generated by magnetic induction.
   Technician B says electricity can be produced by chemical reaction.
   Who is correct?
   A. A only
   B. B only
   C. Both A and B
   D. Neither A nor B

2. Circuit resistance is being discussed:
   Technician A says in a series circuit total resistance is figured by adding together all of the resistances in the circuit.
   Technician B says in a parallel circuit the total resistance is less than the lowest resistor.
   Who is correct?
   A. A only
   B. B only
   C. Both A and B
   D. Neither A nor B

3. While discussing voltage drop:
   Technician A says all of the voltage from the source must be dropped before it returns to the source.
   Technician B says corrosion is not a contributor to voltage drop.
   Who is correct?
   A. A only
   B. B only
   C. Both A and B
   D. Neither A nor B

4. *Technician A* says voltage is the electrical pressure that causes electrons to move.
   Technician B says voltage will exist between any two points in that circuit unless the potential drops to zero.
   Who is correct?
   A. A only
   B. B only
   C. Both A and B
   D. Neither A nor B

5. *Technician A* says wattage is a measure of the total electrical work being performed per unit of time.
Technician B says Watt's law is expressed as $P = R \times I$.
Who is correct?
A. A only
B. B only
C. Both A and B
D. Neither A nor B

6. *Technician A* says a capacitor consumes electrical power.
Technician B says a capacitor induces voltage.
Who is correct?
A. A only
B. B only
C. Both A and B
D. Neither A nor B

7. Types of electrical currents are being discussed.
Technician A says alternating current is produced from a voltage and current that remain constant and flow in the same direction.
Technician B says direct current changes directions from positive to negative.
Who is correct?
A. A only
B. B only
C. Both A and B
D. Neither A nor B

8. The principles of induction are being discussed:
Technician A says induction is the magnetic process of producing a current flow in a wire without any actual contact to the wire.
Technician B says induced voltage only exists when the magnetic field or the conductor is in motion.
Who is correct?
A. A only
B. B only
C. Both A and B
D. Neither A nor B

9. *Technician A* says if the resistance increases and the voltage remains constant, the amperage will increase.
Technician B says Ohm's law can be stated as $I = V \div R$.
Who is correct?
A. A only
B. B only
C. Both A and B
D. Neither A nor B

10. *Technician A* says an insulator is capable of supporting the flow of electricity through it.
Technician B says a conductor is not capable of supporting the flow of electricity.
Who is correct?
A. A only
B. B only
C. Both A and B
D. Neither A nor B

Electrical Components and Meters

Upon completion and review of this chapter, you should be able to:

❏ Explain the proper use of the voltmeter, ammeter, and ohmmeter.

❏ Define circuit defects including opens, shorts, grounds, and excessive voltage drops.

❏ Explain the effects that each type of circuit defect has on the operation of the electrical system.

❏ Explain the purpose of a circuit protection device. Describe the most common types in use.

❏ Describe the common types of electrical system components used and how they affect the electrical system.

❏ Explain the operation of the electrical controls, including switches, relays, and variable resistors.

❏ Describe the basic operating principles of electronic components.

❏ Explain the use of electronic components in the circuit.

Introduction

In this chapter you will be introduced to electrical and electronic components. These components include circuit protection devices, switches, relays, variable resistors, diodes, and different forms of transistors. Today's technician must comprehend the operation of these components and the ways they affect electrical system operation. With this knowledge the technician will be able to accurately and quickly diagnose many electrical failures.

To be able to properly diagnose the components and circuits, the technician must be able to use the test equipment that is designed for electrical system diagnosis. In this chapter you will learn about the various types of test equipment used for diagnosing electrical systems. You will learn the appropriate equipment to use to locate the fault based on the symptoms. In addition, the various types of defects that cause the system to operate improperly are discussed.

Circuit Protection Devices

Most automotive electrical circuits require protection from current draw that would exceed the capacity of the conductors or the load components. The excess current draw can be caused by an overload in the electrical components or by a circuit defect, such as a direct short to ground. To prevent damage to the components and conductors, these circuits use some form of a protection device. If an overload occurs, the protection device opens, preventing current from flowing in the circuit.

Fuses

The most common circuit protector is the in-line fuse (Figure 3-1). The fuses are generally installed in a central fuse box. A common location for the fuse box is under the instrument panel (Figure 3-2). The fuse box can also be located behind kick panels, in the glove box, or on the fender well. Fuse identification and specifications are usually labeled on the fuse box or on the fuse box cover. The in-line fuse is connected in series with the circuit that it is protecting. Battery voltage is applied to the main bus bar, which is connected to one end of the fuse. The other end of the fuse is connected to the component side of the circuit.

Shop Manual
Chapter 3, page 20

The **protection device** is designed to "turn off" the system it protects. This is done by creating an open (like turning off a switch) to prevent a complete circuit.

Excess current flow in a circuit is called an **overload.**

A **fuse** is a replaceable element that will melt if the current passing through it exceeds the fuse rating

Fuse box is the term used to indicate the central location of the fuses contained in a single holding fixture.

Bus bar is a common electrical connection to which all of the fuses are attached. The bus bar is connected to battery voltage

A "blown" fuse is identified by a burned-through metal wire in the capsule (Figure 3-3).

A **fusible link** is made of meltable material with a special heat resistant insulation. When there is an overload in the circuit, the link melts and opens the circuit. To properly test a fusible link, use an ohmmeter or continuity tester.

A   B   C

Figure 3-1 Three types of commonly used fuses: (A) glass cartridge, (B) ceramic, and (C) blade (or mini-fuse).

Figure 3-2 Fuse boxes are usually located under the dash.

When adding accessories to the vehicle, the correct fuse rating must be selected. Use Watt's law to determine the correct fuse rating (watts ÷ volts = amperes). The fuse selected should be rated slightly higher than the actual current draw to allow for current surges (5% to 10%).

⚠ **WARNING:** Fuses are rated by amperage and voltage. Never install a larger rated fuse into a circuit than the one that was designed by the manufacturer. Doing so may damage or destroy the circuit.

In a parallel circuit a single fuse can be used before the first branch (Figure 3-4). Or, an individual fuse can be used with each branch (Figure 3-5).

Fusible Links

A vehicle may have one or several fusible links to provide protection for the main power wires before they are divided into smaller circuits at the fuse box. The fusible links are usually

Figure 3-3 Blown fuses.

Figure 3-4 One fuse to protect the entire parallel circuit.

Figure 3-5 Fuses used to protect each branch of a parallel circuit.

Figure 3-6 Fusible links located near the battery.

located at a main connection near the battery (Figure 3-6). The current capacity of a fusible link is determined by its size. A fusible link is usually four wire sizes smaller (four numbers larger) than the circuit it protects. The smaller the wire, the larger its number. A number 14 circuit would require a number 18 fusible link for protection.

 CAUTION: Do not replace a fusible link with a resistor wire or vice versa.

Maxi-fuses

In place of fusible links, many manufacturers use a maxi-fuse. By using maxi-fuses, manufacturers are able to break down the electrical system into smaller circuits. If a fusible link burns out, many of the vehicle's electrical systems may be affected. By breaking down the electrical system into smaller circuits and installing maxi-fuses, the consequence of a circuit defect will not be as severe as it would have been with a fusible link. In place of a single fusible link, there may be many maxi-fuses, depending on how the circuits are divided. This makes the technician's job of diagnosing a faulty circuit much easier.

Maxi-fuses are used because they are less likely to cause an underhood fire when there is an overload in the circuit. If the fusible link is burned in two, it is possible that the "hot" side of the fuse can come into contact with the vehicle frame and the wire can catch on fire.

Circuit Breakers

A circuit that is susceptible to an overload on a routine basis is usually protected by a circuit breaker. Some circuit breakers require manual resetting by pressing a button. Others must be removed from the power to be reset (Figure 3-7). Cycled circuit breakers are self-resetting. This circuit breaker (Figure 3-8) uses a bimetallic strip that reacts to excessive current. When an overload or circuit defect occurs that causes an excessive amount of current draw, the current flowing through the bimetallic strip causes it to heat. As the strip heats, it bends and opens the contacts. Once the contacts are opened, current can no longer flow. With no current flowing, the strip cools and closes again. If the high current cause is still in the circuit, the breaker will open again. The circuit breaker will continue to cycle open and closed as long as the overload is in the circuit.

Some GM vehicles have the fusible link located at the main connection near the starter motor.

A "blown" fusible link is usually identified by bubbling of the insulator material around the link.

A **maxi-fuse** looks similar to a blade-type fuse except it is larger and has a higher current capacity. It is also referred to as a **cartridge fuse.**

A **bimetallic strip** consists of two different types of metals. One strip will react more quickly to heat than the other, which causes the strip to flex in proportion to the amount of current flow.

Figure 3-7 Noncycling circuit breakers: (A) Manual reset-type circuit breaker; and (B) circuit breaker that requires removal from the power to be reset.

Figure 3-8 The circuit breaker uses a bimetallic strip that opens if current draw is excessive.

☑ **SERVICE TIP:** A circuit breaker, fitted with alligator clips, is useful to bypass a fuse that keeps blowing. The circuit breaker will keep the current flowing through the circuit so that it may be checked for the cause of high current draw while protecting the circuit by cycling on and off (Figure 3-9).

An example of the use of a circuit breaker is in the power window circuit. Because the window is susceptible to jams due to ice buildup on the window, a current overload is possible. If this should occur, the circuit breaker will heat up and open the circuit before the window motor is damaged. If the operator continues to attempt to operate the power window, the circuit breaker will cycle open and closed until the cause of the jam is removed.

Electrical Components

Electrical circuits require different components depending on the type of work they do and how they are to perform it. A light may be wired directly to the battery, but it will remain on until the battery drains. A switch will provide for control of the light circuit. However, if dimming of the light is also required, a rheostat is also needed.

Figure 3-9 A circuit breaker fitted with alligator clips used to diagnose electrical problems.

There are several electrical components that may be incorporated into a circuit to achieve the desired results from the system. These components include switches, relays, buzzers, and various types of resistors.

Switches

Shop Manual
Chapter 3, page 22

Switch controls are designated as to whether they are **normally open (NO)** or **normally closed (NC).**

The term **throw** refers to the number of output circuits. The term **pole** refers to the number of input circuits.

A switch is the most common means of providing control of electrical current flow to an accessory (Figure 3-10). A switch can control the on/off operation of a circuit or direct the flow of current through various circuits. The contacts inside the switch assembly carry the current when they are closed. When they are open, current flow is stopped.

A normally open switch will not allow current flow when it is in its rest position. The contacts are open until they are acted on by an outside force that closes them to complete the circuit. A normally closed switch will allow current flow when it is in its rest position. The contacts are closed until they are acted on by an outside force that opens them to stop current flow.

The simplest type of switch is the single-pole, single-throw (SPST) switch (Figure 3-11). This switch controls the on/off operation of a single circuit. The most common type of SPST switch design is the hinged pawl. The pawl acts as the contact and changes position as directed to open or close the circuit.

Figure 3-10 Common types of switches used in the automotive electrical system.

Figure 3-11 A simplified illustration of a SPST switch.

Some SPST switches are designed to be a momentary contact switch. This switch usually has a spring that holds the contacts open until an outside force is applied and closes them. The horn button on most vehicles is of this design.

Some electrical systems may require the use of a single-pole, double-throw switch (SPDT). The dimmer switch used in the headlight system is usually a SPDT switch. This switch has one input circuit with two output circuits. Depending on the position of the contacts, voltage is applied to the high beam circuit or to the low beam circuit (Figure 3-12).

The most complex switch is the ganged switch used for ignition switches. In Figure 3-13, the five wipers are all ganged together and will move together. Battery voltage is applied to the switch from the starter relay terminal. When the ignition key is turned to the start position, all wipers move to the "S" position. Wipers D and E will complete the circuit to ground to test the instrument panel warning lamps. Wiper B provides battery voltage to the ignition coil. Wiper C supplies battery voltage to the starter relay and the ignition module. Wiper A has no output.

Once the engine starts, the wipers are moved to the RUN position. Wipers D and E are moved out of contact with any output terminals. Wiper A supplies battery voltage to the comfort controls and turn signals, wiper B supplies battery voltage to the ignition coil and other accessories, and wiper C supplies battery voltage to other accessories. The jumper wire between terminals A and R of wiper C indicate that those accessories listed can be operated with the ignition switch in the RUN or ACC position.

The dotted lines used in the symbol indicate the movement of the switch pawl from one position to the other.

Ganged means the wipers all move together.

The **make-before-break wiper** prevents any break in voltage to the ignition coil when the switch is moved from the S position to the R position.

Figure 3-12 A simplified schematic of a headlight system illustrating the SPDT dimmer switch.

Figure 3-13 Illustration of an ignition switch.

Mercury switches are used by many vehicle manufacturers to detect motion. This switch uses a capsule that is partially filled with mercury and has two electrical contacts located at one end. If the switch is constructed as a normally open switch, the contacts are located above the mercury level (Figure 3-14). Mercury is an excellent conductor of electricity. So if the capsule is moved so the mercury touches both of the electrical contacts, the circuit is completed (Figure 3-15). This type of switch is used to illuminate the engine compartment when the hood is opened. While the hood is shut, the capsule is tilted in a position such that the mercury is not able to complete the circuit. Once the hood is opened, the capsule tilts with the hood and the mercury completes the circuit and the light turns on.

Shop Manual
Chapter 3, page 23

A **relay** is a device that uses low current to control a high current circuit.

Relays

Some circuits utilize electromagnetic switches called relays (Figure 3-16). The coil in the relay has a very high resistance, thus it will draw very low current. This low current is used to produce a magnetic field that will close the contacts. Normally open relays have their points closed by the electromagnetic field. Normally closed relays have their points opened by the magnetic field. The contacts are designed to carry the high current required to operate the load component. When current is applied to the coil, the contacts close and heavy battery current flows to the load component that is being controlled.

The illustration (Figure 3-17) shows a relay application in a horn circuit. Battery voltage is applied to the coil. Because the horn button is a normally open-type switch, the current flow to ground is open. Pushing the horn button will complete the circuit, allowing current flow through the coil. The coil develops a magnetic field, which closes the contacts. With the contacts closed, battery voltage is applied to the horn (which is grounded). Used in this manner, the horn relay

OFF

Figure 3-14 A mercury switch in the open position. The mercury does not contact the points.

ON

Figure 3-15 When the mercury switch is tilted, the mercury contacts the points and closes the circuit.

Figure 3-16 A relay uses electrical current to create a magnetic field to draw the contact point closed.

Figure 3-17 A relay can be used in the horn circuit to reduce the size of the conductors required to be installed in the steering column.

becomes a control of the high current necessary to blow the horn. The control circuit may be wired with very thin wire because it will have low current flowing through it. The control unit may have only .25 ampere flowing through it, and the horn may require 24 or more amperes.

Buzzers

A **buzzer**, or **sound generator,** is sometimes used to warn the driver of possible safety hazards by emitting an audio signal (such as when the seat belt is not buckled).

Shop Manual
Chapter 3, page 26

A buzzer is similar in construction to a relay except for the internal wiring (Figure 3-18). The coil is supplied current through the normally closed contact points. When voltage is applied to the buzzer, current flows through the contact points to the coil. When the coil is energized, the contact arm is attracted to the magnetic field. As soon as the contact arm is pulled down, the current flow to the coil is opened, and the magnetic field is dissipated. The contact arm then closes again, and the circuit to the coil is closed. This opening and closing action occurs very rapidly. It is this movement that generates the vibrating signal.

Stepped Resistors

A **stepped resistor** has two or more fixed resistor values. The stepped resistor can have an integral switch or have a switch wired in series.

A stepped resistor is commonly used to control electrical motor speeds (Figure 3-19). By changing the position of the switch, resistance is increased or decreased within the circuit. If the current flows through a low resistance, then higher voltage is applied to the motor and its speed is increased. If the switch is placed in the low speed position, additional resistance is added to the circuit. Less voltage is applied to the motor, which causes it to operate at a reduced speed.

Figure 3-18 A buzzer reacts to the current flow to open and close rapidly to create a noise.

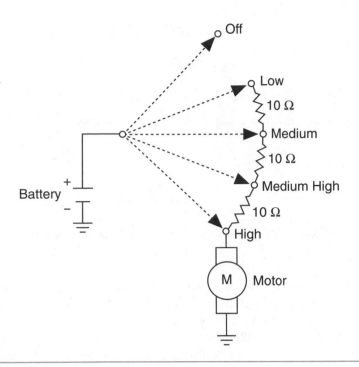

Figure 3-19 The stepped resistor is commonly used to control motor speeds. The total resistance is 30 Ω in the low position, 20 Ω in the medium position, 10 Ω in the medium-high position, and 0 Ω in the high position.

Another use of the stepped resistor is to convert digital to analog signals in the computer circuit. This is accomplished by converting the on/off digital signals into a continuously variable analog signal.

Variable Resistors

The most common types of variable resistors are rheostats and potentiometers. A rheostat has one terminal connected to the fixed end of a resistor and a second terminal connected to a moveable contact called a wiper (Figure 3-20). By changing the position of the wiper on the

Figure 3-20 A rheostat can be used to control the brightness of a lamp.

Shop Manual
Chapter 3, page 26

A **variable resistor** provides for an infinite number of resistance values within a range.

A **rheostat** is a two-terminal variable resistor used to regulate the strength of an electrical current.

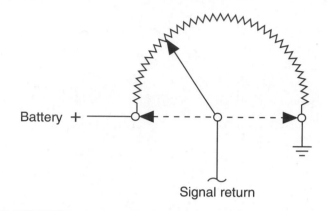

Figure 3-21 A potentiometer is used to send a signal voltage from the wiper.

Shop Manual
Chapter 3, page 28

A **potentiometer** is a three-wire variable resistor that acts as a voltage divider to produce a continuously variable output signal proportional to a mechanical position.

resistor, the amount of resistance can be increased or decreased. The most common use of the rheostat is in the instrument panel lighting switch. As the switch knob is turned, the instrument lights dim or brighten depending on the resistance value.

When a potentiometer is installed into a circuit, one terminal is connected to a power source at one end of the resistor. The second wire is connected to the opposite end of the resistor and is the ground return path. The third wire is connected to the wiper contact (Figure 3-21). The wiper provides a variable voltage drop as it is moved over the resistor. Because the current always flows through the same amount of resistance, the total voltage drop measured by the potentiometer is very stable. For this reason, the potentiometer is a common type of input sensor for the vehicle's onboard computers.

Electronic Components

Diodes

A **diode** is an electrical one-way check valve that will allow current to flow in one direction only.

When N-type materials and P-type materials are joined, the resulting PN junction is a diode (Figure 3-22). When a diode is made, the positive holes from the P region and the negative charges from the N region are drawn toward the junction. Some charges cross over and combine with opposite charges from the other side. When the charges cross over, the two halves are no longer balanced and the diode builds up a network of internal charges opposite to those at the PN junction. The internal EMF between the opposite charges limits the further diffusion of charges across the junction.

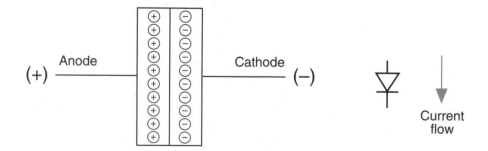

Figure 3-22 A diode and its symbol.

Figure 3-23 Forward-biased voltage causes current flow.

When the diode is incorporated within a circuit and a voltage is applied, the internal characteristics change. If the diode is forward biased there will be current flow (Figure 3-23). In this state the negative region will push electrons across the barrier as the positive region pushes holes across.

If the diode is reverse biased, there will be no current flow (Figure 3-24). The negative region will attract the positive holes away from the junction and the positive region will attract electrons away.

Zener Diodes

As stated, if a diode is reverse biased it will not conduct current. However, if the reverse voltage is increased, a voltage level will be reached at which the diode will conduct in the reverse direction. Reverse current can destroy a simple PN-type diode. But the diode can be doped with materials that will withstand reverse current.

A zener diode is designed to operate in the breakdown region (Figure 3-25). At the point that zener voltage is reached, a large current flows. This prevents the voltage from climbing any higher. This makes the zener diode an excellent component for regulating voltage. If the zener diode is rated at 15 volts, it will conduct in the forward direction. However, it will not conduct in the reverse direction when voltage is below 15 volts. At 15 volts it will conduct and the voltage will not increase over 15 volts.

Forward bias means that a positive voltage is applied to the P-type material and negative voltage to the N-type material.

Reversed bias means that positive voltage is applied to the N-type material and negative voltage is applied to the P-type material.

The voltage reached when the diode conducts in reverse direction is called **zener voltage.**

Figure 3-24 Reverse-biased voltage prevents current flow.

Figure 3-25 Zener diode and its symbol.

The illustration (Figure 3-26) shows a simplified circuit that has a zener diode in it to provide a constant voltage level to the instrument gauge. In this example, the zener diode is connected in series with the resistor and in parallel to the gauge. If the voltage to the gauge must be limited to 7 volts, the zener diode used would be rated at 7 volts. The zener diode maintains a constant voltage drop, and the total voltage drop in a series circuit must equal the amount of source voltage, thus voltage that is greater than the zener voltage must be dropped over the resistor. Even though source voltage may vary (as a normal result of the charging system), causing different currents to flow through the resistor and zener diode, the voltage dropped by the zener diode remains the same.

The zener breaks down when system voltage reaches 7 volts. At this point the zener diode conducts reverse current, causing an additional voltage drop across the resistor. The amount of voltage to the instrument gauge will remain at 7 volts because the zener diode "makes" the resistor drop the additional voltage to maintain this limit.

Light-Emitting Diodes

A **light-emitting diode (LED)** is similar in operation to the diode, except the LED emits light when it is forward biased.

In the light-emitting diode, a small lens is built into the diode so that the light can be seen (Figure 3-27). When the LED is forward biased, the holes and electrons combine. The energy generated is released in the form of light. The material used to make the LED determines the color of the light emitted.

Figure 3-26 Simplified instrument gauge circuit that uses a zener diode to maintain a constant voltage to the gauge.

Figure 3-27 (A) A light-emitting diode uses a lens to emit the generated light. (B) Symbol for LED.

Figure 3-28 A clamping diode in parallel to a coil prevents voltage spikes when the switch is opened.

Clamping Diodes

Whenever the current flow through a coil (such as used in a relay or solenoid) is discontinued, a voltage surge or spike is produced. This spike results when electrons flowing through the coil of the relay do not want to stop and attempt to jump the open. A spark is produced if the electrons jump the open. In some circuits a capacitor can be used as a shock absorber to prevent component damage from this surge. In today's complex electronic systems, a clamping diode is commonly used to prevent the spark. By installing a clamping diode in parallel across the coil, a bypass is provided for the electrons during the time that the circuit is open (Figure 3-28).

An example of the use of clamping diodes is on some air conditioning compressor clutches (Figure 3-29). Because the clutch operates by electromagnetism, opening of the clutch coil produces voltage spikes. If these voltage spikes were left unchecked, they would damage the vehicle's onboard computers. The installation of the clamping diode prevents the voltage spike from reaching the computers.

Transistors

The word *transistor* is a combination of two words, *transfer* and *resist*. The transistor is used to control current flow in the circuit. It can be used to allow a predetermined amount of current flow or to resist this flow.

A **transistor** is a three-layer semiconductor (Figure 3-30). It is used as a very fast switching device.

Figure 3-29 A clamping diode connected across the terminals of an air conditioner compressor clutch.

Figure 3-30 Transistors used in automotive applications.

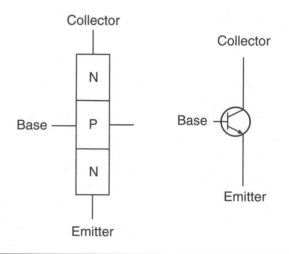

Figure 3-31 A NPN transistor and its symbol.

Figure 3-32 A PNP transistor and its symbol.

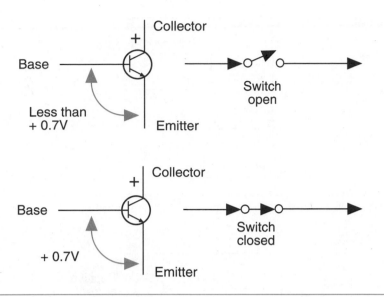

Figure 3-33 NPN transistor action.

The most harmful things to a transistor are excess voltage and heat. If you have a problem with a module that stops operating after the engine is warm, test it by heating it slowly with a hair drier. Two principle uses for transistors are as switches and amplifiers. The average transistor should last 100 years unless it receives some abuse.

Transistors are made by combining P-type and N-type materials in groups of three. The two possible combinations are NPN (Figure 3-31) and PNP (Figure 3-32). In effect, a transistor is two diodes that share a common center layer. No matter how the transistor is connected to the circuit, one of the diodes will be reverse biased and the other will be forward biased.

 WARNING: The PNP-type transistor is the most commonly used transistor in automotive electronics. A PNP transistor cannot be replaced with an NPN transistor.

The three layers of the transistor are designated as emitter, connector, and base. The emitter is the outside layer of the forward-biased diode that has the same polarity as the circuit side to which it is applied. The arrow on the transistor symbol refers to the emitter lead and points in the direction of positive current flow. The collector is the outside layer of the reverse-biased diode. The base is the shared middle layer. Each of these different layers has its own lead for connecting to different parts of the circuit.

In the NPN transistor, the emitter conducts current flow to the collector when the base is forward biased. The transistor cannot conduct unless the voltage applied to the base leg exceeds the emitter voltage by approximately 0.7 volt. This means both the base and collector must be positive with respect to the emitter. With less than 0.7 volt applied to the base leg (compared to the voltage at the emitter), the transistor acts as an opened switch. When the voltage difference is greater than 0.7 volt at the base, compared to the emitter voltage, the transistor acts as a closed switch (Figure 3-33).

When an NPN transistor is used in a circuit, it normally has a reverse bias applied to the base-collector junction. If the emitter-base junction is also reverse biased, no current will flow through the transistor (Figure 3-34). If the emitter-base junction is forward biased (Figure 3-35), current flows from the emitter to the base. Because the base is a thin layer and a positive voltage is applied to the collector, electrons flow from the emitter to the collector.

Figure 3-34 NPN transistor with reverse-biased voltage applied to the base. No current flow.

Figure 3-35 NPN transistor with forward-biased voltage applied to the base. Current flows.

In the PNP transistor, current will flow from the emitter to the collector when the base leg is forward biased with a voltage that is more negative than that at the emitter (Figure 3-36). For current to flow through the emitter to the collector, both the base and the collector must be negative in respect to the emitter. The operation of the PNP transistor is the same as the NPN, except current flow is hole current.

Current flow in a PNP transistor is considered as movement of holes. In the NPN transistor current flow is the movement of electrons.

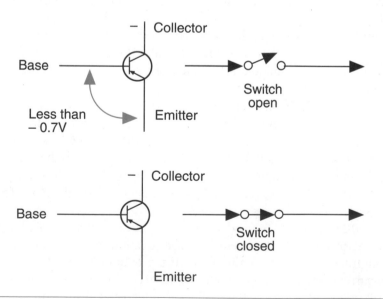

Figure 3-36 PNP transistor action.

Current can be controlled through a transistor. Thus transistors can be used as a very fast electrical switch. It is also possible to control the amount of current flow through the collector. This is because the output current is proportional to the amount of current through the base leg.

A transistor has three operating conditions:

1. **Cutoff:** When reverse-biased voltage is applied to the base leg of the transistor In this condition the transistor is not conducting and no current will flow.

2. **Conduction:** Bias voltage difference between the base and the emitter has increased to the point that the transistor is switched on. In this condition the transistor is conducting. Output current is proportional to that of the current through the base.

3. **Saturation:** This is the point where forward-biased voltage to the base leg is at a maximum. With bias voltage at the high limits, output current is also at its maximum.

These types of transistors are called bipolar because they have three layers of silicon; two of these layers are the same. Another type of transistor is the field-effect transistor (FET). The FET's leads are listed as source, drain, and gate. The source supplies the electrons and is similar to the emitter in the bipolar transistor. The drain collects the current and is similar to the collector. The gate creates the capacitive field that allows electron flow from the source to the drain. It is similar to the base.

The FET transistor does not require bias voltage. Only a voltage need be applied to the gate terminal to get electron flow from the source to the drain. The source and drain are constructed of the same type of doped material. They can be either N-type or P-type materials. The source and drain are separated by a thin layer of either N-type or P-type material.

Using the illustration (Figure 3-37), if the source voltage is held at 0 volts and 6 volts are applied to the drain, no current will flow between the two. However, if a lower positive voltage to the gate is applied, the gate forms a capacitive field between the channel and itself. The voltage of the capacitive field attracts electrons from the source and current will flow through the channel to the higher positive voltage of the drain.

FET-type transistors are common in the onboard computer systems of today's vehicles.

Figure 3-37 An FET uses a positive voltage to the gate terminal to create a capacitive field to allow electron flow.

This type of FET is called an enhancement-type FET because the field effect improves current flow from the source to the drain. This operation is similar to that of a normally open switch. A depletion-type FET is like a normally closed switch, whereas the field effect cuts off current flow from the source to the drain.

▲ **WARNING:** Some forms of FETs have a very thin insulation layer between the gate and channel that static electricity from your hands is able to burn through. Be careful not to touch the connector pins of the computer or the integrated circuits inside of the computer.

Transistor Amplifiers

A transistor can be used in an amplifier circuit to amplify the voltage. This is useful when using a very small voltage for sensing computer inputs, but needing to boost that voltage to operate an accessory (Figure 3-38). The waveform showing the small signal voltage that is applied to the base leg of a transistor may look like that shown (Figure 3-39A). The waveform showing the corresponding signal through the collector will be inverted (Figure 3-39B). Three things happen in an amplified circuit:

1. The amplified voltage at the collector is greater than that of the base voltage.

2. The input current increases.

3. The pattern has been inverted.

The first transistor in a Darlington pair is used as a preamplifier to produce a large current to operate the second transistor. The second transistor is isolated from the control circuit and is the final amplifier. The second transistor boosts the current to the amount required to operate the load component. The Darlington pair is utilized by most control modules used in electronic ignition systems.

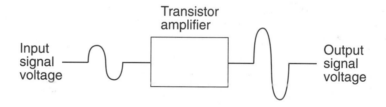

Figure 3-38 A simplified amplifier circuit.

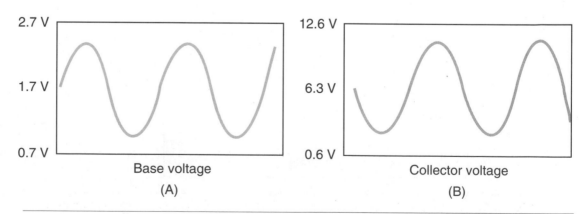

Figure 3-39 (A) Base voltage, (B) Collector voltage.

Figure 3-40 A Darlington pair used to amplify current. T1 acts as a preamplifier that creates a larger base current for T2, which is the final amplifier that creates a larger current.

Figure 3-41 Phototransistor.

Phototransistors

In a phototransistor, a small lens is used to focus incoming light onto the sensitive portion of the transistor. When light strikes the transistor, holes and free electrons are formed. These increase current flow through the transistor according to the amount of light. The stronger the light intensity, the more current that will flow. This type of phototransistor is often used in automatic headlight dimming circuits.

A **phototransistor** is a transistor that is sensitive to light (Figure 3-41).

Thyristors

The most common type of thyristor used in automotive applications is the silicon-controlled rectifier (SCR). Like the transistor, the SCR has three legs. However, it consists of four regions arranged PNPN (Figure 3-42). The three legs of the SCR are called the anode (or P-terminal), the cathode (or N-terminal), and the gate (one of the center regions).

A **thyristor** is a semiconductor switching device composed of alternating N and P layers. It can also be used to rectify current from AC to DC.

Figure 3-42 A forward direction SCR.

The SCR requires only a trigger pulse (not a continuous current) applied to the gate to become conductive. Current will continue to flow through the anode and cathode as long as the voltage remains high enough or until the gate voltage is reversed.

The SCR can be connected into a circuit either in the forward or reverse direction. Using Figure 3-42 of a forward direction connection, the P-type anode is connected to the positive side of the circuit and the N-type cathode is connected to the negative side. The center PN junction blocks current flow through the anode and cathode.

Once a positive voltage pulse is applied to the gate, the SCR turns on. Even if the positive voltage pulse is removed, the SCR will continue to conduct. If a negative voltage pulse is applied to the gate, the SCR will no longer conduct.

The SCR will also block any reverse current from flowing from the cathode to the anode. Because current can flow only in one direction through the SCR, it can rectify AC current to DC current.

Integrated Circuits

An integrated circuit is a complex circuit of thousands of transistors, diodes, resistors, capacitors, and other electronic devices that are formed onto a tiny silicon chip (Figure 3-43). As many as 30,000 transistors can be placed on a chip that is 1/4 inch (6.35 mm) square.

Integrated circuits are constructed by photographically reproducing circuit patterns onto a silicon wafer. The process begins with a large-scale drawing of the circuit. This drawing can be room size. Photographs of the circuit drawing are reduced until they are the actual size of the

☒ P Type
☐ N Type
▨ Poly
▢ Contact
▧ Metal

Figure 3-43 An enlarged illustration of an integrated circuit with thousands of transistors, diodes, resistors, and capacitors. Actual size can be less than 1/4 inch square.

circuit. The reduced photographs are used as a mask. Conductive P-type and N-type materials, along with insulating materials, are deposited onto the silicon wafer. The mask is placed over the wafer and selectively exposes the portion of material to be etched away or the portions requiring selective deposition. The entire process of creating an integrated circuit chip takes over 100 separate steps. Out of a single wafer 4 inches in diameter, thousands of integrated circuits can be produced.

The small size of the integrated chip has made it possible for the vehicle manufacturers to add several computer-controlled systems to the vehicle without taking up much space. Also a single computer is capable of performing several functions.

 WARNING: Integrated circuits can be damaged by static electricity. Use caution when working with these circuits. There are antistatic straps available for the technician to wear to reduce the possibility of destroying the integrated circuit.

 WARNING: Do not connect or disconnect an IC to the circuit with the power on. The arc produced may damage the chip.

The integrated circuit is also called an **IC chip.**

Test Equipment

Electricity is an invisible force, so the proper use of test tools will permit the technician to "see" the flow of electrons. Knowing what is being looked at and being able to interpret various meter types will assist in electrical system diagnosis. To diagnosis and repair electrical circuits correctly, a number of common tools and instruments are used. The most common tools are jumper wires, test lights, voltmeters, ammeters, and ohmmeters.

Jumper Wires

Connecting one end of the jumper wire to battery positive will provide an excellent 12-volt power supply for testing a component (Figure 3-44). Jumper wires can be used to check the load components by bypassing switches, conductors, and connections in the circuit. Jumper wires can also be used to provide the ground to test that portion of the circuit.

A **jumper wire** is simply a wire with an alligator clip on each end.

 WARNING: Never connect a jumper wire across the terminals of the battery. The battery could explode, causing serious injury.

Figure 3-44 Using a jumper wire to bypass a portion of the circuit, and to test the ground circuit.

Test Lights

A test light handle is transparent and contains a light bulb. A sharp probe extends from one end of the handle while a ground wire with a clamp extends from the other end (Figure 3-45). If the circuit is operating properly—clamping the lead of the test light to ground and probing a live circuit—the lamp should light (Figure 3-46).

A test light is limited in that it does not display how much voltage is at the point of the circuit being tested. However, by understanding the effects of voltage drop the technician will be able to interpret the brightness of the test light and relate the results to that which would be expected in a good circuit. If the lamp is connected after a voltage drop, the lamp will light dimly. Connecting the test lamp before the voltage drop should light the lamp brightly. The light should not illuminate at all if it is probing for voltage after the last resistance.

> ▲ **WARNING:** It is not recommended that a test light be used to probe for power in a computer-controlled circuit. The increased draw of the test light may damage the system components.

Another type of circuit tester is the self-powered continuity tester (Figure 3-47). The continuity tester has an internal battery that powers a light bulb—if the circuit is complete between

A **test light** is used when the technician needs to "look" for electrical power in the circuit.

Figure 3-45 A typical test light used to probe for voltage in a circuit.

Figure 3-46 If voltage is present, the test light will illuminate.

Figure 3-47 Typical self-powered continuity tester.

the probe and the ground wire. With the power in the circuit turned off or disconnected, the ground clip is connected to the ground terminal of the load component. By probing the feed wire, the light will illuminate if the circuit is complete (has continuity).

⚠️ **WARNING:** Do not connect a self-powered test light to a circuit that is powered. Doing so will damage the test light.

Voltmeter

A voltmeter is connected in parallel with a circuit and reads directly in volts (Figure 3-49). The voltmeter hookup should parallel the circuit being measured to prevent the high resistance meter from disrupting the circuit.

A **voltmeter** is one of the most used meters in the shop. A voltmeter is used to read the pressure behind the flow of electrons (Figure 3-48).

Figure 3-48 A voltmeter is used to read the amount of voltage potential between two points in a circuit.

Figure 3-49 Connecting a voltmeter in parallel to the circuit.

Figure 3-50 Checking voltage in a closed circuit.

The illustration (Figure 3-50) shows how to check for voltage in a closed circuit. The voltage at point A is 12 volts positive. There is a drop of 6 volts over the 1-ohm resistor. The reading is 6 volts positive at point B. The remaining voltage drops in the motor load and the voltmeter reads 0 at point C, indicating normal motor circuit operation.

When reading voltage in the same circuit that has an open (Figure 3-51), 12 volts will be indicated at any point ahead of the open. This is indicated at points A, B, and C, but not through X. Because the circuit is open, and there is no electrical flow, there is no voltage drop across a resistor or load.

To measure the voltage drop across each load it must be determined what point is positive and what point is negative. A point in the circuit can be either positive or negative, depending on what is being measured. Referring to the illustration (Figure 3-52), if voltage drop across R_1 is being measured, the positive meter lead is placed at point A and the negative lead at point B. The voltmeter will measure the difference in volts between these points. However, to measure the voltage drop across R_2, the polarity of point B is positive and point C is negative. The reason being that point B is the most negative for R_1, yet it is the most positive point for R_2. To measure voltage drop across R_3, point C is positive and point D is negative. The positive lead of the voltmeter should be placed as close as possible to the positive side of the battery in the circuit.

Figure 3-51 Checking voltage in an open circuit.

Figure 3-52 Using a voltmeter to measure voltage drops.

Ohmmeter

By connecting the ohmmeter leads to each end of a wire, an open or excessive resistance can be detected. The meter should read 0 ohms if the wire is good. If the meter indicates an infinity (∞) reading, this usually means there is an open in the circuit.

An **ohmmeter** will measure resistance and continuity (Figure 3-53).

⚠ **WARNING:** The ohmmeter is self-powered. Never use an ohmmeter on a powered circuit.

Most ohmmeters use a multiplier to figure higher resistances. The multiposition switch on the front of the meter indicates four ranges. These ranges are labeled $R \times 1$, $R \times 10$, $R \times 100$, and $R \times 1k$. Each reading must be multiplied by the number to get the actual resistance. If the reading is 22 Ω (resistance) and the switch is on $R \times 1$, the resistance is 22 Ω. If a 65 Ω value is obtained on the $R \times 100$ scale the reading is 6,500 Ω (65 $\times$ 100). If a reading of 40 Ω is obtained on the $R \times 1k$ scale, then the reading is actually 40,000 Ω (40 $\times$ 1,000).

If the resistance is unknown, start on the lowest scale and work up to the higher scales. This will prevent misinterpreting infinity readings.

Figure 3-53 A typical analog, four-range ohmmeter.

Type of Defect	Test Unit	Expected Results
Open	Ohmmeter	∞ infinite resistance between conductor ends
	Test light	No light after open
	Voltmeter	∅ volts at end of conductor after the open
Ground	Ohmmeter	∅ resistance to ground
	Test light	Lights if connected across fuse
	Voltmeter	Generally not used to test for ground
Short	Ohmmeter	Lower than specified resistance through load component
		∅ resistance to adjacent conductor ∞ infinite resistance to ground
	Test light	Light will illuminate on both conductors
	Voltmeter	A voltage will be read on both conductors

Figure 3-54 Circuit test chart.

The test chart shown (Figure 3-54) illustrates the readings that may be expected from an ohmmeter or voltmeter under different conditions. It is important to become familiar with these examples in order to analyze circuits.

Ammeter

An **ammeter** is used to measure current draw (Figure 3-55).

Many styles of ammeters required being connected in series with the load to read the amount of current draw (Figure 3-56). To make a series connection, disconnect the load and reconnect it with all of the current going through the ammeter. Polarity must be followed. Do not connect an ammeter in parallel with the circuit because this can cause damage to the circuit or the meter. To prevent damage to the computers on modern vehicles, use only an induction-type ammeter with a clamp on pickup (Figure 3-57). The ammeter determines the amount of amperage by the strength of the magnetic field that is created by the current flowing through the wire.

Figure 3-55 An analog ammeter.

Figure 3-56 Ammeter connected in series with the circuit.

Figure 3-57 Ammeter with inductive pickup.

CAUTION: Always use an ammeter that can handle the expected current. Excessive current can damage the meter.

Digital Multimeter

With modern vehicles incorporating computer-controlled systems, digital multimeters are required (Figure 3-58). Computer systems have integrated circuits that operate on very low amounts of current. Analog meters will down load computer circuits and burn out the IC chips. The advantage of the digital multimeter (DMM) is its very high input resistance (impedance), which prevents the meter from drawing current when connected to a circuit. Most DMMs have at least 10 megohms (10 million ohms) impedance. This reduces the risk of damaging computer circuits and components.

Most **analog** meters use a needle to indicate the readings on a scale.

Down loading is charging the circuit.

Digital multimeters are also known as **DVOMs** (Digital Volt-Ohm Meters).

Figure 3-58 Digital Multimeter. (Courtesy of TIF Instruments, Inc.)

 WARNING: Not all DMMs are rated at 10 megaohms of impedance. Be sure of the meter that you are using to prevent electronic component damage.

Unlike an analog meter, digital meters are not polarity sensitive. The readout will display + or − to indicate the polarity.

Reading the DVOM

With the increased use of the DVOM, it is important for the technician to be able to accurately read the meter. By becoming proficient in the use of the DVOM, technicians will have confidence in their conclusions and recommended repairs. This will eliminate the replacement of parts that were not faulty. Although there are deviations between the different DVOM manufacturers as to the way the display is presented, most follow the method described here.

When continuity is good, the DVOM will read 0 or close to 0 even on the low ohmmeter scale. If the continuity is very poor, the DVOM will display an infinite reading. This reading is usually shown as a blinking "1.000," a blinking "1," or an "OL."

Referring to Figure 3-58 of a DVOM, the meter is capable of displaying resistance values in different scales. The most common scale granulations are 200, 2K, 20K, 200K, 2M, and 20M. It is important that the correct scale be used to obtain an accurate reading. When the DVOM is connected to a circuit to test its resistance, begin with the lowest scale and scale up until the infinite indicator is no longer displayed. This is true unless the lowest scale does not produce the infinite reading. In this case, stay on the lowest scale. Also, if the DVOM indicates an infinite reading on the highest scale then there is an open in the circuit.

This method of scaling up will put the DVOM to the lowest scale that it is still capable of reading the resistance of the component or circuit. This will assure that the highest possible degree of accuracy is attained.

The number that represents the scale reading is the potential number of units that can be read on that particular scale, before the infinite indicator is displayed. Any letter suffix represents the multiplying factor. On the 200 scale there is no multiplying factor and the meter is capable of reading up to 200 ohms before the infinite indicator is displayed. On the 2K scale the multiplying factor is 1,000. This scale is capable of reading 2,000 ohms before an infinite indicator is shown.

Good continuity means there is very low resistance.

Very poor continuity indicates there is extremely high resistance or an open.

Some DVOMs have automatic scaling. Therefore, this step would not be necessary.

K stands for Kilo and means 1,000.

M stands for Mega and means 1,000,000.

Figure 3-59 DVOM displaying resistance on the 2K scale. The resistance is less than 1,000 ohms, so the first space is blank.

The 20K scale is capable of reading up to 20,000 ohms before the infinite indicator is shown. The 20M scale has a multiplier factor of 1,000,000 and is capable of reading up to 20,000,000 ohms of resistance before the infinite indicator is shown.

If the resistance reading is on the 200 scale, simply read the display as it appears. If the display shows 154, the resistance is 154 ohms. If the display shows 104.4 ohms, the resistance is 104.4 ohms. If the resistance value of the component or circuit is over 200 ohms, the display would show the infinite indicator. If the infinite indicator is shown, then scale up to the next range.

If the meter is set on the 2K scale, the resistance is read by placing the decimal point three places to the right. For example, if the resistance value is 450 ohms the display will read .450. The first space would be blank (Figure 3-59). If the resistance value was 1,230 ohms, this would be displayed directly (Figure 3-60). If the resistance was over 2,000 ohms, the display would show the infinite indicator and the technician would go to the next highest scale.

If the DVOM is on the 20K scale, move the decimal point three places to the right. Do this regardless of whether or not all three places are actually shown on the display. For example, if the display showed 15.00. this would indicate 15,000 ohms of resistance. A reading of 50 ohms would be indicated by 0.05.

The 200K scale is read the same way as the 20K scale. Move the decimal point three places to the right. If the display shows 150.0 the resistance value is 150,000 ohms.

Figure 3-60 DVOM displaying resistance on the 2K scale. The resistance is greater than 1,000 ohms, so the first space is filled.

On the 20M scale move the decimal point six places to the right. A display of 20.00 would actually be 20,000,000 ohms, and a display of 1.456 would be 1,456,000 ohms. If the amount of resistance is higher than 20M ohms, the display will show the infinite indicator. This usually means there is an open in the circuit.

A voltage reading on the DVOM is very simple. The scales are usually 2 V, 20 V and 200 V. On the 2-V scale the display would show up to 2.000 volts. On the 20-V scale the display will be up to 20.00 volts and on the 200-V scale the display will be up to 200.0 volts. Be sure the meter is on the appropriate DC or AC voltage to test the circuit.

Circuit Defects

Electrical circuits may develop an open, a short, a ground, or an excessive voltage drop that will cause the circuit to operate improperly. Understanding the different types of circuit defects will allow the technician to isolate the problem and make the needed repairs to the circuit in the least amount of time.

Open

Shop Manual
Chapter 3, page 29

An **open circuit** is a circuit in which there is a break in continuity.

If the continuity of the circuit is broken, the system is open (Figure 3-61). An open circuit is like turning off the switch, and results in the system not operating. The open can be on either the insulated side or the ground side of the circuit.

Figure 3-61 An open circuit stops all current flow.

Shorts

Shop Manual
Chapter 3, page 30

A **shorted circuit** is a circuit that allows current to bypass part of the normal path.

An example of a shorted circuit could be found in a faulty coil (Figure 3-62). The windings within a coil are insulated from each other. However, if this insulation breaks down a copper-to-copper contact is made between the turns. Because part of the windings will be bypassed, this reduces the number of windings in the coil through which electricity could flow. This results in reducing the effectiveness of the coil. Also, because the current bypasses a portion of the normal circuit resistance, current flow is increased and excess heat can be generated.

Another example of a shorted circuit is if the insulation of two adjacent wires breaks down, and allows a copper-to-copper contact (Figure 3-63). If the short is between points A and B, light 1 would be on all the time. If the short is between points B and C, light 2 would illuminate, along with light 1, when the switch for light 1 was closed.

Figure 3-62 A shorted circuit will reduce the effectiveness of the coil.

Figure 3-63 A short circuit can be a copper-to-copper contact between two adjacent wires.

Figure 3-64 A grounded circuit.

A **grounded circuit** is a condition that allows current to return to ground before it has reached the intended load component (Figure 3-64).

Grounds

SERVICE TIP: A grounded circuit can be checked by removing the fuse and connecting a test lamp in series across the fuse connections. If the lamp lights, the circuit is grounded (Figure 3-65).

A grounded circuit is much like a short in that the load component is bypassed. In a grounded circuit, an insulation breakdown occurs that allows the current to flow to ground before reaching the load component. For example, if the wire leading to the taillight has an insulation breakdown that allows the wire to touch the body or frame, current will flow to ground at this point and return to the source. A grounded circuit may cause excessive current to be drawn from the battery, and has the potential to be very damaging to many components in the electrical system. If the correct fuse is installed in the circuit of the system, the excessive current draw will cause the fuse to "blow." The open fuse will prevent current flow, thus protecting the circuit from the increased amperage.

Figure 3-65 To test for a grounded circuit, remove the fuse and connect a test light across the fuse terminals. If the test light illuminates, there is a ground circuit.

Excessive Voltage Drop

Voltage drop, when considered as a defect, defines the portion of applied voltage that is used up in other points of the circuit rather than that used by the load component. The effect is that the load component, with reduced voltage applied, operates with reduced efficiency. An example would be a taillight circuit with a load component (light bulb) that is rated at 50 watts. To be fully effective this bulb must draw 4.2 amperes at 12 volts ($I = P \div V$). This means that a full 12 volts should appear at the bulb. If resistance is present at other points in the circuit, some of the 12 volts will be dropped. With less voltage being available to the light bulb, the bulb will illuminate with less intensity.

Excessive voltage drop may appear on either the insulated or grounded return side of a circuit. It may also be present in both. To test for voltage drop, the circuit must be active (current flowing). The source voltage must be as specified before voltage drop readings can be valid. Whenever voltage drop is suspected, both sides of the circuit must be checked.

Summary

❏ The protection device is designed to "turn off" the system it protects. This is done by creating an open (like turning off a switch) to prevent a complete circuit.

❏ Fuses are rated by amperage. Never install a larger rated fuse into a circuit than the one that was designed by the manufacturer. Doing so may damage or destroy the circuit.

❏ A switch can control the on/off operation of a circuit or direct the flow of current through various circuits.

❏ A normally open switch will not allow current flow when it is in its rest position. A normally closed switch will allow current flow when it is in its rest position.

❏ A relay is a device that uses low current to control a high current circuit.

❏ A buzzer is sometimes used to warn the driver of possible safety hazards by emitting an audio signal (such as when the seat belt is not buckled).

❏ A stepped resistor has two or more fixed resistor values. It is commonly used to control electrical motor speeds.

❏ A variable resistor provides for a infinite number of resistance values within a range. A rheostat is a two-terminal variable resistor used to regulate the strength of an electrical current. A potentiometer is a three-wire variable resistor that acts as a voltage divider to produce a continuously variable output signal proportional to a mechanical position.

❏ A diode is an electrical one-way check valve that will allow current to flow in one direction only.

❏ Forward bias means that a positive voltage is applied to the P-type material and negative voltage to the N-type material. Reversed bias means that positive voltage is applied to the N-type material and negative voltage is applied to the P-type material.

❏ A transistor is a three-layer semiconductor that is commonly used as a very fast switching device.

❏ An integrated circuit is a complex circuit of thousands of transistors, diodes, resistors, capacitors, and other electronic devices that are formed onto a tiny silicon chip.

❏ An open circuit is a circuit in which there is a break in continuity.

❏ A shorted circuit is a circuit that allows current to bypass part of the normal path.

❏ A grounded circuit is a condition that allows current to return to ground before it has reached the intended load component.

Terms to Know

Ammeter

Bimetallic

Bus bar

Clamping diode

Digital multimeters

Diode

DVOM (Digital Volt-Ohm Meters)

Forward bias

Fuse

Fuse box

Grounded circuit

Jumper wire

Light-emitting diode (LED)

Normally closed (NC)

Normally open (NO)

Ohmmeter

Open circuit

Overload

Phototransistor

Potentiometer

Relay

Reverse bias

Rheostat

Saturation

Shorted circuit

Stepped resistor

Test light

Thyristor

Transistor

Variable resistor

Voltmeter

Zener diode

Review Questions

Short Answer Essays

1. Describe the use of three types of semiconductors.

2. What is the ohmmeter used to test for?

3. Define what is meant by opens, shorts, grounds, and excessive voltage drops.

4. Explain the effects that each type of circuit defect will have on the operation of the electrical system.

5. Explain the purpose of a circuit protection device.

6. Describe the most common types of circuit protection devices.

7. Describe the common types of electrical system components used and how they affect the electrical system.

8. Describe the difference between a rheostat and a potentiometer.

9. Explain the difference between normally open (NO) and normally closed (NC) switches.

10. Describe how to use a DVOM to measure voltage.

Fill-in-the-Blanks

1. Never install a larger rated _____ into a circuit than the one that was designed by the manufacturer.

2. A _____ can control the on/off operation of a circuit or direct the flow of current through various circuits.

3. A normally _____ switch will not allow current flow when it is in its rest position. A normally _____ switch will allow current flow when it is in its rest position.

4. An _____ _____ is a complex circuit of thousands of transistors, diodes, resistors, capacitors, and other electronic devices that are formed onto a tiny silicon chip.

5. When continuity is good, the DVOM will read close to _____ , even on the low scale. If the continuity is very poor, the DVOM will display an _____ reading.

6. A _____ is used in electronic circuits as a very fast switching device.

7. A _____ is an electrical one-way check valve that will allow current to flow in one direction only.

8. A _____ is a device that uses low current to control a high current circuit.

9. A _____ _____ provides for an infinite number of resistance values within a range. A _____ is a two-terminal variable resistor used to regulate the strength of an electrical current.

10. The _____ requires only a trigger pulse applied to the gate to become conductive.

ASE Style Review Questions

1. The use of an ammeter is being discussed:
   Technician A says the ammeter is used to measure current draw.
   Technician B says the ammeter is used to measure resistance.
   Who is correct?
   A. A only
   B. B only
   C. Both A and B
   D. Neither A nor B

2. While discussing protection devices:
   Technician A says a fuse automatically resets after the cause of the overload is repaired.
   Technician B says the protection device creates an open when an overload occurs.
   Who is correct?
   A. A only
   B. B only
   C. Both A and B
   D. Neither A nor B

3. While discussing circuit components:
   Technician A says a switch can control the on/off operation of a circuit or direct the flow of current through various circuits.
   Technician B says a relay is a SPDT-type switch.
   Who is correct?
   A. A only
   B. B only
   C. Both A and B
   D. Neither A nor B

4. While discussing diodes:
   Technician A says the zener diode is an excellent component for regulating voltage.
   Technician B says installing a clamping diode provides a bypass for the electrons when the circuit is opened suddenly.
   Who is correct?
   A. A only
   B. B only
   C. Both A and B
   D. Neither A nor B

5. The use of a DVOM is being discussed:
   Technician A says the number that represents the scale reading is the potential number of units that can be read on that particular scale, before the infinite indicator is displayed.
   Technician B says any letter suffix represents the multiplying factor.
   Who is correct?
   A. A only
   B. B only
   C. Both A and B
   D. Neither A nor B

6. While discussing circuit defects:
   Technician A says an open means there is continuity in the circuit.
   Technician B says a short bypasses a portion of the circuit.
   Who is correct?
   A. A only
   B. B only
   C. Both A and B
   D. Neither A nor B

7. While discussing the use of transistors:
   Technician A says a transistor can be used to control the switching on/off of a circuit.
   Technician B says a transistor can be used to amplify voltage.
   Who is correct?
   A. A only
   B. B only
   C. Both A and B
   D. Neither A nor B

8. Circuit defects are being discussed:
   Technician A says voltage drop can cause a lamp in a parallel circuit to burn brighter than normal.
   Technician B says excessive voltage drop may appear on either the insulated or grounded return side of a circuit.
   Who is correct?
   A. A only
   B. B only
   C. Both A and B
   D. Neither A nor B

9. The DVOM is being used to measure resistance and is set on the 20M scale:

Technician A says to move the decimal point six places to the right.

Technician B says to move the decimal two places to the left.

Who is correct?

A. A only
B. B only
C. Both A and B
D. Neither A nor B

10. Circuit protection devices are being discussed:

Technician A says a "blown" fuse is identified by bubbling of the insulator material around the link.

Technician B say a "blown" fusible link is identified by a burned-through metal wire in the capsule.

Who is correct?

A. A only
B. B only
C. Both A and B
D. Neither A nor B

Wiring and Circuit Diagrams

Upon completion and review of this chapter, you should be able to:

❏ Explain when single-stranded or multistranded wire should be used.

❏ Explain the use of resistive wires in a circuit.

❏ Describe the construction of spark plug wires.

❏ Explain how wire size is determined by the American Wire Gauge (AWG) and metric methods.

❏ Describe how to determine the correct wire gauge to be used in a circuit.

❏ Explain how temperature affects resistance and wire size selection.

❏ Explain the purpose and use of printed circuits.

❏ Explain why wiring harnesses are used and how they are constructed.

❏ Explain the purpose of wiring diagrams.

❏ Identify the common electrical symbols that are used.

❏ Explain the purpose of the component locator.

Introduction

Today's vehicles have a vast amount of electrical wiring that, if laid end to end, can stretch for half a mile. Technicians must therefore be proficient at reading wiring diagrams to be able to sort through this great maze of wires. By being able to combine the knowledge obtained in Chapter 3 and learning the principles presented in this chapter, you should be able to diagnose, locate, and repair any faulty electrical system.

Few areas of today's automobiles are more confusing to the technician than the wiring harness. In this chapter you will learn how wiring harnesses are made, how to read the wiring diagram, how to interpret the symbols used, and how terminals are used. This will reduce the amount of confusion experienced when it comes to performing repairs on any electrical circuit. It is also important for the technician to understand how to determine the correct type and size of wire to carry the anticipated amount of current. It is possible to cause the electrical system to malfunction by simply using the wrong wire. The technician must understand the three factors that cause resistance in a wire—length, diameter, and temperature—to perform repairs correctly.

Automotive Wiring

Primary wiring is the term used for conductors that carry low voltage and low current. The insulation of primary wires is usually thin. Secondary wiring refers to wires used to carry high voltage or high current, such as battery cables and ignition spark plug wires. Secondary wires have extra thick insulation.

Most of the primary wiring conductors used in the automobile are made of several strands of copper wire wound together and covered with a polyvinyl chloride (PVC) insulation (Figure 4-1). Copper has low resistance and can be connected to easily by using crimping connectors or soldered connections. Other types of conductor materials used in automobiles include silver, gold, aluminum, and tin-plated brass.

Copper is used mainly because of its low cost and availability.

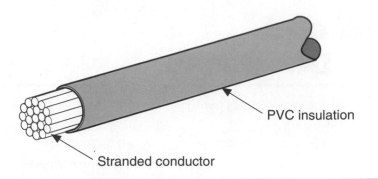

PVC insulation

Stranded conductor

Figure 4-1 Stranded primary wire.

General Motors has used single-stranded aluminum wire in limited applications where no flexing of the wire is expected. For example, it is used in the taillight circuits.

Resistance wire is designed with a certain amount of resistance per foot.

The resistance value of the ballast resistor is usually between 0.8 and 1.2 ohms.

Spark plug wires are often referred to as **television-radio-suppression (TVRS) cables.**

⚠️ **WARNING:** A solid copper wire may be used in low-voltage, low-current circuits where flexibility is not required. Do not use solid wire where high voltage, high current, or flexibility is required.

Stranded wire is used because current flows on the surface of the conductors. Because there is more surface area exposed in a stranded wire (each strand has its own surface), there is less resistance in the stranded wire than in the solid wire (Figure 4-2). The PVC insulation is used because it can withstand temperature extremes and corrosion. PVC insulation is also capable of withstanding battery acid, antifreeze, and gasoline. The insulation protects the wire from shorting to ground and from corrosion.

A ballast resistor is used to protect the ignition primary circuit from excessive voltage. It reduces the current flow through the coil's primary windings when it is not needed, and provides a stable voltage to the coil.

Some automobiles have a resistance wire incorporated into the ignition system. It is most commonly used to limit the amount of current flow through the primary windings of the ignition coil. This wire is called the ballast resistor and is located between the ignition switch and the ignition coil (Figure 4-3).

Spark plug wires also are resistance wires. Whenever a spark occurs, electromagnetic energy is radiated from the spark. This energy can cause radio interference in the vehicle's radio, other radios, and in nearby televisions. Current standards require that all ignition systems control RFI, and most manufacturers do this by using resistance in the spark plug wires.

Most spark plug wires are made of nylon, rayon, fiberglass, or aramid thread impregnated with carbon. This core is surrounded by rubber (Figure 4-4). The carbon-impregnated core provides sufficient resistance to reduce RFI, yet does not affect engine operation. As the spark plug

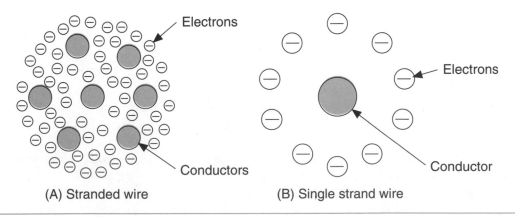

Electrons

Electrons

Conductors

Conductor

(A) Stranded wire

(B) Single strand wire

Figure 4-2 Stranded wire provides more surface area for electron flow than a single-strand wire.

Figure 4-3 Ballast resistor used in some ignition primary wiring circuits.

The interference caused by electromagnetic energy is called **radiofrequency interference (RFI).**

wires wear because of age and temperature changes, the resistance in the wire will change. Most plug wires have a resistance value of 3,000 Ω to 6,000 Ω per foot. However, some have between 6,000 Ω and 12,000 Ω. The accepted value when testing is 10,000 Ω per foot as a general specification.

Because the high voltage within the plug wires can create electromagnetic induction, proper wire routing is important to eliminate the possibility of cross-fire. To prevent cross-fire, the plug wires must be installed in the proper separator. Any two parallel wires next to each other in the firing order should be positioned as far away from each other as possible (Figure 4-5). When induction cross-fire occurs, no spark is jumped from one wire to the other. The spark is the result of induction from another field. Cross-fire induction is most common in two parallel wires that fire one after the other in the firing order.

It is important to check the procedure for testing the plug wires because some manufacturers require that the distributor cap be connected to the wires.

Wire Sizes

An additional amount of consideration must be given for some margin of safety when selecting wire size. There are three major factors that determine the proper size of wire to be used:

1. The wire must be large enough—for the length required—to carry the necessary current for the load components in the circuit to operate properly.

2. The wire must be able to withstand the anticipated vibration.

3. The wire must be able to withstand the anticipated amount of heat exposure.

Cross-fire is the electromagnetic induction spark that can be transmitted in another wire close to the wire carrying the current.

Figure 4-4 Typical spark plug wire.

Cable bracket

Plug cables 7 and 8 separated in cable bracket

Firing orders and cylinder numbering vary among the different engines

Example:
firing order
1-5-4-2-6-3-7-8

5 6 7 8

Left bank engine cylinders

Figure 4-5 Proper spark plug wire routing to prevent cross-fire. (Courtesy of Chrysler Corporation)

The number assigned to a wire to indicate its size is referred to as **gauge.**

Some high current circuits will also use 10- or 12-gauge wire.

Wire size is based on the diameter of the conductor. The larger the diameter, the less the resistance. There are two common size standards used to designate wire size: American Wire Gauge (AWG) and metric.

The AWG standard assigns a number to the wire based on its diameter. The higher the number, the smaller the wire diameter. For example, 20-gauge wire is smaller in diameter than 10-gauge wire. Most electrical systems in the automobile use 14-, 16-, or 18-gauge wire. Most battery cables are 2-, 4-, or 6-gauge cable.

Both wire diameter and wire length affect resistance. Sixteen-gauge wire is capable of conducting 20 amperes for 10 feet with minimal voltage drop. However, if the current is to be carried for 15 feet, 14-gauge wire would be required. If 20 amperes were required to be carried for 20 feet, then 12-gauge wire would be required. The additional wire size is needed to prevent voltage drops in the wire. The illustration (Figure 4-6) lists the wire size required to carry a given amount of current for different lengths.

Another factor to wire resistance is temperature. An increase in temperature creates a similar increase in resistance. A wire may have a known resistance of 0.03 ohms per 10 feet at 70° F. When exposed to temperatures of 170° F, the resistance may increase to 0.04 ohms per 10 feet. Wires that are to be installed in areas that experience high temperatures, as in the engine compartment, must be of a size such that the increased resistance will not affect the operation of the load component. Also, the insulation of the wire must be capable of withstanding the high temperatures.

In the metric system, wire size is determined by the cross-sectional area of the wire. Metric wire size is expressed in square millimeters (mm²). In this system the smaller the number, the smaller the wire conductor. The approximate equivalent wire size of metric to AWG is shown (Figure 4-7).

Terminals and Connectors

To perform the function of connecting the wires from the voltage source to the load component reliably, terminal connections are used. Today's vehicles can have as many as 500 separate circuit connections. The terminals used to make these connections must be able to perform with very low voltage drop. A loose or corroded connection can cause a high voltage drop that results in poor operation of the load component.

Shop Manual
Chapter 4, pages 44, 45, and 52

Total Approximate Circuit Amperes	Wire Gauge (for Length in Feet)								
12 V	3	5	7	10	15	20	25	30	40
1.0	18	18	18	18	18	18	18	18	18
1.5	18	18	18	18	18	18	18	18	18
2	18	18	18	18	18	18	18	18	18
3	18	18	18	18	18	18	18	18	18
4	18	18	18	18	18	18	18	16	16
5	18	18	18	18	18	18	18	16	16
6	18	18	18	18	18	18	16	16	16
7	18	18	18	18	18	18	16	16	14
8	18	18	18	18	18	16	16	16	14
10	18	18	18	18	16	16	16	14	12
11	18	18	18	18	16	16	14	14	12
12	18	18	18	18	16	16	14	14	12
15	18	18	18	18	14	14	12	12	12
18	18	18	16	16	14	14	12	12	10
20	18	18	16	16	14	12	10	10	10
22	18	18	16	16	12	12	10	10	10
24	18	18	16	16	12	12	10	10	10
30	18	16	16	14	10	10	10	10	10
40	18	16	14	12	10	10	8	8	6
50	16	14	12	12	10	10	8	8	6
100	12	12	10	10	6	6	4	4	4
150	10	10	8	8	4	4	2	2	2
200	10	8	8	6	4	4	2	2	1

Note: 18 AWG as indicated above this line could be 20 AWG electrically.
18 AWG is recommended for mechanical strength.

Figure 4-6 The distance the current must be carried is a factor in determining the correct wire gauge to use.

Terminals are constructed of either brass or steel with a coating of tin or lead.

If as little as 10% voltage drop (1.2 V) occurs in a bad connection of a light circuit, it may result in a 30% loss of lighting efficiency.

Metric Size (mm^2)	Wire Size	Ampere Capacity
0.5	20	4
0.8	18	6
1.0	16	8
2.0	14	15
3.0	12	20
5.0	10	30
8.0	8	40
13.0	6	50
19.0	4	60

Figure 4-7 Approximate AWG to metric equivalents.

Figure 4-8 Primary wire terminals used in automotive applications.

Shop Manual
Chapter 4, page 52

Shop Manual
Chapter 4, page 53

Terminals can be either crimped or soldered to the conductor. The terminal makes the electrical connection and, it must be capable of withstanding the stress of normal vibration. The illustration (Figure 4-8) shows several different types of terminals used in the automotive electrical system. In addition, the following connectors are used on the automobile:

1. **Molded connector:** These connectors usually have one to four wires that are molded into a one-piece component (Figure 4-9).
2. **Multiple-wire hard-shell connector:** These connectors usually have a hard plastic shell that holds the connecting terminals of separate wires (Figure 4-10). The wire terminals can be removed from the shell to be repaired.

Figure 4-9 Multiple-circuit wire-molded connector.

Figure 4-10 Multiple-wire hard-shell connector.

Figure 4-11 Bulkhead connector. (Courtesy of Chrysler Corporation)

Shop Manual
Chapter 4, page 54

Shop Manual
Chapter 4, page 55

3. **Bulkhead connectors:** These connectors are used when several wires must pass through the bulkhead (Figure 4-11).

4. **Weather-Pack Connectors:** These connectors have rubber seals on the terminal ends and on the covers of the connector half (Figure 4-12). These connectors are used on computer circuits to protect the circuit from corrosion, which may result in a voltage drop.

5. **Metri-Pack Connectors:** These are like the weather-pack connectors, but do not have the seal on the cover half (Figure 4-13).

Figure 4-12 Weather-pack connector is used to prevent connector corrosion.

Figure 4-13 Metri-pack connector.

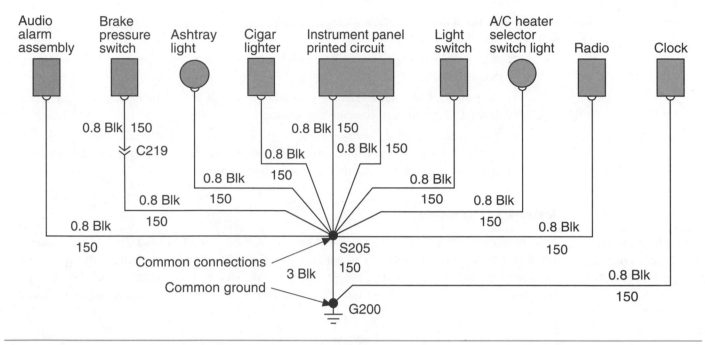

Figure 4-14 Common connections are used to reduce the number of connectors. (Courtesy of General Motors Corporation)

To reduce the number of connectors in the electrical system, a common connection can be used (Figure 4-14). If there are several electrical components that are physically close to each other, a single common connection eliminates using a separate connector for each wire.

Printed Circuits

Most instrument panels use printed circuit boards as circuit conductors. A printed circuit is made of a thin phenolic or fiberglass board that copper (or some other conductive material) has been deposited on. Portions of the conductive metal are then etched or eaten away by acid. The remaining strips of conductors provide the circuit path for the instrument panel lights, warning lights, indicator lights, and gauges of the instrument panel (Figure 4-15). The printed circuit board is attached to the back of the instrument panel housing. An edge connector joins the printed circuit board to the vehicle wiring harness.

Common connections are used to share source of power or a common ground.

Printed circuit boards are used to simplify the wiring of the circuits they operate. Other uses of printed circuit boards include the inside of radios, computers, and some voltage regulators.

Figure 4-15 Printed circuits eliminate bulky wires behind the instrument panel.

Whenever it is necessary to perform repairs on or around the printed circuit board, it is important to follow these precautions:

1. When replacing light bulbs, be careful not to cut or tear the surface of the printed circuit board.

2. Do not touch the surface of the printed circuit with your fingers. The acid present in normal body oils can damage the surface.

3. If the printed circuit board needs to be cleaned, use a commercial cleaning solution designed for electrical use. If this solution is not available, it is possible to clean the board by **lightly** rubbing the surface with an eraser.

Wiring Harness

A **wire harness** is an assembled group of wires that branch out to the various electrical components.

Most manufacturers use wiring harnesses to reduce the amount of loose wires hanging under the hood or dash of an automobile. The wiring harness provides for a safe path for the wires of the vehicle's lighting, engine, and accessory components. The wiring harness is made by grouping insulated wires and wrapping them together. The wires are bundled into separate harness

Figure 4-16 Complex wiring harness. (Courtesy of Chrysler Corporation)

Figure 4-17 Simple wiring harness. (Courtesy of Chrysler Corporation)

assemblies that are joined together by connector plugs. The mutiple-pin connector plug may have more than 60 individual wire terminals.

There are several complex wiring harnesses in a vehicle, in addition to the simple harnesses. The engine compartment harness and the under dash harness are examples of a complex harness (Figure 4-16). Lighting circuits usually use a more simple harness (Figure 4-17). A complex harness serves many circuits. The simple harness services only a few circuits. Some individual circuit wires may branch out of a complex harness to other areas of the vehicle.

Most wiring harnesses now use a flexible tubing to provide for quick wire installation (Figure 4-18). The tubing has a seam that can be opened to accommodate the installation or removal of wires from the harness. The seam will close once the wires are installed, and will remain closed even if the tubing is bent.

Wiring Protective Devices

Often overlooked, but very important to the electrical system, are proper wire protection devices (Figure 4-19). These devices prevent damage to the wiring by maintaining proper wire routing and retention. Special clips, retainers, straps, and supplementary insulators provide additional protection to the conductor over what the insulation itself is capable of providing. Whenever the technician must remove one of these devices to perform a repair, it is important that the device be reinstalled to prevent additional electrical problems.

Figure 4-18 Flexible tubing used to make wiring harnesses.

Figure 4-19 Typical wire protection devices. (Courtesy of Chrysler Corporation)

Whenever it is necessary to install additional electrical accessories, try to support the primary wire in at least 1-foot intervals. If the wire must be routed through the frame or body, use rubber grommets to protect the wire.

CAUTION: Do not use metal clamps to secure wires to the frame or body of the vehicle. The metal clamp may cut through the insulation and cause a short to ground. Use plastic clips in place of metal.

Shop Manual
Chapter 4, page 57

A **wiring diagram** is an electrical schematic that shows a representation of actual electrical or electronic components (by use of symbols) and the wiring of the vehicle's electrical systems.

In place of actual pictures, a variety of **electrical symbols** are used to represent the components in the wiring diagram.

Wiring Diagrams

Perhaps the technician's greatest helpmate in locating electrical problems is the wiring diagram. Correct use of the wiring diagram will reduce the amount of time a technician needs to spend tracing the wires in the vehicle. The wiring diagram will indicate what circuits are interconnected, where circuits receive their voltage source, what color of wires are used in the circuit, and any additional information necessary for the technician to make an accurate diagnosis (Figure 4-20).

The wiring diagram can illustrate the entire vehicle wiring (Figure 4-21) or just one electrical circuit (Figure 4-22). All connections are included to show the routing of the wires. Wiring diagrams also show the color coding used in different circuits.

Wire diagrams are a vital tool to the technician for troubleshooting any electrical system problems. The wiring diagram will illustrate how the various circuits receive their power and what other devices control the circuit. The actual operation of the circuits is not usually described in the diagram. It is generally covered in the text area of the shop manual.

Electrical Symbols

Most shop manuals do not show actual pictures of the components in a circuit on the wiring diagram. Instead, they rely on electrical symbols. A listing of symbols used in automotive circuits is shown (Figure 4-23). Some import manufacturer manuals will use different electrical symbols (Figure 4-24). Many different electrical and wiring symbols are used in automotive repair manuals. It is important to become familiar with them to correctly analyze more involved circuits.

Fuses Gives fuse amperage and fuse cavity.

Circuit identification code, circuit code, wire size, and color code. "A" shows it's a power feed, and it has 14-gauge black wire. You can follow the black wire to…

…a single connector. You see what the connector looks like, and notice it has fusible link wire on the other side of the connector. The connector location is also indicated.

The fusible link wire, is a finer gauge with a lower melting point than the wire it's connected to. Here it's 20-gauge orange between the 14-gauge black and 14-gauge pink wires

A splice symbol indicates the junction of the fusible link with the standard wire in the circuit.

The bulkhead connector symbol tells you the pink wire goes to cavity # 31.

Circuit direction. You are directed to page 47 for the rest of the A-3 circuit.

NOTE: THE CONNECTOR CAVITY MAY BE IDENTIFIED ON SOME DIAGRAMS WITH THE OLDER SYSTEM USING "S.C." (FOR SERVICE CONNECTOR).

This circuit code shows a tracer symbol (*) but not it's color. Here you would look for a 14-gauge pink wire with a tracer which will be black or white.

Tracer color is indicated. Her tracer is/RD/ 12BK/RD*.

Fuse # 13 (5 amp)

*Use cavity # 14 (6 amp) circuit breaker

J2 14DB   # 10

A1   Grd

To starter system (see page 11)

J2 14DB

To ignition switch (see page 29)

Q2 16BK

A2 10GBK

Left headlight ground (left fender shield-rear of battery)

− Black

Battery (front of car left side)

+ Red

G5   20DB•

A1   Grd

A2 6GBK

J2 14DB

J2 14DB

J2   2

J2 14DB

J2   1

J2 14DB

A7 6GBK

A3 14BK

A1 6BK

(Rear of battery)

(Rear of battery)

G5   20DB•

Q2 16BK

A3 20DB

A1 8RD

To deck lid release (see page 79)

To lift gate release (see page 75)

To rear wash wipe (see page 77)

To speed control (see page 30)   # 31

To G5 splice (see page 30.51)

A3 14PK

A3 14PK

Fusible link (Hypalon wire) (rear of battery)

To hazard flasher (see page 471)

To heated rear window (see page 82)

C13 12BK/RD*

75 Amp   # 36

C13 12BK/RD*

Fusible link (Hypalon wire) (left side shield-front)

C13 20DB

A1   Grd

Figure 4-20 Wiring diagrams provide the technician with necessary information to accurately diagnose the electrical systems. (Courtesy of Chrysler Corporation)

Component and connector location is giving on wiring diagram.

Wire separated from component shows connector or terminal that is connected to that component.

Ground symbol indicates body or engine ground connection.

Power feed circuit information works both ways—you can trace the power feed forward from here by going to the pages indicated, or you may be directed back to this point as you check the circuits on pages 11, 13, 14, 28, 29, 33 and 34.

This splice symbol indicates that all these wires are joined to the A1-1 feed circuit splice.

Note:

This is a splice

J2   14DBL

J2   14DBL

These points do not connect

J2 14DBL

J2 14DBL

Voltage regulator (right side shield)

R3   18OG
J2   14DB

J2 14DB

J3 18DG

(Rear of battery)

R3   18DG

J2   18DG

Generator (right side forward of engine)

J2 14DB

R6 8BK

To low oil pressure switch (see page 32)

J2   14DB

R9 8BK*

R2   60BK

R9

Air pump bracket mounting bolt

R9   60BK

C9   12BK

C29   18BK

To air conditioning and heater system (see page 33)

(Rear of battery)

To starter system (see page 11)

R1 12RD

R6   14RD

R6   8BK

Fusable link (Hypalon wire) (left side shield-front)

C13 20OR

C26   20OR

C26   14GY

To air conditioning and heater system (see page 33,34)

R1   8RD

J10   18GY

J10   12PK*

J10   12PK*

Fusable link (Hypalon wire) (left side shield-front)

4

To ignition switch (see page 29)

1   R1

J1   20OR

J1   12RD

J1   12RD

37

J1   14PK

To electronic spark advance system (see page 13,14)

Fusable link (Hypalon wire) (left side shield-front)

R6   18GY

R6   12BK

35

R6   12BK

To   R6   Splice

(see page 28)

Figure 4-20 (continued)

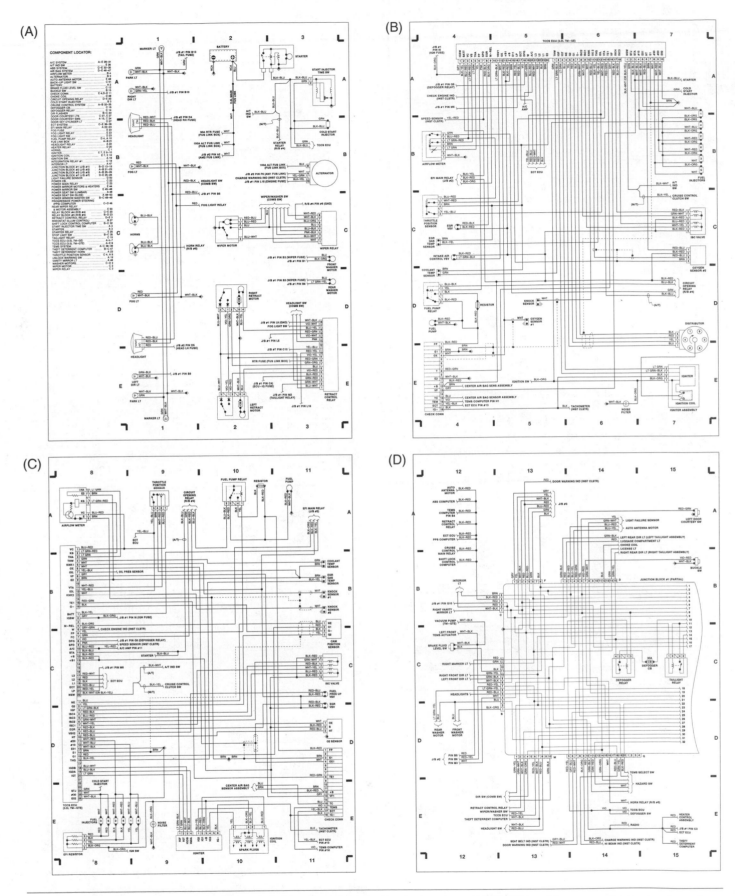

Figure 4-21 Wiring diagram illustrating an entire vehicle's electrical system. (1990 Wiring Diagrams—Supra courtesy of Toyota Motor Manufacturing, USA, Inc.)

Figure 4-21 (continued)

Figure 4-21 (continued)

Figure 4-21 (continued)

Figure 4-22 Wiring diagram illustrating only one specific circuit for easier reference. (Courtesy of Chrysler Corporation)

+	Posiitive	&#8614;	Connector
−	Negative	→	Male connector
Ground symbol	Ground	&#62;	Female connector
Fuse symbol	Fuse		Multiple connector
Circuit breaker symbol	Circuit breaker		Denotes wire continues elsewhere
Capacitor symbol	Capacitor		Splice
Ω	Ohms	-2 2	Splice identification
Resistor symbol	Resistor		Optional Wiring with / Wiring without
Variable resistor symbol	Variable resister		Thermal element bimetal strip
Series resistor symbol	Series resistor		"Y" Windings
Coil symbol	Coil	08:85	Digital readout
Step up coil symbol	Step up coil		Single filament lamp
Open contact symbol	Open contact		Dual filament lamp
Closed contact symbol	Closed contact		LED light emitting diode
Open switch symbol	Open switch		Thermistor
Closed switch symbol	Closed switch		Gauge
Closed ganged switch symbol	Closed ganged switch	Timer	Timer
Open ganged switch symbol	Open ganged switch	M	Motor
Two pole switch symbol	Two pole single throw switch		Armature and brushes
Pressure switch symbol	Pressure switch		Denotes wire goes through grommet
Solenoid switch symbol	Solenoid switch		Denotes wire goes through 40 way disconnect
Mercury switch symbol	Mercury switch	Steering column	Denotes wire goes through 25 way steering column connector
Diode symbol	Diode or rectifier	Instrument panel	Denotes wire goes through 25 way instrument panel connector
Zener diode symbol	Bi directional zener diode		

Figure 4-23 Common electrical symbols used in wiring diagrams. (Courtesy of Chrysler Corporation)

Resistor	Wire connector, detachable	Soldered or welded wire splice
Variable resistor	Semiconductor diode	Wiring cross section (gauge) 16
Electrically operated valve	Electromagnetic relay	Toggle or rocker switch (manually operated)
Spark plug	Alternator	Hydraulically operated switch
Fuse	Motor	Solid-state relay
Light bulb	Wire junction, detachable	Thermally operated (bimetallic) switch
One filament in a multifilament light bulb	Wire crossing (no connection)	Manually operated multi-position switch
Heating element	Wire junction, permanent	Solid-state circuitry
Mechanically operated switch	Battery	Manually operated switch
Meter or gauge	Shielded conductors	Horn

Terminal number code
30 – power from the battery, hot all the time
15 – power when the ignition key is on
50 – power only when operating the starter
X – power when the key is on, losses power when cranking
31 – ground

Color code
Black – BK   Lt. green – LT. G
Brown – BR   Blue – BL
Clear – CL   Violet – V
Red – R   Gray – GY
Yellow – Y   White – W
Green – G

Wire connection code
T1 – SIngle
T2 – double
T3 – 3-point
T4 – 10-point
T5 – 18-point

Figure 4-24 Elecrical symbols used in some import manuals.

Color	Abbreviations		
Aluminum	AL		
Black	BLK	BK	B
Blue (Dark)	BLU DK	DB	DK BLU
Blue (Light)	BLU LT	LB	LT BLU
Brown	BRN	BR	BN
Glazed	GLZ	GL	
Gray	GRA	GR	G
Green (Green)	GRN DK	DG	DK GRN
Green (Light)	GRN LT	LG	LT GRN
Maroon	MAR	M	
Natural	NAT	N	
Orange	ORN	O	ORG
Pink	PNK	PK	P
Purple	PPL	PR	
Red	RED	R	RD
Tan	TAN	T	TN
Violet	VLT	V	
White	WHT	W	WH
Yellow	YEL	Y	YL

Figure 4-25 Common color codes used in automotive applications.

Color Codes and Circuit Numbering

Color codes and circuit numbers are used to make tracing wires easier. Unfortunately, not all manufacturers use the same method of wire identification. The illustration (Figure 4-25) shows the abbreviations commonly used for color codes. The wiring diagrams in most shop manuals will usually list that manufacturer's method of wire identification. It is important that technicians use the color-code chart for the manufacturer of the vehicle they are working on.

In most color codes, the first group of letters designates the base color of the insulation. If a second group of letters is used, it indicates the color of the tracer. For example, a wire designated as WH/BLK would have a white base color with a black tracer.

Ford uses four methods of color coding its wires (Figure 4-26):

1. Solid color.
2. Base color with a stripe (tracer).
3. Base color with hash marks.
4. Base color with dots.

Solid color
Striped
Hashmarked
Dotted

(D) Dot
(H) Hashmark
Stripe is understood

Examples:
BK–Solid black
BR–Y – Brown with yellow stripe
BK–Y H – Black with yellow hashmarks
O–BK D – Orange with blacks dot

Figure 4-26 Four methods that Ford uses to color code its wires. (Reprinted with the permission of Ford Motor Company)

Chrysler uses a numbering method to designate the circuits on the wiring diagram (Figure 4-27). The circuit identification, wire gage, and color of the wire are included in the wire number. Chrysler identifies the main circuits by using a main circuit identification code that corresponds to the first letter in the wire number (Figure 4-28).

General Motors uses numbers that include the wire gage in metric millimeters, the wire color, the circuit number, splice number, and ground identification (Figure 4-29). In this example, the circuit is designated as 120, the wire size is 0.8 mm2, the insulation color is black, the splice is numbered S114, and the ground is designated as G117.

Most manufacturers also number connectors and terminals for identification.

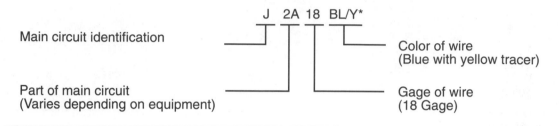

Figure 4-27 Chrysler wiring code identification. (Courtesy of Chrysler Corporation)

Main Circuit Identification Codes

A BATTERY FEED (i.e. Fuselink Feeds, Starter Feeds, Starter Relay)
B Brakes
C Climate Control (A/C, Heater, E.B.L. and Heated Mirror Related Circuits)
D Diagnostic Circuits
E Dimming Illumination Circuits
F Fused Circuits (Non-Dedicated Multi-System Feeds)
G Monitoring Circuits (Gages, Clocks, Warning Devices)
H **OPEN**
I Not used as a circuit designator
J **OPEN**
K Engine Logic Module Control Circuits
L Exterior Lighting Circuits
M Interior Lighting Circuits (Dome, Courtesy Lamps, Cargo Lamps)

N ESA Module Electronic Circuits
O Not used as a circuit designator
P Power Options (Battery Feed) (i.e. Seats, Door Locks, Mirrors, Deck Lid Release, etc.)
Q Power Options (Ignition Feed) (i.e. Windows, Power Top, Power Sun Roof, etc.)
R Passive Restraint
S Suspension and Steering Circuits
T Transmission/Transaxle, Differential, Transfer Case and Starter System Circuits
U **OPEN**
V Speed Control and Wash Wipe Circuit
W **OPEN**
X Sound Systems (i.e. Radio and Horn)
Y **OPEN**
Z Grounds (B−)

Figure 4-28 Chrysler circuit identification codes.

Figure 4-29 GM's method of circuit and wire identification.

Standardized Wiring Designations. The Society of Automotive Engineers (SAE) is attempting to standardize the circuit diagrams used by the various manufacturers. The system that is developed may be similar to the DIN used by import manufacturers. DIN assigns certain color codes to a particular circuit as follows:

- Red wires are used for direct battery-powered circuits and also ignition-powered circuits.
- Black wires are also powered circuits controlled by switches or relays.
- Brown wires are usually the grounds.
- Green wires are used for ignition primary circuits.

A combination of wire colors is used to identify subcircuits. The base color still identifies the circuit's basic purpose. In addition to standardized color coding, DIN attempts to standardize terminal identification and circuit numbering.

Component Locators

The wiring diagrams in most service manuals may not indicate the exact physical location of the components of the circuit. Another shop manual called a component locator is used to find where a component is installed in the vehicle. The component locator will use both drawings and text to lead the technician to the desired component (Figure 4-30).

Many electrical components may be hidden behind kick panels, dash boards, fender wells, and under seats. The use of a component locator will save the technician time in finding the suspected defective unit.

Summary

❑ Most of the primary wiring conductors used in the automobile are made of several strands of copper wire wound together and covered with a polyvinyl chloride (PVC) insulation.

❑ Stranded wire is used becuase current flows on the surface of the conductors. Because there is more surface area exposed in a stranded wire, there is less resistance in the stranded wire than in the solid wire.

❑ There are three major factors that determine the proper size of wire to be used: (1) The wire must be large enough—for the length required—to carry the necessary current for the load components in the circuit to operate properly, (2) The wire must be able to withstand the anticipated vibration, and (3) The wire must be able to withstand the anticipated amount of heat exposure.

❑ Wire size is based on the diameter of the conductor. The higher the number, the smaller the wire diameter.

❑ Factors that affect the resistance of the wire include wire diameter, wire length, and temperature.

❑ Terminals can be either crimped or soldered to the conductor. The terminal makes the electrial connection and it must be capable of withstanding the stress of normal vibration.

❑ Printed circuit boards are used to simplifiy the wiring of the circuits they operate. A printed circuit is made of a thin phenolic or fiberglass board that copper (or some other conductive material) has been deposited on.

❑ A wire harness is an assembled group of wires that branch out to the various electrical components. It is used to reduce the amount of loose wires hanging under the hood or dash. It provides for a safe path for the wires of the vehicle's lighting, engine, and accessory components.

A **trace**r is a thin or dashed line of a different color than the base color of the insulation.

Shop Manual
Chapter 4, page 41

DIN is the abbreviation for Deutsche Institut fuer Normung (German Institute for Standardization) and is the recommended standard for European manufacturers to follow.

A **component locato**r is used to determine the exact location of several of the electrical components.

Terms to Know
Ballast resistor
Bulkhead connectors
Common connections
Component locator
Cross-fire
Electrical symbols
Gauge

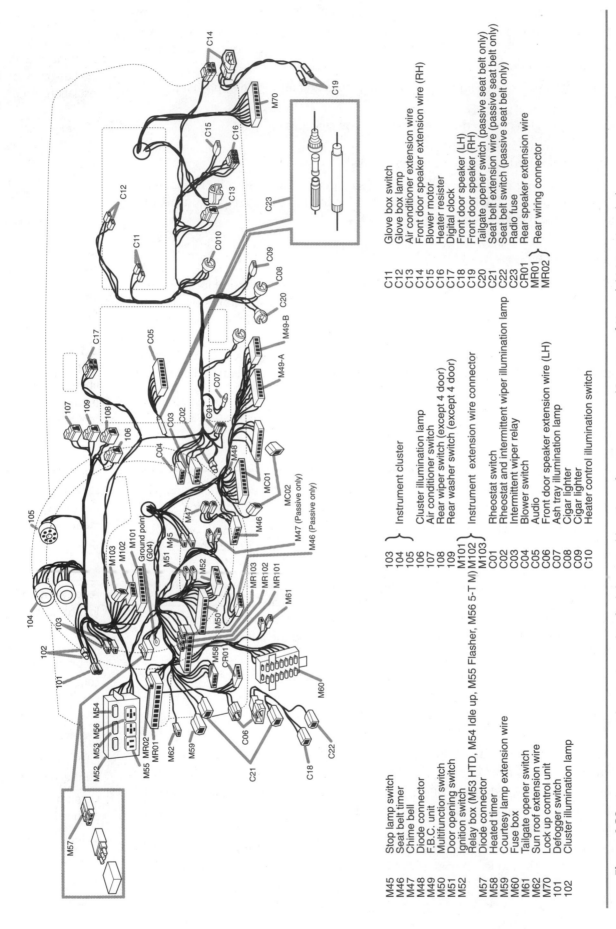

Figure 4-30 The component locator is used to find the actual location of a component. (Courtesy of Hyundai Motor America)

M45	Stop lamp switch
M46	Seat belt timer
M47	Chime bell
M48	Diode connector
M49	F.B.C. unit
M50	Multifunction switch
M51	Door opening switch
M52	Ignition switch
M53	Relay box (M53 HTD, M54 Idle up, M55 Flasher, M56 5-T M)
M57	Diode connector
M58	Heated timer
M59	Courtesy lamp extension wire
M60	Fuse box
M61	Tailgate opener switch
M62	Sun roof extension wire
M70	Lock up control unit
101	Defogger switch
102	Cluster illumination lamp
103	Instrument cluster
104	
105	
106	Cluster illumination lamp
107	Air conditioner switch
108	Rear wiper switch (except 4 door)
109	Rear washer switch (except 4 door)
M101	
M102	Instrument extension wire connector
M103	
C01	Rheostat switch
C02	Rheostat and intermittent wiper illumination lamp
C03	Intermittent wiper relay
C04	Blower switch
C05	Audio
C06	Front door speaker extension wire (LH)
C07	Ash tray illumination lamp
C08	Cigar lighter
C09	Cigar lighter
C10	Heater control illumination switch
C11	Glove box switch
C12	Glove box lamp
C13	Air conditioner extension wire
C14	Front door speaker extension wire (RH)
C15	Blower motor
C16	Heater resister
C17	Digital clock
C18	Front door speaker (LH)
C19	Front door speaker (RH)
C20	Tailgate opener switch (passive seat belt only)
C21	Seat belt extension wire (passive seat belt only)
C22	Seat belt switch (passive seat belt only)
C23	Radio fuse
CR01	Rear speaker extension wire
MR01	Rear wiring connector
MR02	

Figure 4-30 (continued)

❑ The wiring harness is made by grouping insulated wires and wrapping them together. The wires are bundled into separate harness assemblies that are joined together by connector plugs.

❑ A wiring diagram is an electrical schematic that shows a representation of actual electrical or electronic components and the wiring of the vehicle's electrical systems.

❑ The technician's greatest helpmate in locating electrical problems is the wiring diagram. Correct use of the wiring diagram will reduce the amount of time a technician needs to spend tracing the wires in the vehicle.

❑ In place of actual pictures, variety of electrical symbols are used to represent the components in the wiring diagram.

❑ Color codes and circuit numbers are used to make tracing wires easier.

❑ In most color codes, the first group of letters designates the base color of the insulation. If a second group of letters is used, it indicates the color of the tracer.

❑ A component locator is used to determine the exact location of several of the electrical components.

Review Questions

Short Answer Essays

1. Explain the purpose of wiring diagrams.

2. Explain how wire size is determined by the American Wire Gauge (AWG) and metric methods.

3. Explain the purpose and use of printed circuits.

4. Explain the purpose of the component locator.

5. Explain when single-stranded or multistranded wire should be used.

6. Explain how temperature affects resistance and wire size selection.

7. List the three major factors that determine the proper size of wire to be used.

8. List and describe the different types of terminal connectors used in the automotive electrical system.

9. What is the difference between a complex and a simple wiring harness?

10. Describe the methods the three domestic automobile manufacturers use for wiring code identification.

Fill-in-the-Blanks

1. There is _____ resistance in the stranded wire than in the solid wire.

2. _____ _____ is the electromagnetic induction spark that can be transmitted in another wire that is close to the wire carrying the current.

3. Wire size is based on the _____ of the conductor.

4. In the AWG standard, the _____ the number, the smaller the wire _____ .

5. An increase in temperature creates a _____ _____ in resistance.

6. _____ connectors are used when several wires must pass through the bulkhead.

7. _____ _____ _____ are used to prevent damage to the wiring by maintaining proper wire routing and retention.

8. A wiring diagram is an electrical schematic that shows a _____ of actual electrical or electronic components (by use of symbols) and the _____ of the vehicle's electrical systems.

9. In most color codes, the first group of letters designates the _____ _____ of the insulation. The second group of letters indicates the color of the _____ .

10. A _____ _____ is used to determine the exact location of several of the electrical components.

ASE Style Review Questions

1. Automotive wiring is being discussed:
   Technician A says most of the primary wiring conductors are made of several strands of copper wire wound together and covered with an insulation.
   Technician B says other types of conductor materials used in automobiles include silver, gold, aluminum, and tin-plated brass.
   Who is correct?
   A. A only
   B. B only
   C. Both A and B
   D. Neither A nor B

2. Stranded wire use is being discussed:
   Technician A says there is less surface area exposed in a stranded wire for electron flow.
   Technician B says there is more resistance in the stranded wire than in the solid wire.
   Who is correct?
   A. A only
   B. B only
   C. Both A and B
   D. Neither A nor B

3. Spark plug wires are being discussed:
   Technician A says RFI is controlled by using resistances in the conductor of the spark plug wire.
   Technician B says current standards require that all ignition systems control RFI.
   Who is correct?
   A. A only
   B. B only
   C. Both A and B
   D. Neither A nor B

4. Spark plug wire installation is being discussed:
   Technician A says there is little that can be done to correct cross-fire.
   Technician B says the spark plug wires must be installed in the proper separator and any two parallel wires next to each other in the firing order should be positioned as far away from each other as possible to prevent cross-fire.
   Who is correct?
   A. A only
   B. B only
   C. Both A and B
   D. Neither A nor B

5. The selection of the proper size of wire to be used is being discussed:
   Technician A says the wire must be large enough—for the length required—to carry the amount of current necessary for the load components in the circuit to operate properly.
   Technician B says temperature has such little effect on resistance that it is not a factor in wire size selection.
   Who is correct?
   A. A only
   B. B only
   C. Both A and B
   D. Neither A nor B

6. Terminal connectors are being discussed:
   Technician A says terminal connections cannot corrode.
   Technician B says the terminals can be either crimped or soldered to the conductor.
   Who is correct?
   A. A only
   B. B only
   C. Both A and B
   D. Neither A nor B

7. Wire routing is being discussed:
   Technician A says to install additional electrical accessories it is necessary to support the primary wire in at least 10-foot intervals.
   Technician B says if the wire must be routed through the frame or body, use metal clips to protect the wire.
   Who is correct?
   A. A only
   B. B only
   C. Both A and B
   D. Neither A nor B

8. Printed circuit boards are being discussed:
   Technician A says printed circuit boards are used to simplify the wiring of the circuits they operate.
   Technician B says care must be taken not to touch the board with bare hands.
   Who is correct?
   A. A only
   B. B only
   C. Both A and B
   D. Neither A nor B

9. Wiring harnesses are being discussed:
   Technician A says a wire harness is an assembled group of wires that branches out to the various electrical components.
   Technician B says most underhood harnesses are simple harnesses.
   Who is correct?
   A. A only
   B. B only
   C. Both A and B
   D. Neither A nor B

10. Wiring diagrams are being discussed:
    Technician A says wiring diagrams give the exact location of the electrical components.
    Technician B says a wiring diagram will indicate what circuits are interconnected, where circuits receive their voltage source, and what color of wires are used in the circuit.
    Who is correct?
    A. A only
    B. B only
    C. Both A and B
    D. Neither A nor B

Automotive Batteries

Upon completion and review of this chapter, you should be able to:

- ❏ Explain the purposes of the battery.
- ❏ Describe the construction of conventional, maintenance-free, hybrid, and recombination batteries.
- ❏ Define the main elements of the battery.
- ❏ Explain the chemical action that occurs to produce current in a battery.
- ❏ Explain the chemical reaction that occurs in the battery during cycling.
- ❏ Describe the differences, advantages, and disadvantages between different types of batteries.
- ❏ Describe the different types of battery terminals used.

- ❏ Describe the methods used to rate batteries.
- ❏ Determine the correct battery to be installed into a vehicle.
- ❏ Explain the effects of temperature on battery performance.
- ❏ Describe the different loads or demands placed upon a battery during different operating conditions.
- ❏ Explain the major reasons for battery failure.
- ❏ Define battery-related terms such as deep cycle, electrolyte solution, and gassing.

Introduction

An automotive battery is an electrochemical device that provides for and stores electrical energy. When the battery is connected to an external load, such as a starter motor, an energy conversion occurs that results in an electrical current flowing through the circuit. Electrical energy is produced in the battery by the chemical reaction that occurs between two dissimilar plates that are immersed in an electrolyte solution. The automotive battery produces direct current (DC) electricity that flows in only one direction.

When discharging the battery (current flowing from the battery), the battery changes chemical energy into electrical energy. It is through this change that the battery releases stored energy. During charging (current flowing through the battery from the charging system), electrical energy is converted into chemical energy. As a result, the battery can store energy until it is needed.

Shop Manual
Chapter 5, page 63

The battery does not store electricity as electrons. The battery stores energy in chemical form.

The automotive battery has several important functions, including:

1. It operates the starting motor, ignition system, electronic fuel injection, and other electrical devices for the engine during cranking and starting.

2. It supplies all the electrical power for the vehicle accessories whenever the engine is not running or at low idle.

3. It furnishes current for a limited time whenever electrical demands exceed charging system output.

4. It acts as a stabilizer of voltage for the entire automotive electrical system.

5. It stores energy for extended periods of time.

The largest demand placed on the battery occurs when it must supply current to operate the starter motor. The amperage requirements of a starter motor may be over several hundred amperes. This requirement is also affected by temperatures, engine size, and engine condition.

After the engine is started, the vehicle's charging system works to recharge the battery and to provide the current to run the electrical systems. Most AC generators have a maximum output of 60 to 90 amperes. This is usually enough to operate all of the vehicle's electrical systems and meet the demands of these systems. However, under some conditions (such as engine running at idle) alternator output is below its maximum rating. If there are enough electrical accessories turned on during this time (heater, wipers, headlights, and radio) the demand may exceed the AC generator output. The total demand may be 20 to 30 amperes. During this time the battery must supply the additional current.

Even with the ignition switch turned off, there are electrical demands placed on the battery. Clocks, memory seats, engine computer memory, body computer memory, and electronic sound system memory are all examples of key-off loads. The total current draw of key-off loads is usually less than 30 milliamperes.

In the event that the vehicle's charging system fails, the battery must supply all of the current necessary to run the vehicle. Most batteries will supply 25 amperes for approximately 120 minutes before discharging low enough to cause the engine to stop running.

The amount of electrical energy that a battery is capable of producing depends on the size, weight, active area of the plates, and the amount of sulfuric acid in the electrolyte solution.

In this chapter you will study the design and operation of different types of batteries currently used in automobiles. These include conventional batteries, maintenance-free batteries, hybrid batteries, and recombination batteries.

Conventional Batteries

The conventional battery is constructed of seven basic components:

1. Positive plates
2. Negative plates
3. Separators
4. Case
5. Plate straps
6. Electrolyte
7. Terminals

The difference between "3-year" and "5-year" batteries is the amount of material expanders used in the construction of the plates and the number of plates used to build a cell.

A plate, either positive or negative, starts with a grid. The grid has horizontal and vertical grid bars that intersect at right angles (Figure 5-1). An active material made from ground lead oxide, acid, and material expanders is pressed into the grid in paste form. The positive plate is

Conventional
5% antimony

Figure 5-1 Conventional battery grid. (Reprinted with the permission of Ford Motor Company)

Figure 5-2 A battery cell consists of alternate positive and negative plates. (Reprinted with the permission of Ford Motor Company)

given a "forming charge" that converts the lead oxide paste into lead peroxide. The negative plate is given a "forming charge" that converts the paste into sponge lead.

The negative and positive plates are arranged alternately in each cell element (Figure 5-2). Each cell element can consist of 9 to 13 plates. The positive and negative plates are insulated from each other by separators made of microporous materials. The construction of the element is completed when all of the positive plates are connected to each other and all of the negative plates are connected to each other. The connection of the plates is by plate straps (Figure 5-3).

A typical 12-volt automotive battery is made up of six cells connected in series (Figure 5-4). This means the positive side of a cell element is connected to the negative side of the next cell element. This is repeated throughout all six cells. By connecting the cells in series the current

Figure 5-3 Construction of a battery element. (Reprinted with the permission of Ford Motor Company)

Usually, negative plate groups contain one more plate than positive plate groups to help equalize the chemical activity.

Many batteries have envelope-type separators that retain active materials near the plates.

The most common connection used to connect cell elements is through the partition. It provides the shortest path and the least resistance.

Electrolyte consists of sulfuric acid diluted with water. The **electrolyte solution** used in automotive batteries consists of 64% water and 36% sulfuric acid. Electrolyte is both conductive and reactive.

12 Volts

Figure 5-4 The 12-volt battery consists of six 2-volt cells that are wired in series. (Reprinted with the permission of Ford Motor Company)

capacity of the cell is increased, and cell voltage remains the same. The six cells produce 2.1 volts each. Wiring the cells in series produces the 12.6 volts required by the automotive electrical system. The plate straps provide a positive cell connection and a negative cell connection. The cell connection may be one of three types: through the partition, over the partition, or external (Figure 5-5). The cell elements are submerged in a cell case filled with electrolyte solution.

⚠️ **WARNING:** Electrolyte is very corrosive. It can cause severe injury if it comes in contact with skin and/or eyes. If you come into contact with battery acid, wash immediately with a water and baking soda solution (baking soda will neutralize the acid). If you get the acid in your eyes, flush them immediately with cool water or a commercial eye wash. Then seek medical treatment immediately. If you swallow any electrolyte, **do not** induce vomiting. Seek medical treatment immediately.

Intercell connectors

Over the partition   Through-the-partition   External

Figure 5-5 The cell elements can be connected using one of three intercell connection methods. (Reprinted with the permission of Ford Motor Company)

CAUTION: Do not add electrolyte to the battery (after the initial fill) if the cells are low. Add only distilled water. Distilled water has the minerals removed. The minerals in regular tap water can cause the battery cells to short out because they are conductive.

The battery case is made of polypropylene, hard rubber, and plastic base materials. The battery case must be capable of withstanding temperature extremes, vibration, and acid absorption. The cell elements sit on raised supports in the bottom of the case. By raising the cells, chambers are formed at the bottom of the case that trap the sediment that flakes off the plates. If the sediment was not contained in these chambers, it could cause a conductive connection across the plates and short the cell. The case is fitted with a one-piece cover.

Because the conventional battery releases hydrogen gas when it is being charged, the case cover will have vents. The vents are located in the cell caps of a conventional battery (Figure 5-6).

Figure 5-6 The vents of a conventional battery allow the release of gases.

WARNING: The hydrogen gases produced from a charging battery are very explosive. Exploding batteries are responsible for over 15,000 injuries per year that are severe enough to require hospital treatment. Do not smoke, have any open flames, or cause any sparks near the battery. Also, do not lay tools on the battery. They may short across the terminals causing the battery to explode. Always wear eye protection and proper clothing when working near the battery. Also, because most jewelry is an excellent conductor of electricity, do not wear it when performing work on or near the battery.

WARNING: A battery that has been rapidly discharged will create hydrogen gas. Do not attach jumper cables to a weak battery if starting the vehicle has been attempted. Wait for at least 10 minutes before connecting the jumper cable and attempting to start the vehicle.

Chemical Action

Activation of the battery is through the addition of electrolyte. This solution causes the chemical actions to take place between the lead peroxide of the positive plates and the sponge lead of the negative plates. The electrolyte is also the carrier that moves electric current between the positive and negative plates through the separators.

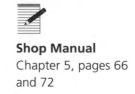

Shop Manual
Chapter 5, pages 66 and 72

119

Figure 5-7 Chemical action that occurs inside of the battery during the discharge cycle.

Specific gravity is the weight of a given volume of a liquid divided by the weight of an equal volume of water. Water has a specific gravity of 1.000.

The automotive battery has a fully charged specific gravity of 1.265 corrected to 80°F. Therefore, a specific gravity of 1.265 for electrolyte means it is 1.265 times heavier than an equal volume of water.

In operation, the battery is being partially discharged and then completely recharged. This represents an actual reversing of the chemical action that takes place within the battery. The constant cycling of the charge and discharge modes slowly wears away the active materials on the cell plates. This action eventually causes the battery plates to oxidize. The battery must be replaced once the oxidizing of plates has reached the point that there is insufficient active plate area.

In the charged state, the positive plate material is essentially pure lead dioxide, PbO_2. The active material of the negative plates is spongy lead, Pb. The electrolyte is a solution of sulfuric acid, H_2SO_4, and water. The voltage of the cell depends on the chemical difference between the active materials.

The illustration(Figure 5-7) shows what happens to the plates and electrolyte during discharge. The lead (Pb) from the positive plate combines with sulfate (SO_4) from the acid, forming

Figure 5-8 Chemical action inside the battery during the charge cycle.

lead sulfate (PbSO₄). While this is occurring, oxygen (O) in the active material of the positive plate joins with the hydrogen from the electrolyte forming water (H$_2$O). This water dilutes the acid concentration.

A similar reaction is occurring in the negative plate. Lead (Pb) is combining with sulfate (SO₄) forming lead sulfate (PbSO₄). The result of discharging is changing the positive plate from lead dioxide into lead sulfate and changing the negative plate into lead sulfate. Discharging a cell makes the positive and negative plates the same. Once they are the same, the cell is dead.

The charge cycle is exactly the opposite (Figure 5-8). The lead sulfate (PbSO₄) in both plates is split into its original forms of lead (Pb) and sulfate (SO₄). The water in the electrolyte splits into hydrogen and oxygen. The hydrogen (H$_2$) combines with the sulfate to become sulfuric acid again (H$_2$SO₄). The oxygen combines with the positive plate to form the lead dioxide. This now puts the plates and the electrolyte back in their original form and the cell is charged.

Maintenance-Free Batteries

The maintenance-free battery contains cell plates made of a slightly different compound. The plate grids contain calcium, cadmium, or strontium to reduce gassing and self-discharge. The antimony used in conventional batteries is not used in maintenance-free batteries because it increases the breakdown of water into hydrogen and oxygen and because of its low resistance to overcharging. The use of calcium, cadmium, or strontium reduces the amount of vaporization that takes place during normal operation. The grid may be constructed with additional supports to increase its strength and to provide a shorter path, with less resistance, for the current to flow to the top tab (Figure 5-9).

Each plate is wrapped and sealed on three sides by an envelope design separator. The envelope is made from microporous plastic. By enclosing the plate in an envelope, the plate is insulated and reduces the shedding of the active material from the plate.

The battery is completely sealed except for a small vent so the electrolyte and vapors cannot escape. An expansion chamber allows internal expansion and contraction to occur. Because the vapors cannot escape from the battery, it is not necessary to add water to the battery on a periodic basis. Containing the vapors also reduces the possibility of corrosion and discharge through the surface because of electrolyte on the surface of the battery.

Shop Manual
Chapter 5, page 70

Maintenance-free means there is no provision for the addition of water to the cells. The battery is sealed.

Gassing is the conversion of the battery water into hydrogen and oxygen gas. This process is also called **electrolysis.**

If electrolyte is allowed to accumulate on the top of the battery case it may create a conductive connection between the positive and negative terminals, resulting in a constant discharge on the battery.

Maintenance Free Grid

Calcium or strontium alloy...
• Adds strength
• Cuts gassing up to 97%
• Resists overcharge

Figure 5-9 Maintenance-free battery grids with support bars give increased strength and faster electrical delivery. (Reprinted with the permission of Ford Motor Company)

Green dot visible (OK)

Dark green dot not visible (charge before testing)

Light or yellow (replace battery)

Sight glass

Top of battery

Visual state-of-charge indicator

Green ball

Figure 5-10 A built-in hydrometer gives indication of battery condition. (Courtesy of Chrysler Corporation)

A **hydrometer** is a test instrument that is used to check the specific gravity of the electrolyte to determine the battery's state of charge.

Some maintenance-free batteries have a built-in hydrometer that shows the state of charge (Figure 5-10). If the dot that is at the bottom of the hydrometer is green, then the battery is fully charged (more than 65% charged). If the dot is black, the battery state of charge is low. If the battery does not have a built-in hydrometer it cannot be tested with a hydrometer because the battery is sealed.

 WARNING: If the dot is yellow, do not atttempt to recharge the battery. If the "eye" is clear, the electrolyte is low. In either case the battery must be replaced.

Grid growth is a condition where the grid grows little metallic fingers that extend through the separators and short out the plates.

Many manufacturers have revised the maintenance-free battery to a "low maintenance battery," in that the caps are removable for testing and electrolyte level checks. Also the grid construction contains about 3.4% antimony. To decrease the distance and resistance of the path that current flows in the grid and to increase its strength, the horizontal and vertical grid bars do not intersect at right angles (Figure 5-11).

Deep cycling is to discharge the battery completely before recharging it.

The **hybrid battery** combines the advantages of the low maintenance and maintenance-free batteries.

Low maintenance 3.4% or less antimony

Figure 5-11 Low maintenance battery grid with vertical grid bars intersecting at an angle. (Reprinted with the permission Ford Motor Company)

The advantages of maintenance-free batteries over conventional batteries include:

1. A larger reserve of electrolyte above the plates.
2. Increased resistance to overcharging.
3. Longer shelf life (approximately 18 months).
4. Ability to be shipped with electrolyte installed, reducing the possibility of accidents and injury to the technician.
5. Higher cold cranking amps rating.

The major disadvantages of the maintenance-free battery include:

1. Grid growth when the battery is exposed to high temperatures.
2. Inability to withstand deep cycling.
3. Low reserve capacity.
4. Faster discharge by parasitic loads.
5. Shorter life expectancy.

Hybrid Batteries

The hybrid battery can withstand six deep cycles and still retain 100% of its original reserve capacity. The grid construction of the hybrid battery consists of approximately 2.75% antimony alloy on the positive plates and a calcium alloy on the negative plates. This allows the battery to withstand deep cycling while retaining reserve capacity for improved cranking performance. Also, the use of antimony alloys reduces grid growth and corrosion. The lead calcium has less gassing than conventional batteries.

Grid construction differs from other batteries in that the plates have a lug located near the center of the grid. In addition, the vertical and horizontal grid bars are arranged in a radial pattern (Figure 5-12). By locating the lug near the center of the grid and using the radial design, the current has less resistance and a shorter path to follow to the lug (Figure 5-13). This means the battery is capable of providing more current at a faster rate.

The separators used are constructed of glass with a resin coating. The glass separators offer low electrical resistance with high resistance to chemical contamination. This type of construction provides for increased cranking performance and battery life.

> **Grid growth** is a condition where the grid grows little metallic fingers that extend through the separators and short out the plates.

> **Deep cycling** is to discharge the battery completely before recharging it.

> The **hybrid battery** combines the advantages of the low maintenance and maintenance-free batteries.

> **Radial** means branching out from a common center

> Some manufacturers are using fiberglass separators.

Grid with active material

100% glass separator

Grid only

Figure 5-12 Hybrid grid and separator construction. (Reprinted with the permission Ford Motor Company)

Hybrid grid radial design and center lug reduces the resistance for current that is produced at points "A" to reach point "B".

Figure 5-13 The hybrid battery grid construction allows for faster current delivery. Electrical energy at point "A" has a shorter distance to travel to get to the tab at point "B".

Recombination Batteries

One of the most recent variations of the automobile battery is the recombination battery (Figure 5-14). The recombination battery does not use a liquid electrolyte. Instead, it uses separators that hold a gel-type material. The separators are placed between the grids and have very low electrical resistance. Because of this design, output voltage and current are higher than in conventional batteries. The extra amount of available voltage (approximately 0.6 V) assists in cold weather starting. Also, gassing is virtually eliminated.

The following are some other safety features and advantages of the recombination battery:

1. Contains no acid. If the case is cracked, no acid will spill.
2. Can be installed in any position, including upside down.

Figure 5-14 The recombination battery is one of the most recent advances in the automotive battery. (Courtesy of Optima Batteries, Inc.)

3. Is corrosion free.

4. Has very low maintenance because there is no electrolyte loss.

5. Can last as much as four times longer than conventional batteries.

6. Can withstand deep cycling without damage.

7. Can be rated over 800 cold cranking amperes.

> **CAUTION:** The recombination battery requires slightly different testing procedures. Refer to the manufacturer's manual before attempting to test the battery.

Battery Terminals

Shop Manual
Chapter 5, page 69

All automotive batteries have two terminals. One terminal is a positive connection, the other is a negative connection. The battery terminals extend through the cover or the side of the battery case. The following are the most common types of battery terminals (Figure 5-15):

1. **Post or top terminals:** Used on most automotive batteries. The positive post will be larger than the negative post to prevent connecting the battery in reverse polarity.

2. **Side terminals:** Positioned in the side of the container near the top. These terminals are threaded and require a special bolt to connect the cables. Polarity identification is by positive and negative symbols.

3. **L terminals:** Used on specialty batteries and some imports.

Battery terminals provide a means of connecting the battery plates to the vehicle's electrical system.

Side terminal

Post or top terminal

"L" terminal

Battery terminals

Figure 5-15 The most common types of automotive battery terminals. (Reprinted with the permission of Ford Motor Company)

Battery Ratings

Battery capacity ratings are established by the Battery Council International (BCI) in conjunction with the Society of Automotive Engineers (SAE). Battery cell voltage depends on the types of materials used in the construction of the battery. Current capacity depends on several factors:

1. The size of the cell plates. The larger the surface area of the plates, the more chemical action that can occur. This means a greater current is produced.

2. The weight of the positive and negative plate active materials.

3. The weight of the sulfuric acid in the electrolyte solution.

The battery's current capacity rating is an indication of its ability to deliver cranking power to the starter motor and of its ability to provide reserve power to the electrical system. The commonly used current capacity ratings are explained in the following sections.

Ampere-Hour Rating

The ampere-hour rating is the amount of steady current that a fully charged battery can supply for 20 hours at 80°F (26.7°C) without the cell voltage falling below 1.75 volts. For example, if a battery can be discharged for 20 hours at a rate of 4.0 amperes before its terminal voltage reads 10.5 volts, it would be rated at 80 ampere-hours.

Cold Cranking Rating

Cold cranking rating is the most common method of rating automotive batteries. It is determined by the load, in amperes, a battery is able to deliver for 30 seconds at 0°F (−17.7°C) without terminal voltage falling below 7.2 volts for a 12-volt battery. The cold cranking rating is given in total amperage and is identified as 300 CCA, 400 CCA, 500 CCA, and so on. Some batteries are rated as high as 1,100 CCA.

Reserve Capacity Rating

The reserve capacity rating is determined by the length of time, in minutes, that a fully charged battery can be discharged at 25 amperes before battery cell voltage drops below 1.75 volts per cell. This rating gives an indication of how long the vehicle can be driven, with the headlights on, if the charging system should fail.

Watt-Hour Rating

The starter motor converts the electrical power supplied by the battery into mechanical power, so some battery manufacturers rate their batteries using watt-hour rating. The watt-hour rating of the battery is determined at 0°F (−17.7°C) because the battery's capability to deliver wattage varies with temperature. Watt-hour rating is determined by calculating the ampere-hour rating of the battery times the battery voltage.

Battery Size Selection

Some of the aspects that determine the battery rating required for a vehicle include engine size, engine type, climatic conditions, vehicle options, and so on. The requirement for electrical energy to crank the engine increases as the temperature decreases. Battery power drops drastically as temperatures drop below freezing (Figure 5-16). The engine also becomes harder to crank due to the tendancy of some oils to thicken when cold, which results in increased friction. As a general rule, it takes 1 ampere of cold cranking power per cubic inch of engine displacement. Therefore, a 200 cubic inch displacement (CID) engine should be fitted with a battery of at least 200 CCA. To convert this into metric, it takes 1 amp of cold cranking power for every 16 cm³ of engine displacement. A 1.6 liter engine should require at least a battery rated at 100 CCA. This rule may not apply to vehicles that have several electrical accessories. The best method of determining the correct battery is to refer to the manufacturer's specifications.

The battery that is selected should fit the battery holding fixture and the hold-down must be able to be installed. It is also important that the height of the battery not allow the terminals to short across the vehicle hood when it is shut. BCI group numbers are used to indicate the physical size and other features of the battery (Figure 5-17) This group number does not indicate the current capacity of the battery.

Temperature	% of Cranking Power
80°F (26.7°C)	100
32°F (0°C)	65
0°F (−17.8°C)	40

Figure 5-16 Temperatures affect the cranking power of the battery.

The ampere-hour rating is also known as the 20-hour discharge rating.

The **cold cranking rating** indicates the battery's ability to deliver a specified amount of current to start an engine at low ambient temperatures.

Cold cranking rating is also called **cold cranking amps (CCA)**

Reserve capacity rating is indicated in the amount of minutes, such as 60, 110, 120, and so on.

The term **watts** is the unit of measure of electrical power and is the equivalent of horsepower. One horsepower is equal to 746 watts.

The largest current capacity rating that can be achieved in a given battery group size may be in the customer's best interests. However, be aware of overkill.

Grp. Size	Vlt.	Cold cranking power—amps for 30 secs. at 0°F*	No. of mo. warranted	Size of battery container in inches (incl. terminals)		
				Lgth.	Wd.	Ht.
17HF	6	400	24	7¼	6¾	9
21	12	450	60	8	6¾	8½
22F	12	430	60	9	6⅞	8⅛
	12	380	55	9	6⅞	8⅛
	12	330	40	9	6⅞	8⅛
22NF	12	330	24	9½	5½	8⅞
24	12	525	60	10¼	6⅞	8⅝
	12	450	55	10¼	6⅞	8⅝
	12	410	48	10¼	6⅞	8⅝
	12	380	40	10¼	6⅞	8⅝
	12	325	36	10¼	6⅞	8⅝
	12	290	30	10¼	6⅞	8⅝
24F	12	525	60	10¼	6⅞	8⅝
	12	450	55	10¼	6⅞	8⅝
	12	410	48	10¼	6⅞	8⅝
	12	380	40	10¼	6⅞	8⅝
	12	325	36	10¼	6⅞	8⅝
	12	290	30	10¼	6⅞	8⅝
27	12	560	60	12	6⅞	8⅝
27F	12	560	60	12	6⅞	9
41	12	525	60	11⁹⁄₁₆	6¹³⁄₁₆	6¹⁵⁄₁₆
42	12	450	60	9⅝	6⅞	6¾
	12	340	40	9⅝	6⅞	6¾
45	12	420	60	9½	5½	8⅞
46	12	460	60	10¼	6⅞	8⅝
48	12	440	60	12	6⅞	7½
49	12	600	60	14½	6⅞	7½
56	12	450	60	10	6	8⅜
	12	380	48	10	6	8⅜
58	12	425	60	9¼	7¼	6⅞
71	12	450	60	8	7¼	8½
	12	395	55	8	7¼	8½
	12	330	36	8	7¼	8½
72	12	490	60	9	7¼	8¼
	12	380	48	9	7¼	8¼
74	12	585	60	10¼	7¼	8¾
	12	525	60	10¼	7¼	8¾
	12	505	60	10¼	7¼	8¾
	12	450	55	10¼	7¼	8¾
	12	410	48	10¼	7¼	8¾
	12	380	40	10¼	7¼	8¾
	12	325	36	10¼	7¼	8¾

*Meets or exceeds Battery Council International rating standards.

Figure 5-17 BCI battery group numbers indicate the size and features of the battery.

Figure 5-18 The battery cable is designed to carry the high current required to start the engine and supply the vehicle's electrical systems.

Battery Cables

Battery cables must be of a sufficient capacity to carry the current required to meet all demands (Figure 5-18). Normal 12-volt cable size is usually 4 or 6 gauge. Various forms of clamps and terminals are used to assure a good electrical connection at each end of the cable. Connections must be clean and tight to prevent arcing, corrosion, and high voltage resistance.

The positive cable is usually red (but not always) and the negative cable is usually black. The positive cable will fasten to the starter solenoid or relay. The negative cable fastens to ground on the engine block. Some manufacturers use a negative cable with no insulation. Sometimes the negative battery cable may have a body grounding wire to help assure that the vehicle body is properly grounded.

CAUTION: Connecting the battery cables in reverse polarity can damage many of the vehicle's computer systems.

Battery Hold-Downs

All batteries must be secured in the vehicle to prevent damage and the possibility of shorting across the terminals if it tips. Normal vibrations cause the plates to shed their active materials. Hold-downs reduce the amount of vibration and help increase the life of the battery.

Shop Manual
Chapter 5, page 66

Battery Failure

Whenever battery failure occurs, first perform some simple visual inspections. Check the case for cracks, check the electrolyte level in each cell, and check the terminals for corrosion. The sulfuric acid that vents out with the battery gases attacks the battery terminals and battery cables. As the sulfuric acid reacts with the lead and copper, deposits of lead sulfate and copper sulfate are created (Figure 5-19). These deposits are resistive to electron flow and limit the amount of

Figure 5-19 Corroded battery terminals reduce the efficiency of the battery.

current that can be supplied to the electrical and starting systems. If the deposits are bad enough, the resistance can increase to a level that prevents the starter from cranking the engine.

One of the most common causes of early battery failure is overcharging. If the charging system is supplying a voltage level over 15.5 volts, the plates may become warped. Warping of the plates results from the excess heat that is generated as a result of overcharging. Overcharging also causes the active material to disintegrate and shed off of the plates.

If the charging system does not produce enough current to keep the battery charged, the lead sulfate can become hard. If this happens, the materials act as a resistance that will oppose recharging. The recharging process converts the sulfate on the plates. If there is an undercharging condition, the sulfate is not converted and it will harden on the plates.

Vibration is another common reason for battery failure. If the battery is not secure, the plates will shed the active material as a result of excessive vibration. If enough material is shed, the sediment at the bottom of the battery can create an electrical connection between the plates. The shorted cell will produce the voltage, resulting in a battery that will have only 10.5 volts across the terminals. With this reduced amount of voltage, the starter usually will not be capable of starting the engine. To prevent this problem, make sure that proper hold-down fixtures are used.

During normal battery operation, the active materials on the plates will shed. The negative plate also becomes soft. Both of these events will reduce the effectiveness of the battery.

> The sulfate that is not converted hardens on the plates. This results in **battery sulfation,** which permanently damages the battery.

Summary

❑ An automotive battery is an electrochemical device that provides for and stores electrical energy.
❑ Electrical energy is produced in the battery by the chemical reaction that occurs between two dissimilar plates that are immersed in an electrolyte solution.
❑ An automotive battery has the following important functions:

  1. It operates the starting motor, ignition system, electronic fuel injection, and other electrical devices for the engine during cranking and starting.

  2. It supplies all the electrical power for the vehicle accessories whenever the engine is not running or at low idle.

Terms to Know

Battery hold-downs

Battery terminals

Cell element

Cold cranking amps (CCA)

Cold cranking rating

3. It furnishes current for a limited time whenever electrical demands exceed charging system output.

4. It acts as a stabilizer of voltage for the entire automotive electrical system.

5. It stores energy for extended periods of time.

❑ Electrical loads that are still placed on the battery when the ignition switch is in the OFF position are called key-off loads.

❑ The amount of electrical energy that a battery is capable of producing depends on the size, weight, and active area of the plates and the amount of sulfuric acid in the electrolyte solution.

❑ The conventional battery is constructed of seven basic components:

1. Positive plates
2. Negative plates
3. Separators
4. Case
5. Plate straps
6. Electrolyte
7. Terminals

❑ Electrolyte solution used in automotive batteries consists of 64% water and 36% sulfuric acid.

❑ The electrolyte solution causes the chemical actions to take place between the lead dioxide of the positive plates and the sponge lead of the negative plates. The electrolyte is also the carrier that moves electric current between the positive and negative plates through the separators.

❑ The automotive battery has a fully charged specific gravity of 1.265 corrected to 80°F.

❑ Grid growth is a condition where the grid grows little metallic fingers that extend through the separators and short out the plates.

❑ Deep cycling is discharging the battery almost completely without recharging it.

❑ In a conventional battery, the positive plate is covered with lead peroxide and the negative plate is covered with sponge lead.

❑ In maintenance-free batteries, the cell plates contain calcium, cadmium, or strontium to reduce gassing and self-discharge.

❑ The grid construction of the hybrid battery consists of approximately 2.75% antimony alloy on the positive plates and a calcium alloy on the negative plates.

❑ The recombination battery uses separators that hold a gel-type material in place of liquid electrolyte.

❑ The three most common types of battery terminals are:

1. Post or top terminals: Used on most automotive batteries. The positive post will be larger than the negative post to prevent connecting the battery in reverse polarity.

2. Side terminals: Positioned in the side of the container near the top. These terminals are threaded and require a special bolt to connect the cables. Polarity identification is by positive and negative symbols.

3. L terminals: Used on specialty batteries and some imports.

❑ The most common methods of battery rating are cold cranking, reserve capacity, ampere-hour, and watt-hour.

Review Questions

Short Answer Essays

1. Explain the purposes of the battery.

2. Describe how a technician is to determine the correct battery to be installed into a vehicle.

3. Describe the methods used to rate batteries.

4. Describe the different types of battery terminals used.

5. Explain the effects that temperature has on battery performance.

6. Describe the different loads or demands that are placed upon a battery during different operating conditions.

7. List and describe the seven main elements of the conventional battery.

8. What are the major reasons that a battery fails?

9. List at least three safety concerns associated with working on or near the battery.

10. Describe the difference in construction of the hybrid battery as compared to the conventional battery.

Fill-in-the-Blanks

1. An automotive battery is an _____ device that provides for and stores _____ energy.

2. When discharging the battery, it changes _____ energy into _____ energy.

3. The assembly of the positive plates, negative plates, and separators is called the _____ or _____ .

4. The electrolyte solution used in automotive batteries consists of _____ water and _____ sulfuric acid.

5. The automotive battery has a fully charged specific gravity of _____ corrected to 80°F.

6. _____ _____ is a condition where the grid grows little metallic fingers that extend through the separators and short out the plates.

7. The _____ _____ rating indicates the battery's ability to deliver a specified amount of current to start an engine at low ambient temperatures.

8. The electrolyte solution causes the chemical actions to take place between the lead peroxide of the _____ plates and the _____ _____ of the _____ plates.

9. Some of the aspects that determine the battery rating required for a vehicle include engine _____ , engine _____ , _____ conditions, and vehicle _____ .

10. Electrical loads that are still present when the ignition switch is in the OFF position are called _____ loads.

ASE Style Review Questions

1. *Technician A* says the battery stores electricity as electrons.
   Technician B says the battery stores energy in chemical form.
   Who is correct?
   A. A only
   B. B only
   C. Both A and B
   D. Neither A nor B

2. *Technician A* says the largest demand on the battery is when it must supply current to operate the starter motor.
   Technician B says the current requirements of a starter motor may be over several hundred amperes.
   Who is correct?
   A. A only
   B. B only
   C. Both A and B
   D. Neither A nor B

3. *Technician A* says even with the ignition switch turned off, there are electrical demands placed on the battery.
   Technician B says after the engine is started, the vehicle's charging system works to recharge the battery and to provide the current to run the electrical systems.
   Who is correct?
   A. A only
   B. B only
   C. Both A and B
   D. Neither A nor B

4. The current capacity rating of the battery is being discussed:
   Technician A says the amount of electrical energy that a battery is capable of producing depends on the size, weight, and active area of the plates.
   Technician B says the current capacity rating of the battery depends on the types of materials used in the construction of the battery.
   Who is correct?
   A. A only
   B. B only
   C. Both A and B
   D. Neither A nor B

5. The construction of the battery is being discussed:

   Technician A says the 12-volt battery consists of six 12-volt cells wired in parallel.

   Technician B says the 12-volt battery consists of six 2-volt cells wired in series.

   Who is correct?
   A. A only
   B. B only
   C. Both A and B
   D. Neither A nor B

6. Maintenance of a conventional battery is being discussed:

   Technician A says to add electrolyte to the battery if the cells are low.

   Technician B says to add only distilled water to the cells.

   Who is correct?
   A. A only
   B. B only
   C. Both A and B
   D. Neither A nor B

7. Battery terminology is being discussed:

   Technician A says grid growth is a condition where the grid grows little metallic fingers that extend through the separators and short out the plates.

   Technician B says deep cycling is discharging the battery almost completely without recharging it.

   Who is correct?
   A. A only
   B. B only
   C. Both A and B
   D. Neither A nor B

8. Battery rating methods are being discussed:

   Technician A says the ampere-hour is determined by the load in amperes a battery is able to deliver for 30 seconds at 0°F (−17.7°C) without terminal voltage falling below 7.2 volts for a 12-volt battery.

   Technician B says the cold cranking rating is the amount of steady current that a fully charged battery can supply for 20 hours at 80°F (26.7°C) without the cell voltage falling below 1.75 volts.

   Who is correct?
   A. A only
   B. B only
   C. Both A and B
   D. Neither A nor B

9. The hybrid battery is being discussed:

   Technician A says the hybrid battery can withstand six deep cycles and still retain 100% of its original reserve capacity.

   Technician B says the grid construction of the hybrid battery consists of approximately 2.75% antimony alloy on the positive plates and a calcium alloy on the negative plates.

   Who is correct?
   A. A only
   B. B only
   C. Both A and B
   D. Neither A nor B

10. *Technician A* says connecting the battery cables in reverse polarity can damage many of the vehicle's computer systems.

   Technician B says the battery must be secured in the vehicle to prevent damage and the possibility of shorting across the terminals if it tips.

   Who is correct?
   A. A only
   B. B only
   C. Both A and B
   D. Neither A nor B

Lighting Circuits

Upon completion and review of this chapter, you should be able to:

❏ Describe the operation and construction of automotive lamps.

❏ Describe the differences between conventional sealed-beam, halogen, and composite headlight lamps.

❏ Describe the operation and controlled circuits of the headlight switch.

❏ Describe the operation of the dimmer switch.

❏ Explain the operation of the most common styles of concealed headlight systems.

❏ Describe the operation of the various exterior light systems, including parking, tail, brake, turn, side, clearance, and hazard warning lights.

❏ Explain the operating principles of the turn signal and hazard light flashers.

❏ Describe the operation of the various interior light systems, including courtesy and instrument panel lights.

Introduction

Today's technician is required to understand the operation and purpose of the various lighting circuits on the vehicle. The addition of computers and their many sensors and actuators (some that interlink to the lighting circuits) make it impossible for mechanics to just bypass part of the circuit and rewire the system to their own standards. If a lighting circuit is not operating properly the safety of the driver, the passengers, people in other vehicles, and pedestrians are in jeopardy. When today's technician performs repairs on the lighting systems, the repairs must meet at least two requirements: They must assure vehicle safety and meet all applicable laws.

The lighting circuits of today's vehicles can consist of more than 50 light bulbs and hundreds of feet of wiring. Incorporated within these circuits are circuit protectors, relays, switches, lamps, and connectors. In addition, more sophisticated lighting systems use computers and sensors. The lighting circuits consist of an array of interior and exterior lights, including headlights, taillights, parking lights, stoplights, marker lights, dash instrument lights, courtesy lights, and so on.

The lighting circuits are largely regulated by federal laws, so the systems are similar between the various manufacturers. However, there are variations. Before attempting to do any repairs on an unfamiliar circuit, the technician should always refer to the manufacturer's service manuals. This chapter provides information about the types of lamps used, describes the headlight circuit, discusses different types of concealed headlight systems, and explores the various exterior and interior light circuits individually.

Lamps

A lamp generates light as current flows through the filament. This causes it to get very hot. The changing of electrical energy to heat energy in the resistive wire filament is so intense that the filament starts to glow and emits light. The lamp must have a vacuum surrounding the filament to prevent it from burning so hot that the filament burns in two. The glass envelope that encloses the filament maintains the presence of vacuum. When the lamp is manufactured, all the air is removed and the glass envelope seals out the air. If air is allowed to enter the lamp, the oxygen would cause the filament to oxidize and burn up.

It is important that any burned-out lamp be replaced with the correct lamp. The technician can determine what lamp to use by checking the lamp's standard trade number (Figures 6-3).

A **lamp** is a device that produces light as a result of current flow through a filament. The filament is enclosed within a glass envelope and is a type of resistance wire that is generally made from tungsten (Figure 6-1).

The process of changing energy forms to produce light is called **incandescence.**

Many lamps are designed to execute more than one function. A **double filament lamp** (Figure 6-2) can be used in the stop light circuit, taillight circuit, and the turn signal circuit combined.

Figure 6-1 A single filament bulb.

Figure 6-2 Double filament lamp.

TYPICAL AUTOMOTIVE LIGHT BULBS

Trade Number	Design Volts	Design Amperes	Watts: P = I x E
37	14.0	0.09	1.3
37E	14.0	0.09	1.3
51	7.5	0.22	1.7
53	14.4	0.12	1.7
55	7.0	0.41	2.9
57	14.0	0.24	3.4
57X	14.0	0.24	3.4
63	7.0	0.63	4.4
67	13.5	0.59	8.0
68	13.5	0.59	8.0
70	14.0	0.15	2.1
73	14.0	0.08	1.1
74	14.0	0.10	1.4
81	6.5	1.02	6.6
88	13.0	0.58	7.5
89	13.0	0.58	7.5
90	13.0	0.58	7.5
93	12.8	1.04	13.3
94	12.8	1.04	13.3
158	14.0	0.24	3.4
161	14.0	0.19	2.7
168	14.0	0.35	4.9

Figure 6-3 Chart of typical automotive light bulbs.

Trade Number	Design Volts	Design Amperes	Watts: P = I x E
192	13.0	0.33	4.3
194	14.0	0.27	3.8
194E-1	14.0	0.27	3.8
194NA	14.0	0.27	3.8
209	6.5	1.78	11.6
211-2	12.8	0.97	12.4
212-2	13.5	0.74	10.0
214-2	13.5	0.52	7.0
561	12.8	0.97	12.4
562	13.5	0.74	10.0
563	13.5	0.52	7.0
631	14.0	0.63	8.8
880	12.8	2.10	27.0
881	12.8	2.10	27.0
906	13.0	0.69	9.0
912	12.8	1.00	12.8
1003	12.8	0.94	12.0
1004	12.8	0.94	12.0
1034	12.8	1.80/0.59	23.0/7.6
1073	12.8	1.80	23.0
1076	12.8	1.80	23.0
1129	6.4	2.63	16.8
1133	6.2	3.91	24.2
1141	12.8	1.44	18.4
1142	12.8	1.44	18.4
1154	6.4	2.63/.75	16.8/4.5
1156	12.8	2.10	26.9
1157	12.8	2.10/0.59	26.9/7.6
1157A	12.8	2.10/0.59	26.9/7.6
1157NA	12.8	2.10/0.59	26.9/7.6
1176	12.8	1.34/0.59	17.2/7.6
1195	12.5	3.00	37.5
1196	12.5	3.00	37.5
1445	14.4	0.135	1.9
1816	13.0	0.33	4.3
1889	14.0	0.27	3.8
1891	14.0	0.24	3.4
1892	14.4	0.12	1.7
1893	14.0	0.33	4.6
1895	14.0	0.27	3.8
2057	12.8	2.10/0.48	26.9/6.1
2057NA	12.8	2.10/0.48	26.9/6.1
P25-1	13.5	1.86	25.1
P25-2	13.5	1.86	25.1
R19/5	13.5	0.37	
R19/10	13.5	0.74	
W10/3	13.5	0.25	

Figure 6-3 (continued)

Figure 6-4 Sealed-beam headlight construction.

Headlights

There are three basic types of headlights used on automobiles today: (1) standard sealed beam, (2) halogen sealed beam, and (3) composite.

Sealed-Beam Headlights

From 1939 to about 1975 the headlights used on vehicles remained virtually unchanged. During this time the headlight was a round lamp. The introduction of the rectangle headlight in 1975 enabled the vehicle manufacturers to lower the hood line of their vehicles. Both the round and rectangle headlights were sealed-beam construction (Figure 6-4). The standard sealed-beam headlight does not surround the filament with its own glass envelope (bulb). The glass lens is fused to the parabolic reflector that is sprayed with vaporized aluminum. The inside of the lamp is filled with argon gas. All oxygen must be removed from the standard sealed-beam headlight to prevent the filament from becoming oxidized. The reflector intensifies the light produced by the filament, and the lens directs the light to form the required light beam pattern.

The lens is designed to produce a broad flat beam. The light from the reflector is passed through concave prisms in the glass lens (Figure 6-5). The illustration (Figure 6-6) shows the horizontal spreading and the vertical control of the light beam to prevent upward glaring.

Figure 6-5 The lens uses prisms to redirect the light.

Shop Manual
Chapter 6, pages 96 and 99

The **sealed-beam** headlight is a self-contained glass unit made up of a filament, an inner reflector, and an outer glass lens.

The vaporized aluminum gives a reflecting surface that is comparable to silver.

Lens prisms redirect the light beam and create a broad, flat beam.

Figure 6-6 The prism directs the beam into (A) a flat horizontal pattern and (B) downward.

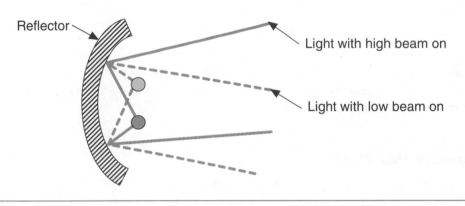

Figure 6-7 Filament placement controls the light beam projection.

> ⚠️ **WARNING:** Because of the construction and placement of prisms in the lens, it is important that the technician install the headlight in its proper position. The lens is usually marked "TOP" to indicate the proper installation position.

By placing the filament in different locations on the reflector, the direction of the light beam is controlled (Figure 6-7). In a dual filament lamp, the lower filament is used for the high beam and the upper filament is used for the low beam.

Halogen Headlights

The halogen lamp most commonly used in automotive applications consists of a small bulb filled with iodine vapor. The bulb is made of a high temperature resistant glass or plastic that surrounds a tungsten filament. This inner bulb is installed in a sealed glass housing (Figure 6-8). With the halogen added to the bulb, the tungsten filament is capable of withstanding higher temperatures than that of conventional sealed-beam lamps. The halogen lamp can withstand higher temperatures and thus is able to burn brighter.

In a conventional sealed-beam headlight, the heating of the filament causes atoms of tungsten to be released from the surface of the filament. These released atoms deposit on the glass envelope and create black spots that affect the light output of the lamp. In a halogen lamp, the iodine vapor causes the released tungsten atoms to be redeposited back onto the filament. This virtually eliminates any black spots. It also allows for increased high beam output of 25% over conventional lamps.

Halogen is the term used to identify a group of chemically related nonmetallic elements. These elements include chlorine, fluorine, and iodine.

Because the filament is contained in its own bulb, cracking or breaking of the lens does not prevent halogen headlight operation. As long as the filament envelope has not been broken, the filament will continue to operate. However, a broken lens will result in poor light quality and should be replaced.

Figure 6-8 Halogen sealed-beam headlight with iodine vapor bulb.

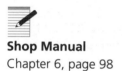

> **WARNING:** It is not recommended that halogen sealed-beam and standard sealed-beam headlights be mixed on the vehicle. Also, if the vehicle was originally equipped with halogen headlights, do not replace these with standard sealed beams. Doing so may result in poor light quality.

Composite Headlights

Shop Manual
Chapter 6, page 98

Many of today's vehicles have a halogen headlight system that uses a replaceable bulb. This system is called **composite headlights.**

By using the composite headlight system, vehicle manufacturers are able to produce any style of headlight lens they desire (Figure 6-9). This improves the aerodynamics, fuel economy, and styling of the vehicle.

Many manufacturers vent the composite headlight housing because of the increased amount of heat developed by these bulbs. Because the housings are vented, condensation may develop inside of the lens assembly. This condensation is not harmful to the bulb and does not affect headlight operation. When the headlights are turned on, the heat generated from the halogen bulbs will

Figure 6-9 A composite headlight system with a replaceable halogen bulb.

Figure 6-10 The correct method of handling the composite bulb during replacement. (Reprinted with the permission of Ford Motor Company)

Halogen headlight bulb

Do not touch bulb with fingers. Handle bulb by base only.

dissipate the condensation quickly. Ford uses integrated nonvented composite headlights. On these vehicles condensation is not considered normal. The assembly should be replaced.

⚠️ **WARNING:** Whenever technicians replace a composite lamp, care must be taken not to touch the envelope with the fingers. Staining the bulb with normal skin oil can substantially shorten the life of the bulb. Handle the lamp only by its base (Figure 6-10). Also dispose of the lamp properly.

Headlight Switches

The headlight switch controls most of the vehicle's lighting systems (Figure 6-12). The most common style of headlight switch is the three-position type with OFF, PARK, and HEADLIGHT positions. The headlight switch will generally receive direct battery voltage to two terminals of the switch. This allows the light circuits to be operated without having the ignition switch in the RUN or ACC (accessory) position.

When the headlight switch is in the OFF position, the open contacts prevent battery voltage from continuing to the lamps (Figure 6-13). When the switch is in the PARK position, battery voltage that is present at terminal 5 is able to be applied through the closed contacts to the side marker, taillight, license plate, and instrument cluster lights (Figure 6-14). This circuit is usually protected by a 15- to 20-ampere fuse that is separate from the headlight circuit.

Shop Manual
Chapter 6, page 107

The headlight switch may be located either on the dash by the instrument panel or on the steering column (Figure 6-11).

A BIT OF HISTORY

The Model T Ford used a headlight system that had a replaceable bulb. The owner's manual warned against touching the reflector except with a soft cloth.

Figure 6-11 (A) Instrument panel-mounted headlight switch. (Reprinted with the permission of Ford Motor Company) (B) Steering column-mounted headlight switch. (Courtesy of Toyota Motor Corporation)

Figure 6-12 Typical dash-mounted headlight switch. Pushing in on the release button allows for removal of the knob.

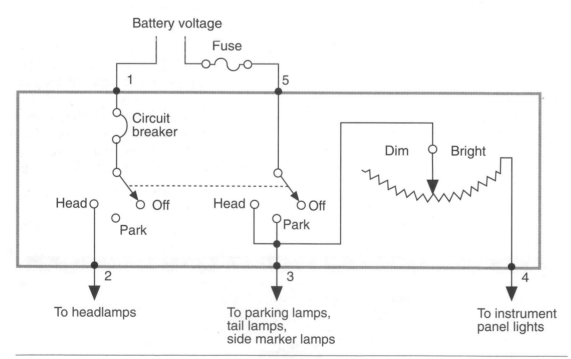

Figure 6-13 Headlight switch in the OFF position.

Figure 6-14 Headlight switch in the PARK position.

When the switch is located in the HEADLIGHT position, battery voltage that is present at terminal 1 is able to be applied through the circuit breaker and the closed contacts to light the headlights. Battery voltage from terminal 5 continues to light the lights that were on in the PARK position (Figure 6-15). The circuit breaker is used to prevent temporary overloads to the system from totally disabling the headlights.

Figure 6-15 Headlight switch in the HEADLIGHT position.

In vehicles that have the headlight switch located in the steering column, the rheostat may be a separate unit located on the dash near the instrument panel (Figure 6-16).

Figure 6-16 Headlight switch mounted on the steering column with a separate control on the dash to control the brightness of the instrument panel illumination lights.

The rheostat is a variable resistor that the driver uses to control the instrument cluster illumination lamp brightness. As the driver turns the light switch knob, the resistance in the rheostat is changed. The greater the resistance, the dimmer he instrument panel illumination lights glow.

Dimmer Switches

Shop Manual
Chapter 6, page 116

In the past, the most common location of the dimmer switch was on the floor board next to the left kick panel. This switch is operated by the driver pressing on it with a foot (Figure 6-17). Positioning the switch on the floor board made the switch subject to damage because of rust, dirt, and so forth. Most newer vehicles locate the dimmer switch on the steering column to prevent early failure and to increase driver accessibility (Figure 6-18).

Headlight Circuits

Shop Manual
Chapter 6, page 103

The complete headlight circuit consists of the headlight switch, dimmer switch, high beam indicator, and the headlights. When the headlight switch is pulled to the HEADLIGHT position, current flows to the dimmer switch through the closed contacts (Figure 6-19). If the dimmer switch is in the LOW position, current flows through the low beam filament of the headlights. When the

The **dimmer switch** provides the means for the driver to select either high or low beam operation, and to switch between the two. The dimmer switch is connected in series within the headlight circuit and controls the current path for high and low beams.

Low-beam wire

Dimmer switch assembly

Wiring harness

Supply wire

Vehicle floor

High-beam wire

Figure 6-17 Floor-mounted dimmer switch. (Reprinted with the permission of Ford Motor Company)

Figure 6-18 Steering column-mounted dimmer switch. (Reprinted with the permission of Ford Motor Company)

Figure 6-19 Headlight circuit indicating current flow with the dimmer switch in the LOW beam position.

Figure 6-20 Headlight circuit indicating current flow with the dimmer switch in the HIGH beam position.

dimmer switch is placed on the HIGH position, current flows through the high beam filaments of the headlights (Figure 6-20).

The headlight circuits just discussed are designed with insulated side switches and grounded bulbs. In this system, battery voltage is present to the headlight switch. The switch must be closed in order for current to flow through the filaments and to ground. The circuit is complete because the headlights are grounded to the vehicle body or chassis. Many import manufacturers use a system design that has insulated bulbs and ground side switches (Figure 6-21). In this system, when the headlight switch is located in the HEADLIGHT position the contacts are closed to complete the circuit path to ground. The headlight switch is located after the headlight lamps in the circuit. Battery voltage is applied directly to the headlights when the relays are closed. But the headlights will not light until the switch completes the ground side of the relay circuits. In this system, both the headlight and dimmer switches complete the circuits to ground.

No matter if the headlights use insulated side switches or ground side switches, each system is wired in parallel to each other. This prevents total headlight failure if one filament burns out.

Figure 6-21 Insulated headlights with ground side switches. (Courtesy of Toyota Motor Corporation)

Concealed Headlights

A vehicle equipped with a concealed headlight system hides the lamps behind doors when the headlights are turned off. When the headlight switch is turned to the HEADLIGHT position, the headlight doors open (Figure 6-22). The headlight doors can be controlled by either electric motors or by vacuum.

Shop Manual
Chapter 6, page 105

Some manufacturers use a **concealed headlight** system to help improve fuel economy and styling of the vehicle.

Figure 6-22 Concealed headlights enhance the vehicle's styling and aerodynamics.

Figure 6-23 A vacuum distribution valve located at the back of the headlight switch.

Vacuum-Controlled Systems

A **vacuum distribution valve** controls the direction of vacuum to various vacuum motors or to vent.

Systems that utilize vacuum to operate the headlight doors use a headlight switch with a vacuum distribution valve (Figure 6-23). The headlight doors are operated by vacuum motors (Figure 6-24). With the headlight switch in the OFF position, engine vacuum is supplied to the vacuum doors to keep them closed. When the headlight switch is pulled out to turn on the headlights, the distribution valve vents the vacuum that is held in the vacuum motors. This allows the springs to open the doors. Using vacuum to close the doors and springs to open the doors as the vacuum is vented assures that the doors will be open if vacuum to the system is lost. The vacuum reservoir stores vacuum to keep the doors closed when the engine is shut off or when low vacuum is supplied from the engine (such as during wide open throttle). Also, a bypass valve is installed into the system to provide a means of manually opening the doors in the event that the system fails (Figure 6-25).

Electrically Controlled Systems

Electrically controlled systems can use either a torsion bar to open both headlight doors (Figure 6-26), or a separate motor for each headlight door. Most systems will use limit switches to stop current flow when the doors are full up or full down. These switches generally operate from a cam on the reaction motor (Figure 6-27). Only one limit switch can be closed at a time. When the door is full up, the opening limit switch opens and the closing limit switch closes. When the door is full down, the closing limit switch is open and the opening limit switch closes. This prepares the reaction motor for the next time that the system is activated or deactivated.

Headlamp door

Vacuum motor

Vacuum motor

Figure 6-24 Vacuum motors are used to open and close the headlight doors.

By-pass valve

Figure 6-25 A bypass valve is used to open the doors if the system fails. (Courtesy of Chrysler Corporation)

Retainer clip

Collar

Torsion bar

Door crank

Motor assembly

Figure 6-26 An electrically operated concealed headlight system that uses one motor and a torsion bar.

Closed limit switch

Cam

Open limit switch

Figure 6-27 Most limit switches operate off a cam on the motor. (Courtesy of Chrysler Corporation)

Figure 6-28 Electrically controlled concealed headlight system with a manual control valve. (Courtesy of General Motors Corporation)

The electrically operated concealed headlight system also will have a provision for manually opening the doors in the event of a system failure (Figure 6-28).

Figure 6-29 illustrates a system that incorporates an integrated chip. Each motor has its own relay and limiting switches. When the limit switches are in the A-B position, the doors are full open. When the switches are in the A-C position, the doors are full closed.

Figure 6-29 Toyota pop-up headlight system. (Courtesy of Toyota Motor Corporation)

Figure 6-30 Operation when the headlight switch is turned to the HEADLIGHT position. (Courtesy of Toyota Motor Corporation)

When the headlights are turned on, terminal 14 is grounded through the headlight switch (Figure 6-30). This signals the IC to bias the leg of transistor TR2 for 10 seconds. When TR2 is biased it closes the circuits for relays 1 and 2, through position A-C of the limit switches and terminal 18. With the relay coils energized, battery voltage is supplied to the motors and they operate until the limit switches close to A-B or the 10-second timer turns off. TR3 and TR4 are also biased to complete the circuit for the headlight and taillight relays. When the relays are energized, the circuit is completed to the headlights and taillights, and they illuminate.

The motors used in this system provide for 360-degree rotation. The first 180 degrees of rotation opens the doors and an additional 180 degrees closes them. The timer circuit is used to protect the motors. The diodes in the motor relays are called clamping diodes. These protect the IC from induced voltage when the relay coils collapse

When the headlights are turned off, ground through terminal 14 is opened by the headlight switch (Figure 6-31). This signals the IC to bias transistor TR1 for 10 seconds. TR1 closes the circuit to ground for the relay circuit through the A-B positions of the limit switches and terminal 18. With the relays energized, battery voltage is sent to the motors. Also the IC ceases to bias TR3 and TR4. As a result, the relays are deenergized and the lamps turn off.

Figures 6-33 through 6-35 illustrate one of the methods used by the Chrysler Corporation to operate the electric motors for their concealed headlight system. When the ignition switch is in the RUN position but the headlight switch is off, current flows through the ignition switch to the

Figure 6-31 Operation when the headlight switch is returned to the OFF position from the HEADLIGHT position. (Courtesy of Toyota Motor Corporation)

Figure 6-32 Current flow with the headlight switch OFF and the headlight doors closed.

Figure 6-33 Current flow with the headlight switch in the HEADLIGHT position. The headlight doors are open.

relay. The relay is energized because the coil is grounded through the headlight filaments (Figure 6-32). With the coil energized the relay points close. However, the door closing limit switch is open. This results in a deenergized door closing field winding.

When the headlight switch is turned to the HEADLIGHT position, current continues to flow to the relay coil through the ignition switch. However, current is also sent to the other side of the relay coil from the headlight switch (Figure 6-33). Voltage is equal on both sides of the relay coil, so there is no voltage potential and the coil is deenergized. The relay contact points close to the door opening field winding. With the door opening limit switch closed, the motor operates until the limit switch is opened.

When the headlights are turned off again, voltage is applied to only one side of the coil through the ignition switch. Ground is provided through the headlight filaments. This energizes the relay, closing the contact point to the door closing winding. Since the door closing limit switch is closed, the motor operates until the limit switch opens again (Figure 6-34).

Flash to Pass

Most steering column-mounted dimmer switches have an additional feature called "flash to pass." This circuit illuminates the high beam headlights even with the headlight switch in the OFF or PARK position (Figure 6-35). In this illustration, battery voltage that is supplied to terminal "B1" of the headlight switch is also provided to the dimmer switch through the wire designated as L2 14LG/BK. Battery voltage is available to the dimmer switch through this wire in both the OFF and PARK positions of the headlight switch. When the driver activates the flash to pass feature, the contacts in the dimmer switch complete the circuit to the high beam filaments.

Chrysler calls this feature **optical horn.**

Figure 6-34 Current flow with the headlight switch returned to the OFF position from the HEADLIGHT position. The headlight doors are closing.

Exterior Lights

CHMSL is the abbreviation for center high mounted stop light. It is also referred to as a **collision avoidance light.**

Shop Manual
Chapter 6, pages 118 and 121

Parking lights can also be referred to as running lights.

When the headlight switch is pulled to the PARK or HEADLIGHT position, the front parking lights, taillights, side marker lights, and rear license plate light are all turned on. The front parking lights usually use dual filament bulbs. The other filament is used for the turn signals and hazard lights.

Most taillight assemblies include the brake, parking, rear turn signal, and rear hazard lights. The CHMSL, back-up lights, and license plate lights can be included as part of the taillight circuit design. Depending on the manufacturer, the taillight assembly can be wired to use single filament or dual filament bulbs. When single filament bulbs are used, the taillight assembly is wired as a three-bulb circuit. A three-bulb circuit uses one bulb each for the tail, brake, and turn signal lights on each side of the vehicle. When dual filament bulbs are used, the system is wired as a two-bulb circuit. Each bulb can perform more than one function.

Taillight Assemblies

Parking and taillights are controlled by the headlight switch. They can be turned on without having to turn on the headlights. Usually the first detent on the headlight switch is provided for this function. Figure 6-36 illustrates a parking and taillight circuit. This circuit is controlled by the headlight switch. Thus the lights can be operated with the ignition switch in the OFF position.

Figure 6-35 Flash to pass feature added to the headlight circuit. (Courtesy of Chrysler Corporation)

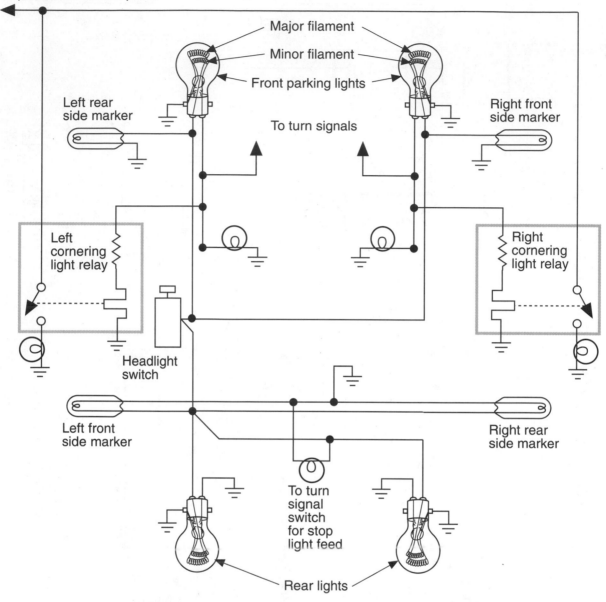

To power distribution panel

Major filament

Minor filament

Front parking lights

Left rear side marker

To turn signals

Right front side marker

Left cornering light relay

Right cornering light relay

Headlight switch

Left front side marker

Right rear side marker

To turn signal switch for stop light feed

Rear lights

Figure 6-36 Parking and taillight circuit. (Reprinted with the permission of Ford Motor Company)

In a three-bulb taillight system, the brake lights are controlled directly by the brake light switch (Figure 6-37). In many applications, the brake light switch is attached to the brake pedal, with a small clearance between the pedal arm pin and the eye of the pushrod (Figure 6-38). When the brakes are applied, the pedal moves down and the switch plunger moves away from the pushrod. This closes the contact points and lights the brake lights. On some vehicles the brake light switch may be a pressure sensitive switch located in the brake master cylinder. When the brakes are applied, the pressure developed in the master cylinder closes the switch to light the lamps.

The brake light switch receives direct battery voltage through a fuse, which allows the brake lights to operate when the ignition switch is in the OFF position. Once the switch is closed, voltage is applied to the brake lights. The brake lights on both sides of the vehicle are wired in parallel. The bulb is grounded to complete the circuit.

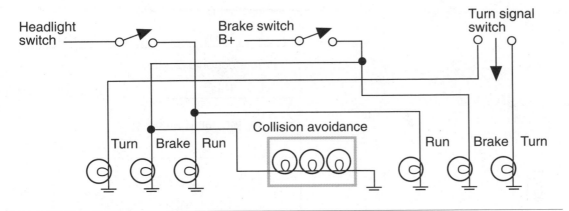

Figure 6-37 The three-bulb taillight circuit. One bulb is used for each function.

Most brake light systems use dual filament bulbs that perform multifunctions. Usually the filament of the dual filament bulb, which is also used by the turn signal and hazard lights, is used for the brake lights (the high intensity filament). In this type of circuit, the brake lights are wired through the turn signal and hazard switches (Figure 6-39). If neither turn signal is on, the current is sent to both of the brake lights (Figure 6-40). If the left turn signal is on, current for the right brake light is sent to the lamp through the turn signal switch and wire designated as 18BR/RD. The left brake light does not receive any voltage from the brake switch because the turn signal switch opens that circuit (Figure 6-41).

All brake lights must be red and, starting in 1986, the vehicle must have a center high mounted stop lamp (CHMSL). This lamp must be located on the center line of the vehicle and no lower than 3 inches below the bottom of the rear window (6 inches on convertibles). In a three-bulb system, wiring for the CHMSL is in parallel to the brake lights (Figure 6-42).

Because the turn signal switches used in a two-bulb system also control a portion of the operation of the brake lights, they have a complex system of contact points. The technician must remember that many brake light problems are caused by worn contact points in the turn signal switch.

Studies indicate that locating a brake light at eye level significantly reduces rear-end collisions.

Figure 6-38 Operation of a brake light switch. (Reprinted with the permission of Ford Motor Company)

Figure 6-39 Turn signal switch used in a two-bulb taillight circuit. (Courtesy of Chrysler Corporation)

Figure 6-40 Brake light operation with the turn signals in the neutral position. (Courtesy of Chrysler Corporation)

Figure 6-41 Brake light operation with the turn signal in the left turn position. (Courtesy of Chrysler Corporation)

Figure 6-42 Wiring of a CHMSL in a three-bulb circuit.

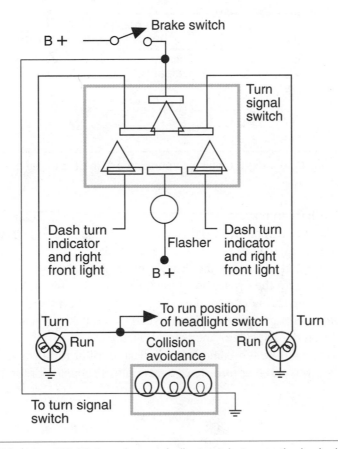

Figure 6-43 Wiring the CHMSL into the two-bulb circuit between the brake light switch and the turn signal.

In a two-bulb circuit the CHMSL can be wired in one of two common methods. The first method is to connect to the brake light circuit between the brake light switch and the turn signal switch (Figure 6-43). This method is simple to perform. However, it increases the number of conductors needed in the harness.

The most common method used by manufacturers is to install diodes in the conductors that are connected between the left and right side bulbs (Figure 6-44). If the brakes are applied with the turn signal switch in the neutral position, the diodes will allow voltage to flow to the CHMSL. If the turn signal switch is placed in the left turn position, the left light must receive a pulsating voltage from the flasher. However, the steady voltage being applied to the right brake light

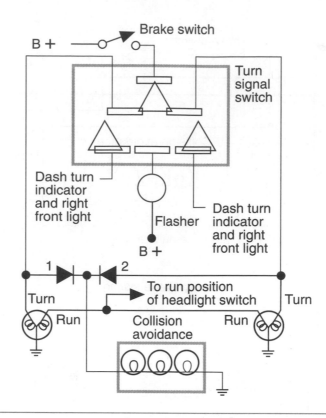

Figure 6-44 Two-bulb taillight circuit incorporating a CHMSL into the brake lights system.

would cause the left light to burn steady if the diode was not used. Diode 1 will block the voltage from the right lamp, preventing it from reaching the left light. Diode 2 will allow this voltage from the right brake light circuit to be applied to the CHMSL.

Turn signals are used to indicate the driver's intention to change direction or lanes. Figures 6-47 through 6-49 illustrate the operation of the turn signal circuit. In the neutral position, the contacts are opened, preventing current flow (Figure 6-46). When the driver moves the turn signal lever to indicate a left turn, the turn signal switch closes the contacts to direct voltage to the front and rear lights on the left side of the vehicle (Figure 6-47).

When the turn signal switch is moved to indicate a right turn, the contacts are moved to direct voltage to the front and rear turn signal lights on the right side of the vehicle (Figure 6-48).

Most turn signal switches receive their voltage from the ignition switch when it is in the RUN position only. This prevents the turn signals from operating while the ignition switch is in the OFF position.

The turn signal switch is located in the steering column behind the lock and horn plates (Figure 6-45).

Figure 6-45 Typical turn signal switch location. (Courtesy of Chrysler Corporation)

Figure 6-46 Turn signal circuit with switch in neutral position. (Courtesy of Chrysler Corporation)

Figure 6-47 Turn signal circuit with the switch in the left turn position. (Courtesy of Chrysler Corporation)

Figure 6-48 Turn signal circuit with the switch in the right turn position. (Courtesy of Chrysler Corporation)

Figure 6-49 A turn signal flasher located in the fuse box. (Courtesy of Ford Motor Company)

Flasher schematic

Figure 6-50 The flasher uses a bimetallic strip and a heating coil to flash the turn signal lights. (Courtesy of Ford Motor Company)

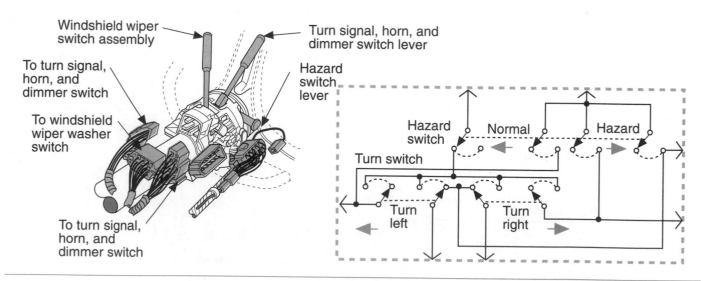

Figure 6-51 The hazard warning system is incorporated into the turn signal system. (Reprinted with the permission of Ford Motor Company)

SERVICE TIP: If the turn signals operate properly in one direction but do not flash in the other, the problem is not in the flasher unit. A burned-out lamp filament will not cause enough current to flow to sufficiently heat the bimetallic strip to cause it to open. Thus, the lights do not flash. Locate the faulty bulb and replace it.

With the contacts closed, power flows from the flasher through the turn signal switch to the lamps. The flasher (Figure 6-49) consists of a set of normally closed contacts, a bimetallic strip, and a coil heating element (Figure 6-50). These three components are wired in series. As current flows through the heater element, it increases in temperature, which heats the bimetallic strip. The strip then bends and opens the contact points. Once the points are open, current flow stops. The bimetallic strip cools and the contacts close again. With current flowing again the process is repeated. Because the flasher is in series with the turn signal switch, this action causes the turn signal lights to turn on and off.

WARNING: The incorrect selection of the turn signal flasher may result in fast, slow, or no turn signal operation.

The hazard warning system is part of the turn signal system (Figure 6-51). It has been included on all vehicles sold in the United States since 1967. All four turn signal lamps flash when the hazard warning switch is turned on. Depending on the manufacturer, a separate flasher can be used for the hazard lights than the one used for the turn signal lights. The operation of the hazard flasher is identical to that of the turn signal. The only difference is that the hazard flasher is capable of carrying the additional current drawn by all four turn signals. And, it receives its power source directly from the battery. Figure 6-52 shows the current flow through the hazard warning system

Cornering Lights

Vehicles equipped with cornering lights have an additional set of contacts in the turn signal switch. These contacts operate the cornering light circuit only. The contacts can receive voltage from either the ignition switch or the headlight switch. If the ignition switch provides the power, the cornering lights will be activated any time the turn signals are used (Figure 6-54). If the contacts receive the voltage from the headlight switch, the cornering lights do not operate unless the headlight switch is in the PARK or HEADLIGHT position (Figure 6-55).

Backup Lights

All vehicles sold in the United States after 1971 are required to have backup lights. Backup lights illuminate the road behind the vehicle and warn other drivers and pedestrians of the driver's intention to back up. Figure 6-56 illustrates a backup light circuit. Power is supplied through the ignition switch when it is in the RUN position. When the driver shifts the transmission into reverse, the backup light switch contacts are closed and the circuit is completed.

Many automatic transmission equipped vehicles incorporate the backup light switch into the neutral safety switch. Most manual transmissions are equipped with a separate switch.

Cornering lights are lamps that illuminate when the turn signals are activated. They burn steady when the turn signal switch is in a turn position to provide additional illumination of the road in the direction of the turn (Figure 6-53).

Figure 6-52 Current flow when the hazard warning system is activated. (Courtesy of Chrysler Corporation)

Figure 6-53 Cornering lights are used to provide additional illumination during turns.

Either style of switch can be located on the steering column, on the floor console, or on the transmission (Figure 6-57). Depending on the type of switch used, there may be a means of adjusting the switch to assure that the lights are not on when the vehicle is in a forward gear selection.

Side Marker and Clearance Lights

Side marker lights are installed on all vehicles sold in the United States since 1969. These lamps permit the vehicle to be seen when entering a roadway from the side. This also provides a means for other drivers to determine vehicle length. The front side marker light lens must be amber and the rear lens must be red. Vehicles that use wrap-around headlight and taillight assemblies also use this lens for the side marker lights (Figure 6-58). Vehicles that surpass certain length and height limits are also required to have clearance lights that face both to the front and rear of the vehicle.

The common method of wiring the side marker lights is in parallel with the parking lights. Wired in this manner, the side marker lights would only illuminate when the headlight switch was in the PARK or HEADLIGHT position.

Many vehicle manufacturers use a method of wiring in the side marker lights so that they flash when the turn signals are activated. This system uses a special high resistance bulb for the side marker light. The side marker light is wired across the parking light and turn signal light (Figure 6-59). If the parking lights are on, voltage is applied to the side marker light from the parking light circuit. Ground for the side marker light is provided through the turn signal filament. Because the turn signal filament has less resistance than the side marker light, it will not illuminate. In this condition the side marker light stays on constantly (Figure 6-60).

If the parking lights are off and the turn signal is activated, the side marker light receives its voltage source from the turn signal circuit. Ground for the side marker light is provided through the parking light filament. The voltage drop over the side marker light is so high that the parking light will not illuminate. The side marker light will flash with the turn signal light (Figure 6-61).

Figure 6-54 Cornering light circuit powered through the ignition switch. (Courtesy of Chrysler Corporation)

Figure 6-54 (continued)

If the turn signal is activated while the parking lights are illuminated, the side marker light will flash alternately with the turn signal light. When both the turn signal light and the parking light are on, there is equal voltage applied to both sides of the side marker light. There is no voltage potential across the bulb, so the light does not illuminate (Figure 6-62). The turn signal light turns off as a result of the flasher opening. Then the turn signal light filament provides a ground path and the side marker light comes on. The side marker light will stay on until the flasher contacts close to turn on the turn signal light again.

Figure 6-55 Cornering light circuit powered when the taillights are on.

Figure 6-56 Backup light circuit.

Figure 6-57 A combination backup and neutral safety switch installed on an automatic transmission.

Figure 6-58 Wrap-around headlights serve as side marker lights

Figure 6-59 Side marker light wired across two circuits.

Figure 6-60 Current flow to the side marker light with the parking light on.

Figure 6-61 Side marker operation with the turn signal switch activated.

Figure 6-62 Side marker light with the turn signal light and parking light on.

Figure 6-63 Courtesy lights using ground side switches.

Interior Lights

Interior lighting includes courtesy lights, map lights, and instrument panel lights.

Courtesy Lights

Courtesy lights operate from the headlight and door switches and receive their power source directly from a fused battery connection. The switches can be either ground switch circuit (Figure 6-63) or insulated switch circuit design (Figure 6-64). In the insulated switch circuit, the

Courtesy lights
illuminate the vehicle interior when the doors are open.

Figure 6-64 Courtesy lights using insulated side switches.

switch is used as the power relay to the lights. In the grounded switch circuit, the switch controls the grounding portion of the circuit for the lights. The courtesy lights may also be activated by the headlight switch. When the headlight switch knob is turned to the extreme counterclockwise position, the contacts in the switch close and complete the circuit.

Shop Manual
Chapter 6, page 126

Instrument Cluster and Panel Lights

Consider the following three types of lighting circuits within the instrument cluster:

1. **Warning lights** alert the driver to potentially dangerous conditions such as brake failure or low oil pressure.

2. **Indicator lights** include turn signal indicators.

3. **Illumination lights** provide indirect lighting to illuminate the instrument gauges, speedometer, heater controls, clock, ashtray, radio, and other controls.

The power source for the instrument panel lights is provided through the headlight switch. The contacts are closed when the headlight switch is located in the PARK or HEADLIGHT position. The current must flow through a variable resistor (rheostat) that is either a part of the headlight switch or a separate dial on the dash. The resistance of the rheostat is varied by turning the knob. By varying the resistance, changes in the current flow to the lamps control the brightness of the lights (Figure 6-65).

SERVICE TIP: On some vehicles the instrument cluster illumination light fuse is located after the headlight switch. On these circuits the headlight switch must be turned on when using a test light or digital volt-ohm meter (DVOM) to check the fuse.

Figure 6-65 A rheostat controls the brightness of the instrument panel lights.

Lighting System Complexity

Today's vehicles have a sophisticated lighting system and electrical interconnections. It is possible to have problems with lights and accessories that cause them to operate when they are not supposed to. This is through a condition called feedback. If there is an open in the circuit, electricity will seek another path to follow. This may cause any lights or accessories in that path to turn on.

Examples of feedback and how it may cause undesired operation are illustrated in Figures 6-66 through 6-73. The illustration (Figure 6-66) shows a system that has the dome light, tail light,

Feedback occurs when electricity seeks a path of lower resistance. This alternate path operates another component than the one intended. Feedback can be classified as a short.

Figure 6-66 A normally operating circuit.

Figure 6-67 An open (blown) dome light fuse can cause feedback into other circuits when the headlights are turned on.

and brake light circuits on one fuse; the cigar lighter circuit has its own fuse. The two fuses are located in the main fuse block and share a common bus bar on the power side.

If the dome light fuse blew, and the headlight switch was in the PARK or HEADLIGHT position, the courtesy lights, dome light, taillight, parking lights, and instrument lights would all be very dimly lit (Figure 6-67). Current would flow through the cigar lighter fuse to the courtesy light and on to the door light switch. Current will then continue through the dome light to the headlight switch. Because the headlight switch is now closed, the instrument panel lights are also in the circuit. The lights are dim because all the bulbs are now connected in series.

Figure 6-68 Feedback with a blown dome light fuse and the door switch closed.

Figure 6-69 Feedback when brake light switch is closed.

If the dome light fuse is blown and the headlight switch is in the OFF position, all lights will turn off. However, if the door is opened, the courtesy lights will come on but the dome light will not (Figure 6-68).

With the same blown fuse and the brake light switch closed, the dome light, courtesy light, and brake light will all illuminate dimly because the loads are in series (Figure 6-69).

In this example, if the dome light and courtesy lights come on dimly when the cigar lighter is pushed in, the problem can be caused by a blown cigar lighter fuse (Figure 6-70). With the cigar lighter pushed in, a path to ground is completed. The lights and cigar lighter are now in

Figure 6-70 Feedback as a result of the cigar lighter fuse being blown.

Figure 6-71 Opening the door will cause the courtesy light to go out and the dome light to get brighter.

series, thus the lights are dim and there is not enough current to heat and release the cigar lighter. If the cigar lighter was left in this position the battery would eventually drain down.

A blown cigar lighter fuse will also cause the dome light to get brighter when the doors are open, and the courtesy lights will go out (Figure 6-71). Also, if the lighter is pushed in and the brake light switch is closed, the dome and courtesy lights will go out (Figure 6-72).

Feedback can also be the result of a conductive corrosion that is developed at a connection. If the corrosion allows for current flow from one conductor to an adjacent conductor in the

Figure 6-72 Dome and courtesy lights go out when the brakes are applied.

Figure 6-73 A corroded common connection can cause feedback.

connection, the other circuit will also be activated. The illustration (Figure 6-73) shows how corrosion in a common connector can cause the dome light to illuminate when the wiper motor is turned on. Because the wiper motor has a greater resistance than the light bulb, more voltage will flow through the bulb than through the motor. The bulb will light brightly, but the motor will turn very slowly or not at all. The same effect will result if the courtesy light switch is turned on with the motor switch off.

Dual filament light bulb sockets are subjectable to corrosion that can cause feedback. The most common indicator of this problem is parking lights that illuminate when the brake pedal is applied.

Summary

❏ The most commonly thought of light circuit is the headlights. But there are many lighting systems in the vehicle.

❏ Different types of lamps are used to provide illumination for the systems. The lamp may be either a single filament bulb that performs a single function, or a double filament that performs several functions.

❏ The headlight lamps can be one of three designs: standard sealed beam, halogen sealed beam, or composite.

❏ The headlight filament is located on a reflector that intensifies the light, which is then directed through the lens. The lens is designed to change the circular light pattern into a broad, flat light beam. Placement of the filament in the reflector provides for low and high beam light patterns.

❏ Some manufacturers use concealed headlights to improve the aerodynamics of the vehicle. The concealed headlight doors can operate from vacuum or by electrically controlled motors. Some systems incorporate the use of IC chips into the concealed headlight door control.

❏ In addition to the headlight system, the lighting systems include:
Stop lights
Turn signals
Hazard lights
Parking lights
Taillights

Terms to Know
CHMSL
Composite bulb
Cornering lights
Courtesy lights
Dimmer switch
Double filament lamp
Feedback
Filament
Halogen
Illumination lights
Incandescence
Indicator lights
Lamp
Limit switches
Optical horn
Prism lens

**Terms to Know
(continued)**

Reflector

Sealed beam

Vacuum distribution
valve

Warning lights

Backup lights

Side marker lights

Courtesy lights

Instrument panel lights

❑ The headlight switch can be used as the control of many of these lighting systems. Most headlight switches have a circuit breaker that is an integral part of the switch. The circuit breaker provides protection of the headlight system without totally disabling the headlight operation if a circuit overload is present.

❑ A rheostat is used in conjunction with the headlight switch to control the brightness of the instrument panel illumination lights.

Review Questions

Short Answer Essays

1. What lighting systems are controlled by the headlight switch?

2. How is the brightness of the instrument cluster lamps controlled?

3. What is CHMSL?

4. What is the purpose of the lamp filament?

5. What three lighting circuits are incorporated within the instrument cluster?

6. List and describe the three types of headlight lamps used.

7. Describe the influence that the turn signal switch has on the operation of the brake lights in a two-bulb taillight assembly.

8. What is the purpose of the diodes on some CHMSL circuits?

9. How are most cornering light circuits wired to allow the cornering light to be on steady when the turn signal switch is activated?

10. Describe what the term *feedback* means and how it can affect the operation of the electrical system.

Fill-in-the-Blanks

1. When today's technician performs repairs on the lighting systems, the repairs must meet at least two requirements: They must assure vehicle _____ and meet all _____ _____ .

2. A _____ is a device that produces light as a result of current flow through a _____ .

3. _____ _____ redirect the light beam and create a broad, flat beam.

4. The _____ _____ controls most of the vehicle's lighting systems.

5. The _____ _____ provides the means for the driver to select either high or low beam operation.

6. The complete headlight circuit consists of the _____ _____ , _____ _____ , _____ _____ _____ , and the _____ .

7. The headlight doors of a concealed system can be controlled by either _____ _____ or by _____ .

8. On vehicles equipped with cornering lights, the turn signal switch has an additional set of _____ that operate the cornering light circuit only.

9. Most limit switches operate off of a _____ on the motor.

10. In most automatic transmission equipped vehicles, the backup light switch is part of the _____ _____ _____ . Most manual transmissions are equipped with a _____ switch.

ASE Style Review Questions

1. Two-bulb taillight assemblies are being discussed:
   Technician A says the brake lights use the high intensity filament of the taillight bulb.
   Technician B says the current from the brake lights flows through the turn signal switch before going to the brake lights.
   Who is correct?
   A. A only
   B. B only
   C. Both A and B
   D. Neither A nor B

2. Composite headlights are being discussed:
   Technician A says composite headlights have replaceable bulbs.
   Technician B says a cracked or broken lens will prevent the operation of the composite headlight.
   Who is correct?
   A. A only
   B. B only
   C. Both A and B
   D. Neither A nor B

3. The brake light circuit is being discussed:
   Technician A says the brake light switch receives current from the ignition switch.
   Technician B says the brake light switch receives current from the headlight switch.
   Who is correct?
   A. A only
   B. B only
   C. Both A and B
   D. Neither A nor B

4. The turn signal circuit is being discussed:
   Technician A says the dimmer switch is a part of the circuit.
   Technician B says the flasher uses a bimetallic strip to open and close the circuit.
   Who is correct?
   A. A only
   B. B only
   C. Both A and B
   D. Neither A nor B

5. The turn signals work properly in one direction, but in the other direction the indicator light stays on steadily:
Technician A says a burned out light bulb may be the fault.
Technician B says the flasher is at fault.
Who is correct?
   A. A only
   B. B only
   C. Both A and B
   D. Neither A nor B

6. The concealed headlight system is being discussed:
Technician A says the system can use vacuum to operate the doors.
Technician B says the system can use electric motors to operate the doors.
Who is correct?
   A. A only
   B. B only
   C. Both A and B
   D. Neither A nor B

7. The CHMSL circuit is being discussed:
Technician A says the diodes are used to assure proper turn signal operation.
Technician B says the diodes are used to prevent radio static when the brake light is activated.
Who is correct?
   A. A only
   B. B only
   C. Both A and B
   D. Neither A nor B

8. The exterior lights of a vehicle are being discussed:
Technician A says the cornering lights use an additional set of contacts in the turn signal switch.
Technician B says the cornering light circuit can receive its voltage from the ignition switch.
Who is correct?
   A. A only
   B. B only
   C. Both A and B
   D. Neither A nor B

9. *Technician A* says the side marker lights can be wired to flash with the turn signals.
Technician B says wrap-around lens can be used for side marker lights.
Who is correct?
   A. A only
   B. B only
   C. Both A and B
   D. Neither A nor B

10. *Technician A* says feedback does not affect the operation of the electrical system.
Technician B says feedback is a form of a short.
Who is correct?
   A. A only
   B. B only
   C. Both A and B
   D. Neither A nor B

Conventional Analog Instrumentation, Indicator Lights, and Warning Devices

Upon completion and review of this chapter, you should be able to:

❑ Describe the operation of mechanical speedometers and odometers.

❑ Describe the function and operation of the tachometer.

❑ Explain the purpose of an instrument voltage regulator.

❑ Describe the operation of bimetallic gauges.

❑ Describe the operation of electromagnetic gauges, including d'Arsonval, three coil, two coil, and air core.

❑ Explain the function and operation of the various gauge sending units, including thermistors, piezoresistive, and mechanical variable resistors.

❑ Explain the operation of various warning lamp circuits.

❑ Explain the operation of various audible warning systems.

Introduction

Analog instrument gauges and indicator lights monitor the various vehicle operating systems. They provide information to the driver about their current operation (Figure 7-1). Warning devices also provide information to the driver, however, these are usually associated with an audible signal. Some vehicles use a voice module to alert the driver to certain conditions.

This chapter details the operation of analog electrical gauges, indicator lights, and warning devices.

Indicator/Warning Light Key

1. Turn signals
2. Charging system (AMP)
3. Door ajar
4. Malfunction of anti-lock brake system
5. High beam
6. Brake
7. Engine temp. gauge
8. Fuel gauge
9. Seat belt
10. Check engine
11. Speedometer
12. Tachometer
13. Boost gauge
14. Low Fuel *
15. Low oil pressure*
16. Trac-control active

* Low oil pressure/hi coolant temp/low fuel (below 1/8) redundant with gauges

Figure 7-1 Instrument panel. (Courtesy of Chrysler Corporation)

Figure 7-2 The main elements of a conventional-type speedometer.

The **speedometer** is used to indicate the speed of the vehicle.

The aluminum drum is not attracted to the magnetic field. However, it is a conductor of electric current.

Shop Manual
Chapter 7, page 141

Eddy currents are small induced currents

Speedometers

A conventional speedometer (Figure 7-2) uses a cable that is connected to the output shaft of the transmission (or transfer case if four-wheel drive). The rotation of the output shaft causes the speedometer cable to rotate within its housing (Figure 7-3). The cable then transfers rotation to the speedometer assembly. In the speedometer assembly, the cable is connected to a permanent magnet that is surrounded by an aluminum drum. The speedometer needle is attached to the drum. There is no solid or mechanical connection between the speedometer needle and the cable.

The rotating permanent magnet produces a rotating magnetic field around the drum. The rotating magnetic field generates circulating currents in the drum. These eddy currents produce a small magnetic field that interacts with the field of the rotating magnet. This interaction of the two magnetic fields pulls the drum and needle around with the rotating magnet. A fine hairspring holds back the drum to prevent the needle from bouncing. As the drum rotates, the needle moves across the speedometer scale (Figure 7-4).

Shop Manual
Chapter 7, page 146

Odometers

The odometer is driven by the speedometer cable through a worm gear (Figure 7-5). The odometer usually has six wheels; each wheel is numbered 0 through 9. The wheels are geared together so that as the right wheel makes one full revolution, the next wheel to the left moves one position. This action is repeated for all of the wheels.

A BIT OF HISTORY

One of the early styles of speedometers used a regulated amount of air pressure to turn a speed dial. The air pressure was generated in a chamber containing two intermeshing gears. The gears were driven by a flexible shaft that was connected to a front wheel or the driveshaft. The air was applied against a vane inside of the speed dial. The amount of air applied was proportional to the speed of the vehicle.

WARNING: Federal and state laws prohibit tampering with the correct mileage as indicated on the odometer. If the odometer must be replaced, it must be set to the reading of the original odometer. Or, a door sticker must be installed indicating the reading of the odometer when it was replaced.

The **odometer** is a mechanical counter in the speedometer unit that indicates total miles accumulated on the vehicle. Many vehicles also have a second odometer that can be reset to zero. It is referred to as a **trip odometer.**

A **worm gear** is a spiral cut gear on a shaft.

Some manufacturers use an odometer with seven wheels to display mileage over 100,000 miles.

Speedometer driven gear retainer

Speedometer driven gear

O Ring

Speedometer cable

Mounting bolt   Mounting clip

Figure 7-3 Speedometer cable connection to the transmission.

Pointer

Speedometer cable

Aluminum drum

Figure 7-4 Eddy currents cause the needle to move across the scale.

Speedometer spiral gear

Gear train

Odometer

Figure 7-5 Odometer gears and wheels.

Figure 7-6 Electrical tachometer wired into the ignition system.

A **tachometer** is an instrument that measures the speed of the engine in revolutions per minute (rpm).

Shop Manual
Chapter 7, page 146

Tachometers

An electrical tachometer receives voltage pulses from the ignition system—usually the coil (Figure 7-6). Each of the voltage pulses represents the generation of one spark at the spark plug. The rate of spark plug firing is in direct relationship to the speed of the engine. A circuit within the tachometer converts the ignition pulse signal into a varying voltage. The voltage is applied to a voltmeter that serves as the engine speed indicator.

Shop Manual
Chapter 7, page 147

Gauges

Most instrument panels will include at least one gauge. The electromechanical gauge acts as an ammeter because the gauge reading changes with variations in the sender unit resistance. There are two basic types of electromechanical gauges: the bimetallic gauge and the electromagnetic gauge. The basic principles of operation of electrical gauges are very simple. Once these principles are mastered, the technician should have no difficulty in locating and repairing a faulty gauge circuit.

A **gauge** is a device that displays the measurement of a monitored system by the use of a needle or pointer that moves along a calibrated scale.

> **WARNING:** These gauges are called analog because they use needle movement to indicate current levels. However, many newer instrument panels use computer driven analog gauges that operate under different principles. It is important that the technician follow the manufacturer's procedures for testing the gauges or gauge damage will result.

Instrument Voltage Regulator

Shop Manual
Chapter 7, page 150

Some gauge systems require the use of an instrument voltage regulator (IVR) that provides a constant voltage to the gauge so it will read accurately under all charging conditions. The IVR consists of a set of normally closed contacts and a heating coil wrapped around a bimetallic strip (Figure 7-7). When voltage is applied to the IVR, current flows through the contacts and the heating coil. Because the heating coil is connected to a ground, the flowing current heats the coil and the bimetallic strip bends. When the strip bends, the contacts open and current flows through the IVR and the heater coil stops. With no current flowing through the coil, the bimetallic strip cools and straightens. This closes the contact points and the process is repeated. This constant opening

Figure 7-7 Instrument voltage regulator.

The gauge is called an **electro-mechanical device** because it is operated electrically. However, its movement is mechanical.

The **sender unit** is the sensor for the gauge. It is a variable resistor that changes resistance values with changing monitored conditions.

The **instrument voltage regulator (IVR)** provides a constant voltage to the gauge regardless of the voltage output of the charging system.

Opened is the term used to mean that current flow is stopped. The path for electron flow is broken by opening the circuit. **Closed circuit** means there are no breaks in the path and current will flow.

and closing of the contact points causes a pulsating DC current with a varying potential equivalent in heating effects to approximately 5 volts. The equivalent voltage is constant, and is applied to the gauge. The IVR output is approximately 5 volts, regardless of the alternator output.

Bimetallic Gauges

Bimetallic gauges (or thermoelectric gauges) are simple dial and needle indicators that transform the heating effect of electricity into mechanical movement. The movement of the needle is slow and smooth, so the needle avoids responding to sudden changes that could cause a flickering needle. This prevents the gauges from constantly moving as a result of vehicle movement (as would be the case with a fuel gauge for example).

The construction of the bimetallic gauge features an indicating needle that is linked to the free arm of a U-shaped bimetallic strip (Figure 7-8). The free arm has a heater coil that is connected to the gauge terminal posts. When current flows through the heater coil, it heats the bimetallic arm. This causes the arm to bend and moves the needle across the gauge dial.

The amount that the bimetallic strip bends is proportional to the heat produced in the heater coil. When the current flow through the heater coil is small, less heat is created and needle movement is slight. If the current through the heater coil is increased, more heat is created

Figure 7-8 Bimetallic gauge construction. (Reprinted with the permission of Ford Motor Company)

Figure 7-9 Typical bimetallic fuel gauge circuit. (Courtesy of Chrysler Corporation)

A **bimetallic strip** consists of two different types of metals. Heating one of the metals more rapidly than the other causes the strip to flex in proportion to the amount of heat.

Opening and closing of the contact points creates induced voltage (like that in an ignition coil). This voltage is directed through a **radio choke** that absorbs it and prevents static in the vehicle's radio.

The bimetallic gauge has the advantage that it is not affected by changes in the charging system because gauge input is controlled by the IVR.

A **variable resistor** provides for an infinite number of resistance values within a range.

Electromagnetic gauges produce needle movement by magnetic forces instead of heat.

and the needle will move more. The variable resistance used to control the current flow through the heater coil is in the sending unit (Figure 7-9).

The bimetallic gauge uses heat to move the needle. Thus it is influenced by changes as a result of high or low ambient temperatures. Change in ambient temperatures is compensated for by the U-shape of the bimetallic element. When ambient temperature bends the free arm, it also affects the fixed arm. The effect on the fixed arm is equal to the free arm but in the opposite direction. This action then cancels the effects of outside temperatures.

Electromagnetic Gauges

There are four types of electromagnetic gauges: the d'Arsonval, the three coil, the two coil, and the air core.

The d'Arsonval Gauge. The d'Arsonval gauge consists of a permanent horseshoe-type magnet that surrounds a moveable electromagnet (armature) that is attached to a needle (Figure 7-10). When current flows through the armature it becomes an electromagnet and is repelled by the permanent magnet. When current flow through the armature is low, the strength of the electromagnet is weak and needle movement is small. When the current flow is increased, the magnetic

Figure 7-10 d'Arsonval gauge needle movement. (Reprinted with the permission of Ford Motor Company)

Figure 7-11 Three-coil gauge.

field created in the armature is increased and needle movement is greater. The armature has a small spring attached to it to return the needle to zero when current is not applied to the armature. An IVR is used because voltage to the armature must remain constant to give accurate readings.

The Three-Coil Gauge. The three-coil gauge consists of a permanent magnet with a needle attached to it. The permanent magnet is surrounded by three electromagnets. There may also be a quantity of silicone dampening fluid to restrict needle movement due to vehicle movement (Figure 7-11).

The three coils of fine wire are wound on a square plastic frame. The needle shaft is supported by a bearing sleeve extending from the frame. The needle shaft connects the pointer to a circular permanent magnet, which is surrounded by the coil windings.

The three coils are the low-reading coil, a bucking coil, and a high-reading coil (Figure 7-12). When voltage is applied to the gauge, there are two paths for current flow. One path is

Figure 7-12 Three-coil gauge circuit.

The **d'Arsonval gauge** uses the interaction of a permanent magnet and an electromagnet, and the total field effect to cause needle movement.

The **three-coil** gauge uses the interaction of three electromagnets and the total field effect upon a permanent magnet to cause needle movement.

The three-coil gauge is also known as a magnetic bobbin gauge.

The **bucking coil** produces a magnetic field that bucks or opposes the low-reading coil. The **low-reading coil** and the bucking coil are wound together, but in opposite directions. The **high-reading coil** is positioned at a 90-degree angle to the low-reading and bucking coils.

Figure 7-13 With sending unit resistance low, the needle is attracted to the low-reading coil.

through the low-reading coil and through the sending unit to ground (Figure 7-13). The second path is through the low-reading coil to the bucking coil and the high-reading coil to ground (Figure 7-14). The amount of resistance that the sending unit has determines the path. If there is less resistance to ground through the sending unit than through the bucking and high-reading coils, the current will take the path through the sending unit. If the resistance through the sending unit is greater than the resistance through the coils, the current will not flow through the sending unit.

When sending unit resistance is low, more current flows through the low-reading coil than through the bucking and high-reading coils. This causes the needle to be attracted to the left and

Figure 7-14 With sending unit resistance high, the needle is attracted to the high-reading coil.

Figure 7-15 A two-coil temperature gauge.

the gauge reads toward zero. When sending unit resistance is high, very little current will flow through the sending unit. The current now flows through the three coils. The magnetic field created by the bucking coil cancels the magnetic field of the low-reading coil. The high-reading coil's magnetic field then attracts the needle and it swings toward maximum.

At an intermediate sending unit resistance value, the current can flow through both paths. If resistance was equal in the two paths, the needle would point at the midrange. As the magnetic field(s) changes as the result of resistance change in the sending unit, the needle will swing toward the more powerful magnetic field.

Variation in the charging system output will not affect the gauge readings. This is because of the current flowing through both the low-reading and high-reading coils. Any variation in charging system output affects the strength of both coils. Also, it is normal for the three-coil gauge needle to remain in its last position when the ignition switch is turned off.

The Two-Coil Gauge. There are different designs of the two-coil gauge, depending on the gauge application. For example, in a coolant temperature gauge (Figure 7-15), both coils receive battery voltage. One of the coils is grounded directly, and the other is grounded through the sender unit. As the resistance in the sender unit varies as a result of temperature changes, so too does the current flow through that coil. The two magnetic fields have different strengths depending on the amount of current flow through the sender unit. Electricity always flows the path of least resistance, so the sender unit resistance dictates the needle movement. The strength of the "H" coil's magnetic field changes with the amount of resistance in the sender unit. The stronger of the two magnetic fields causes the armature, with the needle attached to it, to move in proportion to the engine coolant temperature.

> The **two-coil** gauge uses the interaction of two electromagnets and the total field effect on an armature to cause needle movement.

With the engine temperature cold, the sender unit resistance is high. More current will flow through the "C" coil than the "H" coil. This will cause the needle to be attracted to the "C" coil's magnetic field and indicate a cold temperature on the gauge face. As the resistance in the sender unit decreases, more current will flow through the "H" coil. This will result in needle movement toward the hot temperature range on the gauge face.

A two-coil gauge that is constructed to be used as a fuel gauge will use a different method (Figure 7-16). The "E" coil receives battery voltage. At the end of the coil, the voltage is divided. One path is through the "F" coil to ground; the other is through the sender unit to ground. With the fuel level low, there is less resistance in the sender unit resistor than in coil "F." Current flow will be through coil "E," to the sender unit, through the variable resistor, and to ground. Because most of the current is flowing through coil "E," it will produce a stronger magnetic field and attract the needle toward it. Higher sender unit resistance causes more current to flow through

> The two-coil gauge does not require the use of an IVR. It is normal for the gauge to remain at its last position when the ignition is turned off.

Figure 7-16 A two-coil fuel gauge.

the "F" coil. As more current bypasses the sender unit and flows through the "F" coil, the magnetic field becomes stronger and the needle moves toward the full position.

The **air core** gauge uses the interaction of two electro-magnets and the total field effect upon a permanent magnet to cause needle movement.

The Air Core Gauge. The air core gauge works on the same principle as the two coil. However, the pointer is connected to a permanent magnet (Figure 7-17). Two windings are placed at different angles, one wound around the other. There is no core inside of the windings. Instead, the permanent magnet is placed inside of the windings. The magnet aligns itself to a resultant field, in the field windings, according to the resistance of the sender unit. The sender unit resistance varies the strength of the field winding, which opposes the strength of the reference winding. The strength of the electromagnetic field depends on the resistance in the sending unit. Figure 7-17 illustrates an air core fuel gauge.

The air core gauge does not require an IVR. It is normal for the gauge to remain at its last position when the ignition is turned off.

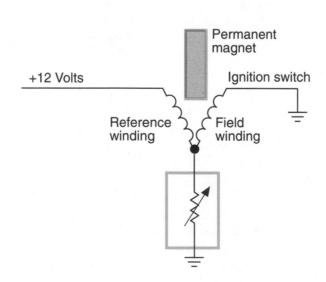

Figure 7-17 Air core gauge needle movement.

Figure 7-18 A thermistor used to sense engine temperature.

Gauge Sending Units

There are three types of sending units associated with the gauges just described: (1) a thermistor, (2) a piezoresistive sensor, and (3) a mechanical variable resistor.

In the coolant temperature sensing circuit, current is sent from the gauge unit into the top terminal of the sending unit, through the variable resistor (thermistor), and to the engine block (ground). The resistance value of the thermistor changes in proportion to coolant temperature (Figure 7-18). As the temperature rises, the resistance decreases and the current flow through the gauge increases. As the coolant temperature lowers, the resistance value increases and the current flow decreases.

The piezoresistive sensor sending unit is threaded into the oil delivery passage of the engine. The pressure exerted by the oil causes the flexible diaphragm to move (Figure 7-19). The diaphragm movement is transferred to a contact arm that slides along the resistor. The position of the sliding contacts on the arm in relation to the resistance coil determines the resistance value, and the amount of current flow through the gauge to ground.

Figure 7-19 Piezoresistive sensor used for measuring engine oil pressure.

Shop Manual
Chapter 7, page 152

Generally, the sensor is threaded into the engine block or cooling system, with the tip projected into the coolant passage.

The **thermistor** is a resistor whose resistance changes in relation to changes in temperature. It is often used as a coolant temperature sensor.

A **piezoresistive sensor** is sensitive to pressure changes. Its most common use is to measure the engine oil pressure.

A fuel level sending unit is an example of a mechanical variable resistor (Figure 7-20). The sending unit is located in the fuel tank and has a float that is connected to the wiper of a variable resistor. The floating arm rises and falls with the difference in fluid level. This movement of the float is transferred to the sliding contacts. The position of the sliding contacts on the resistor determines the resistor value.

A sending unit that is used with bimetallic gauges will have a low resistance value when the fuel level is high. The low resistance value causes a high current to flow through the gauge, thus heating the bimetallic strip and causing the needle to move toward FULL. A sending unit used with an electromagnetic gauge has high resistance when the float level is high.

Figure 7-20 Fuel gauge sending unit. (Courtesy of Chrysler Corporation)

WARNING: It is important to know that the sending unit operation is different for electromagnetic gauges than bimetallic gauges. When resistance is low in most bimetallic gauges the gauge reads high; with many electromagnetic gauges the gauge reads low.

Shop Manual
Chapter 7, page 154

A **warning light** is a lamp that is illuminated to warn the driver of a possible problem or hazardous condition.

Warning Lamps

A warning light may be used to warn of low oil pressure, high coolant temperature, defective charging system, or a brake failure. A warning light can be operated by two methods: a sending unit circuit or controlling the voltage being applied to the lamp.

Sending Unit Controlled Lights

Unlike gauge sending units, the sending unit for a warning light is nothing more than a simple switch. The style of switch can be either normally open or normally closed, depending on the monitored system.

Figure 7-21 (A) Oil pressure light sending unit. (B) Oil pressure warning lamp circuit.

Most oil pressure warning circuits use a normally closed switch (Figure 7-21). A diaphragm in the sending unit is exposed to the oil pressure. The switch contacts are controlled by the movement of the diaphragm. When the ignition switch is turned to the RUN position with the engine not running, the oil warning light turns on. Because there is no pressure to the diaphragm, the contacts remain closed and the circuit is complete to ground. When the engine is started, oil pressure builds and the diaphragm moves the contacts apart. This opens the circuit and the warning light goes off. The amount of oil pressure required to move the diaphragm is about 3 psi. If the oil warning light comes on while the engine is running, it indicates that the oil pressure has dropped below the 3 psi limit.

Most coolant temperature warning light circuits use a normally open switch (Figure 7-22). The temperature sending unit consists of a fixed contact and a contact on a bimetallic strip. As the coolant temperature increases, the bimetallic strip bends. As the strip bends, the contacts move closer to each other. Once a predetermined temperature level has been exceeded, the contacts are closed and the circuit to ground is closed. When this happens the warning light is turned on.

Figure 7-22 Temperature indicator light circuit.

Figure 7-23 A prove-out circuit included in normally open (NO) coolant temperature light system.

A **prove-out circuit** completes the warning light circuit to ground through the ignition switch when it is in the START position. The warning light will be on during engine cranking to indicate to the driver that the bulb is working properly.

Shop Manual
Chapter 7, page 156

With normally open-type switches, the contacts are not closed when the ignition switch is turned to ON. In order to perform a bulb check on normally open switches a prove-out circuit is included (Figure 7-23).

It is possible to have more than one sender unit connected to a single bulb. The illustration (Figure 7-24) shows a wiring circuit of a dual purpose warning light. The light will come on whenever oil pressure is low or coolant temperature is too high.

Another system that is monitored with a warning light is the braking system. The illustration (Figure 7-25) shows a brake system combination valve. The center portion of the valve senses differences in the hydraulic pressures on both sides of the valve. With the differential valve centered, the plunger on the warning light switch is in the recessed area of the valve. If the pressure drops in either side of the brake system, the differential valve will be forced to move by hydraulic pressure. When the differential valve moves, the switch plunger is pushed up and the switch contacts close.

Opposing Voltage-Controlled Lights

A lamp lights when there is a voltage drop or potential across its terminals. If equal voltage is applied to both sides of the lamp, the lamp remains off because current cannot flow. This is the basic principle of most charging system indicator lights (Figure 7-26).

When the ignition switch is turned to the ON position and the engine is off, the light is "proofed." The current flows through the ignition switch and warning light to the input terminal 1.

Figure 7-24 One warning lamp used with two sensors.

Rear brake pressure is applied here.

Front brake pressure is applied here.

A leak in either system drops pressure to that system.

The piston moves toward the reduced pressure side.

Trigger is pushed into close switch and illuminate brake warning light on instrument panel.

Piston is normally held centered by equal pressure at both ends. Switch trigger extends into groove and switch is open.

Figure 7-25 Brake warning light switch as part of the combination valve.

The current continues to the common connector at R_1 and through the field coil. Transistor TR1 is biased to conduct through R_1 and the circuit is completed to ground. When the engine is started, the AC Generator begins to produce voltage. The voltage produced in the stator is sent through the diode trio. This places output voltage at the common connection at R_1, putting equal voltage to both sides of the indicator light. Because there is no potential difference, current cannot flow and the light goes out. The resistor is wired in parallel to the light to assure that field current will flow if the lamp burns out.

If the indicator light comes on while the engine is running, it indicates that charging system output voltage has dropped. With a potential at both light terminals, the lamp lights.

Figure 7-26 Some charging systems use opposing voltage to control operation of the warning light.

Audible Warning Systems

Many warning systems also include an audible signal to alert the driver of potentially dangerous conditions. This could include seatbelt warning systems, low oil pressure, key in ignition, headlights on, and so forth.

Seatbelt Warning Systems

On many Ford vehicles the light and buzzer come on regardless of whether or not the seatbelts are fastened.

When the ignition switch is turned on and the seatbelt is not fastened, a buzzer will sound and a warning light will come on for approximately 8 seconds. The seatbelt switch is a normally closed switch to ground (Figure 7-27). When the seatbelt is fastened, the switch is opened. With the key in the RUN position, battery voltage is supplied to the timer. If the seatbelt is not buckled, the circuit is complete to ground, and the buzzer and light operate. When the driver's seatbelt is not fastened, the bimetallic strip heats up and opens the circuit. Because battery current flows through the heater as long as the ignition switch is in the RUN position, the bimetallic strip stays hot enough to remain open until the ignition switch is turned to the OFF position.

A **timer circuit** uses a bimetallic strip that opens as a result of the heat being generated by the current flow.

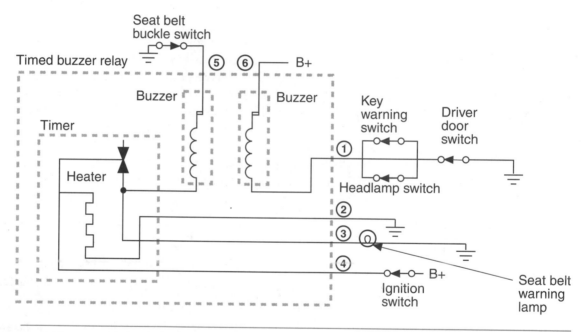

Figure 7-27 Seatbelt warning system. (Courtesy of Chrysler Corporation)

Headlight and Key-In Ignition Warning Systems

Ford uses normally open switches.

If drivers fail to turn off the headlights and they open the door, a buzzer or chime will sound. The driver door switch is a normally closed switch to ground. The switch opens when the door is closed. If the headlight switch is in the HEADLIGHT or PARK position, battery voltage is applied through the buzzer and the headlight switch to the driver door switch (Figure 7-27). If the driver's door is opened, the circuit is completed and the buzzer sounds until either the headlight switch is turned off or the driver door is shut.

The "key in ignition" warning system operates in the same manner. When the ignition key is inserted into the ignition switch tumblers, the key warning switch is closed. If the driver's door is opened while the key is in the ignition switch, the circuit is completed and the buzzer will sound.

Summary

❏ Through the use of gauges and indicator lights, the driver is capable of monitoring several engine and vehicle operating systems.

❏ The gauges include speedometer, odometer, tachometer, oil pressure, charging indicator, fuel level, and coolant temperature.

❏ Some gauge types require the use of an IVR to assure constant voltage to the gauge coils. This assures accurate gauge readings.

❏ The most common types of gauges are the bimetallic, d'Arsonval, three coil, two coil, and air core.

❏ All gauges require the use of a variable resistance sending unit. Styles of sending units include thermistors, piezoresistive sensors, and mechanical variable resistors.

❏ In the absence of gauges, important engine and vehicle functions are monitored by warning lamps. These circuits generally use an On-Off switch-type sensor. The exception would be the use of voltage-controlled warning lights that use the principle of voltage drop.

Review Questions

Short Answer Essays

1. What are the most common types of electromagnetic gauges?

2. What type of electromagnetic gauge uses an IVR?

3. Describe the operation of the IVR.

4. Describe the operation of the piezoresistive sensor.

5. Describe the operation of the conventional speedometer.

6. Where do most tachometers receive the signal from?

7. Describe the principle of operation of the bimetallic gauge.

8. Describe what occurs in the warning light circuit of the charging system when the light is being proofed.

9. What is a thermistor used for?

10. What is meant by electromechanical?

Fill-In-The-Blanks

1. The purpose of the tachometer is to indicate _____ _____

2. A piezoresistive sensor is used to monitor _____ changes.

3. The most common style of fuel level sending unit is _____ variable resistor.

4. If equal voltage is applied to both sides of a lamp, the lamp is

_____

5. The brake warning light is activated by _____ pressure in the brake hydraulic system.

6. The IVR sends a constant _____ to the gauges, regardless of _____ output.

7. _____ gauges transform the heating effect of electricity into mechanical movement.

8. In a three-coil gauge, the _____ _____ produces a magnetic field that bucks or opposes the low-reading coil. The _____ _____ coil and the bucking coil are wound together, but in opposite directions. The _____ _____ coil is positioned at a 90-degree angle to the low-reading and bucking coils.

9. The _____ gauge consists of a permanent horseshoe-type magnet that surrounds a moveable electromagnet (armature), which is attached to a needle.

10. A _____ _____ circuit completes the warning light circuit to ground through the ignition switch when it is in the START position.

ASE Style Review Questions

1. Odometer replacement is being discussed:
   Technician A says it is permissible to turn back the reading on an odometer as long as the customer is notified.
   Technician B says if an odometer is replaced it must be set to the same reading as the original odometer.
   Who is correct?
   A. A only
   B. B only
   C. Both A and B
   D. Neither A nor B

2. The IVR is being discussed:
   Technician A says an IVR is used to assure a constant 12 volts is applied to the gauge coils.
   Technician B says an IVR is used on bimetallic gauges.
   Who is correct?
   A. A only
   B. B only
   C. Both A and B
   D. Neither A nor B

3. The operation of the speedometer is being discussed:
   Technician A says there is a mechanical link between the speedometer cable and the needle.
   Technician B says the system operates on magnetism.
   Who is correct?
   A. A only
   B. B only
   C. Both A and B
   D. Neither A nor B

4. Electromagnetic gauges are being discussed:
   Technician A says the d'Arsonval gauge uses the interaction of a permament magnet and an electromagnet, and the total field effect to cause needle movement.
   Technician B says the three-coil gauge uses the interaction of three electromagnets and the total field effect upon a permanent magnet to cause needle movement.
   Who is correct?
   A. A only
   B. B only
   C. Both A and B
   D. Neither A nor B

5. Electric tachometers are being discussed:
   Technician A says the tachometer receives its signal from the + side of the ignition coil.
   Technician B says the tachometer is used to measure drive shaft speed.
   Who is correct?
   A. A only
   B. B only
   C. Both A and B
   D. Neither A nor B

6. *Technician A* says the three-coil gauge uses the principle that electricity seeks the path of least resistance.
   Technician B says the three coils used are the low-reading coil, a bucking coil, and a high-reading coil.
   Who is correct?
   A. A only
   B. B only
   C. Both A and B
   D. Neither A nor B

7. Sending unit operation is being discussed:
   Technician A says in most bimetallic gauges if sending unit resistance is low, the gauge reads high.
   Technician B says with most electromagnetic gauges if sending unit resistance is low, the gauge reads low.
   Who is correct?
   A. A only
   B. B only
   C. Both A and B
   D. Neither A nor B

8. Warning light circuits are being discussed:
   Technician A says most oil pressure warning circuits use a normally closed switch.
   Technician B says most coolant temperature warning light circuits use a normally open switch.
   Who is correct?
   A. A only
   B. B only
   C. Both A and B
   D. Neither A nor B

9. The brake failure warning system is being discussed:
   Technician A says if the pressure drops in either side of the brake system, the switch plunger is pushed up and the switch contacts close.
   Technician B says the warning light comes on if the pressure is equal on both sides of the brake system.
   Who is correct?
   A. A only
   B. B only
   C. Both A and B
   D. Neither A nor B

10. *Technician A* says the trip odometer is able to be reset to zero.
    Technician B says the odometer is driven by the speedometer cable through a worm gear.
    Who is correct?
    A. A only
    B. B only
    C. Both A and B
    D. Neither A nor B

Direct Current Motors and the Starting System

Upon completion and review of this chapter, you should be able to:

❑ Explain the purpose of the starting system.

❑ List and identify the components of the starting system.

❑ Explain the principle of operation of the DC motor.

❑ Describe the purpose and operation of the armature.

❑ Describe the purpose and operation of the field coil.

❑ Explain the differences between the types of magnetic switches used.

❑ Identify and explain the differences between starter drive mechanisms.

❑ Describe the differences between the positive engagement and solenoid shift starter.

❑ Describe the operation and features of the permanent magnet starter.

Introduction

The internal combustion engine must be rotated before it will run under its own power. The starting system is a combination of mechanical and electrical parts that work together to start the engine. The starting system is designed to change the electrical energy, which is being stored in the battery, into mechanical energy. To accomplish this conversion, a starter or cranking motor is used. The starting system includes the following components:

1. Battery

2. Cable and wires

3. Ignition switch

4. Starter solenoid or relay

5. Starter motor

6. Starter drive and flywheel ring gear

7. Starting safety switch

Components in a simplified cranking system circuit are shown (Figure 8-1). This chapter examines both this circuit and the fundamentals of electric motor operation.

Shop Manual
Chapter 8, page 167

Figure 8-1 Major components of the starting system. The solid line represents the starting circuit. The dashed line indicates the starter control circuit.

In the early days of the automobile, the vehicle did not have a starter motor. The operator had to use a starting crank to turn the engine by hand. Charles F. Kettering invented the first electric "self-starter," which was developed and built by the Delco Electrical Plant. The self-starter first appeared on the 1912 Cadillac and was actually a combination starter and generator.

Classroom Manual
Chapter 2, page 41.

Shop Manual
Chapter 8, page 188

The **armature** is the moveable component of the motor that consists of a conductor wound around a laminated iron core. It is used to create a magnetic field.

Pole shoes are made of high-magnetic permeability material to help concentrate and direct the lines of force in the field assembly.

Motor Principles

DC motors use the interaction of magnetic fields to convert the electrical energy into mechanical energy. Magnetic lines of force flow from the north pole to the south pole of a magnet (Figure 8-2). If a current carrying conductor is placed within the magnetic field, two fields will be present. On the left side of the conductor the lines of force are in the same direction. This will concentrate the flux density of the lines of force on the left side. This will produce a strong magnetic field, because the two fields will reinforce each other. The lines of force oppose each other on the right side of the conductor. This results in a weaker magnetic field. The conductor will tend to move from the strong field to the weak field. This principle is used to convert electrical energy into mechanical energy in a starter motor by electromagnetism.

A simple electromagnet-style starter motor is shown (Figure 8-3). The inside windings are called the armature. The armature rotates within the stationary outside windings, called the field, which has windings coiled around pole shoes.

When current is applied to the field and the armature, both produce magnetic flux lines. The direction of the windings will place the left pole at a south polarity and the right side at a north polarity. The lines of force move from north to south in the field. In the armature, the flux lines circle in one direction on one side of the loop and in the opposite direction on the other side. Current will now set up a magnetic field around the loop of wire, which will interact with the north and south fields and put a turning force on the loop. This force will cause the loop to turn in the direction of the weaker field (Figure 8-4). However, the armature is limited in how far it is able to turn. When the armature is halfway between the shoe poles, the fields balance one another.

For the armature to continue rotating, the current flow in the loop must be reversed. To accomplish this, a split-ring commutator is in contact with the ends of the armature loops. Current enters and exits the armature through a set of brushes that slide over the commutator's sections. As the brushes pass over one section of the commutator to another, the current flow in the armature

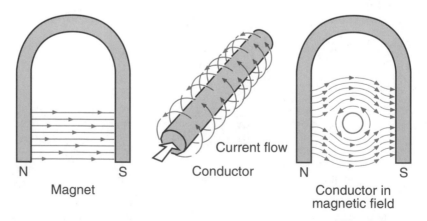

Figure 8-2 Magnetic field interaction.

Figure 8-3 Simple electromagnetic motor.

Figure 8-4 Rotation of the conductor is in the direction of the weaker field.

is reversed. The position of the magnetic fields are the same. However, the direction of current flow through the loop has been reversed. This will continue until the current flow is turned off.

A single loop motor would not produce enough torque to rotate an engine. Power can be increased by the addition of more loops or pole shoes. An armature with its many windings, with each loop attached to corresponding commutator sections is shown (Figure 8-5). In a typical starter motor (Figure 8-6) there are four brushes that make the electrical connections to the commutator. Two of the brushes are grounded to the starter motor frame, and two are insulated from the frame. Also, the armature is supported by bushings at both ends.

CAUTION: The high amount of current required to operate the starter motor generates heat very quickly. Continuous operation of the starter motor for longer than 30 seconds causes serious heat damage. The starter motor should not be operated for more than 30 seconds at a time and should have a 2-minute wait between cranking attempts.

Figure 8-5 Starter armature.

The point at which the fields balance is called the **static neutral point.**

The **commutator** is a series of conducting segments located around one end of the armature.

Brushes are electrically conductive sliding contacts, usually made of copper and carbon.

The number of field coils and brushes varies between manufacturers.

Figure 8-6 Starter and solenoid components. (Courtesy of Robert Bosch Corporation)

The stampings of the armature core are called **laminations.**

The construction of the armature from individual stampings is called **laminated construction.**

Shop Manual
Chapter 8, page 188

Counter voltages induced in a core are called **eddy currents**. These cause heat to build up in the core and waste energy.

The wave-winding pattern is the most commonly used due to its lower resistance.

Armature

The armature is constructed with a core made of several thin iron stampings that are attached to each other (Figure 8-7). Laminated construction is used because in a solid iron core the magnetic fields would generate eddy currents. By using laminated construction, and insulating the laminations, eddy currents in the core are minimized.

The slots on the outside diameter of the laminations hold the armature windings. The windings loop around the core and are connected to the commutator. Each commutator segment is insulated from the adjacent segments. A typical armature can have more than 30 commutator segments.

A steel shaft is fitted into the center hole of the core laminations. The commutator is also insulated from the shaft.

Two basic winding patterns are used in the armature: lap winding and wave winding. In the lap winding, the two ends of the winding are connected to adjacent commutator segments (Figure 8-8). In this pattern, the wires passing under a pole field have their current flowing in the same direction

In the wave winding pattern, each end of the winding connects to commutator segments that are 90 or 180 degrees apart (Figure 8-9). In this pattern design some windings will have no

Figure 8-7 Lamination construction of a typical motor armature.

Figure 8-8 Lap winding diagram. (Courtesy of Delco Remy Division—GMC)

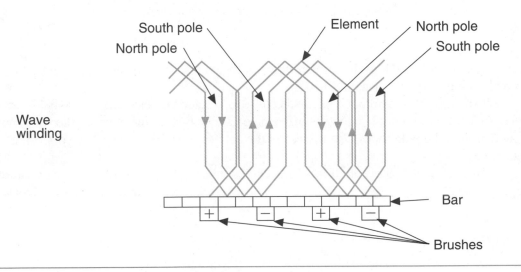

Figure 8-9 Wave-wound armature. (Courtesy of Delco Remy Division—GMC)

current flow at certain positions of armature rotation. This occurs because the segment ends of the winding loop are in contact with brushes that have the same polarity.

Field Coils

The field coils are electromagnets constructed of wire coils wound around a pole shoe (Figure 8-10). The field coils are attached to the inside of the starter housing (Figure 8-11). The

Shop Manual
Chapter 8, page 187

The pole shoes are constructed of heavy iron.

Most starter motors use four field coils.

Figure 8-10 Field coil wound around a pole shoe.

Figure 8-11 Field coils mounted to the inside of starter housing.

iron pole shoes and the iron starter housing work together to increase and concentrate the field strength of the field coils (Figure 8-12).

When current flows through the field coils, strong stationary electromagnetic fields are created. The fields have a north and south magnetic polarity based on the direction the windings are wound around the pole shoes. The polarity of the field coils alternate to produce opposing magnetic fields.

In any DC motor, there are three methods of connecting the field coils to the armature: in series, in parallel (shunt), and a compound connection that uses both series and shunt coils.

Series-Wound Motors

Most starter motors are series-wound with current flowing first to the field windings, then to the brushes, through the commutator and the armature winding contacting the brushes at that time,

Figure 8-12 Magnetic fields in a four-pole starter motor. (Courtesy of Robert Bosch Corporation)

Figure 8-13 Series-wound motor schematic.

then through the grounded brushes back to the battery source (Figure 8-13). This design permits all of the current that passes through the field coils to also pass through the armature.

A series-wound motor will develop its maximum torque output at the time of initial start. As the motor speed increases, the torque output of the motor will decrease. This decrease of torque output is the result of counter electromotive force.

Shunt-Wound Motors

Electric motors, or shunt motors, have the field windings wired in parallel across the armature (Figure 8-14). A shunt motor does not decrease in its torque output as speeds increase. This is because the CEMF produced in the armature does not decrease the field coil strength. Due to a shunt motor's inability to produce high torque, it is not used as a starter motor. However, shunt motors may be found as wiper motors, power window motors, power seat motors, and so on.

Compound Motors

In a compound motor some of the field coils are connected to the armature in series, and some field coils are connected in parallel with the battery and the armature (Figure 8-15). This configuration allows the compound motor to develop good starting torque and constant operating speeds. The field coil that is shunt wound is used to limit the speed of the starter motor. Also, on Ford's positive engagement starters, the shunt coil is used to engage the starter drive. This is possible because the shunt coil is energized as soon as battery voltage is sent to the starter.

Figure 8-14 Shunt-wound motor schematic.

Figure 8-15 Compound motor uses both series and shunt coils.

Counter electromotive force (CEMF) is current produced in the starter motor itself. This current acts against the supply current from the battery. CEMF is produced by electromagnetic induction.

Shunt means there is more than one path for current to flow.

A shunt-wound field is used to limit the speed that the motor can turn.

A starter motor that uses the characteristics of a series motor and a shunt motor is called a **compound motor.**

Starter Drives

The **starter drive** is the part of the starter motor that engages the armature to the engine flywheel ring gear.

The **ratio** of the starter drive is determined by dividing the number of teeth on drive gear (pinion gear) into the number of teeth on the driven gear (flywheel).

Inertia is the tendency of an object that is at rest to stay at rest, and an object that is in motion to stay in motion.

The purpose of the **drive spring** is to absorb the initial shock of engagement.

A starter drive includes a pinion gear set that meshes with the flywheel ring gear on the engine's crankshaft (Figure 8-16). To prevent damage to the pinion gear or the ring gear, the pinion gear must mesh with the ring gear before the starter motor rotates. To help assure smooth engagement, the end of the pinion gear is tapered (Figure 8-17). Also, the action of the armature must always be from the motor to the engine. The engine must not be allowed to spin the armature. The ratio of the number of teeth on the ring gear and the starter drive pinion gear is usually between 15:1 and 20:1. This means the starter motor is rotating 15 to 20 times faster than the engine. Normal cranking speed for the engine is about 200 rpm. If the starter drive had a ratio of 18:1, the starter would be rotating at a speed of 3,600 rpm. If the engine started and was accelerated to 2,000 rpm, the starter speed would increase to 36,000 rpm. This would destroy the starter motor if it was not disengaged from the engine.

Bendix Inertia Drive

The bendix drive depends on inertia to provide meshing of the drive pinion with the ring gear (Figure 8-18). The screwshaft threads are a part of the armature, and will turn at armature speed. At the end of the pinion and barrel is the pinion gear that will mesh with the ring gear. The pinion and barrel have internal threads that match those of the screwshaft. When current flows through the starter motor, the armature will begin to spin. Torque from the armature is transmitted via a shock-absorbing spring and drive head to the screwshaft. This causes the screwshaft to rotate. However, the barrel does not rotate. The barrel has a weight on one side to increase its inertial effect. The barrel tends to stay at rest, and the screwshaft rotates inside the barrel. As a result, the barrel is threaded down the length of the screwshaft to the end. At the end of the screwshaft, the pinion gear engages the ring gear. Here the pinion gear locks to the screwshaft and transfers torque from the armature to the ring gear and engine.

Once the engine starts and is running under its own power, it will rotate faster than the armature. This causes the barrel to screw back down the screwshaft and bring the pinion gear out of engagement with the ring gear

There are a couple different variations of the inertia drive. One of these variations is the barrel-type drive (Figure 8-19). The barrel-type starter drive is similar to the inertia drive except:

1. The pinion is mounted on the end of the barrel.

2. It has a higher gear ratio.

3. It works directly off screw threads at the end of the armature, instead of a screwshaft.

Figure 8-16 Starter drive pinion gear is used to turn the engine's flywheel.

Figure 8-17 The pinion gear teeth are tapered to allow for smooth engagement.

Figure 8-18 Bendix inertia drive. (Courtesy of Delco Remy Division—GMC)

Figure 8-19 Bendix barrel-type starter drive. (Courtesy of Delco Remy Division—GMC)

Another variation is the folo-thru drive. This drive is much like the barrel drive with the addition of a detent pin and a detent clutch (Figure 8-20).

When the pinion barrel has moved to the end of the screwshaft, the detent pin locks the barrel to the screwshaft. The detent pin operates on centrifugal force. As the shaft is turning rapidly, centrifugal force throws the pin into engagement between the barrel and the screwshaft.

The detent clutch disengages the sections of the screwshaft when the engine is running faster than the armature, and the drive is still engaged. Disengaging the clutch protects the motor from being damaged.

Figure 8-20 Bendix folo-thru starter drive. (Courtesy of Delco Remy Division—GMC)

Figure 8-21 Overrunning clutch starter drive. (Reprinted with the permission of Ford Motor Company)

Overrunning Clutch Drive

The most common type of starter drive is the overrunning clutch. The overrunning clutch is a roller-type clutch that transmits torque in one direction only and freewheels in the other direction. This allows the starter motor to transmit torque to the ring gear, but prevents the ring gear from transferring torque to the starter motor.

In a typical overrunning-type clutch (Figure 8-21), the clutch housing is internally splined to the starter armature shaft. The drive pinion turns freely on the armature shaft within the clutch housing. When torque is transmitted through the armature to the clutch housing, the spring-loaded rollers are forced into the small ends of their tapered slots (Figure 8-22). They are then wedged tightly against the pinion barrel. The pinion barrel and clutch housing are now locked together; torque is transferred through the starter motor to the ring gear and engine.

When the engine starts and is running under its own power, the ring gear attempts to drive the pinion gear faster than the starter motor. This unloads the clutch rollers and releases the pinion gear to rotate freely around the armature shaft.

Cranking Motor Circuits

The starting system of the vehicle consists of two circuits: the starter control circuit and the motor feed circuit. These circuits are separate but related. The control circuit consists of the starting portion of the ignition switch, the starting safety switch (if applicable), and the wire conductor to connect these components to the relay or solenoid. The motor feed circuit consists of heavy battery cables from the battery to the relay and the starter or directly to the solenoid if the starter is so equipped.

Figure 8-22 When the armature turns, it locks the rollers into the tapered notch. (Courtesy of Robert Bosch Corporation)

Starter Control Circuit Components

Magnetic Switches

The starter motor requires large amounts of current (300 to 400 amperes) to generate the torque needed to turn the engine. The conductors used to carry this amount of current (battery cables) must be large enough to handle the current with very little voltage drop. It would be impractical to place a conductor of this size into the wiring harness to the ignition switch. To provide control of the high current, all starting systems contain some type of magnetic switch. There are two basic types of magnetic switches used: the solenoid and the relay.

Solenoids. In the solenoid-actuated starter system, the solenoid is mounted directly on top of the starter motor (Figure 8-23). The solenoid switch on a starter motor performs two functions: It

Figure 8-23 Solenoid-operated starter has the solenoid mounted directly on top of the motor.

Shop Manual
Chapter 8, page 176

A **solenoid** is an electromagnetic device that uses movement of a plunger to exert a pulling or holding force.

Some manufacturers use a starter relay in conjunction with a solenoid relay. The relay is used to reduce the amount of current flow through the ignition switch.

Shop Manual
Chapter 8, pages 168 and 178

Figure 8-24 The solenoid uses two windings. Both are energized to draw the plunger, then only the hold-in winding is used to hold the plunger in position.

closes the circuit between the battery and the starter motor. Then it shifts the starter motor pinion gear into mesh with the ring gear. This is accomplished by a linkage between the solenoid plunger and the shift lever on the starter motor. The most common method of energizing the solenoid is directly from the battery through the ignition switch.

When the circuit is closed and current flows to the solenoid, current from the battery is directed to two separate windings (Figure 8-24). Because it requires more magnetic force to pull the plunger in than to hold it in position, both windings are energized to create a combined magnetic

The two windings of the solenoid are called the **pull-in** and the **hold-in windings.** Their names explain their function.

Figure 8-25 Schematic of solenoid-operated starter motor circuit.

field that pulls the plunger. Once the plunger is moved, the current required to hold the plunger is reduced. This allows the current that was used to pull the plunger in to be used to rotate the starter motor.

When the ignition switch is placed in the START position, current is applied to the S terminal of the solenoid (Figure 8-25). The hold-in winding has its own ground to the case of the solenoid. The pull-in winding's ground is through the starter motor. Current will flow through both windings to produce a strong magnetic field. When the plunger is moved into contact with the main battery and motor terminals, the pull-in winding is de-energized. The pull-in winding is not energized because the contact places battery voltage on both sides of the coil (Figure 8-26). The current that was directed through the pull-in winding is now sent to the motor.

Because the contact disc does not close the circuit from the battery to the starter motor until the plunger has moved the shift lever, the pinion gear is in full mesh with the flywheel before the armature starts to rotate.

After the engine is started, releasing the key to the RUN position opens the control circuit. Current no longer is supplied to the hold-in windings; the return spring causes the plunger to return to its neutral position.

A common problem with the control circuit is that low system voltage or an open in the hold-in windings will cause an oscillating action to occur. The combination of the pull-in winding and the hold-in winding is sufficient to move the plunger. However, once the contacts are closed, there is insufficient magnetic force to hold the plunger in place. This condition is recognizable by a series of clicks when the ignition switch is turned to the START position. Before replacing the solenoid, check the battery condition; a low battery charge will cause the same symptom.

> The amount of current drawn by the two windings can be as high as 50 amperes.

> The R terminal provides current to the ignition bypass circuit, which is used to provide for full battery voltage to the ignition coil while the engine is cranking. This circuit bypasses the ballast resistor. The bypass circuit is not used on most ignition systems today.

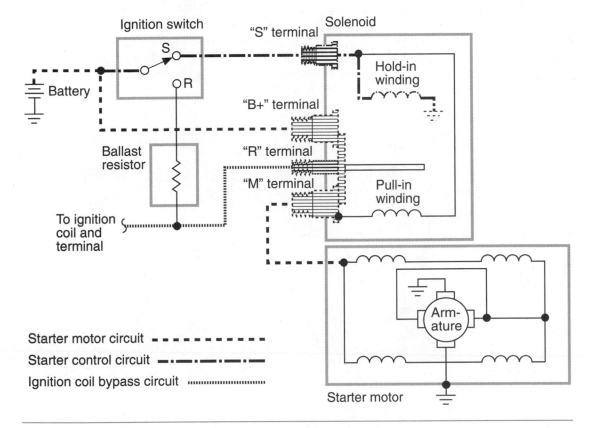

Figure 8-26 Once the contact disc closes the terminals, the hold-in winding is the only one that is energized.

Figure 8-27 Typical starter relay. (Courtesy of Chrysler Corporarion)

Starter Relays. Many manufacturers use a starter relay instead of a solenoid (Figure 8-27). The relay is usually mounted near the battery on the fender well or radiator support (Figure 8-28). Unlike the solenoid, the relay does not move the pinion gear into mesh with the flywheel ring gear.

When the ignition switch is turned to the START position, current is supplied through the switch to the relay coil. The coil produces a magnetic field, so it pulls the moveable core into contact with the internal contacts of the battery and starter terminals (Figure 8-29). With the contacts closed, full battery current is supplied to the starter motor.

A secondary function of the starter relay is to provide for an alternate path for current to the ignition coil during cranking. This is done by an internal connection that is energized by the relay core when it completes the circuit between the battery and the starter motor.

Figure 8-28 Typical starter relay location. (Reprinted with the permission of Ford Motor Company)

Figure 8-29 Current flow when the starter relay is energized.

Ignition Switch

The ignition switch is the power distribution point for most of the vehicle's primary electrical systems (Figure 8-30). Most ignition switches have five positions:

1. ACCESSORIES: Supplies current to the vehicle's electrical accessory circuits. It will not supply current to the engine control circuits, starter control circuit, or the ignition system.

2. LOCK: Mechanically locks the steering wheel and transmission gear selector. All electrical contacts in the ignition switch are open. Most ignition switches must be in this position to insert or remove the key from the cylinder.

3. OFF: All circuits controlled by the ignition switch are opened. The steering wheel and transmission gear selector are unlocked.

4. ON or RUN: The switch provides current to the ignition, engine controls, and all other circuits controlled by the switch.

5. START: The switch provides current to the starter control circuit, ignition system, and engine control circuits.

The ignition switch is spring loaded in the START position. This momentary contact automatically moves the contacts to the RUN position when the driver releases the key. All other ignition switch positions are detent positions.

From starter relay battery terminal

37 Y

To headlight switch

A – Accessory
L – Lock
O – Off
R – Run
S – Start

977 PK-W

41 BK-LBH
297 BK-LB H

297 BK-LBH
32 R-LB

20 W-LBH
16 R-LB
262 BR-PK

687 GY-Y
904 LG-R

Low-vacuum warning light

Gauges CV unit

Alternator warning light

Ignition module

Ignition coil

Charging system warning light

PC-instrument warning lights

Brake warning light

W/S wiper & washer

Power windows

Speed control anti skid

Horn HTD breaklight

Starter relay

Ignition module

Ignition coil

Seatbelt warning

Warning lights

Heater A/C

Turn signal

Lamps

Figure 8-30 Ganged ignition switch. (Reprinted with the permission of Ford Motor Company)

Figure 8-31 The neutral safety switch can be combined with the back-up light switch and installed in the transmission case.

Starting Safety Switch

Actual location of the neutral safety switch depends on the kind of transmission and the location of the shift lever. Some manufacturers place the switch in the transmission case (Figure 8-31).

Vehicles equipped with automatic transmissions require a means of preventing the engine from starting while the transmission is in gear. Without this feature the vehicle would lunge forward or backward once it was started, causing personal or property damage. The normally open neutral safety switch is connected in series in the starting system control circuit and is usually operated by the shift lever (Figure 8-32). When in the PARK or NEUTRAL position, the switch is closed, allowing current to flow to the starter circuit. If the transmission is in a gear position, the switch is opened and current cannot flow to the starter circuit.

A-Locking washer
B-Switch attaching nut
C-Switch adjusting bolt
D-Neutral safety switch

Figure 8-32 Neutral safety switch attached to the shift lever on the console.

Many vehicles equipped with manual transmissions use a similar type of safety switch. The start/clutch interlock switch is usually operated by movement of the clutch pedal (Figure 8-33). When the clutch pedal is pushed downward, the switch closes and current can flow through the starter circuit. If the clutch pedal is left up, the switch is open and current cannot flow.

Some General Motors vehicles use a mechanical linkage that blocks movement of the ignition switch cylinder unless the transmission is in PARK or NEUTRAL (Figure 8-34).

Cranking Motor Designs

The most common type of starter motor used today incorporates the overrunning clutch starter drive instead of the old inertia-engagement bendix drive. There are four basic groups of starter motors:

1. Direct drive
2. Gear reduction
3. Positive-engagement (moveable pole)
4. Permanent magnet

Figure 8-33 Start/clutch interlock switch installation. (Reprinted with the permission of Ford Motor Company)

Figure 8-34 Mechanical linkage used to prevent starting the engine while the transmission is in gear. (Courtesy of Cadillac Motor Division—GMC)

Figure 8-35 Solenoid-operated Delco MT series starter motor. (Courtesy of General Motors Corporation)

Direct Drive Starters

The most common type of starter motor is the solenoid-operated direct drive unit (Figure 8-35). Although there are construction differences between applications, the operating principles are the same for all solenoid-shifted starter motors.

When the ignition switch is placed in the START position, the control circuit energizes the pull-in and hold-in windings of the solenoid. The solenoid plunger moves and pivots the shift lever, which in turn locates the drive pinion gear into mesh with the engine flywheel.

When the solenoid plunger is moved all the way, the contact disc closes the circuit from the battery to the starter motor. Current now flows through the field coils and the armature. This develops the magnetic fields that cause the armature to rotate, thus turning the engine.

The direct drive starter motor can be either series-wound or compound motors.

Gear Reduction Starters

Some manufacturers use a gear reduction starter to provide increased torque (Figure 8-36). The gear reduction starter differs from most other designs in that the armature does not drive the

Most gear reduction starter motors are compound motors.

Figure 8-36 Gear reduction starter motor construction. (Reprinted with the permission of Ford Motor Company)

pinion gear directly. In this design, the armature drives a small gear that is in constant mesh with a larger gear. Depending on the application, the ratio between these two gears is between 2:1 and 3.5:1. The additional reduction allows for a small motor to turn at higher speeds and greater torque with less current draw.

The solenoid operation is similar to that of the solenoid-shifted direct drive starter in that the solenoid moves the plunger, which engages the starter drive.

Positive-engagement Starters

One of the most commonly used starters on Ford applications is the positive-engagement starter (Figure 8-37). Positive-engagement starters use the shunt coil windings of the starter motor to engage the starter drive. The high starting current is controlled by a starter relay mounted close to the battery. When the relay is closed, current flows through a drive coil. The drive coil creates an electromagnetic field that attracts a moveable pole shoe. The moveable pole shoe is attached to the starter drive through the plunger lever. When the moveable pole shoe moves, the drive gear engages the engine flywheel.

Figure 8-37 Positive-engagement starters use a moveable pole shoe. (Reprinted with the permission of Ford Motor Company)

As soon as the starter drive pinion gear contacts the ring gear, a contact arm on the pole shoe opens a set of normally closed grounding contacts (Figure 8-38). With the return to ground circuit opened, all the starter current flows through the remaining three field coils and through the brushes to the armature. The starter motor then begins to rotate. To prevent the starter drive from disengaging from the ring gear if battery voltage drops while cranking, the moveable-pole shoe is held down by a holding coil. The holding coil is a smaller coil inside the main drive coil and is strong enough to hold the starter pinion gear engaged.

Permanent Magnet Starters

The permanent magnet starter design provides for less weight, simpler construction, and less heat generation as compared to conventional field coil starters (Figure 8-39). Because there are no field coils, current is delivered directly to the armature through the commutator and brushes.

Figure 8-38 Schematic of a positive-engagement starter.

Figure 8-39 The PMGR motor uses a planetary gear set and permanent magnets.(Courtesy of Delco Remy Division—GMC)

Figure 8-40 Comparison of the electrical circuits used in field coil and PMGR starters. (Courtesy of Chrysler Corporation)

The greatest amount of gear reduction from a planetary gear set is accomplished by holding the ring gear, inputing the sun gear, and outputing the carrier

The permanent magnet starter also uses gear reduction through a planetary gear set. The planetary gear train transmits power between the armature and the pinion shaft. This allows the armature to rotate at greater speed and increased torque. The planetary gear assembly consists of a sun gear on the end of the armature, and three planetary carrier gears inside a ring gear. The ring gear is held stationary. When the armature is rotated, the sun gear causes the carrier gears to rotate about the internal teeth of the ring gear. The planetary carrier is attached to the output shaft. The gear reduction provided for by this gear arrangement is 4.5:1. By providing for this additional gear reduction, the demand for high current is lessened.

The electrical operation between the conventional field coil and PMGR starters remains basically the same (Figure 8-40).

CAUTION: Special care must be taken when handling the PMGR starter. The permanent magnets are very brittle and are easily destroyed if the starter is dropped or struck by another object.

Summary

Terms to Know

Armature

Bendix drive

Brushes

❑ The starting system is a combination of mechanical and electrical parts that work together to start the engine.

❑ The starting system components include the battery, cable and wires, the ignition switch, the starter solenoid or relay, the starter motor, the starter drive and flywheel ring gear, and the starting safety switch.

❑ The armature is the moveable component of the motor that consists of a conductor wound around a laminated iron core. It is used to create a magnetic field.

❑ Pole shoes are made of high magnetic permeability material to help concentrate and direct the lines of force in the field assembly.

❑ The magnetic forces will cause the armature to turn in the direction of the weaker field.

❑ Within an electromagnetic style of starter motor, the inside windings are called the armature. The armature rotates within the stationary outside windings, called the field, which has windings coiled around pole shoes.

❑ The commutator is a series of conducting segments located around one end of the armature.

❑ A split-ring commutator is in contact with the ends of the armature loops. So, as the brushes pass over one section of the commutator to another, the current flow in the armature is reversed.

❑ Two basic winding patterns are used in the armature: lap winding and wave winding.

❑ The field coils are electromagnets constructed of wire coils wound around a pole shoe.

❑ When current flows through the field coils, strong stationary electromagnetic fields are created.

❑ In any DC motor, there are three methods of connecting the field coils to the armature: in series, in parallel (shunt), and a compound connection that uses both series and shunt coils.

❑ A starter drive includes a pinion gear set that meshes with the engine flywheel ring gear on the engine.

❑ To prevent damage to the pinion gear or the ring gear, the pinion gear must mesh with the ring gear before the starter motor rotates.

❑ The bendix drive depends on inertia to provide meshing of the drive pinion with the ring gear.

❑ The most common type of starter drive is the overrunning clutch. This is a roller-type clutch that transmits torque in one direction only and freewheels in the other direction.

❑ The starting system consists of two circuits called the starter control circuit and the motor feed circuit.

❑ The components of the control circuit include the starting portion of the ignition switch, the starting safety switch (if applicable), and the wire conductor to connect these components to the relay or solenoid.

❑ The motor feed circuit consists of heavy battery cables from the battery to the relay and the starter or directly to the solenoid if the starter is so equipped.

❑ There are four basic groups of starter motors: direct drive, gear reduction, positive engagement (moveable pole), and permanent magnet.

Review Questions

Short Answer Essays

1. What is the purpose of the starting system?

2. List and describe the purpose of the major components of the starting system.

3. Explain the principle of operation of the DC motor.

4. Describe the types of magnetic switches used in starting systems.

5. List and describe the operation of the different types of starter drive mechanisms.

6. Describe the differences between the positive-engagement and solenoid shift starter.

7. Explain the operating principles of the permanent magnet starter.

8. Describe the purpose and operation of the armature.

9. Describe the purpose and operation of the field coil.

10. Describe the operation of the two circuits of the starter system.

Fill-in-the-Blanks

1. DC motors use the interaction of magnetic fields to convert the _____ energy into _____ energy.

2. The _____ is the moveable component of the motor, which consists of a conductor wound around a _____ iron core and is used to create a _____ field.

3. Pole shoes are made of high magnetic _____ material to help concentrate and direct the _____ _____ _____ in the field assembly.

4. The starter motor electrical connection that permits all of the current that passes through the field coils to also pass through the armature is called the _____ motor.

5. _____ _____ _____ is current produced in the starter motor itself. This current acts against the supply current from the battery.

6. A starter motor that uses the characteristics of a series motor and a shunt motor is called a _____ motor.

7. The _____ _____ is the part of the starter motor that engages the armature to the engine flywheel ring gear.

8. The _____ _____ is a roller-type clutch that transmits torque in one direction only and freewheels in the other direction.

9. The two circuits of the starting system are called the _____ _____ circuit and the _____ _____ circuit.

10. There are two basic types of magnetic switches used in starter systems: the _____ and the _____ .

ASE Style Review Questions

1. The purpose of the starter system is being discussed:
   Technician A says the starting system is a combination of mechanical and electrical parts that work together to start the engine.
   Technician B says the starting system is designed to change the mechanical energy into electrical energy.
   Who is correct?
   A. A only
   B. B only
   C. Both A and B
   D. Neither A nor B

2. The components of the starting system are being discussed:
   Technician A says the drive belt is part of the starting system.
   Technician B says the starter drive and flywheel ring gear are components of the starting system.
   Who is correct?
   A. A only
   B. B only
   C. Both A and B
   D. Neither A nor B

3. The operation of the DC motor is being discussed:
   Technician A says DC motors use the interaction of magnetic fields.
   Technician B says DC motors use a mechanical connection to the engine that turns the armature.
   Who is correct?
   A. A only
   B. B only
   C. Both A and B
   D. Neither A nor B

4. The starter motor armature is being discussed:
   Technician A says the armature is the stationary component of the motor that consists of a conductor wound around a pole shoe.
   Technician B says the commutator is a series of conducting segments located around one end of the armature.
   Who is correct?
   A. A only
   B. B only
   C. Both A and B
   D. Neither A nor B

5. The starter motor field coils are being discussed:
   Technician A says the field coil is made of wire wound around a non-magnetic pole shoe.
   Technician B says the field coils are always shunt wound to the armature.
   Who is correct?
   A. A only
   B. B only
   C. Both A and B
   D. Neither A nor B

6. The starter solenoid is being discussed:
   Technician A says the solenoid is an electromagnetic device that uses movement of a plunger to exert a pulling or holding force.
   Technician B says the solenoid makes the electrical connection, but it does not move the pinion gear into mesh with the flywheel ring gear.
   Who is correct?
   A. A only
   B. B only
   C. Both A and B
   D. Neither A nor B

7. *Technician A* says both windings of the solenoid are energized anytime the ignition switch is in the START position.
   Technician B says the two windings of the solenoid are called the pull-in and the hold-in windings.
   Who is correct?
   A. A only
   B. B only
   C. Both A and B
   D. Neither A nor B

8. Permanent magnet starters are being discussed:
   Technician A says the permanent magnet starter uses four or six permanent magnet field assemblies in place of field coils.
   Technician B says the permanent magnet starter uses a planetary gear set.
   Who is correct?
   A. A only
   B. B only
   C. Both A and B
   D. Neither A nor B

9. *Technician A* says the R terminal of the starter solenoid provides current to the ignition bypass circuit.
Technician B says the ignition switch is a component of the starter feed circuit.
Who is correct?
A. A only
B. B only
C. Both A and B
D. Neither A nor B

10. A customer's no-start complaint is being discussed:
Technician A says the problem may be that the starter safety switch needs adjusting.
Technician B says the battery should be tested before condemning starter system components.
Who is correct?
A. A only
B. B only
C. Both A and B
D. Neither A nor B

Charging Systems

Upon completion and review of this chapter, you should be able to:

❏ Explain the purpose of the charging system.

❏ Identify the major components of the charging system.

❏ Explain the function of the major components of the AC generator.

❏ Describe the two styles of stators.

❏ Describe how AC current is rectified to DC current in the AC generator.

❏ Describe the three principle circuits used in the AC generator.

❏ Explain the relationship between regulator resistance and field current.

❏ Explain the relationship between field current and AC generator output.

❏ Identify the differences between A circuit, B circuit, and isolated circuit.

❏ Explain the operation of charge indicators, including lamps, electronic voltage monitors, ammeters, and voltmeters.

Introduction

The automotive storage battery is not capable of supplying the demands of the electrical system for an extended period of time. Every vehicle must be equipped with a means of replacing the current being drawn from the battery. A charging system is used to restore the electrical power to the battery that was used during engine starting. In addition, the charging system must be able to react quickly to high load demands required of the electrical system. It is the vehicle's charging system that generates the current to operate all of the electrical accessories while the engine is running.

Two basic types of charging systems have been used. The first was a DC generator, which was discontinued in the 1960s. Since that time the AC alternator has been the predominant charging device. The DC generator and the AC alternator both use similar operating principles.

The purpose of the charging system is to convert the mechanical energy of the engine into electrical energy to recharge the battery and run the electrical accessories. When the engine is first started, the battery supplies all the current required by the starting and ignition systems.

As the battery drain continues, and engine speed increases, the charging system is able to produce more voltage than the battery can deliver. When this occurs, the electrons from the charging device are able to flow in a reverse direction through the battery's positive terminal. The charging device is now supplying the electrical system's load requirements; the reserve electrons build up and recharge the battery (Figure 9-1).

If there is an increase in the electrical demand and a drop in the charging system's output equal to the voltage of the battery, the battery and charging system work together to supply the required current.

In an attempt to standardize terminology in the industry, the term alternator is being replaced with generator. In this text, the alternator will be referred to as an AC generator.

Figure 9-1 Current flow when the AC generator is operating.

The ignition switch is considered a part of the charging system because it closes the circuit that supplies current to the indicator lamp and stimulates the field coil.

As illustrated (Figure 9-2), the entire charging system consists of the following components:

1. Battery
2. AC or DC generator
3. Drive belt
4. Voltage regulator
5. Charge indicator (lamp or gauge)
6. Ignition switch
7. Cables and wiring harness
8. Starter relay (some systems)
9. Fusible link (some systems)

Figure 9-2 Components of the charging system. (Reprinted with the permission of Ford Motor Company)

Figure 9-3 Simplified alternator indicating electromagnetic induction.

Principle of Operation

All charging systems use the principle of electromagnetic induction to generate electrical power (Figure 9-3). Electromagnetic principle states that a voltage will be produced if motion between a conductor and a magnetic field occurs. The amount of current produced is affected by:

1. The speed at which the conductor passes through the magnetic field.

2. The strength of the magnetic field.

3. The number of conductors passing through the magnetic field.

To see how electromagnetic induction produces an AC current, refer to the illustration (Figure 9-4). When the conductor is parallel with the magnetic field, the conductor is not cut by

Shop Manual
Chapter 9, pages
202, 205, and 208

Figure 9-4 Alternating current is produced as the conductor is rotated.

any flux lines (Figure 9-4A). At this point in the revolution there is zero voltage and current being produced.

As the conductor is rotated 90 degrees, the magnetic field is at a right angle to the conductor (Figure 9-4B). At this point in the revolution the maximum number of flux lines cut the conductor at the north pole. With the maximum amount of flux lines cutting the conductor, voltage and current are at maximum positive values.

When the conductor is rotated an additional 90 degrees, the conductor returns to being parallel with the magnetic field (Figure 9-4C). Once again no flux lines cut the conductor, and voltage and current drop to zero.

An additional 90-degree revolution of the conductor results in the magnetic field being reversed at the top conductor (Figure 9-4D). At this point in the revolution, the maximum number of flux lines cuts the conductor at the south pole. Voltage and current are now at maximum negative values.

When the conductor completes one full revolution, it returns to a parallel position with the magnetic field. Voltage and current return to zero. The **sine wave** is determined by the angle between the magnetic field and the conductor. It is based on the trigonometry sine function of angles. The sine wave shown (Figure 9-5) plots the voltage generated during one revolution.

It is the function of the drive belt to turn the conductor. Drive belt tension should be checked periodically to assure proper charging system operation. A loose belt can inhibit charging system efficiency, and a belt that is too tight can cause early bearing failure.

DC Generators

The DC generator is similar to the DC starter motor used to crank the engine. The housing contains two field coils that create a magnetic field. Output current is generated in the wire loops of the armature as it rotates inside the magnetic field. This current is sent to the battery through the brushes.

The components must be polarized whenever a replacement DC generator or voltage regulator is installed. To polarize an externally grounded field circuit (A-type field circuit), use a jumper wire and connect between the BAT terminal and the ARM terminal of the voltage regulator. Make this jumper connection for just an instant. Do not hold the jumper wire on the terminals. For an internally grounded field circuit (B-type), jump the F terminal and the BAT terminal.

The sine wave produced by a single conductor during one revolution is called **single-phase voltage.**

Polarizing will make sure that the polarity is the same for both the generator and the regulator.

Most generator terminals are identified as BAT for battery output, F for field, and ARM for armature.

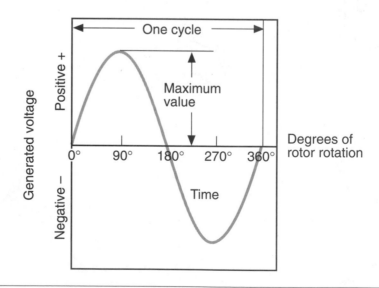

Figure 9-5 Sine wave produced in one revolution of the conductor.

Figure 9-6 Components of an AC generator. (Reprinted with the permission of Ford Motor Company)

AC Generators

The DC generator was unable to produce the sufficient amount of current required when the engine was operating at low speeds. With the addition of more electrical accessories and components, the AC (alternating current) generator, or alternator, replaced the DC generator. The main components of the AC generator are:

1. The rotor
2. Brushes
3. The stator
4. The rectifier bridge
5. The housing
6. Cooling fan

These components of the AC generator are illustrated (Figure 9-6).

Rotors. The rotor is constructed of several turns of copper wire around an iron core. There are metal plates bent over the windings at both ends of the rotor windings (Figure 9-7). The poles do not come into contact with each other, but they are interlaced. When current passes through the coil (1.5 to 3.0 amperes), a magnetic field is produced. The strength of the magnetic field is dependent on the amount of current flowing through the coil.

The poles will take on the polarity (north or south) of the side of the coil they touch. The right-hand rule will show whether a north or south pole magnet is created. When the rotor is

Shop Manual
Chapter 9, page 226

The **rotor** creates the rotating magnetic field of the AC generator. It is the portion of the AC generator that is rotated by the drive belt.

The metal plates are called **fingers** or **poles.**

The current flow through the coil is referred to as **field current.**

Shaft

Pole piece

Coil

Pole piece

Figure 9-7 Components of a typical AC generator rotor.

Figure 9-8 Rotor field north and south poles alternate.

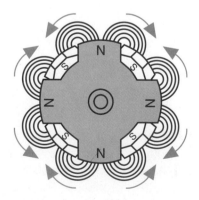

Figure 9-9 Magnetic flux lines move in opposite directions between the rotor poles. (Reprinted with the permission of Ford Motor Company)

Figure 9-10 The slip rings and brushes provide a current path to the rotor coil.

assembled, the poles alternate north-south around the rotor (Figure 9-8). As a result of this alternating arrangement of poles, the magnetic flux lines will move in opposite directions between adjacent poles (Figure 9-9). This arrangement provides for several alternating magnetic fields to intersect the stator as the rotor is turning. These individual magnetic fields produce a current by induction in the stationary stator windings.

The wires from the rotor coil are attached to two slip rings that are insulated from the rotor shaft. The insulated stationary carbon brush passes field current into a slip ring, then through the field coil, and back to the other slip ring. Current then passes out of the grounded stationary brush (Figure 9-10).

Brushes. The field winding of the rotor receives current through a pair of brushes that ride against the slip rings. The brushes and slip rings provide a means of maintaining electrical continuity between stationary and rotating components. The brushes (Figure 9-11) ride the surface of the slip rings on the rotor and are held tight against the slip rings by spring tension provided by the brush holders. The AC generator brushes conduct only the field current (2 to 5 amperes). The low current that the brushes must carry contributes to their longer life.

Most rotors have twelve to fourteen poles.

The slip rings function much like the armature commutator in the starter motor, except they are smooth.

Shop Manual
Chapter 9, page 225

Brushes are electrically conductive sliding contacts, usually made of copper and carbon.

The brushes used in the DC generator conduct the output voltage of the generator.

Figure 9-11 Brushes are the stationary electrical contact to the rotor's slip rings.

Figure 9-12 Components of a typical stator. (Reprinted with the permission of Ford Motor Company)

Direct current from the battery is supplied to the rotating field through the field terminal and the insulated brush. The second brush is the ground brush, which is attached to the AC generator housing.

Stators. The stator contains three main sets of windings wrapped in slots around a laminated, circular iron frame (Figure 9-12). Each of the three windings has the same number of coils as the rotor has pairs of north and south poles. The coils of each winding are evenly spaced around the core. The three sets of windings alternate and overlap as they pass through the core (Figure 9-13). The overlapping is needed to produce the required phase angles.

Shop Manual
Chapter 9, page 226

The **stator** is the stationary coil in which current is produced.

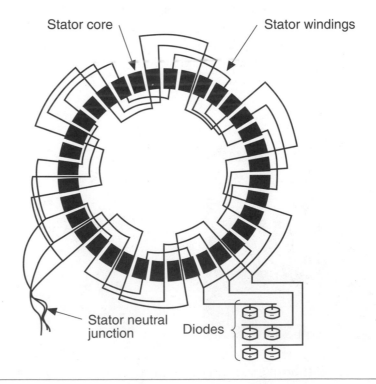

Figure 9-13 Overlapping stator windings produce required phase angles.

Figure 9-14 A small air gap between the rotor and the stator maximizes the magnetic force.

The rotor is fitted inside the stator (Figure 9-14). A small air gap (approximately 0.015 inch) is maintained between the rotor and the stator. This gap allows the rotor's magnetic field to energize all of the windings of the stator at the same time and to maximize the magnetic force.

Each group of windings has two leads. The first lead is for the current entering the winding. The second lead is for current leaving. There are two basic means of connecting the leads. The most common method is called the wye connection (Figure 9-15). In the wye connection one lead from each winding is connected to one common junction. From this junction the other leads branch out in a Y pattern. The other method of connecting the windings is called the delta connection (Figure 9-16). The delta connection connects the lead of one end of the winding to the lead at the other end of the next winding.

Each group of windings occupies one third of the stator, or 120 degrees of the circle. As the rotor revolves in the stator, a voltage is produced in each loop of the stator at different phase angles. The resulting overlap of sine waves that is produced is shown (Figure 9-17). Each of the

The **wye wound connection** receives its name from its resemblance to the letter Y.

The common junction in the wye connected winding is called the **stator neutral junction**.

The **delta connection** receives its name from its resemblance to the Greek letter delta (Δ).

Stator neutral junction

To diodes

To diodes

"Y" connection

To diodes

To diodes

To diodes

Stator neutral junction

To diodes

Figure 9-15 Wye connected stator winding.

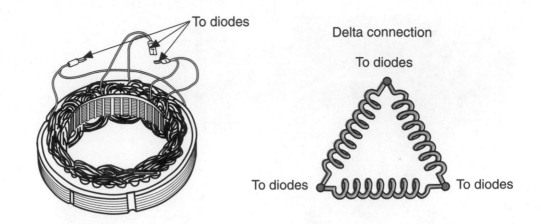

Figure 9-16 Delta connected stator winding.

sine waves is at a different phase of its cycle at any given time. As a result, the output from the stator is divided into three phases.

Diode Rectifier Bridge. The battery and the electrical system cannot accept or store AC voltage. For the vehicle's electrical system to be able to use the voltage and current generated in the AC generator, the AC current needs to be converted to DC current. A split-ring commutator cannot be used to rectify AC current to DC current because the stator is stationary in the AC generator. Instead, a diode rectifier bridge is used to change the current in an AC generator (Figure 9-18).

Shop Manual
Chapter 9, pages
217, 228 and 230

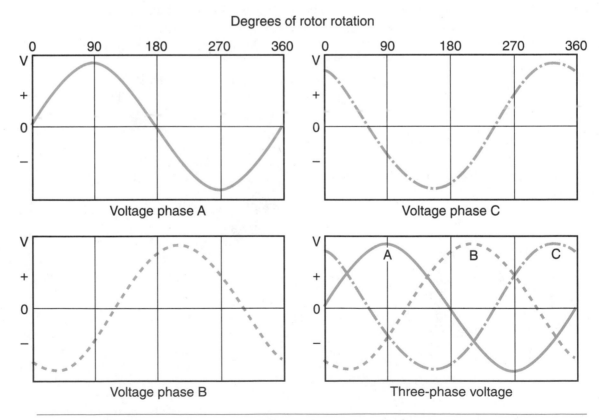

Figure 9-17 The voltage produced in each stator winding is added together to create a three-phase voltage.

Figure 9-18 General Motors rectifier bridge.

Acting as a one-way check valve, the diodes switch the current flow back and forth so that it flows from the AC generator in only one direction.

When AC current reverses itself, the diode blocks and no current flows (Figure 9-19). If AC voltage passes through a positively biased diode, the diode will block off the negative pulse. The result is the scope pattern shown in Figure 9-19. The AC current has been changed to a pulsing DC current.

An AC generator usually uses a pair of diodes for each stator winding, for a total of six diodes (Figure 9-20). Three of the diodes are positive biased and are mounted in a heat sink (Figure 9-21). The three remaining diodes are negative biased and are attached directly to the

The **diode rectifier bridge** provides reasonably constant DC voltage to the vehicle's electrical system and battery.

The converting of AC current to DC current is called **rectification.**

Diodes are electrical one-way check valves that permit current to flow in one direction only.

The passing of half of the AC pulses is called **half-wave rectification.**

Figure 9-19 AC current rectified to a pulsating DC current after passing through a positive biased diode.

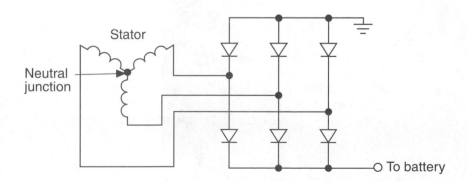

Figure 9-20 A simplified schematic of the AC generator windings connected to the diode rectifier bridge.

Figure 9-21 The positive biased diodes are mounted into a heat sink to provide protection.

The use of three positive biased and three negative biased diodes provides for **full-wave rectification.**

The diodes of the rectifier bridge produce heat, thus they are mounted in **heat sinks** to dissipate the heat.

Not only do the diodes rectify stator output, but they also block battery drain back when the engine is not running.

The circuit is called **full-wave rectification** because both halves of the sine wave are used.

The rectifier bridge is also known as a **rectifier stack.**

frame of the AC generator (Figure 9-22). By using a pair of diodes that are reversed biased to each other, rectification of both sides of the AC sine wave is achieved (Figure 9-23). The negative biased diodes allow for conducting current from the negative side of the AC sine wave and putting this current into the circuit. Diode rectification changes the negative current into positive output.

With each stator winding connected to a pair of diodes, the resultant waveform of the rectified voltage would be similar to that shown (Figure 9-24). With six peaks per revolution, the voltage will vary by only a couple of volts during each cycle.

The examples used so far have been for single-pole rotors in a three-winding stator. Most AC generators use either a twelve- or fourteen-pole rotor. Each pair of poles produces one complete sine wave in each winding per revolution. During one revolution a fourteen-pole rotor will produce seven sine waves. The rotor generates three overlapping sine wave voltage cycles in the stator. The total output of a fourteen-pole rotor per revolution would be twenty-one sine wave cycles (Figure 9-25). With final rectification, the waveform would be similar to the one shown (Figure 9-26).

Figure 9-22 Negative biased diodes pressed into the AC generator housing.

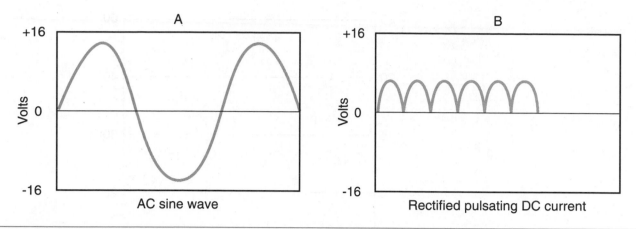

Figure 9-23 Full-wave rectification uses both sides of the AC sine wave to create a pulsating DC current.

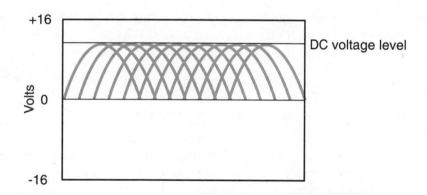

Figure 9-24 With three-phase rectification, the DC voltage level is uniform.

Figure 9-25 Sine wave cycle of a fourteen-pole rotor and three-phase stator.

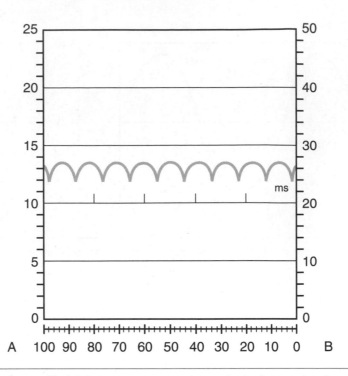

Figure 9-26 The rectified AC generator output has a ripple that can be shown on an oscillo-scope.

Full-wave rectification is desired because using only half-wave rectification wastes the other half of the AC current. Full-wave rectification of the stator output uses the total potential by redirecting the current from the stator windings so that all current is in one direction.

A wye wound stator with each winding connected to a pair of diodes is shown (Figure 9-27). Each pair of diodes has one negative and one positive diode. During rotor movement two stator windings will be in series and the third winding will be neutral. As the rotor revolves it will energize a different set of windings. Also, current flow through the windings is reversed as the rotor passes. Current in any direction through two windings in series will produce DC current.

Figure 9-27 Current flow through a wye wound stator.

Figure 9-28 Current flow through a delta wound stator.

The action that occurs when the delta wound stator is used is shown (Figure 9-28). Instead of two windings in series, the three windings of the delta stator are in parallel. This makes more current available because the parallel paths allow more current to flow through the diodes.

AC Generator Housing and Cooling Fan. Most AC generator housings are a two-piece construction, made from cast aluminum (Figure 9-29). The two end frames provide support of the rotor and the stator. In addition, the end frames contain the diodes, regulator, heat sinks, terminals, and other components of the AC generator. The two end pieces are referred to as:

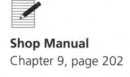

Shop Manual
Chapter 9, page 202

1. The drive end housing: This housing holds a bearing to support the front of the rotor shaft. The rotor shaft extends through the drive end housing and holds the drive pulley and cooling fan.

2. The slip ring end housing: This housing also holds a rotor shaft support bearing. In addition, it contains the brushes and has all of the electrical terminals. If the AC generator has an integral regulator, it is also contained in this housing.

The cooling fan draws air into the AC generator through the openings at the rear of the AC generator housing. The air leaves through openings behind the cooling fan (Figure 9-30).

Figure 9-29 Typical two-piece AC generator housing. (Courtesy of Chrysler Corporation)

Figure 9-30 The cooling fan draws air in from the rear of the AC generator to keep the diodes cool. (Courtesy of Robert Bosch Corporation)

CAUTION: Do not pry on the AC generator housing because any excess force can damage the housing.

Shop Manual
Chapter 9, pages 228 and 230

If the battery is completely discharged, the vehicle cannot be push started because there is no excitation of the field coil.

The **diode trio** is used by some manufacturers to rectify the stator current so that it can be used to create the magnetic field in the field coil of the rotor. This eliminates extra wiring.

AC Generator Currents

There are three principle circuits used in the AC generator:

1. The charging circuit: Consists of the stator windings and rectifier circuits.

2. The excitation circuit: Consists of the rotor field coil and the electrical connections to the coil.

3. The preexcitation circuit: Supplies the initial current for the field coil that starts the buildup of the magnetic field.

For the AC generator to produce current, the field coil must develop a magnetic field. The AC generator creates its own field current in addition to its output current.

For excitation of the field to occur, the voltage induced in the stator rises to a point that it overcomes the forward voltage drop of at least two of the rectifier diodes. Before the diode trio

Figure 9-31 The diode trio connects the phase windings to the field. To conduct, there must be 0.6 V more positive on the anode side of the diodes.

Figure 9-32 Charging circuit wiring diagram.

can supply field current, the anode side of the diode must be at least 0.6 volt more positive than the cathode side (Figure 9-31). When the ignition switch is turned on, the warning lamp current acts as a small magnetizing current through the field (Figure 9-32). This current preexcites the field, reducing the speed required to start its own supply of field current.

AC Generator Operation Overview

When the engine is running, the drive belt spins the rotor inside the stator windings. This magnetic field inside the rotor generates a current in the windings of the stator. Field current flowing through the slip rings to the rotor creates alternating north and south poles on the rotor.

The induced current in the stator is an alternating current because the magnetic fields are alternating. As the magnetic field begins to induce current in the stator's windings, the induced current starts to increase. The amount of current will peak when the magnetic field is the strongest. As the magnetic field begins to move away from the stator windings, the amount of current will start to decrease. Each of the three windings of the stator generates current, so the three combine to form a three-phase voltage output.

The most common type of stator is the wye connection (Figure 9-33). The output terminals (A, B, and C) apply voltage to the rectifier. Because only two stator windings apply voltage (because the third winding is always connected to diodes that are reverse biased), the voltages come from points A to B, B to C, and C to A.

To determine the amount of voltage produced in the two stator windings, find the difference between the two points. For example, to find the voltage applied from points A and B subtract the voltage at point B from the voltage at point A. If the voltage at point A is 8 volts positive and the voltage at point B is 8 volts negative, the difference is 16 volts. This procedure can be performed for each pair of stator windings at any point in time to get the sine wave patterns

Alternating current is constantly changing, so this formula would have to be performed at several different times.

Figure 9-33 Wye connected stator windings attached to the rectifier bridge.

(Figure 9-34). The voltages in the windings are designated as V_A, V_B, and V_C. Designations of V_{AB}, V_{BC}, and V_{CA} refer to the voltage difference in the two stator windings. In addition, the numbers refer to the diodes used for the voltages generated in each winding pair.

The current induced in the stator passes through the diode rectifier bridge consisting of three positive and three negative diodes. At this point there are six possible paths for the current to follow. The path that is followed depends on the stator terminal voltages. If the voltage from points A and B is positive (point A is positive in respect to point B), current is supplied to the

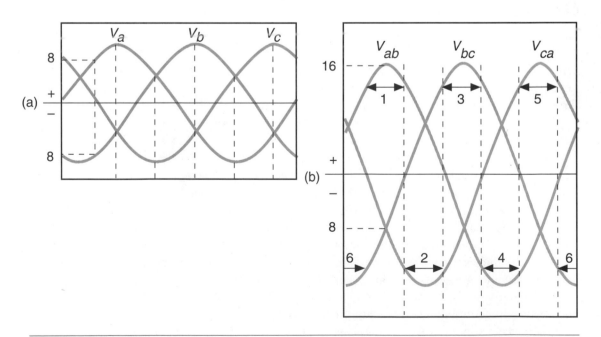

Figure 9-34 (A) Individual stator winding voltages; (B) voltages across the stator terminals A, B, and C.

Figure 9-35 Current flow when terminals AB are positive.

positive terminal of the battery from terminal A through diode 2 (Figure 9-35). The negative return path is through diode 3 to terminal B.

Both diodes 2 and 3 are forward biased. The stator winding labeled C does not produce current because it is connected to diodes that are reverse biased. The stator current is rectified to DC current to be used for charging the battery and supplying current to the vehicle's electrical system.

When the voltage from terminals C and A is negative (point C is negative in respect to point A), current flow to the battery positive terminal is from terminal A through diode 2 (Figure 9-36). The negative return path is through diode 5 to terminal C.

This procedure is repeated through the four other current paths (Figures 9-37 through 9-40)

Figure 9-36 Current flow when terminals C and A are negative.

Figure 9-37 Current flow when terminals B and C are positive.

Figure 9-38 Current flow when terminals A and B are negative.

Figure 9-39 Current flow when terminals C and A are positive.

Figure 9-40 Current flow when terminals B and C are negative.

Shop Manual
Chapter 9, page 217

The **voltage regulator** controls the output voltage of the generator, based on charging system demands, by controlling field current.

The opposing current is called **inductive reactance.**

The regulator must have system voltage as an input in order to regulate the output voltage. The input voltage to the AC generator is called **sensing voltage.**

Shop Manual
Chapter 9, page 209

The **A circuit** is called an **external grounded field circuit.** It is always an electronic-type regulator.

Regulation

The battery, and the rest of the electrical system, must be protected from excessive voltages. To prevent early battery and electrical system failure, regulation of the charging system is very important. Also the charging system must supply enough current to run the vehicle's electrical accessories when the engine is running.

AC generators do not require current limiters, because they limit their own current output. Current limit is the result of the constantly changing magnetic field because of the induced AC current. As the magnetic field changes, an opposing current is induced in the stator windings. The inductive reactance in the AC generator limits the maximum current that the AC generator can produce. Even though current (amperage) is limited by its operation, voltage is not. The AC generator is capable of producing as high as 250 volts, if it were not controlled.

Regulation of voltage is done by varying the amount of field current flowing through the rotor. The higher the field current, the higher the output voltage. By controlling the amount of resistance in series with the field coil, control of the field current and the AC generator output is obtained. To insure a full battery charge, and operation of accessories, most regulators are set for a system voltage between 13.5 and 14.5 volts.

If sensing voltage is below the regulator setting, an increase in charging output results by increasing field current. Higher sensing voltage will result in a decrease in field current and system output. A vehicle being driven with no accessories on and a fully charged battery will have a high sensing voltage. The regulator will reduce the charging voltage, and current, until it is at a level to run the ignition system while trickle charging the battery (2 to 4 amperes). If a heavy load is turned on (such as the headlights) the additional draw will cause a drop in the battery voltage. The regulator will sense this low system voltage and will reduce the field circuit resistance. This will allow more current to the field windings. With the increase of field current, the magnetic field is stronger and AC generator output is increased. When the load is turned off, the regulator senses the rise in system voltage and cuts back the amount of field current and ultimately AC generator output.

Another input that affects regulation is temperature. Because ambient temperatures influence the rate of charge that a battery can accept, regulators are temperature compensated (Figure 9-41). Temperature compensation is required because the battery is more reluctant to accept a charge at lower ambient temperatures. The regulator will increase the system voltage until it is at a high enough level that the battery will accept it.

Field Circuits

To properly test and service the charging system, it is important to identify the field circuit being used. Automobile manufacturers use three basic types of field circuits. The first type is called the A circuit. It has the regulator on the ground side of the field coil. The B+ for the field coil is picked up

Temperature	Volts	
	Minimum	Maximum
20° F	14.3	15.3
80° F	13.8	14.4
140° F	13.3	14.0
Over 140° F	Less than 13.3	–

Figure 9-41 Chart indicating the relationship between temperature and charge rate.

from inside the AC generator (Figure 9-42). By placing the regulator on the ground side of the field coil, the variable resistance will allow the control of field current by varying the current flow to ground. A resistance can be located anywhere in the series circuit and have the same effect.

The second type of field circuit is called the B circuit. In this case, the voltage regulator controls the power side of the field circuit. Also the field coil is grounded from inside the AC generator (Figure 9-43).

The third type of field circuit is called the isolated field. The AC generator has two field wires attached to the outside of the case. The voltage regulator can be located on either the ground (A circuit) or on the B+ (B circuit) side (Figure 9-44).

Figure 9-42 Simplified diagram of an A circuit field.

Figure 9-43 Simplified diagram of a B circuit field.

Figure 9-44 In the isolated circuit field AC generator the regulator can be installed on either side of the field.

Usually the B circuit regulator is mounted externally of the AC generator. The B circuit is an **internally grounded circuit.**

Sensing voltage is what determines the amount of system output, so the condition and voltage of the battery determines the charge rate. This is why a charging system cannot be tested with a bad battery. System testing must be done with a known good battery that is at least 75% charged. Testing with a defective battery may suggest a faulty AC generator or regulator when these units are good.

Isolated field AC generators pick up B+ and ground externally.

Figure 9-45 An external electromechanical regulator. (Reprinted with the permission of Ford Motor Company)

Shop Manual
Chapter 9, page 209

The electromechanical regulators were discontinued by most manufacturers by 1978.

The **field relay** applies battery voltage to the AC generator field coil after the engine has started. The **voltage limiter** is connected through the resistor network and determines whether the field will receive high, low, or no voltage. It automatically controls the field voltage for the required amount of charging.

Electromechanical Regulators

There are two basic types of regulators: electromechanical and electronic. Also, on many newer model vehicles regulation is controlled by the computer. Even though the electromechanical regulator is obsolete, a study of its operation will help you to understand the more complex systems.

The external electromechanical regulator is a vibrating contact point design (Figure 9-45). The regulator uses electromagnetics to control the opening and closing of the contact points. Inside the regulator are two coils. One coil is the field relay and the second is the voltage regulator. The field relay coil and contact with no current flowing through the coil are shown (Figure 9-46). The contact points are open, preventing current flow. An electromagnetic field develops when current flows through the field relay coil. It pulls the contact arm down (Figure 9-47). Once the contact points close, current will flow.

The voltage regulator coil uses an electromagnetic field to open the contact points. With the points closed, current flows from the battery to the rotor. Current also flows to the regulator coil. As the battery charges, the battery's voltage increases. This increase in voltage strengthens the coil's attraction for the contact points. At a preset voltage level, the coil will overcome the contact point spring tension and open the points. This will prevent current from flowing to the rotor. Once the points open, voltage output of the AC generator drops, and the battery will start to discharge. As the battery voltage decreases, so does the regulator coil's magnetic strength. Spring tension will overcome the magnetic attraction and the points will close again. Once again current flows through the rotor and the AC generator is producing voltage. This action occurs several times per second.

When the ignition switch is in the RUN position with the engine off, the regulator will be in the position shown (Figure 9-48). With the ignition switch in RUN, current flow for the field will go through the ignition switch through the resistor and bulb, through the lower contacts of the voltage regulator (closed), and out of the F terminal to the AC generator, through the field coil, and to ground. The indicator lamp bulb will light because the bulb is in series with the field coil.

Once the engine is started, the AC generator will begin to produce voltage. At this time the system voltage may be below 13.5 volts, however, because the AC generator rotor is revolving, there is some production of voltage. This allows voltage out of the R terminal to energize the

Figure 9-46 Schematic of an electromechanical regulator with no current flow through the coil. (Reprinted with the permission of Ford Motor Company)

Figure 9-47 Regulator circuit with current flowing through the coil. (Reprinted with the permission of Ford Motor Company)

Figure 9-48 Regulator circuit with the ignition switch in the RUN position and the engine not running.

Figure 9-49 Regulator circuit with the engine running and system voltage less than 13.5 volts. Voltage limiter contacts close to allow current flow to the field coil.

Figure 9-50 Regulator circuit with the system voltage between 13.5 and 14.5 volts. Voltage contacts are in the neutral position and field current flows through the resistor.

field relay coil (Figure 9-49). With the relay coil energized, the contact points close and direct battery voltage flows through terminal 3 and out terminal 4. The bulb will go out with battery voltage on both sides of the bulb. Simultaneously, battery voltage flows through the voltage regulator contact points to the field coil in the AC generator. Because the voltage regulator coil is also connected to the battery (above terminal 4), the lower than 13.5 volts is unable to produce a sufficient electromagnetic field to pull the contact points open. This condition will allow maximum AC generator output.

As the battery receives a charge from the AC generator, the battery voltage will increase to over 13.5 volts (Figure 9-50). The increased voltage will strengthen the electromagnetic field of the voltage regulator coil. The coil will attract the points and cause the lower contacts to open. Current will now flow through the resistor and out terminal F. Because an additional series resistance is added to the field coil circuit of the AC generator, field current is reduced, and AC generator output is also reduced to one half its rating.

If the AC generator is producing more voltage than the system requires, both battery and system voltage will increase. As this voltage increases to a level above 14.5 volts, the magnetic strength of the coil increases. This increase in magnetic strength will close the top set of contact points and apply a ground to the F terminal and the AC generator's field coil

Maximum AC generator output is called **full field current.**

When current flows through the series resistor to the field coil, it is called **half field current.**

Figure 9-51 Regulator circuit when system voltage is over 14.5 volts. The voltage limiter contacts close to ground preventing current flow to the field coil.

Figure 9-51). Both sides of the field coil are grounded, thus no current will flow through it and there is no output.

Once the engine is shut off, there is no current from the R terminal; the field relay coil is deenergized, allowing the points to open. This prevents battery draw into the charging system.

Electronic Regulators

The second type of regulator is the electronic regulator. Electronic regulators can be mounted either externally or internally of the AC generator. There are no moving parts, so it can cycle between 10 and 7,000 times per second. This quick cycling provides more accurate control of the field current through the rotor. Electronic regulation control is through the ground side of the field current (A circuit).

Pulse width modulation controls AC generator output by varying the amount of time the field coil is energized. For example, assume that a vehicle is equipped with a 100-ampere alternator. If the electrical demand placed on the charging system requires 50 amperes of current, the regulator would energize the field coil for 50% of the time (Figure 9-52). If the electrical system's demand was increased to 75 amperes, the regulator would energize the field coil 75% of the cycle time (Figure 9-53).

The electronic regulator uses a zener diode that blocks current flow until a specific voltage is obtained, at which point it allows the current to flow. A simplified electronic regulator is shown (Figure 9-54).

Classroom Manual
Chapter 3, page 61

Shop Manual
Chapter 9, page 228

An **electronic regulator** uses solid-state circuitry to perform the regulatory functions.

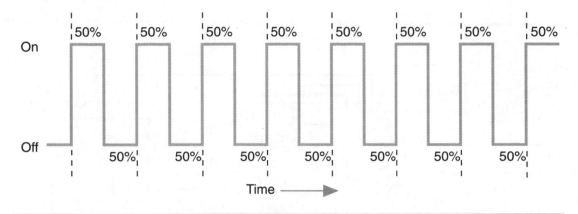

Figure 9-52 Pulse width modulation with 50% on time.

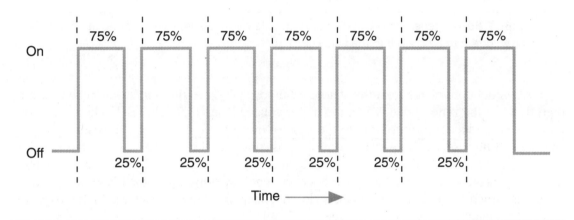

Figure 9-53 Pulse width modulation with 75% on time.

The on/off cycling is called **pulse width modulation.** The period of time for each cycle does not change. Only the amount of on time in each cycle changes.

Figure 9-54 A simplified circuit diagram of an electronic regulator utilizing a zener diode.

Figure 9-55 AC generator circuit diagram with internal regulator, using a diode trio to rectify stator current to be applied to the field coil.

The thermistor changes resistance with temperature.

AC generator voltage from the stator and diodes first goes through a thermistor. Current then flows to the zener diode. When the upper voltage limit (14.5 volts) is reached, the zener diode will conduct current to flow to the base of transistor 1. This turns transistor 1 on and switches off transistor 2. Transistor 2 controls field current to the AC generator. If transistor 2 is off, no current can flow through the field coil and the AC generator will not have any output. When no voltage is applied to the zener diode, current flow stops, transistor 1 is turned off, transistor 2 is turned on, and the field circuit is closed. The magnetic field is restored in the rotor, and the AC generator produces output voltage.

Many manufacturers are installing the voltage regulator internally in the AC generator. This eliminates some of the wiring needed for external regulators. The diode trio rectifies AC current from the stator to DC current that is applied to the field windings (Figure 9-55).

Current flow with the engine off and the ignition switch in the RUN position is illustrated (Figure 9-56). Battery voltage is applied to the field through the common point above R1. TR1 conducts the field current coming from the field coil, producing a weak magnetic field. The indicator lamp lights because TR1 directs current to ground and completes the lamp circuit.

The resistor above the indicator lamp is used to ensure that current will flow through terminal 1 if the lamp burns out.

Current flow with the engine running is illustrated (Figure 9-57). When the AC generator starts to produce voltage, the diode trio will conduct and battery voltage is available for the field and terminal 1 at the common connection. Placing voltage on both sides of the lamp removes any voltage potential, and the lamp goes out.

Current flow as AC generator output is being regulated is illustrated (Figure 9-58). The sensing circuit from terminal 2 passes through a thermistor to the zener diode (D2). When the system voltage reaches the upper voltage limit of the zener diode, the zener diode conducts current to TR2. When TR2 is biased it opens the field coil circuit and current stops flowing through the field coil. Regulation of this switching on and off is based on the sensing voltage received through terminal 2. With the circuit to the field coil opened, the sensing voltage decreases and the zener diode stops conducting. TR2 is turned off and the circuit for the field coil is closed.

Figure 9-56 Current flow to the rotor with the ignition switch in the RUN position and the engine off.

Figure 9-57 Current flow with the engine running and AC generator producing current.

Figure 9-58 When the system voltage is high enough to allow the zener diode to conduct, TR2 is turned on and opens the field circuit.

Shop Manual
Chapter 9, page 209

Duty-cycle is the percentage of on time to total cycle time.

Computer-Controlled Regulation

On many vehicles after the mid-1980s, the regulator function has been incorporated into the vehicle's engine computer (Figure 9-59). The operation is the same as the internal electronic regulator. Regulation of the field circuit is through the ground (A circuit).

The logic board's decisions, concerning voltage regulation, are based on output voltages and battery temperature. When the desired AC generator output voltage is obtained (based on battery temperature) the logic board duty-cycles a switching transistor. This transistor grounds the AC generator's field to control output voltage.

General Motors introduced an AC generator called the CS (charging system) series. This AC generator is smaller than previous designs (Figure 9-60). Additional features include two cooling fans (one external and one internal), and terminals designed to permit connections to an onboard computer through terminals L and F (Figure 9-61). The voltage regulator switches the field current on and off at a fixed frequency of about 400 times per second. Varying the on and off time of the field current controls voltage output.

Charging Indicators

There are four basic methods of informing the driver of the charging system's condition: indicator lamps, electronic voltage monitor, ammeter, and voltmeter.

Indicator Light Operation

As discussed earlier, most indicator lamps operate on the basis of opposing voltages. If the AC generator output is less than battery voltage, there is an electrical potential difference in the lamp circuit and the lamp will light. In the electromechanical regulator system, if the stator is

Figure 9-59 Computer-controlled voltage regulator circuit diagram. (Courtesy of Chrysler Corporation)

Figure 9-60 General Motors CS series AC generator.

Figure 9-61 CS series AC generator circuit diagram.

Figure 9-62 Electromechanical regulator with indicator light on with no AC generator output.

Figure 9-63 Electromechanical regulator with indicator light off when the AC generator has output.

not producing a sufficient amount of current to close the field relay contact points the lamp will light (Figure 9-62). If the voltage at the battery is equal to the output voltage, the two equal voltages on both sides of the lamp result in no electrical potential and the lamp goes out (Figure 9-63).

Electronic regulators that use an indicator lamp operate on the same principle. If there is no stator output through the diode trio, then the lamp circuit is completed to ground through the rotor field and TR1 (Figure 9-64).

On most systems, the warning lamp will be "proofed" when the ignition switch is in the RUN position before the engine starts. This indicates that the bulb and indicator circuit are operating properly. Proofing the bulb is accomplished because there is no stator output without the rotor turning.

Electronic Voltage Monitor

The electronic voltage monitor module is used to monitor the system voltage (Figure 9-65). The lamp will remain off if the system voltage is above 11.2 volts. Once system voltage drops below 11.2 volts, a transistor amplifier in the module turns on the indicator lamp. This system can use either a lamp or a light-emitting diode.

Figure 9-64 Electronic regulator with an indicator light on due to no AC generator output.

Figure 9-65 Electronic voltage monitor module. (Courtesy of Chrysler Corporation)

Classroom Manual
Chapter 7, page 190

The **ammeter** measures charging and discharging current in amperes.

Ammeter Operation

In place of the indicator light, some manufacturers install an ammeter. The ammeter is wired in series between the AC generator and the battery (Figure 9-66). Most ammeters work on the principle of d'Arsonval movement.

The movement of the ammeter needle under different charging conditions is illustrated (Figure 9-67). If the charging system is operating properly, the ammeter needle will remain within the normal range. If the charging system is not generating sufficient current, the needle will swing toward the discharge side of the gauge. When the charging system is recharging the battery, or is called on to supply high amounts of current, the needle deflects toward the charge side of the gauge.

It is normal for the gauge to read a high amount of current after initial engine start up. As the battery is recharged, the needle should move more toward the normal range.

Figure 9-66 Ammeter connected in series to indicate charging system operation.

Ammeter conditions

Discharging

Battery is being discharged. AC generator is not charging or is not keeping up with vehicle's electrical needs.

High charge

Battery has been partially discharged and AC generator is recharging it.

Normal

Battery charge is normal and AC generator is supplying vehicle's electrical needs.

Figure 9-67 Ammeter needle movement indicates charging conditions. (Reprinted with the permission of Ford Motor Company)

Voltmeter Operation

Because the ammeter is a complicated gauge for most people to understand, many manufacturers use a voltmeter to indicate charging system operation. The voltmeter is usually connected between the battery positive and negative terminals (Figure 9-68).

When the engine is started, it is normal for the voltmeter to indicate a reading between 13.2 and 15.2 volts. If the voltmeter indicates a voltage level that is below 13.2, it may mean that the battery is discharging. If the voltmeter indicates a voltage reading that is above 15.2 volts, the charging system is overcharging the battery. The battery and electrical circuits can be damaged as a result of higher than normal charging system output.

The **voltmeter** indicates the amount of voltage potential between two points of a circuit.

Figure 9-68 Voltmeter connected to the charging circuit to monitor operation.

AC Generator Differences

Although all AC generators operate on the same principles, there are differences in the styles and construction.

General Motors 10SI Series

The 10SI series AC generator uses an internal voltage regulator that is mounted to the inside of the slip ring end frame (Figure 9-69). There are three terminals on the rear-end frame of the AC generators:

- **Terminal number 1:** Connects to the field through one brush and slip ring and to the output of the diode trio. In addition, this terminal is connected to a portion of the regulator circuitry.

- **Terminal number 2:** Connects to the regulator to supply battery voltage to a portion of the regulator circuitry.

- **BAT terminal:** Connects to the output of the stator windings and supplies the battery with charging voltage.

Figure 9-69 10SI AC generator. (Courtesy of General Motors Corporation)

Figure 9-70 The four types of AC generators used by Ford. (Reprinted with the permission of Ford Motor Company)

Ford AC Generators

There are four different designs of AC generators that Ford used (Figure 9-70). For many years Ford used the common rear or side terminal AC generator. The rear terminal AC generators used two different types of rectifiers. One rectifier has a single plate that contains all six of the diodes. The diodes are built into the plate (Figure 9-71).

The second type of rectifier uses two plates that are stacked on top of each other (Figure 9-72). One plate contains the positive diodes and the other contains the negative diodes.

Shop Manual
Chapter 9, page 206

This style of rectifier is called **flat-type rectifier.**

Figure 9-71 Flat-type rectifier has single plate containing all six diodes.

Figure 9-72 Stacked-type rectifier with two plates.

On the rear-terminal AC generator there are four terminals on the end frame:

- **BAT terminal:** Stator output connection that supplies charging voltage to the battery.
- **FLD terminal:** Connects one side of the field winding through the insulated brush and the slip ring.
- **STA terminal:** Connects to the neutral stator junction.
- **GRD terminal:** Provides a connection for the ground wire from the regulator.

The Ford side-terminal AC generator is larger and has higher output capacities. The same four terminals are used, however, they are arranged differently.

In 1984, Ford introduced an integral alternator regulator (IAR) AC generator. The regulator is mounted on the exterior of the rear-end frame, which simplifies testing and replacement of the regulator. The F and A terminals are used to test the charging system. Additional modifications include the brushes being a part of the regulator.

When the ignition switch is in the RUN position, voltage is sent to the I terminal of the regulator (Figure 9-73). Regulator terminal A senses system voltage. Field current is drawn through this terminal also.

Ford's EVR charging system uses a solid-state external regulator. This style AC generator is built either with rear or side terminals. The side-terminal AC generator provides higher output by using delta wound stators.

Figure 9-73 IAR charging system schematic.

Figure 9-74 Rear-end frame of a Chrysler AC generator.

Chrysler AC Generators

The Chrysler AC generator (Figure 9-74) uses separate heat sinks for the positive and negative diodes. Both heat sinks are attached to the rear-end frame. Also, the brushes are attached to the exterior of the end frame. This allows for brush replacement without having to disassemble the AC generator (in fact the brushes can usually be replaced without having to remove the AC generator from the vehicle).

> **CAUTION:** Do not attempt to replace the brushes without first disconnecting the battery negative terminal. Failure to disconnect the battery may result in damage to the charging system or injury to the technician.

The three terminals on the rear-end frame are connected as follows:

- **BAT terminal:** Connects the stator output to the battery to supply charging voltage.
- **FLD terminal:** There are two field terminals. Battery voltage is applied to one of the field terminals; the regulator connects to the second field terminal.

In 1985 Chrysler introduced a delta-wound, dual-output, computer-controlled charging system (Figure 9-75). This system has some unique capabilities:

1. The system is capable of varying charging system output based on the ambient temperature and the system's voltage needs.
2. The computer monitors the charging system and is capable of self-diagnosis.

In recent years Chrysler combined the logic and power module into a single unit.

A BIT OF HISTORY

Chrysler equipped its vehicles with AC generators in the late 1950s making it the first manufacturer to use an AC generator. Chrysler introduced the dual-output AC generator (40 or 90 amperes) with computer control in 1985.

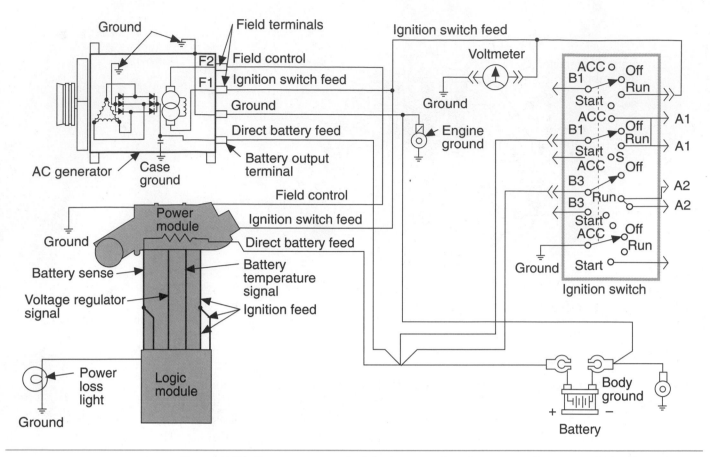

Figure 9-75 Computer-controlled dual-output charging system. (Courtesy of Chrysler Corporation)

When the ignition switch is in the RUN position, the logic module checks the ambient temperature and signals the power module to turn on the AC generator field circuit. Based on inputs to the logic module relating to temperature and system requirements, it signals the power module when current output adjustments are required.

Mitsubishi AC Generator

The Mitsubishi AC generator uses an internal voltage regulator (Figure 9-76). It also has two separate wye connected stator windings (Figure 9-77). Each of the stator windings have their own set of six diodes for rectification.

Figure 9-76 Mitsubishi AC generator terminals. (Courtesy of Chrysler Corporation)

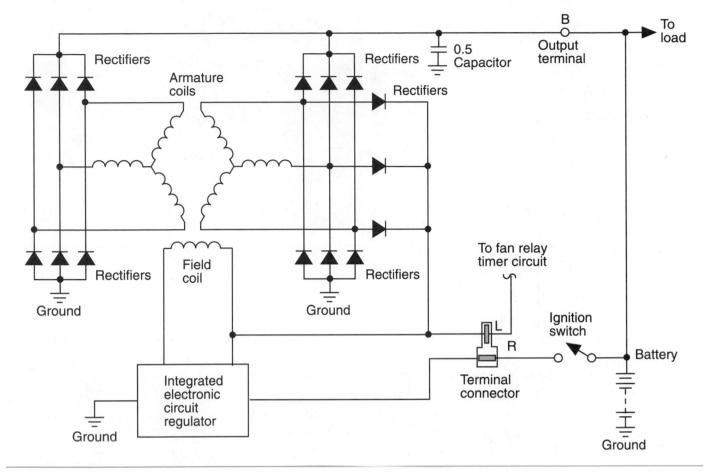

Figure 9-77 The Mitsubishi AC generator uses two separate stator windings and a total of fifteen diodes.

This AC generator also uses a diode trio to rectify stator voltage to be used in the field winding. The three terminals are connected as follows:

- **B terminal:** Connects the output of both stator windings to the battery, supplying charging voltage.

- **R terminal:** Supplies 12 volts to the regulator.

- **L terminal:** Connects to the output of the diode trio to provide rectified stator voltage to designated circuits.

Brushless AC Generators

Some manufacturers have developed AC generators that do not require the use of brushes or slip rings. In these AC generators, the field winding and the stator winding are stationary (Figure 9-78). A screw terminal is used to make the electrical connection. The rotor contains the pole pieces and is fitted between the field winding and the stator winding.

The magnetic field is produced when current is applied to the field winding. The air gaps in the magnetic path contain a nonmetallic ring to divert the lines of force into the stator winding.

The pole pieces on the rotor concentrate the magnetic field into alternating north and south poles. When the rotor is spinning, the north and south poles alternate as they pass the stator winding. The moving magnetic field produces an electrical current in the stator winding. The alternating current is rectified in the same manner as in conventional AC generators.

Figure 9-78 Brushless AC generator with stationary field and stator windings.

Summary

Terms to Know

A circuit

B circuit

Brushes

Delta connection

Diode rectifier bridge

Diode trio

Duty-cycle

External grounded
field circuit

Field current

Field relay

Full field current

Full-wave
rectification

Half field current

Half-wave
rectification

Heat sink

Inductive reactance

Internally grounded
circuit

Polarizing

Pulse width
modulation

Rectification

❑ The purpose of the charging system is to convert the mechanical energy of the engine into electrical energy to recharge the battery and run the electrical accessories.

❑ The charging system consists of the battery, AC or DC generator, drive belt, voltage regulator, charge indicator (lamp or gauge), ignition switch, cables and wiring harness, starter relay (some systems), and fusible links (some systems).

❑ All charging systems use the principle of electromagnetic induction to generate the electrical power.

❑ Electromagnetic principle states that a voltage will be produced if motion between a conductor and a magnetic field occurs. The amount of current produced is affected by the speed that the conductor passes through the magnetic field, the strength of the magnetic field, and the number of conductors passing through the magnetic field.

❑ The main components of the AC generator are the rotor, the brushes, the stator, the rectifier bridge, the housing, and the cooling fan.

❑ The rotor creates the rotating magnetic field of the AC generator. It is the portion of the AC generator that is rotated by the drive belt.

❑ The insulated stationary carbon brush passes field current into a slip ring, then through the field coil, and back to the other slip ring. Current then passes out of the grounded stationary brush.

❑ The stator is the stationary coil in which current is produced.

❑ The stator contains three main sets of windings wrapped in slots around a laminated, circular iron frame.

❑ The most common method of stator connection is called the wye connection. In the wye connection, one lead from each winding is connected to one common junction. From this junction the other leads branch out in a Y pattern.

❑ Another method of stator connection is called the delta connection. The delta connection connects the lead of one end of the winding to the lead at the other end of the next winding.

❑ The diode rectifier bridge provides reasonably constant DC voltage to the vehicle's electrical system and battery. The diode rectifier bridge is used to change the current in an AC generator.

❑ The converting of AC current to DC current is called rectification.

❑ Most AC generator housings are two-piece construction, made from cast aluminum. The two end frames provide support of the rotor and the stator. In addition, the end frames contain the diodes, regulator, heat sinks, terminals, and other components of the AC generator.

❑ The cooling fan draws air into the AC generator through the openings at the rear of the AC generator housing. The air leaves through openings behind the cooling fan.

❑ The three principle circuits used in the AC generator are the charging circuit, which consists of the stator windings and rectifier circuits; the excitation circuit, which consists of the rotor field coil and the electrical connections to the coil; and the preexcitation circuit, which supplies the initial current for the field coil that starts the buildup of the magnetic field.

❑ The voltage regulator controls the output voltage of the AC generator, based on charging system demands, by controlling field current. The higher the field current, the higher the output voltage.

❑ The regulator must have system voltage as an input in order to regulate the output voltage. The input voltage to the regulator is called sensing voltage.

❑ Because ambient temperatures influence the rate of charge that a battery can accept, regulators are temperature compensated.

❑ The A circuit is called an external grounded field circuit, and is always an electronic-type regulator. In the A circuit, the regulator is on the ground side of the field coil. The B+ for the field coil is picked up from inside the AC generator.

❑ Usually the B circuit regulator is mounted externally of the AC generator. The B circuit is an internally grounded circuit. In the B circuit, the voltage regulator controls the power side of the field circuit.

❑ Isolated field AC generators pick up B+ and ground externally. The AC generator has two field wires attached to the outside of the case. The voltage regulator can be located on either the ground (A circuit) or on the B+ (B circuit) side.

❑ There are two basic types of regulators: electromechanical and electronic. Also, on many newer model vehicles regulation is controlled by the computer.

❑ In the electromechanical regulator, the field relay applies voltage to the field coil. The voltage limiter is connected through the resistor network and determines whether the field will receive high, low, or no voltage.

❑ An electronic regulator uses solid-state circuitry to perform the regulatory functions. Electronic regulators can be mounted either externally or internally of the AC generator. Because there are no moving parts, this type of regulator can cycle between 10 and 7,000 times per second.

❑ The electronic regulator uses a zener diode that blocks current flow until a specific voltage is obtained, at which point it allows the current to flow.

❑ On many vehicles after the mid-1980s, the regulator function has been incorporated into the vehicle's engine computer. Regulation of the field circuit is through the ground (A circuit).

❑ There are three basic methods of informing the driver of the charging system's condition: indicator lamps, ammeter, and voltmeter.

❑ Most indicator lamps operate on the basis of voltage drop. If the charging system output is less than battery voltage, there is an electrical potential difference in the lamp circuit and the lamp will light.

❑ The ammeter measures charging and discharging current in amperes. The ammeter is wired in series between the AC generator and the battery.

❑ The voltmeter is usually connected between the battery positive and negative terminals.

Terms to Know (continued)

Rotor

Sensing voltage

Sine wave

Single-phase voltage

Stator

Stator neutral junction

Voltage limiter

Voltage regulator

Wye connection

Review Questions

Short Answer Essays

1. List the major components of the charging system.
2. List and explain the function of the major components of the AC generator.
3. How does the regulator resistance affect field coil current?
4. What is the relationship between field current and AC generator output?
5. Identify the differences between A, B, and isolated circuits.
6. Explain the operation of charge indicator lamps.
7. Describe the two styles of stators.
8. List and describe the three principle circuits used in the AC generator.
9. Describe how AC current is rectified to DC current in the AC generator.
10. What is the purpose of the charging system?

Fill-in-the-Blanks

1. The charging system converts the _____ energy of the engine into _____ energy to recharge the battery and run the electrical accessories.

2. All charging systems use the principle of _____ _____ to generate the electrical power.

3. The _____ creates the rotating magnetic field of the AC generator.

4. _____ are electrically conductive sliding contacts, usually made of copper and carbon.

5. In the _____ connection stator, one lead from each winding is connected to one common junction.

6. The _____ _____ controls the output voltage of the AC generator, based on charging system demands, by controlling _____ current.

7. In an electronic regulator, _____ _____ _____ controls AC generator output by varying the amount of time the field coil is energized.

8. In most electronic regulators that use an indicator lamp, if there is no stator output through the _____ _____ , then the lamp circuit is completed to ground.

9. Full-wave rectification in the AC generator requires _____ pair of diodes.

10. The _____ is the stationary coil that current is produced in the AC generator.

ASE Style Review Questions

1. The purpose of the charging system is being discussed:
   Technician A says the charging system is used to restore the electrical power to the battery that was used during engine starting.
   Technician B says the charging system must be able to react quickly to high load demands required of the electrical system.
   Who is correct?
   A. A only
   B. B only
   C. Both A and B
   D. Neither A nor B

2. The operation of the charging system is being discussed:
   Technician A says battery condition has no affect on the charging system operation.
   Technician B says the stator is the rotating component that creates the magnetic field.
   Who is correct?
   A. A only
   B. B only
   C. Both A and B
   D. Neither A nor B

3. Rectification is being discussed:
   Technician A says the AC generator uses a segmented commutator to rectify AC current.
   Technician B says the AC generator uses a set of diodes to rectify AC current.
   Who is correct?
   A. A only
   B. B only
   C. Both A and B
   D. Neither A nor B

4. Rotor construction is being discussed:
   Technician A says the poles will take on the polarity of the side of the coil that they touch.
   Technician B says the magnetic flux lines will move in opposite directions between adjacent poles.
   Who is correct?
   A. A only
   B. B only
   C. Both A and B
   D. Neither A nor B

5. Stator construction is being discussed:
   Technician A says the wye connection is the most common.
   Technician B says the wye connection connects the lead of one end of the winding to the lead at the other end of the next winding.
   Who is correct?
   A. A only
   B. B only
   C. Both A and B
   D. Neither A nor B

6. Charging system regulation is being discussed:
   Technician A says AC generators require current limiters.
   Technician B says the higher the field current, the lower the output voltage.
   Who is correct?
   A. A only
   B. B only
   C. Both A and B
   D. Neither A nor B

7. Indicator lamp operation is being discussed:
   Technician A says in a system with an electronic regulator, the lamp will light if there is no stator output through the diode trio.
   Technician B says when there is stator output the lamp circuit has voltage applied to both sides and the lamp will not light.
   Who is correct?
   A. A only
   B. B only
   C. Both A and B
   D. Neither A nor B

8. AC generator differences are being discussed:
   Technician A says the Mitsubishi AC generator uses two separate wye connected stator windings.
   Technician B says Ford rear-terminal AC generators use two different types of rectifiers.
   Who is correct?
   A. A only
   B. B only
   C. Both A and B
   D. Neither A nor B

9. *Technician A* says only two stator windings apply voltage because the third winding is always connected to diodes that are reverse biased.
   Technician B says AC generators that use half-wave rectification are the most efficient.
   Who is correct?
   A. A only
   B. B only
   C. Both A and B
   D. Neither A nor B

10. The operation of the electromechanical regulator is being discussed:
    Technician A says the field relay applies battery voltage to the AC generator field coil after the engine has started.
    Technician B says the voltage limiter is connected through the resistor network and determines whether the field will receive high, low, or no voltage.
    Who is correct?
    A. A only
    B. B only
    C. Both A and B
    D. Neither A nor B

Electrical Accessories

Upon completion and review of this chapter, you should be able to:

❑ Describe the operation and function of the horn circuit.

❑ Explain and detail the operation of standard two- and three-speed wiper motors, both permanent magnet and electromagnetic field designs.

❑ Describe the operation of intermittent wipers.

❑ Explain how depressed-park wipers operate.

❑ Explain the operation of windshield washer pump systems.

❑ Describe the operation and methods used to control blower fan motor speeds.

❑ Describe the operation of electric defoggers.

❑ Describe operational principles of power mirrors.

❑ Explain the principles of operation for power windows, power seats, and power locks.

Introduction

Electrical accessories provide additional safety and comfort. There are many electrical accessories that can be installed into today's vehicles. This chapter explains the principles of operation for some of the most common electrical accessories. Systems not discussed here are similar in concept.

This chapter explores the operation of safety accessories, such as the horn, windshield wipers, and windshield washers. Comfort accessories explored in this chapter include the blower motor, electric defoggers, power mirrors, power windows, power seats, and power door locks.

Horns

Automotive electrical horns operate on an electromagnetic principle that vibrates a diaphragm to produce a warning signal. Most electrical horns consist of an electromagnet, a moveable armature, a diaphragm, and a set of normally closed contact points (Figure 10-1). The contact points are wired in series with the field coil. One of the points is attached to the armature. When current flows through the field coil, a magnetic field is developed that attracts the moveable

Shop Manual
Chapter 10,
pages 243 and 246

A **horn** is a device that produces an audible warning signal.

The **diaphragm** is a thin, flexible, circular plate that is held around its outer edge by the horn housing, allowing the middle to flex.

Figure 10-1 Horn construction. The internal resistor allows a weak magnetic field to remain after the contacts open, reducing the amount of time required to rebuild the field when the contacts close again.

279

Figure 10-2 When the armature pulls the diaphragm up, the contacts open.

armature (Figure 10-2). The diaphragm is attached to and moves with the armature. Movement of the armature results in the contact points opening, which breaks the circuit. The diaphragm is released and returns to its normal position. The contact points close again, and the cycle repeats. This vibration of the diaphragm, is repeated several times per second.

As the diaphragm vibrates, it causes a column of air in the horn to vibrate. The vibration of the column of air produces the sound.

Most vehicles are equipped with two horns that are wired in parallel with each other and in series with the switch. One of the horns will have a slightly lower pitch than the other. The design and shape of the horn determines the frequency and tone of the sound (Figure 10-3). Pitch is controlled by the number of times the diaphragm vibrates per second. The faster the vibration, the higher the pitch. The horn pitch can be adjusted by changing the spring tension of the armature. This alters the magnetic pull on the armature and changes the rate of vibrations. The adjustment is made on the outside of the horn (Figure 10-4).

When two horns are used on a vehicle, one is called the **low-note horn** and the other is called the **high-note horn.**

Shop Manual
Chapter 10,
page 244

Horn Switches

Horn switches are either installed in the steering wheel or as a part of the multifunction switch. Most horn switches are normally open switches.

The steering wheel-mounted horn switch can be a single button in the middle of the steering wheel (Figure 10-5). Another design is to have multiple buttons in the horn pad (Figure 10-6).

Figure 10-3 Horn design affects sound quality.

Figure 10-4 Horn pitch adjustment screw.

Figure 10-5 Single button-type horn pad. (Reprinted with the permission of Ford Motor Company)

Figure 10-6 Multiple button horn pad. (Courtesy of General Motors Corporation)

Figure 10-7 Slip ring contact provides horn continuity in all steering wheel positions. (Reprinted with the permission of Ford Motor Company)

Switches mounted on the steering wheel require the use of sliding contacts (Figure 10-7). The contacts provide continuity for the horn control in all steering wheel positions. The contacts consist of a circular contact in the steering wheel that slides against a spring-loaded contact in the steering column.

Horn switches that are a part of the multifunction switch usually operate by a pushbutton on the end of the lever (Figure 10-8).

Figure 10-8 The horn switch button may be a part of the multifunction switch. (Reprinted with the permission of Ford Motor Company)

Hot at all times

Fuse panel

20 A

Cigar lighter

Horn switch

Low pitch horn

High pitch horn

Figure 10-9 Insulated side switch without relay. (Reprinted with the permission of Ford Motor Company)

Horn Circuits

There are two methods of circuit control: with or without a relay. If the horn circuit does not use a relay, the horns must be of low current design because the horn switch carries the total current. Depressing the horn switch completes the circuit from the battery to the horns (Figure 10-9).

The most common type of circuit control is to use a relay (Figure 10-10). Most circuits have battery voltage present to the lower contact plate of the horn switch. When the switch is depressed, the contacts close and complete the circuit to ground. Only low current is required to operate the relay coil, so the horn switch does not have to carry the heavy current requirements of the horns. When the horn switch is closed, it energizes the relay core. The core attracts the relay armature, which closes the contacts and completes the horn circuit. Current flows from the battery to the grounded horns.

Windshield Wipers

There are two types of windshield wiper systems being used today:

1. A standard two- or three-speed system

2. A two- or three-speed system with an intermittent feature.

On most models, the same motor is used for either the standard or intermittent system. Both can have a depressed-park feature.

A single-speed rear window wiper and washer is used on many vehicles. In addition, headlight wipers are installed on many luxury vehicles that operate in union with the windshield wipers (Figure 10-11). The operation of these accessories is the same as the windshield wipers.

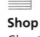

Shop Manual
Chapter 10, pages 243 and 245

Classroom Manual
Chapter 8

Shop Manual
Chapter 10, page 246

Figure 10-10 Relay-controlled horn circuit. The horn button completes the relay coil circuit.

Figure 10-11 Headlight wipers.

Wiper Motors

Most windshield wiper motors use permanent magnet fields. Motor speed is controlled by the placement of the brushes on the commutator. Three brushes are used: common, high speed, and low speed. The common brush carries current whenever the motor is operating. The low speed and high speed brushes are placed in different locations, based on motor design:

1. The high speed and common brushes oppose each other, with the low speed brush offset (Figure 10-12).

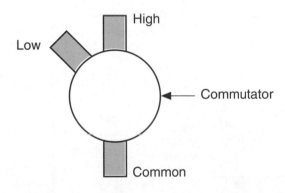

Figure 10-12 One style of brush arrangement has the high speed brush opposite the common brush.

A BIT OF HISTORY

The first windshield wipers were hand operated. Most of the early powered wiper systems were operated by engine vacuum. Many times the wipers would not operate when the vehicle was driven up a hill because of the loss of engine vacuum under those conditions. In 1968 federal law mandated that all vehicles must be equipped with a two-speed wiper and washer system. American Motors Corporation continued to use a two speed vacuum motor until the 1970s; all other manufacturers converted to electric motors.

Windshield wipers are mechanical arms that sweep back and forth across the windshield to remove water, snow, or dirt.

Intermittent means the wipers start and stop at intervals.

In systems equipped with **depressed park,** the blades drop down below the lower windshield molding to hide them.

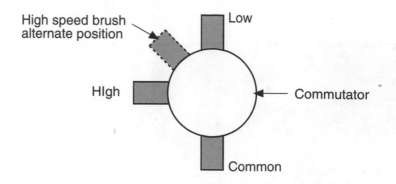

Figure 10-13 The most common brush arrangement is to place the low-speed brush opposite the common brush.

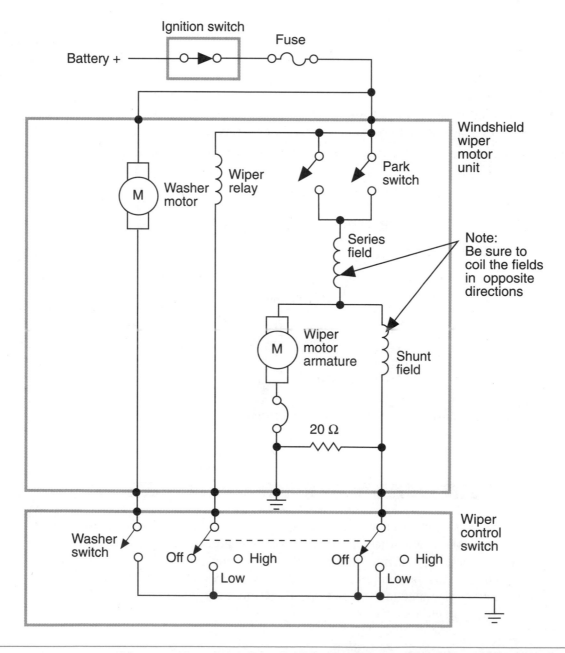

Figure 10-14 Schematic of wiper system using an electromagnetic field motor.

2. The low speed and common brushes oppose each other with the high speed brush offset or centered between them (Figure 10-13). This is the most common brush arrangement.

The placement of the brushes determines how many armature windings are connected in the circuit. There are fewer armature windings connected between the common and high speed brushes. When battery voltage is applied to fewer windings there is less magnetism in the armature and a lower counterelectromotive force (CEMF). With less CEMF in the armature, there is greater armature current. The greater armature current results in higher speeds.

There are more armature windings connected in the circuit between the common and low speed brushes. With more windings, the magnetic field in the armature is increased. This results in greater CEMF. The increased CEMF reduces the amount of current in the armature and slows the speed of the motor.

Some two-speed, and all three-speed wiper motors use two electromagnetic field windings instead of permanent magnets (Figure 10-14). The two field coils are wound in opposite directions so that their magnetic fields will oppose each other. The series field is wired in series with the motor brushes and commutator. The shunt field forms a separate circuit branch off the series field to ground. The strength of the total magnetic field will determine the speed of the motor.

Permanent Magnet Wiper Circuits

A set of park contacts are incorporated into the motor assembly and operate off a cam or latch arm on the motor gear (Figure 10-15). The park switch changes position with each revolution of the motor. The switch remains in the RUN position for approximately 90% of the revolution. It is in the PARK position for the remaining 10% of the revolution. This does not affect the operation of the motor until the wiper control switch is placed in the PARK position.

Most wiper circuits use a circuit breaker to prevent temporary overloads from totally disabling the windshield wipers.

Shop Manual
Chapter 10,
page 250

Figure 10-15 Park switch components.

Park contacts are located inside of the motor assembly, and supply current to the motor after the wiper control switch has been turned to the PARK position. This allows the motor to continue operating until the wipers have reached their park position.

When the wiper control switch is in the HIGH SPEED position, battery voltage is supplied through wiper 1 to the high speed brush (Figure 10-16). Wiper 2 moves with wiper 1, but does not complete any circuits. Current continues to flow through the armature and common brush to ground. Because the ground connection is before the park switch, the park switch position has no effect on motor operation.

When the switch is placed in the LOW SPEED position, battery voltage is supplied through wiper 1 to the low speed brush. Wiper 2 also moves to the LOW position, but does not complete any circuits. Current continues to flow through the armature and common brush to ground (Figure 10-17). Park switch position has no effect on motor operation.

Figure 10-16 Current flow in HIGH, using a permanent magnet motor. (Reprinted with the permission of Ford Motor Company)

Figure 10-17 Current flow in LOW position. (Reprinted with the permission of Ford Motor Company)

When the switch is returned to the OFF position, wiper 1 opens. Battery voltage is applied to the park switch. Wiper 2 is closed to allow current to flow to the low speed brush, through the armature, and to ground (Figure 10-18). When the wiper blades are in their lowest position, the park switch is moved to the PARK position. This opens the circuit to the low speed brush and the motor shuts off.

Electromagnetic Field Wiper Circuits

Electromagnetic field motors use two fields that are wired in opposite direction: the series field and the shunt field. Resistors are used in series with one of the fields to control the strength of the total magnetic field. The wiper control switch directs the current flow through the resistors to obtain the desired motor speed. Circuit operation varies between two- and three-speed systems.

Figure 10-18 Current flow when the wipers are parking. (Reprinted with the permission of Ford Motor Company)

Shop Manual
Chapter 10,
page 248

Two-speed Motors. The ground side switch will determine the current path. One path is directly to ground after the field coil, the other is through a 20-ohm resistor.

With the switch in the OFF position, switch wiper 1 breaks the circuit through the relay to ground. Because the relay is not energized, current is not supplied to the motor(Figure 10-19).

When the switch is placed in the LOW SPEED position, wiper 1 completes the relay coil circuit to ground. The energized relay closes the contacts and applies current to the motor, through the series field and shunt field coils. Wiper 2 provides the ground path for the shunt field coil (Figure 10-20). Because there is less resistance to ground through wiper 2, the 20-ohm resistor is bypassed. With no resistance in the shunt field coil, the shunt field is very strong and bucks the magnetic field of the series field. The result is slow motor operation.

Figure 10-19 Simplified diagram of an electromagnetic field, two-speed wiper system.

Figure 10-20 Current flow in the LOW SPEED position. Wiper 2 provides the ground path, bypassing the 20-ohm resistor.

Figure 10-21 Current flow in the HIGH SPEED position. Wiper 2 opens, causing the current to flow through the resistor.

Figure 10-22 Current flow when the wipers are parking.

When the switch is located in the HIGH SPEED position, wiper 1 completes the relay coil circuit to ground. This closes the relay contacts to the series field and shunt field coils. Wiper 2 opens the circuit to ground and current must now pass through the 20-ohm resistor to ground (Figure 10-21). The resistor reduces the current flow and strength of the shunt field. With less resistance from the shunt field, the series field is able to turn the motor at an increased speed.

When the switch is returned to the OFF position, wiper 1 opens the relay coil circuit. The relay is de-energized, but the contact points to the series and shunt field coils are manually held closed by the park switch. The park switch is closed until the wipers are in their lowest position. Wiper 2 closes the circuit path to ground. As long as the park switch is closed, current flows through the series field, shunt field, and wiper 2 to ground (Figure 10-22). Once the wipers are in their lowest point of travel, the park switch opens and the motor turns off.

Three-Speed Motors. The three-speed motor system offers a low, medium, and high speed selection. The wiper control switch position determines what resistors, if any, will be connected to the circuit of one of the fields (Figure 10-23).

When the wiper control switch is placed in the LOW SPEED position, both field coils receive equal current (Figure 10-24). Both field coils have the same amount of current flow, so the total magnetic field is weak and the motor speed is slow.

When the switch is placed in the MEDIUM SPEED position, the current flows through a resistor before flowing to the shunt field (Figure 10-25). The resistor weakens the strength of the shunt coil, but strengthens the total magnetic field of the motor. The speed is increased over that of the LOW SPEED position.

Shop Manual
Chapter 10,
pages 247, 249,
and 250

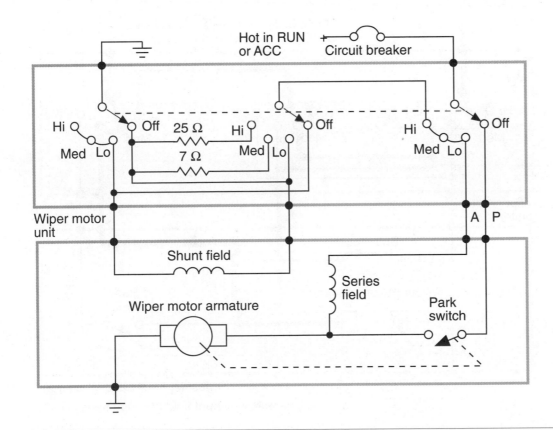

Figure 10-23 Three-speed wiper motor schematic.

Figure 10-24 Current flow in LOW position.

Figure 10-25 Current flow in MEDIUM position.

Series field (full battery voltage)

Shunt field (through resistor)

Figure 10-26 Current flow in HIGH position.

When the switch is placed in the HIGH SPEED position, a resistor of greater value is connected into the shunt field circuit (Figure 10-26). The resistor weakens the magnetic field of the shunt coil, allowing a stronger total field to rotate the motor at a high speed.

Intermittent Wipers

Many wiper systems offer an intermittent mode that provides a variable interval between wiper sweeps. Many of these systems use a module located in the steering column (Figure 10-27). If the

Figure 10-27 Intermittent wiper module. (Reprinted with the permission of Ford Motor Company)

Shop Manual
Chapter 10,
page 253

Many manufacturers are incorporating this function into the body computer. Also, some manufacturers are equipping their vehicles with speed sensitive wiper systems. The delay between wiper sweeps is determined by the speed of the vehicle.

Figure 10-28 Intermittent wiper system schematic. (Reprinted with the permission of Ford Motor Company)

Figure 10-29 Current flow when intermittent wiper mode is initiated. (Reprinted with the permission of Ford Motor Company)

intermittent wiper mode is initiated when the wipers are in their parked position, the park switch is in the ground position. Current is sent to the solid-state module to the timer activate terminal (Figure 10-28). The internal timer unit "triggers" the electronic switch to close the circuit for the governor relay, which then closes the circuit to the low speed brush (Figure 10-29). The wiper will operate until the park switch swings back to the PARK position.

The delay between wiper sweeps is determined by the amount of resistance the driver puts into the potentiometer control. By rotating the intermittent control knob, the resistance value is altered. The module contains a capacitor that is charged through the potentiometer. Once the capacitor is saturated, the electronic switch is "triggered" to send current to the wiper motor. The capacitor discharge is long enough to start the wiper operation and the park switch is returned to the RUN position. The wiper will continue to run until one sweep is completed and the park switch opens. The amount of time between sweeps is based on the length of time required to saturate the capacitor. As more resistance is added to the potentiometer, it takes longer to saturate the capacitor.

Figure 10-30 Depressed-park wiper system in LOW SPEED position.

Depressed Wiper Systems

Systems that have a depressed-park feature use a second set of contacts with the park switch. These contacts are used to reverse the rotation of the motor for about 15 degrees after the wipers have reached the normal park position. The circuitry of the depressed circuit is different from that of standard wiper motors.

The operation of a depressed-park wiper system in the LOW SPEED position is shown (Figure 10-30). Current flows through the number 3 wiper to the common brush. Ground is provided through the low speed brush and switch wiper 2.

When the switch is placed in the OFF position, current is supplied through the park switch wiper B and switch wiper 3 (Figure 10-31). Ground is supplied through the low speed brush and switch wiper 1, then to park switch wiper A.

When the wipers reach their park position, the park switch swings to the PARKING position (Figure 10-32). Current flow is through the park switch wiper A, to switch wiper 1. Wiper 1 directs the current to the low speed brush. The ground path is through the common brush, switch wiper 3, and park switch wiper B. This reversed current flow is continued until the wipers reach the depressed-park position, when park switch wiper A swings to the PARKED position.

Washer Pumps

Windshield washers spray a washer fluid solution onto the windshield and work in conjunction with the wiper blades to clean the windshield of dirt. Some vehicles that have composite headlights

Note the difference in operation between the depressed-park wiper system and the one shown in Figure 10-16.

Shop Manual
Chapter 10,
page 256

Figure 10-31 Current flow when the switch is turned to OFF after operation (parking).

Figure 10-32 Current flow when wipers are parking into the depressed position.

incorporate a headlight washing system along with the windshield washer (Figure 10-33). Most systems have the washer pump motor installed into the reservoir (Figure 10-34). General Motors uses a pulse-type washer pump that operates off the wiper motor (Figure 10-35).

The system is activated by holding the washer switch (Figure 10-36). If the wiper/washer system also has an intermittent control module, a signal is sent to the module when the washer switch is activated (Figure 10-37). An override circuit in the module operates the wipers on low speed for a programmed length of time. The wipers will either return to the parked position or will operate in intermittent mode, depending on system design.

Figure 10-33 Headlight washer system may operate with the windshield washer or have a separate switch.

Figure 10-34 Washer motor installed into the reservoir. (Reprinted with the permission of Ford Motor Company)

Figure 10-35 General Motors' pulse-type washer system incorporates the washer motor into the wiper motor.

Figure 10-36 Windshield washer motor circuit.

Figure 10-37 Input signal alerts the module that the washers are activated. (Courtesy of Chrysler Corporation)

Figure 10-38 The blower motor is usually installed into the heater assembly. Mode doors control if vent, heater, or A/C cooled air is blown by the motor cage.

Shop Manual
Chapter 10, pages
258 and 259

The **resistor block**
consists of two or
three helically
wound wire resistors
wired in series.

Blower Motor Circuit

The blower motor is used to move air inside the vehicle for air conditioning, heating, defrost, and ventilation. The motor is usually a permanent magnet, single-speed motor and is located in the heater housing assembly (Figure 10-38). A blower motor switch mounted on the dash controls the fan speed (Figure 10-39). The switch position directs current flow to a resistor block that is wired in series between the switch and the motor (Figure 10-40).

The blower motor circuit includes the control assembly, blower switch, resistor block, and the blower motor (Figure 10-41). This system uses an insulated side switch and a grounded motor. Battery voltage is applied to the control head when the ignition switch is in the RUN or ACC positions. The current can flow from the control head to the blower switch and resistor block in any control head position except OFF.

When the blower switch is in the LOW position, the blower switch wiper opens the circuit. Current can only flow to the resistor block directly through the control head. The current must

Figure 10-39 Comfort control assembly. (Courtesy of Chrysler Corporation)

Figure 10-40 Fan motor resistor block. (Reprinted with the permission of Ford Motor Company)

Figure 10-41 Blower motor circuit. (Courtesy of Chrysler Corporation)

Figure 10-42 Current flow in the LOW position. (Courtesy of Chrysler Corporation)

Many of today's vehicles are using the body computer to control fan speed by pulse width modulation.

pass through all the resistors before reaching the motor. With the voltage dropped over the resistors, the motor speed is slowed (Figure 10-42).

When the blower switch is placed in the MED 1, MED 2, or HIGH position, the current flows through the blower switch to the resistor block. Depending on the speed selection, the current must pass through one, two, or none of the resistors (Figure 10-43). With more applied voltage to the motor, the fan speed is increased as the amount of resistance decreases.

Current through the circuit will remain constant; varying the amount of resistance changes the voltage applied to the motor. Because the motor is a single-speed motor, it obtains its fastest rotational speed with full battery voltage. The resistors drop the amount of voltage to the motor, resulting in slower speeds.

Some manufacturers use ground side switching with an insulated motor (Figure 10-44). The switch completes the circuit to ground. Depending on wiper position, current flow is directed through the resistor block. The operating principles are identical to that of the insulated switch already discussed.

Figure 10-43 Current flow in the different speed selections. (Courtesy of Chrysler Corporation)

Electric Defoggers

When electrons are forced to flow through a resistance, heat is generated. Rear window defoggers use this principle of controlled resistance to heat the glass. The resistance is through a grid that is baked on the inside of the glass (Figure 10-45). The terminals are soldered to the vertical bus bars. One terminal supplies the current from the switch; the other provides the ground (Figure 10-46).

The system may incorporate a timer circuit that controls the relay (Figure 10-47). The timer is used due to the high amount of current required to operate the system (approximately 30 amperes). If this drain was allowed to continue for extended periods of time, battery and charging system failure could result. Because of the high current draw, most vehicles equipped with a rear window defogger use a high output AC generator.

Shop Manual
Chapter 10,
page 260

Electric defoggers
heat the rear window to remove ice and/or condensation. Some vehicles use the same circuit to heat the outside driver's side mirror.

Figure 10-44 Ground side switch to control the blower motor system. (Reprinted with the permission of Ford Motor Company)

The rear window defogger **grid** is a series of horizontal ceramic silver-compounded lines baked into the surface of the window.

Figure 10-45 Rear window defogger grid.

Figure 10-46 Rear window defogger circuit schematic.

Figure 10-47 Defogger circuit using a solid-state timer.

Figure 10-48 Current flow through the defogger circuit.

The ON indicator can be either a bulb or light-emitting diode (LED).

The control switch is a three-position, spring-loaded switch that returns to the center position after making momentary contact to the ON or OFF terminals. Activation of the switch energizes the electronic timing circuit, which energizes the relay coil. With the relay contacts closed, direct battery voltage is sent to the heater grid (Figure 10-48). At the same time, voltage is applied to the ON indicator. The timer is activated for 10 minutes. At the completion of the timed cycle, the relay is de-energized and the circuit to the grid and indicator light is broken. If the switch is activated again, the timer will energize the relay for 5 minutes.

The timer sequence can be aborted by moving the switch to the OFF position or by turning off the ignition switch. If the ignition switch is turned off while the timer circuit is activated, the rear window defogger switch will have to be returned to the ON position to activate the system again.

Ambient temperatures have an effect on electrical resistance, thus the amount of current flow through the grid depends on the temperature of the grid. As the ambient temperature

Power mirror
control switch

Figure 10-49 Control switch for power mirrors. (Reprinted with the permission of Ford Motor Company)

decreases, the resistance value of the grid also decreases. A decrease in resistance increases the current flow and results in quick warming of the window. The defogger system tends to be self-regulated to match the requirements for defogging.

Power Mirrors

The electrically controlled mirror allows the driver to position the outside mirrors by use of a switch (Figure 10-49). The mirror assembly will use built-in dual drive, reversible permanent magnet (PM) motors (Figure 10-50).

A single switch for controlling both the left and right side mirrors is used. On many systems, selection of the mirror to be adjusted is by rotating the knob counterclockwise for the left

Power mirrors are outside mirrors that are electrically positioned from the inside of the driver compartment.

Motor

Mirror glass

Figure 10-50 Power mirror motor.

Figure 10-51 Mirror selection from the control switch. (Reprinted with the permission of Ford Motor Company)

Figure 10-52 Power mirror logic table. (Reprinted with the permission of Ford Motor Company)

Power mirror logic table

Mirror operational mode	Directional movement	Left hand mirror		Right hand mirror	
		Positive voltage (+)	Ground (-)	Positive voltage (+)	Ground (-)
Vertical	Up	541	542	544	565
Vertical	Down	542	541	545	544
Horizontal	Left	540	542	543	545
Horizontal	Right	542	540	565 545 Exp	543

mirror and clockwise for the right mirror (Figure 10-51). After the mirror is selected, movement of the joystick (up, down, left, or right) moves the mirror in the corresponding direction. The illustration (Figure 10-52) shows a logic table for the mirror switch and motors.

Automatic Rear View Mirror

Some manufacturers have developed interior rear view mirrors that automatically tilt when the intensity of light that strikes the mirror is sufficient enough to cause discomfort to the driver.

The system has two photocells mounted in the mirror housing. One of the photocells is used to measure the intensity of light inside the vehicle. The second is used to measure the intensity of light being received by the mirror. When the intensity of the light striking the mirror is greater than that of ambient light, by a predetermined amount, a solenoid is activated that tilts the mirror.

Electrochromic Mirrors

Electrochromic mirrors are available that automatically adjust the amount of reflectance based on the intensity of glare (Figure 10-53). The process is similar to that used by photo-gray or photochromic sunglasses. If the glare is heavy, the mirror darkens to about 6% reflectivity. The electrochromic mirror has the advantage that it provides a comfort zone where the mirror will provide 20% to 30% reflectivity. When no glare is present, the mirror changes to the daytime reflectivity rating of up to 85%. The reduction of the glare by darkening of the mirror does not impair visibility.

A

B

C

Figure 10-53 Electrochromic mirror operation: (A) day time, (B) mild glare, (C) high glare. (Courtesy of Gentex Corporation)

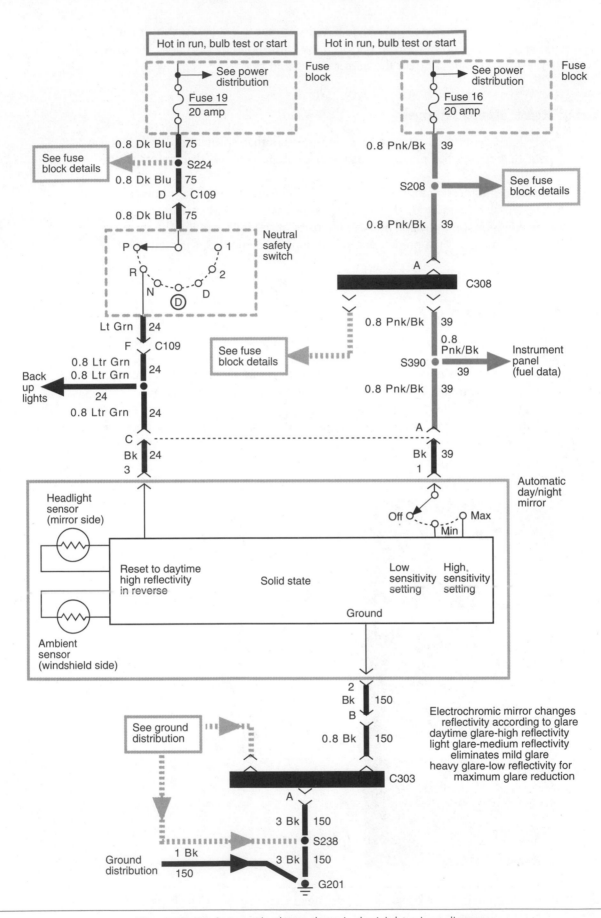

Figure 10-54 Automatic electrochromic day/night mirror diagram.

Electrochromic mirrors are also installed as inside mirrors. The mirror is constructed of a thin layer of electrochromic material that is placed between two plates of conductive glass. There are two photocell sensors that measure light intensity in front and in back of the mirror. During night driving, the headlight beam striking the mirror causes the mirror to gradually become darker as the light intensity increases. The darker mirror absorbs the glare. Sensitivity of the mirror can be adjusted by the driver through a three-position switch (Figure 10-54).

When the ignition switch is placed in the RUN position, battery voltage is applied to the three-position switch. If the switch is in the MIN position battery voltage is applied to the solid-state unit, and sets the sensitivity to a low level. The MAX setting causes the mirror to darken more at a lower glare level. When the transmission is placed in reverse, the reset circuit is activated. This returns the mirror to daytime setting for clearer viewing to back-up.

The MIN position is used for city driving.

Power Windows

Many luxury vehicles replace the conventional window crank with electric motors that operate the side windows. In addition, most station wagon models are equipped with electric rear tail-gate windows. The motor used in the power window system is a reversible PM or two-field winding motor.

The power window system usually consists of the following components:

1. Master control switch
2. Individual control switches
3. Individual window drive motors

Another design is to use rack-and-pinion gears. The rack is a flexible strip of gear teeth with one end attached to the window (Figure 10-55).

Shop Manual Chapter 10, page 262

Power windows are raised and lowered by use of electrical motors.

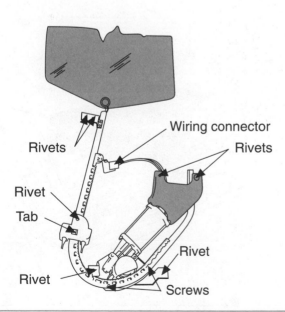

Figure 10-55 Rack-and-pinion-style power window motor and regulator. (Courtesy of Chrysler Corporation)

Figure 10-56 Window regulator. (Courtesy of Chrysler Corporation)

A **window regulator** converts the rotary motion of the motor into the vertical movement of the window.

The **sector gear** is the section of gear teeth on the regulator.

The motor operates the window regulator either through a cable or directly. On direct drive motors, the motor pinion gear meshes with the sector gear (Figure 10-56). As the window is lowered, the spiral spring is wound. The spring unwinds as the window is raised to assist in raising the window. The spring reduces the amount of current that would be required to raise the window by the motor itself.

The master control switch provides the overall control of the system (Figure 10-57). Power to the individual switches is provided through the master switch. The master switch may also have a safety lock switch to prevent operation of the windows by the individual switches. When the safety switch is activated, it opens the circuit to the other switches and control is only by the master switch. As an additional safety feature, some systems prevent operation of the individual switches unless the ignition switch is in the RUN or ACC position (Figure 10-58).

Wiring circuits depend on motor design. Most PM-type motors are insulated, with ground provided through the master switch (Figure 10-59). When the master control switch is placed

Figure 10-57 Power window master control switch. (Reprinted with the permission of Ford Motor Company)

Figure 10-58 Power window wiring diagram.

Figure 10-59 Typical power window circuit using PM motors.

Figure 10-60 Current flow with the L/R window master control switch in the UP position.

in the UP position, current flow is from the battery, through the master switch wiper, through the individual switch wiper, to the top brush of the motor. Ground is through the bottom brush and circuit breaker to the individual switch wiper, to the master switch wiper and ground (Figure 10-60).

When the window is raised from the individual switch, battery voltage is supplied directly to the switch and wiper from the ignition switch. The ground path is through the master control switch (Figure 10-61).

When the window is lowered from the master control switch, the current path is reversed (Figure 10-62). In the illustration shown (Figure 10-63) current flows through the individual switch to lower the window.

Some manufacturers use a two-field coil motor that is grounded with insulated side switches. The two field coils are wired in opposite directions, and only one coil is energized at a time. Direction of the motor is determined by which coil is activated (Figure 10-64).

Power Seats

Shop Manual
Chapter 10,
page 267

The power seat system is classified by the number of ways in which the seat is moved. The most common classifications are:

1. Two-way: Moves the seat forward and backward.

2. Four-way: Moves the seat forward, backward, up, and down.

3. Six-way: Moves the seat forward, backward, up, down, front tilt, and rear tilt.

Figure 10-61 Current flow when R/R window switch is in the UP position.

Figure 10-62 Current flow when L/R window master control switch is placed in the DOWN position.

Figure 10-63 Current flow through the individual switch to lower the R/R window.

Figure 10-64 Wiring diagram of power window circuit using electromagnetic motors.

Figure 10-65 Trimotor power seat installation. (Reprinted with the permission of Ford Motor Company)

All modern six-way power seats use a reversible, permanent magnet trimotor (Figure 10-65). The motor may transfer rotation to a rack-and-pinion or to a worm gear drive transmission. A typical control switch consists of a four-position knob and a set of two position switches (Figure 10-66). The four-position knob controls the forward, rearward, up, and down movement of the seat. The separate two-position switches are used to control the front tilt and rear tilt of the seat.

The three armature motor is called a **trimotor**.

Early General Motors six-way power seats used a single motor. Solenoids were used to connect the motor to one of three transmissions that would move the seat.

Figure 10-66 Power seat control switch. (Reprinted with the permission of Ford Motor Company)

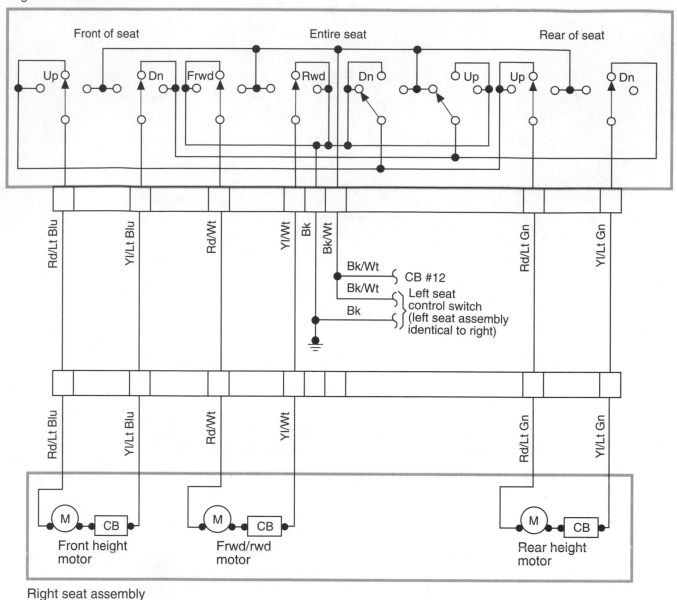

Figure 10-67 Six-way power seat circuit diagram.

Current direction through the motor determines the rotation direction of the motor. The switch wipers control the direction of current flow (Figure 10-67). If the driver pushes the four-way switch into the down position, the entire seat lowers (Figure 10-68). Switch wipers 3 and 4 are swung to the left and battery voltage is sent through wiper 4 to wipers 6 and 8. These wipers direct the current to the front and rear height motors. The ground circuit is provided through wipers 5 and 7, to wiper 3 and ground.

Some manufacturers equip their seats with adjustable support mats that shape the seat to fit the driver (Figure 10-69). The lumbar support mat provides the driver with additional comfort by supporting the back curvature. The system uses air that is pumped into the mats.

Figure 10-68 Current flow in the seat lower position.

Insulated side ——————
Ground side ⫴⫴⫴⫴⫴⫴⫴

Power Door Locks

Some manufacturers use a **child safety latch** in the door lock system that prevents the door from being opened from the inside, regardless of the position of the door lock knob. The child safety latch is activated by a switch designed into the latch bellcrank (Figure 10-70).

Electric power locks use either a solenoid or a permanent magnet reversible motor. Due to the high current demands of solenoids, most modern vehicles use PM motors (Figure 10-71).

Shop Manual
Chapter 10,
page 268

Figure 10-69 Adjustable seat cushions increase drive comfort and safety. (Reprinted with the permission of Nissan Motor Corporation in USA)

Figure 10-70 Child safety latch. (Reprinted with the permission of Ford Motor Company)

Figure 10-71 PM power door lock motor. (Courtesy of Chrysler Corporation)

Figure 10-72 Power door lock circuit using a relay.

Depending on circuit design, the system may incorporate a relay (Figure 10-72). The relay has two coils and two sets of contacts to control current direction. In this system the door lock switch energizes one of the door lock relay coils to send battery voltage to the motor. If the door lock switch is placed in the LOCK position, current flow is that shown (Figure 10-73). In the illustration (Figure 10-74), current flows when the door lock switch is placed in the UNLOCK position.

A system that does not use relays is shown (Figure 10-75). The switch provides control of current flow in the same manner as power seats or windows.

Many vehicles are equipped with automatic door locks that are activated when the gear shift lever is placed in the DRIVE position. The doors unlock when the selector is returned to the PARK position.

Some seat back latches use a solenoid to lock the seat unless the door is open. The solenoid is controlled by the door jam switch.

Figure 10-73 Current flow in the LOCK position.

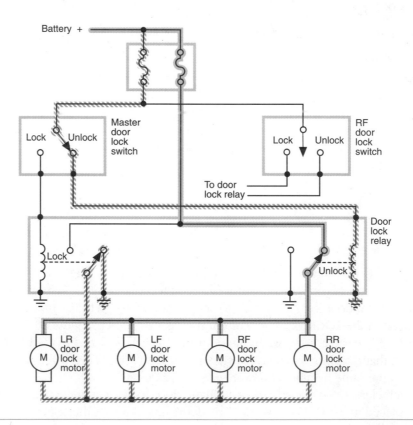

Figure 10-74 Current flow in the UNLOCK position.

Figure 10-75 Electronic door lock circuit diagram. (Courtesy of Chrysler Corporation)

Summary

- ❏ Automotive electrical horns operate on an electromagnetic principle that vibrates a diaphragm to produce a warning signal.
- ❏ Horn switches are either installed in the steering wheel or as a part of the multi function switch. Most horn switches are normally open switches.
- ❏ Horn switches that are mounted on the steering wheel require the use of sliding contacts. The contacts provide continuity for the horn control in all steering wheel positions.
- ❏ The most common type of horn circuit control is to use a relay.
- ❏ Most two-speed windshield wiper motors use permanent magnet fields whereby the motor speed is controlled by the placement of the brushes on the commutator.
- ❏ Some two-speed, and all three-speed wiper motors use two electromagnetic field windings: series field and shunt field. The two field coils are wound in opposite directions so that their magnetic fields will oppose each other. The strength of the total magnetic field will determine what speed the motor will operate.
- ❏ Park contacts are located inside the wiper motor assembly, and supply current to the motor after the switch has been turned to the PARK position. This allows the motor to continue operating until the wipers have reached the PARK position.
- ❏ Intermittent wiper mode provides a variable interval between wiper sweeps and is controlled by a solid-state module.

Terms to Know

Child safety latch

Depressed park

Diaphragm

Electric defoggers

Grid

High-note horn

Horn

Intermittent

Low-note horn

Park contacts

Power mirrors

Power windows

Resistor block

Sector gear

❑ Systems that have a depressed-park feature use a second set of contacts with the park switch, which are used to reverse the rotation of the motor for about 15 degrees after the wipers have reached the normal park position.

❑ Blower fan motors use a resistor block that consists of two or three helically wound wire resistors that are connected in series to control fan speed.

❑ The blower motor circuit includes the control assembly, blower switch, resistor block, and the blower motor.

❑ Electric defoggers heat the rear window by means of a resistor grid.

❑ Electric defoggers may incorporate a timer circuit to prevent the high current required to operate the system from damaging the battery or charging system.

❑ The electrically controlled mirror allows the driver to position the outside mirrors by use of a switch that controls dual drive, reversible PM motors.

❑ Power windows, seats, and door locks usually use reversible PM motors, whereby motor rotational direction is determined by the direction of current flow through the switch wipers.

Review Questions

Short Answer Essays

1. Describe the operation of a relay-controlled horn circuit.

2. Explain how brush placement determines the speed of a two-speed, permanent magnet motor.

3. How do wiper motor systems that use a three-speed, electromagnetic motor control wiper speed?

4. What is the purpose of the capacitor in some intermittent wiper systems?

5. Describe the method used to control blower fan motor speeds.

6. Describe the operation of electric defoggers.

7. Briefly explain the principles of operation for power windows.

8. Describe the operation of a six-way, trimotor power seat.

9. Explain how depressed-park wipers operate.

10. What is the advantage of PM motors over solenoids in the power lock system?

Fill-in-the-Blanks

1. Electrical accessories provide for additional _____ and

   _____ .

2. The _____ is a thin, flexible, circular plate that is held around its

   outer edge by the horn housing, allowing the middle to flex.

3. Horn switches that are mounted on the steering wheel require the use of

   _____ _____ to provide continuity in all steering

   wheel positions.

4. In systems equipped with _____ _____ , the blades drop down below the lower windshield molding to hide them.

5. PM windshield wiper motors use _____ brushes.

6. The operational speed of electromagnetic field winding motors used in wiper systems depends on the strength of the _____ _____ _____ .

7. Most blower motor fan speeds are controlled through a _____ _____ that is wired in series.

8. Electric defoggers operate on the principle that when electrons are forced to flow through a _____ , heat is generated.

9. A window _____ converts the rotary motion of the motor into the vertical movement of the window.

10. The three armature motor is called a _____ .

ASE Style Review Questions

1. The sound generation from the horn is being discussed:
   Technician A says electrical horns operate by the generation of heat to vibrate a diaphragm.
   Technician B says the vibration of the column of air in the horn produces the sound.
   Who is correct?
   A. A only
   B. B only
   C. Both A and B
   D. Neither A nor B

2. The horn circuit is being discussed:
   Technician A says if the circuit does not use a relay, the horn switch carries the total current requirements of the horns.
   Technician B says most systems that use a relay have battery voltage present to the lower contact plate of the horn switch and the switch closes the path for the relay coil.
   Who is correct?
   A. A only
   B. B only
   C. Both A and B
   D. Neither A nor B

3. Permanent magnet wiper motors are being discussed:
   Technician A says motor speed is controlled by the placement of the brushes on the commutator.
   Technician B says the motor uses two electromagnetic fields.
   Who is correct?
   A. A only
   B. B only
   C. Both A and B
   D. Neither A nor B

4. Technician A says if there are more armature windings connected between the common and high speed brushes, there is less magnetism in the armature and a lower counterelectromotive force, thus the motor turns faster.
   Technician B says with less CEMF in the armature, the greater the armature current.
   Who is correct?
   A. A only
   B. B only
   C. Both A and B
   D. Neither A nor B

5. Electromagnetic field wiper motors are being discussed:
   Technician A says the two field coils are wound in opposite directions so that their magnetic fields will oppose each other.
   Technician B says the strength of the total magnetic field will determine the speed of the motor.
   Who is correct?
   A. A only
   B. B only
   C. Both A and B
   D. Neither A nor B

6. Intermittent wiper systems are being discussed:
   Technician A says the system uses a solid-state module or is incorporated into the body computer.
   Technician B says the capacitor operates the wiper motor directly until it is fully discharged.
   Who is correct?
   A. A only
   B. B only
   C. Both A and B
   D. Neither A nor B

7. The blower motor circuit is being discussed:
   Technician A says the motor is usually a permanent magnet, single-speed motor.
   Technician B says the switch position directs current flow to one of the three different brushes in the motor.
   Who is correct?
   A. A only
   B. B only
   C. Both A and B
   D. Neither A nor B

8. *Technician A* says a resistor block that is wired in series between the switch and the motor controls fan speed.
   Technician B says the thermal limiter acts as a circuit breaker to protect the circuit if the resistor block gets too hot.
   Who is correct?
   A. A only
   B. B only
   C. Both A and B
   D. Neither A nor B

9. The electric rear window defogger is being discussed:
   Technician A says the grid is a series of controlled voltage amplifiers.
   Technician B says the system may incorporate a timer circuit to protect the vehicle's electrical system.
   Who is correct?
   A. A only
   B. B only
   C. Both A and B
   D. Neither A nor B

10. *Technician A* says the master control switch for the power windows provides the overall control of the system.
    Technician B says current direction through the power seat motor determines the rotation direction of the motor.
    Who is correct?
    A. A only
    B. B only
    C. Both A and B
    D. Neither A nor B

Introduction to the Body Computer

Upon completion and review of this chapter, you should be able to:

- Describe the principle of analog and digital voltage signals.
- Explain the principle of computer communications.
- Describe the basics of logic gate operation.
- Describe the basic function of the central processing unit (CPU).
- Explain the basic method by which the CPU is able to make determinations.

- List and describe the differences in memory types.
- List and describe the functions of the various sensors used by the computer.
- List and describe the operation of output actuators.
- Explain the principle of multiplexing.

Introduction

This chapter introduces the basic theory and operation of the digital computer used to control many of the vehicle's accessories. The aura of mystery surrounding automotive computers is so great that some technicians are afraid to work on them. Knowledge is key to dispelling this myth. Although it is not necessary to understand all of the concepts of computer operation to service the systems they control, knowledge of the digital computer will make you feel more comfortable when working on these systems.

The use of computers on automobiles has expanded to include control and operation of several functions, including climate control, lighting circuits, cruise control, antilock braking, electronic suspension systems, and electronic shift transmissions. Some of these are functions of what is known as a body computer (BCM). Some body computer-controlled systems include direction lights, rear window defoggers, illuminated entry, intermittent wipers, and other systems once thought of as basic.

A computer processes the physical conditions that represent information (data). The operation of the computer is divided into four basic functions:

1. *Input:* A voltage signal sent from an input device. This device can be a sensor or a button activated by the driver or technician.

2. *Processing:* The computer uses the input information and compares it to programmed instructions. The logic circuits process the input signals into output demands.

3. *Storage:* The program instructions are stored in an electronic memory. Some of the input signals are also stored for later processing.

4. *Output:* After the computer has processed the sensor input and checked its programmed instructions, it will put out control commands to various output devices. These output devices may be the instrument panel display or a system actuator. The output of one computer can also be used as an input to another computer.

Understanding these four functions will help today's technician organize the troubleshooting process. When a system is tested, the technician will be attempting to isolate the problem to one of these functions.

A **computer** is an electronic device that stores and processes data. It is capable of operating other devices.

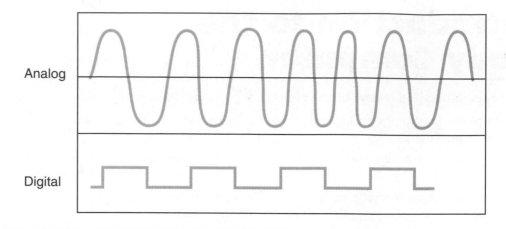

Figure 11-1 Analog voltage signals are constantly variable. Digital voltage patterns are either on or off, high or low; digital signals are referred to as a square wave.

Analog and Digital Principles

Voltage does not flow through a conductor; current flows and voltage is the pressure that "pushes" the current. However, voltage can be used as a signal, for example, difference in voltage levels, frequency of change, or switching from positive to negative values can be used as a signal.

The computer is capable of reading only voltage signals. The programs used by the computer are "burned" into IC chips using a series of numbers. These numbers represent various combinations of voltages that the computer can understand. The voltage signals to the computer can be either analog or digital. Most of the inputs from the sensors are analog variables. For example, ambient temperature sensors do not change abruptly. The temperature varies in infinite steps from low to high. The same is true for several other inputs such as engine speed, vehicle speed, fuel flow, and so on.

Compared to an analog voltage representation, digital voltage patterns are square-shaped because the transition from one voltage level to another is very abrupt (Figure 11-1). A digital signal is produced by an on/off or high/low voltage. The simplest generator of a digital signal is a switch (Figure 11-2). If 5 volts is applied to the circuit, the voltage sensor will read close to 5 volts (a high voltage value) when the switch is open. Closing the switch will result in the voltage sensor reading close to 0 volts. This measuring of voltage drops sends a digital signal to the computer. The voltage values are represented by a series of digits, which create a binary code.

A **program** is a set of instructions the computer must follow to achieve desired results.

Analog means a voltage signal is infinitely variable, or can be changed, within a given range.

Digital means a voltage signal that is one of two states either on-off, yes-no, or high-low.

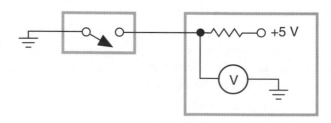

Figure 11-2 Simplified voltage sensing circuit that indicates whether the switch is opened or closed.

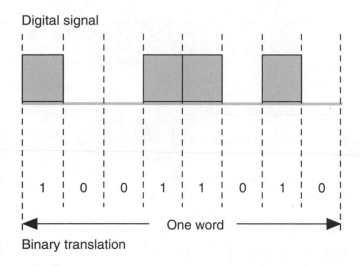

Digital signal

1 | 0 | 0 | 1 | 1 | 0 | 1 | 0

◄——————— One word ———————►

Binary translation

Figure 11-3 Each binary 1 and 0 is one bit of information. Eight bits equal one byte. (Courtesy of General Motors Corporation)

Binary Numbers

A transistor that operates as a relay is the basis of the digital computer. As the input signal switches from off to on, the transistor output switches from cutoff to saturation. The on and off output signals represent the binary digits 1 and 0.

The computer converts the digital signal into binary code by translating voltages above a given value to 1, and voltages below a given value to 0. As shown (Figure 11-3), when the switch is open and 5 volts is sensed, the voltage value is translated into a 1 (high voltage). When the switch is closed, lower voltage is sensed and the voltage value is translated into a 0. Each 1 or 0 represents one bit of information.

In the binary system, whole numbers are grouped from right to left. Because the system uses only two digits, the first portion must equal a 1 or a 0. To write the value of 2, the second position must be used. In binary, the value of 2 would be represented by 10 (one two and zero ones). To continue, a 3 would be represented by 11 (one two and one one). Figure 11-4 illustrates the conversion of binary numbers to digital base ten numbers. If a thermistor is sensing

Binary numbers are represented by the numbers 1 and 0. Any number and word can be translated into a combination of binary 1's and 0's.

Decimal number	Binary number code 8 4 2 1	Binary to decimal conversion
0	0000	= 0 + 0 = 0
1	0001	= 0 + 1 = 1
2	0010	= 2 + 0 = 2
3	0011	= 2 + 1 = 3
4	0100	= 4 + 0 = 4
5	0101	= 4 + 1 = 5
6	0110	= 4 + 2 = 6
7	0111	= 4 + 2 + 1 = 7
8	1000	= 8 + 0 = 8

Figure 11-4 Binary number code conversion to base ten numbers.

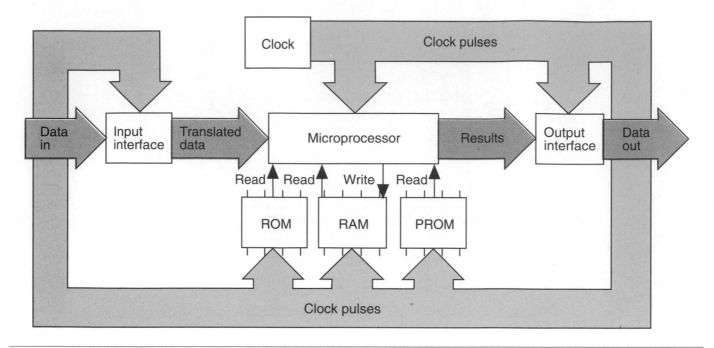

Figure 11-5 Interaction of the main components of the computer. All of the components monitor clock pulses. (Courtesy of General Motors Corporation)

150 degrees, the binary code would be 10010110. If the temperature increases to 151 degrees, the binary code changes to 10010111.

The computer contains a crystal oscillator or clock that delivers a constant time pulse The clock maintains an orderly flow of information through the computer circuits by transmitting one bit of binary code for each pulse (Figure 11-5). In this manner the computer is capable of distinguishing between the binary codes such as 101 and 1001.

Signal Conversion

For the computer to receive information from the sensor, and to give commands to actuators, it requires an interface. The computer will have two interface circuits: input and output. The digital computer cannot accept analog signals from the sensors and requires an input interface to convert the analog signal to digital. Also, some of the controlled actuators may require an analog signal. In this instance, an output digital to analog (D/A) converter is used (Figure 11-6).

Logic Gates

Logic gates are the thousands of field effect transistors (FET) incorporated into the computer circuitry. The FETs use the incoming voltage patterns to determine the pattern of pulses leaving the gate. The following are some of the most common logic gates and their operation. The symbols represent functions and not electronic construction:

1. **NOT gate:** A NOT gate simply reverses binary 1's to 0's and vice versa (Figure 11-7). A high input results in a low output and a low input results in a high output.

The **clock** is a crystal that electrically vibrates when subjected to current at certain voltage levels. As a result, the chip produces very regular series of voltage pulses.

An **interface** is used to protect the computer from excessive voltage levels and to translate input and output signals.

The input interface is used as an analog to digital (A/D) convertor.

Figure 11-6 The interface converts analog inputs into digital signals so the computer can use the voltage signal. Some output actuators require analog signals; the D/A convertor converts the digital commands of the computer into analog voltages. (Courtesy of General Motors Corporation)

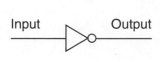

A truth table shows all of the possible outputs from the gate for all possible inputs.

Truth table	
Input	Output
0	1
1	0

Figure 11-7 The NOT gate symbol and truth table. The NOT gate inverts the input signal.

The NOT gate is also called an **inverter**.

Figure 11-8 The AND gate symbol and truth table. The AND gate operates similarly to switches in series.

These circuits are called **logic gates** because they act as gates to output voltage signals depending on different combinations of input signals.

2. **AND gate:** The AND gate will have at least two inputs and one output. The operation of the AND gate is similar to two switches in series to a load (Figure 11-8). The only way the light will turn on is if switches A *and* B are closed. The output of the gate will be high only if both inputs are high. Before current can be present at the output of the gate, current must be present at the base of both transistors (Figure 11-9).

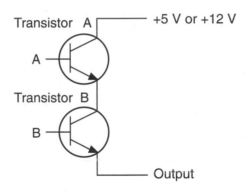

Figure 11-9 The AND gate circuit.

Figure 11-10 OR gate symbol and truth table. The OR gate is similar to parallel switches.

Truth table		
A	B	Output
0	0	1
0	1	1
1	0	1
1	1	0

Truth table		
A	B	Output
0	0	1
0	1	0
1	0	0
1	1	0

Figure 11-11 Symbols and truth tables for NAND and NOR gates. The small circle represents an inverted output on any logic gate symbol.

3. **OR gate:** The OR gate operates similarly to two switches that are wired in parallel to a light (Figure 11-10). If switch A *or* B is closed, the light will turn on. A high signal to either input will result in a high output.

4. **NAND** and **NOR gates:** A NOT gate placed behind an OR or AND gate inverts the output signal (Figure 11-11).

5. **Exclusive-OR (XOR) gate:** A combination of gates that will produce a high output signal only if the inputs are different (Figure 11-12).

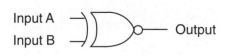

Truth table		
A	B	Output
0	0	0
0	1	1
1	0	1
1	1	0

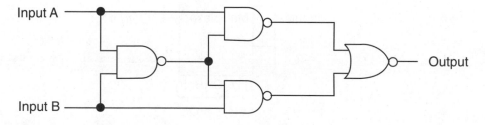

Figure 11-12 XOR gate symbol and truth table. An XOR gate is a combination of NAND and NOR gates.

Figure 11-13 Simplified temperature sensing circuit that will turn on the air conditioning compressor when inside temperatures reach a predetermined value.

These different gates are combined to perform the processing function. The following are some of the most common combinations:

1. **Decoder circuit:** A combination of AND gates used to provide a certain output based on a given combination of inputs (Figure 11-13). When the correct bit pattern is received by the decoder, it will produce the high voltage signal to activate the relay coil.

2. **Multiplexer (MUX):** The basic computer is not capable of looking at all of the inputs at the same time. A multiplexer is used to examine one of many inputs depending on a programmed priority rating (Figure 11-14).

3. **Demultiplexer (DEMUX):** Operates similar to the MUX except that it controls the order of the outputs (Figure 11-15).

4. **RS and clocked RS flip-flop circuits:** Logic circuits that remember previous inputs and do not change their outputs until they receive new input signals. The illlustration (Figure 11-16) shows a basic RS flip-flop circuit. The clocked flip-flop circuit has an inverted clock signal as an input so that circuit operations occur in the proper order (Figure 11-17).

The process that the MUX and DEMUX operate on is called **sequential sampling.** This means the computer will deal with all of the sensors and actuators one at a time.

Flip-flop circuits are called **sequential logic circuits** because the output is determined by the sequence of inputs. A given input affects the output produced by the next input.

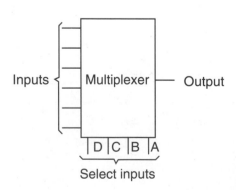

Figure 11-14 Selection at inputs DCBA will determine which data input will be processed.

Figure 11-15 Block diagram representation of the MUX and DEMUX circuit.

(A) (B) (C)

Figure 11-16 (A) RS flip-flop symbol. (B) Truth table. (C) Logic diagram. Variations of the circuit may include NOT gates at the inputs. If used, the truth table outputs would be reversed.

Figure 11-17 Clocked RS flip-flop symbol.

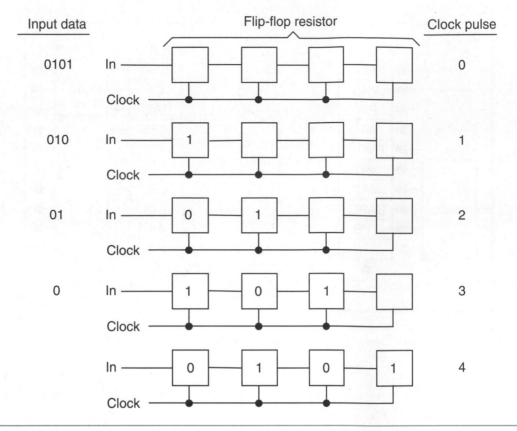

Input data		Flip-flop resistor				Clock pulse
0101	In					0
	Clock					
010	In	1				1
	Clock					
01	In	0	1			2
	Clock					
0	In	1	0	1		3
	Clock					
	In	0	1	0	1	4
	Clock					

Figure 11-18 It takes four clock pulses to load four bits into the register.

5. **Registers:** Used in the computer to temporarily store information. A register is a combination of flip-flops that transfer bits from one to another every time a clock pulse occurs (Figure 11-18).

6. **Accumulators:** Registers designed to store the results of logic operations that can become inputs to other modules.

Central Processing Unit

The terms microprocessor and central processing unit are basically interchangeable.

The central processing unit (CPU) is the brain of the computer. The CPU is constructed of thousands of transistors that are placed on a small chip. The CPU brings information into and out of the computer's memory. The input information is processed in the CPU and checked against the program in memory. The CPU also checks memory for any other information regarding programmed parameters. The information obtained by the CPU can be altered according to the program instructions. The program may have the CPU apply logic decisions to the information. Once all calculations are made, the CPU will deliver commands to make the required corrections or adjustments to the operation of the controlled system.

The CPU has several main components (Figure 11-19). The registers used include the accumulator, the data counter, the program counter, and the instruction register. The control unit implements the instructions located in the instruction register. The arithmetic logic unit (ALU) performs the arithmetic and logic functions.

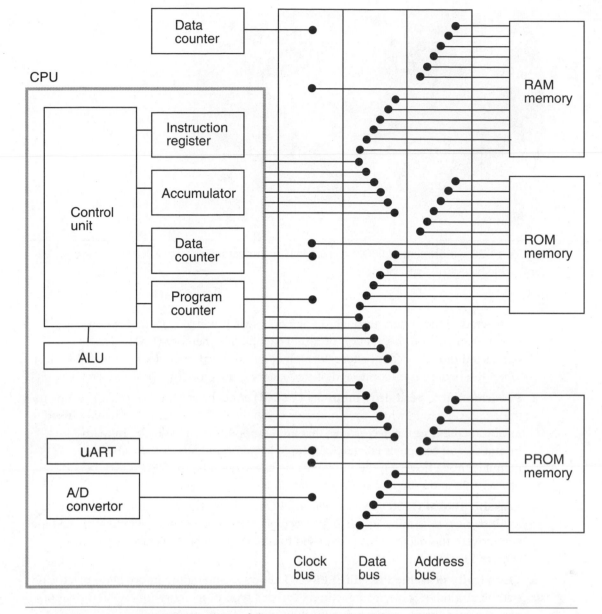

CPU

Figure 11-19 Main components of the computer and the CPU.

Computer Memory

The computer requires a means of storing both permanent and temporary memory. Several types of memory chips are used in the body computer:

1. **Read only memory (ROM)** contains a fixed pattern of 1's and 0's that represent permanent stored information. This information is used to instruct the computer on what to do in response to input data. The CPU reads the information contained in ROM, but it cannot write to it or change it.

2. **Random access memory (RAM)** is constructed from flip-flop circuits formed into the chip. The RAM will store temporary information that can be read from or written to by the CPU. RAM can be designed as volatile or nonvolatile. In volatile RAM, the data will be retained as long as current flows through the memory. RAM that is

The terms ROM, RAM, and PROM are used fairly consistently in the computer industry. However, the names vary between automobile manufacturers.

Figure 11-20 Assortment of PROM chips. Many manufacturers design PROMS that are removable by use of a special tool.

connected to the battery through the ignition switch will lose its data when the switch is turned off. A variation of RAM is keep alive memory (KAM). This is connected directly to the battery through circuit protection devices. KAM will be lost when the battery is disconnected, if the battery drains too low, or if the circuit opens.

3. **Programmable read only memory (PROM)** contains specific data that pertains to the exact vehicle in which the computer is installed. This information may be used to inform the CPU of the accessories that are equipped on the vehicle. In many instances, the computer is interchangeable between models of the same manufacturers; however, the PROM is not. Consequently, the PROM may be replaceable and plug into the computer (Figure 11-20).

4. **Erasable PROM (EPROM)** is similar to PROM except that its contents can be erased to allow new data to be installed. A piece of Mylar tape covers a window. If the tape is removed, the microcircuit is exposed to ultraviolet light that erases its memory (Figure 11-21).

5. **Electrically erasable PROM (EEPROM)** allows changing the information electrically one bit at a time. Some manufacturers use this type of memory to store information concerning mileage, vehicle identification number, and options.

6. **Nonvolatile RAM (NVRAM)** is a combination of RAM and EEPROM into the same chip. During normal operation, data is written to and read from the RAM portion of the chip. If the power is removed from the chip, or at programmed timed intervals, the data is transferred from RAM to the EEPROM portion of the chip. When the power is restored to the chip, the EEPROM will write the data back to the RAM.

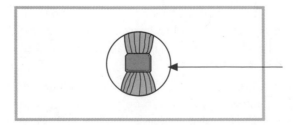

The erasable PROM has a window such as this that the micro-circuitry can be viewed through. This is normally covered by a piece of Mylar™-type material so that the information in it will not be erased by exposing it to ultraviolet light rays.

Figure 11-21 EPROM memory is erased when ultraviolet rays contact the microcircuitry.

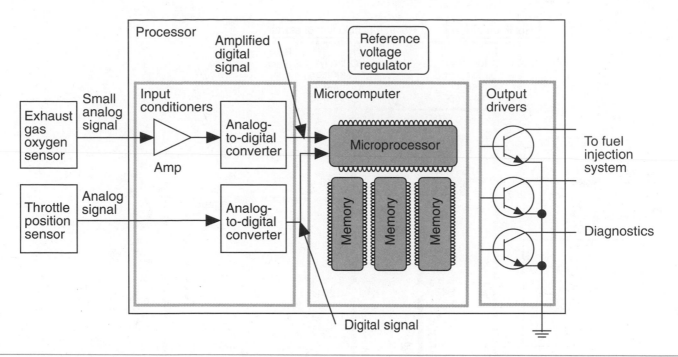

Figure 11-22 The input signals are processed in the microprocessor. The microprocessor directs the output drivers to activate actuators as instructed by the program.

CAUTION: Installing a PROM chip backward will immediately destroy the chip. In addition, **electrostatic discharge (ESD)** will destroy the chip. There are static straps available that will prevent ESD while you are working on the unit.

Inputs

As discussed earlier, the CPU receives inputs that it checks with programmed values. Depending on the input, the computer will control the actuator(s) until the programmed results are obtained (Figure 11-22). The inputs can come from other computers, the driver, the technician, or through a variety of sensors.

Driver input signals are usually provided by momentarily applying a ground through a switch. The computer receives this signal and performs the desired function. For example, if drivers wish to reset the trip odometer on a digital instrument panel, they would push the reset switch. This switch will provide a momentary ground that the computer receives as an input and sets the trip odometer to zero (Figure 11-23).

Switches can be used as an input for any operation that only requires a yes-no, or on-off, condition. Other inputs include those supplied by means of a sensor and those signals returned to the computer in the form of feedback.

Sensors

There are many different designs of sensors. Some are nothing more than a switch that completes the circuit. Others are complex chemical reaction devices that generate their own voltage under different conditions. Repeatability, accuracy, operating range, and linearity are all requirements of a sensor.

Shop Manual
Chapter 11,
page 290

Figure 11-23 The switches in the switch assembly provide driver input to the computer to display the desired information.

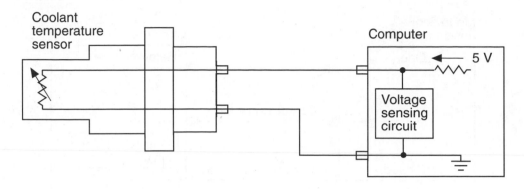

Figure 11-24 A thermistor is used to measure temperature. The sensing unit measures the resistance change and translates the data into temperature values.

Thermistors. A thermistor is used to sense engine coolant or ambient temperatures. By monitoring the thermistor's resistance value, the computer is capable of observing very small changes in temperature. The computer sends a reference voltage to the thermistor (usually 5 volts) through a fixed resistor. As the current flows through the thermistor resistance to ground, a voltage sensing circuit measures the voltage drop (Figure 11-24). Using its programmed values, the computer is able to translate the voltage drop into a temperature value.

Wheatstone Bridges. The illustration (Figure 11-25) shows the construction of the Wheatstone bridge. Usually three of the resistors are kept at exactly the same value and the fourth is the sensing resistor. When all four resistors have the same value, the bridge is balanced and the voltage sensor will indicate a value of 0 volts. If there is a change in the resistance value of the sense resistor, a change will occur in the circuit's balance. The sensing circuit will receive a voltage reading that is proportional to the amount of resistance change. If the Wheatstone bridge is used to measure temperature, temperature changes will be indicated as a change in voltage by the sensing circuit. Wheatstone bridges are also used to measure pressure (piezoresistive) and mechanical strain.

Figure 11-25 Wheatstone bridge.

Mode door position switch

A Open

Wiper

Closed

C

Computer

Reference ← 5 V

B

Voltage sensing circuit

D

Sensor signal →

Ground →

Figure 11-26 A potentiometer sensor circuit measures the amount of voltage drop to determine position.

The **Wheatstone bridge** is a series-parallel arrangement of resistors between an input terminal and ground.

A **potentiometer** is a variable resistor that provides accurate voltage drop readings to the computer.

Shop Manual
Chapter 11,
page 290

Potentiometers. The potentiometer usually consists of a wire wound resistor with a moveable center wiper (Figure 11-26). A constant voltage value (usually 5 volts) is applied to terminal A. If the wiper (which is connected to the shaft or moveable component of the unit that is being monitored) is located close to this terminal, there will be low voltage drop represented by high voltage signal back to the computer through terminal B. As the wiper is moved toward the C terminal, the sensor signal voltage to terminal B decreases. The computer interprets the different voltage value into different shaft positions. The potentiometer can measure linear or rotary movement. As the wiper is moved across the resistor, the position of the unit can be tracked by the computer.

Shop Manual
Chapter 11,
page 292

Magnetic Pulse Generators. Magnetic pulse generators are commonly used to send data to the computer about the speed of the monitored component. This data provides information about vehicle speed and individual wheel speed. The signals from the speed sensors are used for computer-driven instrumentation, cruise control, antilock braking, speed sensitive steering, and automatic ride control systems. The magnetic pulse generator is also used to inform the computer of the position of a monitored component. This is common in engine controls where the computer needs to know the position of the crankshaft in relation to rotational degrees.

Magnetic pulse generators use the principle of magnetic induction to produce a voltage signal.

The magnetic pulse generator is also called a **permanent magnet (PM) generator.**

Alternating current sine wave

+ Voltage

0

− Voltage

Figure 11-27 Pulse signal sine wave.

Figure 11-28 A strong magnetic field is produced in the pick-up coil as the teeth align with the core.

The components of the pulse generator are:

1. A timing disc that is attached to the rotating shaft or cable. The number of teeth on the timing disc is determined by the manufacturer and depends on application. The teeth will cause a voltage generation that is constant per revolution of the shaft. For example, a vehicle speed sensor may be designed to deliver 4,000 pulses per mile. The number of pulses per mile remains constant regardless of speed. The computer calculates how fast the vehicle is going based on the frequency of the signal.

2. A pick-up coil consists of a permanent magnet that is wound around by fine wire.

An air gap is maintained between the timing disc and the pick-up coil. As the timing disc rotates in front of the pick-up coil, the generator sends a pulse signal (Figure 11-27). As a tooth on the timing disc aligns with the core of the pick-up coil, it repels the magnetic field. The magnetic field is forced to flow through the coil and pick-up core (Figure 11-28). When the tooth passes the core, the magnetic field is able to expand (Figure 11-29). This action is repeated every time a tooth passes the core. The moving lines of magnetic force cut across the coil windings and induce a voltage signal.

The **timing disc** is known as an armature, reluctor, trigger wheel, pulse wheel, or timing core. It is used to conduct lines of magnetic force.

The **pick-up coil** is also known as a stator, sensor, or pole piece. It remains stationary while the timing disc rotates in front of it. The changes of magnetic lines of force generate a small voltage signal in the coil.

Figure 11-29 The magnetic field expands (weakens) as the teeth pass the core.

Alternating current sine wave

+ Voltage

0

− Voltage

Figure 11-30 A positive voltage swing is produced as the tooth approaches the core.

When a tooth approaches the core, a positive current is produced as the magnetic field begins to concentrate around the coil (Figure 11-30). When the tooth and core align, there is no more expansion or contraction of the magnetic field (thus no movement) and the voltage drops to zero (Figure 11-31). When the tooth passes the core, the magnetic field expands and a negative current is produced (Figure 11-32). The resulting pulse signal is amplified, digitalized, and sent to the microprocessor.

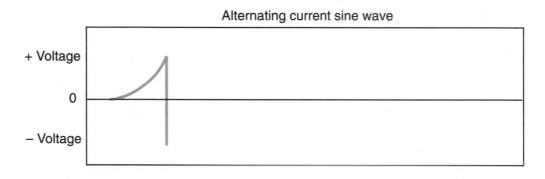

Alternating current sine wave

+ Voltage

0

− Voltage

Figure 11-31 There is no magnetic movement and no voltage when the tooth aligns with the core.

Alternating current sine wave

+ Voltage

0

− Voltage

Figure 11-32 A negative waveform is created as the tooth passes the core.

No magnet
No Hall effect

Increasing magnetism
Increasing Hall voltage

Decreasing magnetism
Decreasing Hall voltage

Figure 11-33 Hall-effect principles of voltage induction.

Hall-Effect Switches. The Hall-effect switch performs the same functions as the magnetic pulse generator. It contains a permanent magnet and a thin semiconductor layer made of gallium arsenate crystal (Hall layer), and a shutter wheel (Figure 11-34). The Hall layer has a negative and a positive terminal connected to it. Two additional terminals located on either side of the Hall layer are used for the output circuit.

The permanent magnet is located directly across from the Hall layer so that its lines of flux will bisect at right angles to the current flow. The permanent magnet is mounted so that a small air gap is between it and the Hall layer.

Shop Manual
Chapter 1,
page 292

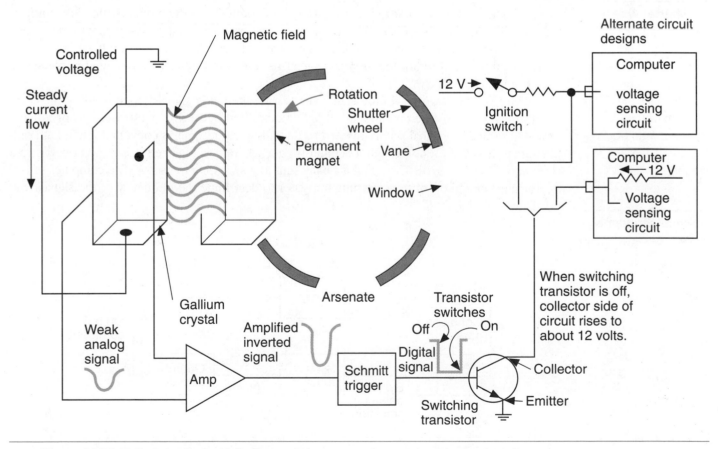

Figure 11-34 Typical circuit of a Hall-effect switch.

U_H = Hall volatage
B = Magnetic field (flux density)
I_V = Constant supply current
A_1, A_2 = Hall layer

Figure 11-35 The magnetic field causes the electrons from the supply current to gather at the Hall layer negative terminal. This creates a voltage potential.

Hall-effect switches operate on the principle that if a current is allowed to flow through thin conducting material that is exposed to a magnetic field, another voltage is produced (Figure 11-33).

The **shutter wheel** consists of a series of alternating windows and vanes. It creates a magnetic shunt that changes the strength of the magnetic field from the permanent magnet.

A **Schmitt trigger** is an A/D convertor.

A steady current is applied to the crystal of the Hall layer. This produces a signal voltage that is perpendicular to the direction of current flow and magnetic flux. The signal voltage produced is a result of the effect the magnetic field has on the electrons. When the magnetic field bisects the supply current flow, the electrons are deflected toward the Hall layer negative terminal (Figure 11-35). This results in a weak voltage potential being produced in the Hall switch.

A shutter wheel is attached to a rotational component. As the wheel rotates, the shutters (vanes) will pass in this air gap. When a shutter vane enters the gap, it intercepts the magnetic field and shields the Hall layer from its lines of force. The electrons in the supply current are no longer disrupted and return to a normal state. This results in low voltage potential in the signal circuit of the Hall switch.

The signal voltage leaves the Hall layer as a weak analog signal. To be used by the computer, the signal must be conditioned. It is first amplified because it is too weak to produce a desirable result. The signal is also inverted so that a low input signal is converted into a high output signal. It is then sent through a Schmitt trigger where it is digitized and conditioned into a clean square wave signal. The signal is finally sent to a switching transistor. The computer senses the turning on and off of the switching transistor to determine the frequency of the signals and calculates speed.

Figure 11-36 Principle of feedback signals.

Feedback Signals

If the computer sends a command signal to open a blend door in an automatic climate control system, a feedback signal may be sent back from the actuator to inform the computer the task was performed. The feedback signal will confirm both the door position and actuator operation (Figure 11-36). Another form of feedback is for the computer to monitor voltage as a switch, relay, or other actuator is activated. Changing states of the actuator will result in a predictable change in the computer's voltage sensing circuit. The computer may set a diagnostic code if it does not receive the correct feedback signal.

Feedback means that data concerning the effects of the computer's commands are fed back to the computer as an input signal.

Outputs

Once the computer's programming instructs that a correction or adjustment must be made in the controlled system, an output signal is sent to an actuator. This involves translating the electronic signals into mechanical motion.

An output driver is used within the computer to control the actuators. The curcuit driver usually applies the ground circuit of the actuator. The ground can be applied steadily if the actuator must be activated for a selected amount of time. For example, if the BCM inputs indicate that the automatic door locks are to be activated, the actuator is energized steadily until the locks are latched. Then the ground is removed.

Other systems require the actuator to either be turned on and off very rapidly or for a set amount of cycles per second. It is duty cycled if it is turned on and off a set amount of cycles per second. Most duty cycled actuators cycle ten times per second. To complete a cycle it must go from off to on to off again. If the cycle rate is ten times per second, one actuator cycle is completed in one tenth of a second. If the actuator is turned on for 30% of each tenth of a second and off for 70%, it is referred to as a 30% duty cycle (Figure 11-37).

Duty cycle is the percentage of on-time to total cycle time.

If the actuator is cycled on and off very rapidly, the pulse width can be varied to provide the programmed results. For example, the computer program will select an illumination level of the digital instrument panel based on the intensity of the ambient light in the vehicle. The illumination level is achieved through pulse width modulation of the lights. If the lights need to be bright, the pulse width is increased, which increases the length of on- time. As the light intensity needs to be reduced, the pulse width is decreased (Figure 11-38).

Pulse width is the length of time in milliseconds that an actuator is energized.

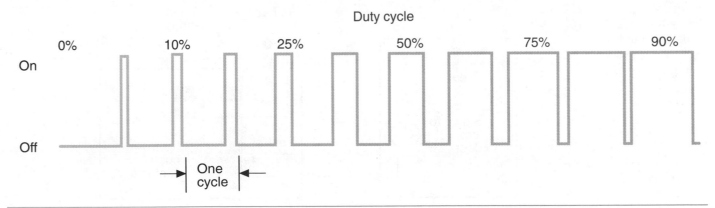

Figure 11-37 Duty cycle is the percentage of on-time per cycle. Duty cycle can be changed. However, total cycle time remains constant.

Figure 11-38 Pulse width is the duration of on time: (A) pulse width modulation to achieve dimmer dash lights, (B) pulse width modulation to achieve brighter dash illumination.

Shop Manual
Chapter 1,
page 290

Actuators perform the actual work commanded by the computer. They can be in the form of a motor, relay, switch, or solenoid.

A **stepper motor** contains a permanent magnet armature with two, four, or more field coils (Figure 11-41).

Actuators

Most computer-controlled actuators are electromechanical devices that convert the output commands from the computer into mechanical action. These actuators are used to open and close switches, control vacuum flow to other components, and operate doors or valves depending on the requirements of the system.

Although they do not fall into the strict definition of an actuator, the BCM can also control lights, gauges, and driver circuits.

Relays. A relay allows control of a high current draw circuit by a very low current draw circuit. The computer usually controls the relay by providing the ground for the relay coil (Figure 11-39). The use of relays protects the computer by keeping the high current from passing through it. For example, the motors used for power door locks require a high current draw to operate them. Instead of having the computer operate the motor directly, it will energize the relay. With the relay energized, a direct circuit from the battery to the motor is completed (Figure 11-40).

Figure 11-39 The computer's output driver applies the ground for the relay coil.

Figure 11-40 The computer controls the operation of the door lock motors by controlling the relays. (Courtesy of Chrysler Corporation)

Figure 11-41 Typical stepper motor.

Figure 11-42 Reversible permanent magnet motor.

Single module engine controller (S.M.E.C.)

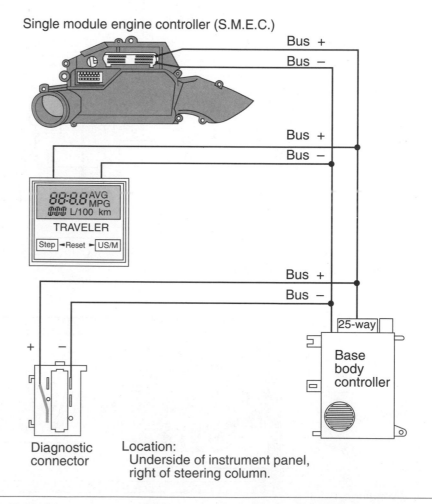

Figure 11-43 Computers use multiplexing to reduce the number of conductors that would be required. (Courtesy of Chrysler Corporation)

Solenoids. Computer control of the solenoid is usually provided by applying the ground through the output driver. A solenoid is commonly used as an actuator because it operates well under duty cycling conditions.

One of the most common uses of the solenoid is to control vacuum to other components. Many automatic climate control systems use vacuum motors to move the blend doors. The computer can control the operation of the doors by controlling the solenoid.

Motors. Many computer-controlled systems use a stepper motor to move the controlled device to whatever location is desired. By applying voltage pulses to selected coils of the motor, the armature will turn a specific number of degrees. When the same voltage pulses are applied to the opposite coils, the armature will rotate the same number of degrees in the opposite direction.

Some applications require the use of a permanent magnet field motor (Figure 11-42). The polarity of the voltage applied to the armature windings determines the direction the motor rotates. The computer can apply a continuous voltage to the armature until the desired result is obtained.

Multiplexing

A multiplex wiring system uses bus data links that connect each module. Each module can transmit and receive digital codes over the bus data links (Figure 11-43). This method allows the modules to share their information. The signal sent from a sensor can go to any of the control modules. And it can be used by any other module (Figure 11-44). This eliminates the need for having conductors exit the sensor and go to each module individually.

A chip is used to prevent the digital codes from overlapping by allowing only one code to be transmitted at a time. Each digital message is proceeded by an identification code that establishes its priority. If two modules attempt to send a message at the same time, the message with a higher priority code is transmitted first.

Summary

❑ A computer is an electronic device that stores and processes data and is capable of operating other devices.

❑ The operation of the computer is divided into four basic functions: input, processing, storage, and output.

❑ Binary numbers are represented by the numbers 1 and 0. A transistor that operates as a relay is the basis of the digital computer. As the input signal switches from off to on, the transistor output switches from cutoff to saturation. The on and off output signals represent the binary digits 1 and 0.

❑ Logic gates are the thousands of field effect transistors that are incorporated into the computer circuitry. The FETs use the incoming voltage patterns to determine the pattern of pulses that leave the gate. The most common logic gates are NOT, AND, OR, NAND, NOR, and XOR gates.

❑ There are several types of memory chips used in the body computer; ROM, RAM, and PROM are the most common types.

❑ ROM (read only memory) contains a fixed pattern of 1's and 0's representing permanent stored information used to instruct the computer on what to do in response to input data.

❑ RAM (random access memory) will store temporary information that can be read from or written to by the CPU.

A **servomotor** produces rotation of less than a full turn. A feedback mechanism is used to position itself to the exact degree of rotation required.

Shop Manual
Chapter 11, page 287

Terms to Know

Actuator

Analog

Binary numbers

Body computer module (BCM)

Central processing unit (CPU)

Computer

Digital

Duty cycle

Feedback

Hall-effect switch

Interface

Linearity

Logic gate

Multiplexing is a system in which electrical signals are transmitted by a peripheral serial bus instead of conventional wires. This allows several devices to share signals on a common conductor.

To reduce the effects of electromagnetic interference, the multiplex wiring system uses a twisted pair design or shielded wires.

Figure 11-44 Any of the input signals to the individual computers can be shared by other computers that may require the information. (Courtesy of Chrysler Corporation)

❏ PROM (programmable read only memory) contains specific data that pertains to the exact vehicle in which the computer is installed.

❏ EPROM (Erasable PROM) is similar to PROM except its contents can be erased to allow new data to be installed.

❏ EEPROM (Electrically erasable PROM) allows changing the information electrically one bit at a time.

❏ NVRAM (Nonvolatile RAM) is a combination of RAM and EEPROM into the same chip.

- Inputs provide the computer with system operation information or driver requests.
- Driver input signals are usually provided by momentarily applying a ground through a switch.
- Switches can be used as an input for any operation that only requires a yes-no, or on-off, condition.
- Sensors convert some measurement of vehicle operation into an electrical signal. There are many different designs of sensors: thermistors, Wheatstone bridge, potentiometers, magnetic pulse generator, and Hall-effect switches.
- A thermistor is a solid-state variable resistor made from a semiconductor material that changes resistance in realtion to temperature changes. Negative temperature coefficient (NTC) thermistors reduce their resistance as the temperature increases. Positive temperature coefficient (PTC) thermistors increase their resistance as the temperature increases.
- The Wheatstone bridge is a series-parallel arrangement of resistors between an input terminal and ground. Usually three of the resistors are kept at exactly the same value while the fourth is the sensing resistor. When all four resistors have the same value, the bridge is balanced and the voltage sensor will indicate a value of 0 volts. If there is a change in the resistance value of the sense resistor, a change will occur in the circuit's balance. The sensing circuit will receive a volatage reading that is proportional to the amount of resistance change.
- A potentiometer is a variable resistor that usually consists of a wire-wound resistor with a moveable center wiper.
- Magnetic pulse generators use the principle of magnetic induction to produce a voltage signal and are commonly used to send data concerning the speed of the monitored component to the computer.
- Hall-effect switches operate on the principle that if a current is allowed to flow through thin conducting material that is exposed to a magnetic field, another voltage is produced.
- Actuators are devices that perform the actual work commanded by the computer. They can be in the form of a motor, relay, switch, or solenoid.
- A servomotor produces rotation of less than a full turn. A feedback mechanism is used to position itself to the exact degree of rotation required.
- A stepper motor contains a permanent magnet armature with two, four, or more field coils. It is used to move the controlled device to whatever location is desired by applying voltage pulses to selected coils of the motor.
- Multiplexing is a system in which electrical signals are transmitted by a peripheral serial bus instead of conventional wires. This allows several devices to share signals on a common conductor.

Terms to Know (continued)

Nonvolatile

Pick-up coil

Positive temperature coefficient (PTC)

Program

PROM

Pulse width

RAM

ROM

Schmitt trigger

Sensor

Servomotor

Stepper motor

Thermistor

Volatile

Review Questions

Short Answer Essays

1. What is binary code?

2. Describe the basics of NOT, AND, and OR logic gate operation.

3. List and describe the four basic functions of the computer.

4. What is the difference between ROM, RAM, and PROM?

5. Explain the principle of multiplexing.

6. How does the Hall-effect switch generate a voltage signal?

7. Describe the basic function of a stepper motor.

8. What is meant by feedback as it relates to computer control?

9. What is the difference between duty cycle and pulse width?

10. What are the purposes of the interface?

Fill-in-the-Blanks

1. In binary code, the number 4 is represented by _____ .

2. The _____ is a crystal that electrically vibrates when subjected to current at certain voltage levels.

3. _____ are registers designed to store the results of logic operations.

4. The _____ _____ _____ is the heart of the computer.

5. _____ contains specific data that pertains to the exact vehicle in which the computer is installed.

6. _____ convert some measurement of vehicle operation into an electrical signal.

7. Negative temperature coefficient (NTC) thermistors _____ their resistance as the temperature increases.

8. _____ switches operate on the principle that if a current is allowed to flow through thin conducting material exposed to a magnetic field, another voltage is produced.

9. Magnetic pulse generators use the principle of _____ _____ to produce a voltage signal.

10. _____ means that data concerning the effects of the computer's commands are fed back to the computer as an input signal.

ASE Style Review Questions

1. *Technician A* says during the processing function the computer uses the input information and compares it to programmed instructions. *Technician B* says during the output function the computer will put out control commands to various output devices.
   Who is correct?
   A. A only
   B. B only
   C. Both A and B
   D. Neither A nor B

2. *Technician A* says analog means the voltage signal is either on-off, yes-no, or high-low. *Technician B* says digital means the voltage signal is infinitely variable within a given range.
   Who is correct?
   A. A only
   B. B only
   C. Both A and B
   D. Neither A nor B

3. Logic gates are being discussed:
   Technician A says NOT gate operation is similar to that of two switches in series to a load. *Technician B* says an AND gate simply reverses binary 1's to 0's and vice versa.
   Who is correct?
   A. A only
   B. B only
   C. Both A and B
   D. Neither A nor B

4. Computer memory is being discussed:
   Technician A says ROM can be written to by the CPU.
   Technician B says RAM will store temporary information that can be read from or written to by the CPU.
   Who is correct?
   A. A only
   B. B only
   C. Both A and B
   D. Neither A nor B

5. *Technician A* says volatile RAM is erased when it is disconnected from its power source. *Technician B* says nonvolatile RAM will retain its memory if removed from its power source.
   Who is correct?
   A. A only
   B. B only
   C. Both A and B
   D. Neither A nor B

6. *Technician A* says EPROM memory is erased if the tape is removed and the microcircuit is exposed to ultraviolet light. *Technician B* says electrostatic discharge will destroy the memory chip.
   Who is correct?
   A. A only
   B. B only
   C. Both A and B
   D. Neither A nor B

7. *Technician A* says negative temperature coefficient thermistors reduce their resistance as the temperature decreases. *Technician B* says positive temperature coefficient thermistors increase their resistance as the temperature increases.
   Who is correct?
   A. A only
   B. B only
   C. Both A and B
   D. Neither A nor B

8. *Technician A* says magnetic pulse generators are commonly used to send data to the computer concerning the speed of the monitored component. *Technician B* says a switch sends a digital signal to the computer.
   Who is correct?
   A. A only
   B. B only
   C. Both A and B
   D. Neither A nor B

9. *Technician A* says the timing disc is stationary and the pick-up coil rotates in front of it. *Technician B* says the number of pulses produced per mile increases as rotational speed increases.
Who is correct?
   A. A only
   B. B only
   C. Both A and B
   D. Neither A nor B

10. *Technician A* says the Hall-effect switch uses a steady supply current to generate a signal. *Technician B* says the switch consists of a permanent magnet wound with a wire coil.
Who is correct?
   A. A only
   B. B only
   C. Both A and B
   D. Neither A nor B

Advanced Lighting Circuits and Electronic Instrumentation

Upon completion and review of this chapter, you should be able to:

❏ Explain the operation of the most common types of automatic headlight dimming systems.

❏ Describe the operation of twilight systems that are body computer controlled.

❏ Explain the use and function of fiber optics.

❏ Describe the different methods used to provide lamp outage indicators.

❏ Describe the operating principles of the digital speedometer.

❏ Explain the operation of IC chip and stepper motor odometers.

❏ Describe the operation of electronic fuel, temperature, oil, and voltmeter gauges.

❏ Explain the use and operation of light emitting diodes, liquid crystal, vacuum fluorescent, and CRT displays in electronic instrument clusters.

❏ Describe the operation of quartz analog instrumentation.

❏ Explain the operation of body computer-controlled instrument panel illumination light dimming.

Advanced Lighting Circuits Introduction

With the addition of solid-state circuitry in the automobile, manufacturers have been able to incorporate several different lighting circuits or modify the existing ones. Some of the refinements that were made to the lighting system include automatic headlight washers, automatic headlight dimming, automatic on/off with timed delay headlights, and illuminated entry systems. Some of these systems use sophisticated body computer-controlled circuitry and fiber optics.

Some manufacturers have included such basic circuits as turn signals into their body computer to provide for pulse width dimming in place of a flasher unit. The body computer can also be used to control instrument panel lighting based on inputs, including if the side marker lights are on or off. By using the body computer to control many of the lighting circuits, the amount of wiring has been reduced. In addition, the use of computer control has provided a means of self-diagnosis in some applications.

Computer-Controlled Concealed Headlights

The body computer has been utilized by some manufacturers to operate the concealed headlight system. The body computer will receive inputs from the headlight and flash-to-pass switches (Figure 12-1). When the headlight switch is turned on, the body computer receives a signal that the headlights are being activated. To open the headlight doors, the computer energizes the open door relay. The contacts of the open relay are closed and battery voltage is applied to the door motor (Figure 12-2). Battery voltage to operate the door motor is supplied from the 30-ampere circuit breaker. The computer energizes the door open relay through circuit L50, which moves the normally open relay contact arm. Ground is provided through the door close relay contact.

Shop Manual
Chapter 12,
page 299

Figure 12-1 Computer-controlled concealed headlight door circuit. (Courtesy of Chrysler Corporation)

Figure 12-2 Concealed headlight door circuit operation with doors opening. (Courtesy of Chrysler Corporation)

Figure 12-3 Concealed headlight door operation circuit with doors closing. (Courtesy of Chrysler Corporation)

When the headlight switch is turned off, the computer energizes the close door relay through circuit L51. With the door close relay energized, the contacts provide battery voltage to the door motor. The ground is supplied through the door open relay (Figure 12-3). Reversing the polarity through the door motor closes the door.

If the flash-to-pass option is activated, the body computer receives a high (on) signal and energizes the door open relay. When the switch is released, the computer receives a low (off) signal and activates the door close relay. The computer delays the activation of the door close relay for 3 seconds.

Automatic Headlight Dimming

Modern automatic headlight dimming systems use solid-state circuitry and electromagnetic relays to control the beam switching. Most systems consist of the following major components:

1. Light sensitive photocell and amplifier unit
2. High-low beam relay
3. Sensitivity control
4. Dimmer switch
5. Flash-to-pass relay
6. Wiring harness

The photocell-amplifier is usually mounted behind the front grill, but ahead of the radiator. The sensitivity control sets the intensity level at which the photocell-amplifier will energize. This control is set by the driver and is located next to, or is a part of, the headlight switch assembly (Figure 12-4). The driver is able to adjust the sensitivity level of the system by rotating the control knob. An increase in the sensitivity level will make the headlights switch to the low beams sooner (approaching vehicle is further away). A decrease in the sensitivity level will switch the headlights to low beams when the approaching vehicle is closer. If the knob is rotated to the full counterclockwise position, the system goes into manual override.

Automatic headlight dimming automatically switches the headlights from high beams to low beams under two different conditions: when light from oncoming vehicles strikes the photocell-amplifier, or light from the taillights of a vehicle being passed strikes the photocell-amplifier.

The **photocell** is like a variable resistor that uses light to change resistance.

The **sensitivity control** is a potentiometer that allows the driver to adjust the sensitivity of the automatic dimmer system to surrounding ambient light conditions.

Figure 12-4 The drive sets the sensitivity of the automatic headlight dimmer system by rotating the potentiometer to change resistance values. (Courtesy of Chilton Book Company)

Figure 12-5 Automatic headlight dimming circuit uses a high-low beam relay to switch beam settings. (Reprinted with the permission of Ford Motor Company)

The high-low relay is a single-pole, double-throw unit that provides the switching of the headlight beams (Figure 12-5). The relay also contains a clamping diode for electrical transient damping to protect the photocell and amplifier assembly.

The dimmer switch is usually a flash-to-pass design. If the turn signal lever is pulled partway up, the flash-to-pass relay is energized. The high beams will stay on as long as the lever is held in this position, even if the headlights are off. In addition, the driver can select either low beams or automatic operation through the dimmer switch.

Although the components are similar in most systems, there are differences in system operations. Systems differ in how the manufacturer uses the relay to do the switching from high beams to low beams. The system can use either an energized relay to activate the high beams or an energized relay to activate the low beams. If the system uses an energized relay to activate the high beams, the relay control circuit is opened when the dimmer switch is placed in the low

Figure 12-6 Automatic headlight dimming circuit with the dimmer switch located in the low beam position. (Reprinted with the permission of Ford Motor Company)

beam position or the driver manually overrides the system (Figure 12-6). With the headlight switch in the ON position and the dimmer switch in the low beam position, battery voltage is applied to the relay coil through circuit 221. The relay coil is not energized because there is no ground provided. The automatic feature is bypassed when the dimmer switch is in the low beam position.

With the dimmer switch in the automatic position, ground is provided for the relay coil through the sensor-amplifier (Figure 12-7). The energized coil closes the relay contacts to the high beams and battery voltage is applied to the headlamps. When the photocell sensor receives enough light to overcome the sensitivity setting, the amplifier opens the relay's circuit to ground. This de-energizes the relay coil and switches battery voltage from high beam to low beam position.

Figure 12-7 Automatic headlight dimming circuit with the dimmer switch located in the automatic position with no oncoming light sensed. (Reprinted with the permission of Ford Motor Company)

If the system uses an energized relay to switch to low beams, placing the dimmer switch in the low beam position will energize the relay (Figure 12-8). With the headlights turned on and the dimmer switch in the automatic position, battery voltage is applied to the photocell-amplifier, one terminal of the high-low control, and through the relay contacts to the high beams. The voltage drop through the high-low control is an input to the photocell-amplifier. When enough light strikes the photocell-amplifier to overcome the sensitivity setting, the amplifier allows battery current to flow through the high-low relay closing the contact points to the low beams. Once the light has passed, the photocell-amplifier opens battery voltage to the relay coil and the contacts close to the high beams.

When flash-to-pass is activated, the switch closes to ground. This bypasses the sensitivity control and de-energizes the relay to switch from low beams to high beams.

Figure 12-8 System that uses an energized relay to switch to low beams. (Reprinted with the permission of Ford Motor Company)

Automatic On/Off
with Time Delay

This system is given
several different
names by the various
manufacturers.
Some of the more
common names
include: Twilight
Sentinel, Auto-
lamp/Delayed Exit,
and Safeguard
Sentinel.

The common components of the automatic on/off with time delay include:

1. Photocell and amplifier

2. Power relay

3. Timer control

In a typical system, a photocell is located inside the vehicle's dash to sense outside light (Figure 12-9). In most systems, the headlight switch must be in the OFF position to activate the automatic mode (Figure 12-10). Battery voltage is applied to the normally open headlight contacts of the relay through the headlight switch. Battery voltage is also supplied to the normally open exterior light contacts through the fuse panel (Figure 12-11).

To activate the automatic on/off feature, the photocell and amplifier must receive voltage from the ignition switch (circuit 640). As the ambient light level decreases, the internal resistance of the photocell increases. When the resistance value reaches a predetermined value, the photocell and amplifier trigger the sensor-amplifier module. The sensor-amplifier module energizes the relay, turning on the headlights and exterior parking lights (Figure 12-12).

Figure 12-9 Most automatic on/off headlight systems have the photocell located in the dash to sense incoming light levels. (Courtesy of General Motors Corporation)

Figure 12-10 Schematic of automatic headlight on/off with time delay system.

Figure 12-11 Current flow in automatic mode with the headlights off.

The **automatic on/off with time delay** has two functions: to turn on the headlights automatically when ambient light decreases to a predetermined level and to allow the headlights to remain on for a certain amount of time after the vehicle has been turned off. This system can be used in combination with automatic dimming systems.

The **timer control** is a potentiometer that is a part of the headlight switch in most systems. The timer control unit controls the automatic operation of the system and the length of time that the headlights stay on after the ignition switch is turned off.

The Twilight Sentinel System is overridden when the delay control switch is in the OFF position. The delay control switch is located on the left switch panel.

Figure 12-12 Current flow in the automatic mode with the headlights on.

Some systems provide a time delay feature that allows drivers to set a timer circuit to control how long the headlights remain on after they leave the vehicle. The control is a potentiometer that signals the sensor-amplifier module to energize the relay for the requested amount of time.

If the headlights are on when the ignition switch is turned off, the photocell and amplifier's voltage from circuit 640 is opened. This activates a timer circuit in the amplifier. The amplifier still receives battery voltage from the headlight switch, and uses this voltage to keep the relay energized for the requested time interval. When the preset length of time has passed, the amplifier module removes power to the relay and the headlights (and exterior lights) turn off.

The driver can override the automatic on/off feature by placing the headlight switch in the ON position. This bypasses the relay and sends battery voltage directly to the headlight circuit (Figure 12-13).

Depending on model application, General Motors' Twilight Sentinel System can use the body computer to control system operation (Figure 12-14). The body computer module (BCM) senses the voltage drop across the photocell and the delay control switch. The delay control switch resistance is wired in series with the photocell. If the ambient light level drops below a specific value, the BCM grounds the headlamp and parklamp relay coils. The BCM also keeps the headlights on for a specific length of time after the ignition switch is turned off.

Figure 12-13 Current flow with the automatic headlight control bypassed.

Illuminated Entry Systems

Most modern illuminated entry systems incorporate solid-state circuitry that includes an illuminated entry actuator and side door switches in the door handles. Illumination of the door lock tumblers can be provided by the use of fiber optics or light emitting diodes.

When either of the front door handles are lifted a switch in the handle will close the ground path from the actuator. This signals the logic module to energize the relay (Figure 12-15). With the relay energized, the contacts close and the interior and door lock lights come on. A timer circuit is incorporated that will turn off the lights after 25 to 30 seconds. If the ignition switch is placed in the RUN position before the timer circuit turns off the interior lights, the timer sequence is interrupted and the interior lights turn off.

Some manufacturers have incorporated the illuminated entry actuator into their body computer (Figure 12-17). Activation of the system is identical as discussed. The signal from the door handle switch can also be used as a "wake-up" signal to the body computer.

The signal from the door handle switch informs the body computer to activate the courtesy light relay control circuit. Some systems use a pair of door jam switches that signal the body computer to keep the courtesy lights on when the door is open. When the door is closed and the ignition switch is in the RUN position, the lights are turned off.

Some manufacturers use the twilight photocell to inform the body computer of ambient light conditions. If the ambient light is bright, the photocell signals the body computer that courtesy lights are not required.

Shop Manual
Chapter 12,
page 30

The **illuminated entry system** turns on the courtesy lights before opening the doors.

A **wake-up signal** is used to notify the body computer that an engine start and operation of accessories is going to be initiated soon. This signal is used to warm up the circuits that will be processing information (Figure 12-16).

Figure 12-14 Some General Motors' Twilight Sentinel systems use the BCM to sense inputs from the photocell and delay control switch. (Courtesy of Chilton Book Company)

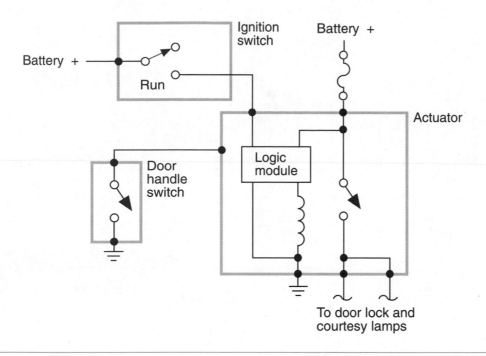

Figure 12-15 Illuminated entry actuator circuit.

Figure 12-16 The illuminated entry system can also send a wake-up signal to the body computer. (Courtesy of Chilton Book Company)

Figure 12-17 Body computer control of the illuminated entry system. (Courtesy of Chrysler Corporation)

Figure 12-18 The dimming control and photocell are inputs to the BCM to control instrument panel dimming. (Courtesy of General Motors Company)

In the computer-controlled **instrument panel dimming** system, the headlight switch dimming control is used as an input to the computer instead of having direct control of the illumination lights.

Shop Manual
Chapter 12, page 315

Fiber optics is the transmission of light through polymethylmethacrylate plastic that keeps the light rays parallel even if extreme bends are in the plastic.

Instrument Panel Dimming

The body computer uses inputs from the panel dimming control and photocell to determine the illumination level of the instrument panel lights (Figure 12-18). With the ignition switch in the RUN position, a 5-volt signal is supplied to the panel dimming control potentiometer. The wiper of the potentiometer returns the signal to the body computer.

When the dimmer control is moved toward the dimmer positions, the increased resistance results in a decreased voltage signal to the body computer. By measuring the voltage that is returned, the body computer is able to determine the resistance value of the potentiometer. The body computer controls the intensity level of the illumination lamps by pulse width modulation.

Fiber Optics

The invention of fiber optics has provided a means of providing illumination of several objects by a single light source (Figure 12-19). Plastic fiber optic strands are used to transmit light from the source to the object to be illuminated. The strands of plastic are sheathed by a polymer that insulates the light rays as they travel within the strands. The light rays travel through the strands by means of internal reflections.

Fiber optics are commonly used as indicator lights to show the driver that certain lights are functioning. Many vehicles with fender-mounted turn signal indicators use fiber optics from the turn signal light to the indicator (Figure 12-20). The indicator will only show light if the turn signal light is on and working properly.

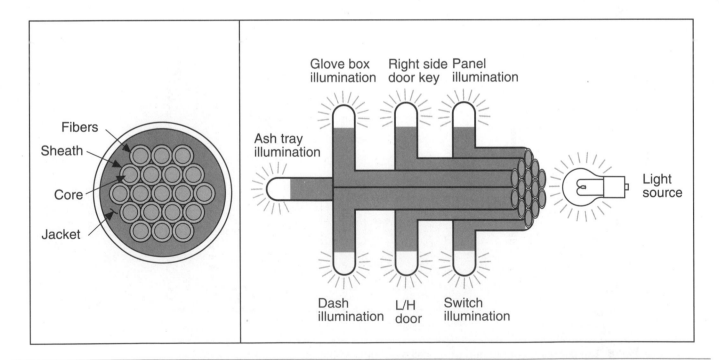

Figure 12-19 One light source can illuminate several areas by using fiber optics.

Fiber-optic conductors

Housing

Readout

Gasket

Hexnut

Seal

Figure 12-20 Fiber optics can be used to indicate the operation of exterior lights to the driver. (Courtesy of General Motors Corporation)

Some manufacturers use fiber optics to provide illumination of the lock cylinder "halo" during illuminated entry operation (Figure 12-21). When the illuminated entry system is activated, the light collector provides the source light to the fiber optics and the halo lens receives the light from the fiber optic cable.

The advantage of fiber optics is it can be used to provide light in areas where bulbs would be inaccessible for service. Other uses of fiber optics include:

- Lighting ash trays
- Illuminating instrument panels
- Dash lighting over switches

Some manufacturers send battery voltage to the dimming rheostat, which uses the voltage to the BCM as an input for illumination level. An input of approximately 1 volt indicates a request for high illumination level; higher voltage level inputs indicate less intensity.

Figure 12-21 Fiber optics used in an illuminated entry system. (Courtesy of Chrysler Corporation)

Figure 12-22 Most vehicle information systems may use a graphic display to indicate warning areas to the driver. (Courtesy of General Motors Corporation)

Lamp Outage Indicators

The most common lamp outage indicator uses a translucent drawing of the vehicle (Figure 12-22). If one of the monitored systems fails, or is in need of driver attention, the graphic display illuminates a light to indicate the location of the problem.

The basic lamp outage indicator system is used to monitor the stop light circuit. This system consists of a reed switch and opposing electromagnetic coils (Figure 12-23). When the ignition

Opposing magnetic fields are created because the coils are wound in opposite directions.

Figure 12-23 Stop light lamp outage indicator circuit. (Courtesy of General Motors Corporation)

switch is turned to the RUN position, battery voltage is applied to the normally open reed switch. When the brake light switch is closed, current flows through the coils on the way to the stop light bulbs. If both bulbs are operating properly, the coils create opposing magnetic fields that keep the reed switch in the open position. If one of the stop light bulbs burns out, current will only flow through one of the coils which attracts the reed switch contacts and closes them. This completes the stop light warning circuit and illuminates the warning light on the dash. The warning light will remain on as long as the stop light switch is closed.

The lamp outage module can be used alone or in conjunction with the vehicle's body computer. If the module is a "stand-alone" unit, it will operate the warning light directly. The module monitors the voltage drop of the resistors. If the circuits are operating properly, there is a 0.5-volt input signal to the module. If one of the monitored bulbs burns out, the voltage input signal drops to about 0.25 volt. The module completes the ground circuit to the warning light to alert the driver that a bulb has burned out. The module is capable of monitoring several different light circuits.

Figure 12-24 The computer-driven vehicle information center keeps the driver aware of the condition of monitored systems. (Courtesy of General Motors Corporation)

Many vehicles today use a computer-driven information center to keep the driver informed of the condition of monitored circuits (Figure 12-24). The vehicle information center usually receives its signals from the vehicle's body computer circuit (Figure 12-25). In this system the lamp outage module is used to send signals to the body computer (Figure 12-26). The body computer will either illuminate a warning light, give a digital message, or activate a voice warning device to alert the driver that a light bulb is burned out.

A burned out light bulb means there is a loss of current flow in one of the resistors of the lamp outage module. A monitoring chip in the module compares the voltage drop across the resistor (Figure 12-27). If there is no voltage drop across the resistor, there is an open in the circuit (burned out light bulb). When the chip measures no voltage drop across the resistor, it signals the body computer, which then gives the necessary message to the vehicle information center (Figure 12-28).

A **lamp outage module** is a current measuring sensor that contains a set of resistors, wired in series with the power supply to the headlights, taillights, and stop lights.

The bulbs are monitored only when current is supplied to them.

Figure 12-25 The body computer can be used to receive signals from various inputs and to give signals to control the information center. (Courtesy of Chrysler Corporation)

Figure 12-26 Lamp outage module. (Courtesy of Chrysler Corporation)

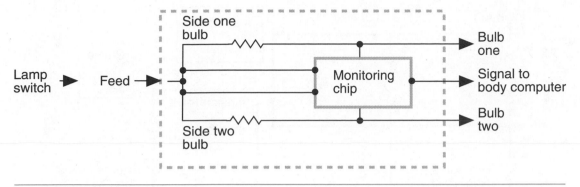

Figure 12-27 One section of the lamp outage module circuit. The monitoring chip compares voltage on both sides of the resistors to measure voltage drop changes. (Courtesy of Chrysler Corporation)

Figure 12-28 Lamp outage indicator circuit. (Courtesy of Chrysler Corporation)

Figure 12-29 Lamp monitor module circuit.

General Motors uses the lamp monitor module to connect the light circuits to ground (Figure 12-29). When the circuits are operating properly, the ground connection in the module causes a low circuit voltage. Input from the lamp circuits are through two equal resistance wires. The module output to the bulbs is from the same module terminals as the inputs.

If a bulb burns out, the voltage at the lamp monitor module terminal will increase. The module will open the appropriate circuit from the BCM, signaling the BCM to send a communication to the IPC computer, which displays the massage in the information center.

Electronic Instrumentation Introduction

Computer-driven instruments are becoming increasingly popular on today's vehicle. These instruments provide far more accurate readings than their conventional analog counterparts. Today's technician will be required to service these systems on a more frequent basis as they grow in popularity. This section introduces you to the most commonly used computer-driven instrumentation systems. These systems include the speedometer, odometer, fuel, oil, and temperature gauges.

The computer-driven instrument panel uses a microprocessor to process information from various sensors and to control the gauge display. Depending on the manufacturer, the

Figure 12-30 Inputs and outputs of the electronic instrument panel. (Courtesy of Chrysler Corporation)

microprocessor can be a separate computer that receives direct information from the sensors and makes the calculations, or it may use the body computer to perform all functions. The illustration (Figure 12-30) shows the different inputs and outputs to the computer-driven instrument panel. The computer may control a digital instrument or an analog cluster.

In addition, there are many types of information systems used today. These systems are used to keep the driver informed of a variety of monitored conditions, including vehicle maintenance, trip information, and navigation.

Digital Instrumentation

Digital instrumentation is far more precise than conventional analog gauges. Analog gauges display an average of the readings received from the sensor; a digital display will present exact readings. In some systems the information to the gauge is updated as often as 16 times per second.

Most digital instrument panels provide for display in English or metric values. Also, many gauges are a part of a multigauge system. Drivers select which gauges they wish to have displayed. Most of these systems will automatically display the gauge to indicate a potentially dangerous situation. For example, if the driver has chosen the oil pressure gauge to be displayed and the engine temperature increases above set limits, the temperature gauge will automatically be displayed to warn the driver. A warning light and/or a chime will also activate to get the driver's attention.

Most electronic instrument panels have self-diagnostic capablities. The tests are initiated through a scan tool or by pushing selected buttons on the instrument panel. The instrument panel cluster also initiates a self-test every time the ignition switch is turned to ACC or RUN.

Shop Manual
Chapter 12,
page 315

Digital instrument clusters use digital and linear displays to notify the drive of monitored system conditions
(Figure 12-31).

International Standards Organization (ISO) symbols are used to represent the gauge function
(Figure 12-32).

Figure 12-31 Digital instrument cluster. (Courtesy of Chrysler Corporation)

Iso symbols

Figure 12-32 A few of the ISO symbols used to identify the gauge. (Courtesy of Chrysler Corporation)

Usually the entire dash is illuminated and every segment of the display is lighted. ISO symbols generally flash during this test. At the completion of the test, all gauges will display current readings. A code is displayed to alert the driver if a fault is found.

Speedometers

Shop Manual
Chapter 12,
page 321

The electronic speedometer receives voltage signals from the vehicle speed sensor (VSS). This sensor can be a PM generator, Hall-effect switch, or an optical sensor.

Ford, GM, and Toyota have used optical vehicle speed sensors. The Ford and Toyota optical sensors are operated from the conventional speedometer cable. The cable rotates a slotted wheel between an LED and a phototransistor (Figure 12-33). As the slots in the wheel break the light, the transistor conducts an electronic pulse signal to the speedometer. An integrated circuit rectifies the analog input signal from the optical sensor and counts the pulses per second. The value is calculated into mph and displayed in the digital readout. The display is updated every 1/2 second. If the driver selected the readout to be in kilometers per hour, the computer makes an additional calculation to convert the readout. These systems may use a conventional gear-driven odometer.

The early style of GM speed sensor also operated from the conventional speedometer cable (Figure 12-34). The LED directs its light onto the back of the speedometer cup. The cup is painted black, and the drive magnet has a reflective surface applied to it. As the drive magnet rotates in front of the LED, its light is reflected back to a phototransistor. A small voltage is created every time the phototransistor is hit with the reflective light.

The illustration (Figure 12-35) is a schematic of an instrument panel cluster that uses a PM generator for the VSS. As the PM generator is rotated, it causes a small AC voltage to be induced in its coil. This AC voltage signal is sent to the engine control module (ECM) and is shared with the body computer module (BCM). The signal is rectified into a digital signal that is

Figure 12-33 Optical speed sensor. (Courtesy of Chilton Book Company)

Figure 12-34 Optical vehicle speed sensor. (Courtesy of General Motors Corporation)

Figure 12-35 The instrument panel cluster module receives its instructions from the BCM, which shares the signals from the VSS with the ECM. (Courtesy of General Motors Corporation)

All display segments
go on and off

Figure 12-36 During the first portion of the self-test all segments of the speedometer display are lighted.

used to control the output to the instrument panel cluster (IPC) module. The body computer calculates the vehicle speed and provides this information to the IPC module through the serial data link. The IPC module turns on the proper display.

The microprocessor will initiate a self-check of the electronic instrument cluster anytime the ignition switch is placed in the ACC or RUN position. The self-check usually runs for about 3 seconds. The most common sequence for the self-check is as follows:

1. All display segments are illuminated (Figure 12-36).
2. All displays go blank.
3. 0 mph or 0 km/h is displayed (Figure 12-37).

Odometers

If the speedometer uses an optical sensor, the odometer may be of conventional design. Two other types of odometer are used with electronic displays: the electromechanical type with a stepper motor, and the electronic design using an IC chip.

Stepper Motor. The electromechanical odometer uses a DC stepper motor that receives control signals from the speedometer circuit (Figure 12-38). The digital signal impulses from the speedometer are processed through a circuit that will halve the signal. The stepper motor receives one-half of the VSS signals sent to the instrument panel cluster. As the stepper motor is activated, the rollers are rotated to accurately display accumulated mileage.

Shop Manual
Chapter 12,
page 323

A **stepper motor** moves in incremental steps between no voltage to full voltage positions.

Speed is displayed
in MPH or Km/H

Figure 12-37 At the completion of the self-test the current speed is indicated.

Figure 12-38 Stepper motor used to rotate the odometer dial.

Figure 12-39 The stepper motor receives its control signals through the speedometer circuit. (Courtesy of General Motors Corporation)

General Motors controls the stepper motor through the same impulses that are sent to the speedometer (Figure 12-39). The stepper motor uses these signals to turn the odometer drive IC on and off. An H-gate arrangement of transistors is used to drive the stepper motor by alternately activating a pair of its coils (Figure 12-40). The H-gate is constantly reversing system polarity, causing the permanent magnet poles to rotate in the same direction.

An **H-gate** is a set of four transistors that reverse current to the motor windings to keep the motor rotating in one direction.

Figure 12-40 The **H-gate** energizes two coils at a time and constantly reverses system polarity.

Figure 12-41 The trip reset button provides a ground signal to the logic circuit, which is programmed to erase the trip odometer memory while retaining total accumulated mileage in the odometer.

Tool C-4817

Cluster

Odometer memory chip

Figure 12-42 Removing the odometer memory chip. (Courtesy of Chrysler Corporation)

IC Chip. The IC chip-type odometer uses a nonvolatile RAM that receives distance information from the speedometer circuit or from the engine controller. The controller can update the odometer display every 1/2 second.

Many instrument panel clusters cannot display both trip mileage and odometer readings at the same time. Drivers must select which function they wish to have displayed (Figure 12-41). By depressing the trip reset button, a ground is applied as an input to the microprocessor. The microprocessor clears the trip odometer readings from memory and returns the display to zero. The trip odometer will continue to store trip mileage even if this function is not selected for display.

If the IC chip fails, some manufacturers provide for replacement of the chip (Figure 12-42). Depending on the manufacturer, the new chip may be programmed to display the last odometer reading. Most replacement chips will display an X, S, or * to indicate the odometer has been changed. It is impossible to "turn back" an IC odometer. If the odometer IC chip cannot be programmed to display correct accumulated mileage, a door sticker must be installed to indicate the odometer has been replaced. IC odometer reading corrections or changes can only be performed in the first 10 miles of operation.

If an error occurs in the odometer circuit, the display will change to notify the driver. The form of error message differs between manufacturers. The illustration (Figure 12-43) shows one method that Ford uses.

In most systems distance is updated to the RAM every 10 miles and whenever the ignition switch is turned off.

Federal Motor Vehicle Safety Standards require the odometer be capable of storing up to 500,000 miles in nonvolatile memory. Most odometer readouts are up to 199,999.9 miles.

Miles

Figure 12-43 Error message alerts the driver that the odometer function is not operating properly.

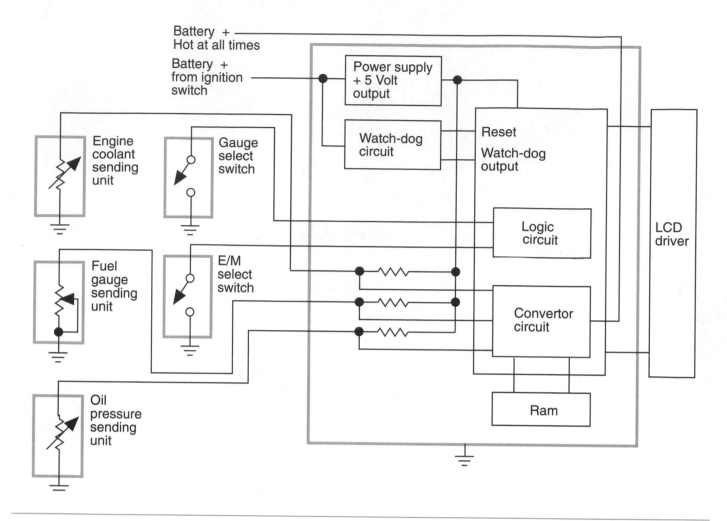

Figure 12-44 Multigauge schematic with tachometer function.

Tachometers

The tachometer can be a separate function that is displayed at all times, or a part of a multigauge display. Ford uses a multigauge that sequentially changes the gauge between four different gauges (Figure 12-44). The tachometer receives its voltage signals from the ignition system and displays the readout in a bar graph. The Ford multigauge has a built in power supply that provides a 5-volt reference signal to the other monitored systems for the gauge. Also, the gauge has a "watchdog" circuit incorporated in it.

General Motors uses the signal from the direct ignition system (DIS) module to the ECM. The signal is sent from the ECM to the BCM on the serial data link. The IPC does not receive this signal directly, but it eavesdrops on the data link communications (Figure 12-45). The IPC uses this reference signal to calculate and display the tachometer reading.

Electronic Fuel Gauges

Most digital fuel gauges use a fuel level sender that decreases resistance value as the fuel level decreases. This resistance value is converted to voltage values by the microprocessor. A voltage-controlled oscillator changes the signal into a cycles-per-second signal. The microprocessor counts the cycles and sends the appropriate signal to operate the digital display (Figure 12-46).

An *F* is displayed when the tank is full and an *E* is displayed when less than 1 gallon is remaining in the tank. Other warning signals include incandescent lamps, a symbol on the dash,

The **power on/off watchdog circuit** supplies a reset voltage to the microprocessor in the event that pulsating output signals from the microprocessor are interrupted.

An **oscillator** creates a rapid back-and-forth movement of voltage.

Figure 12-45 The IPC "listens in" on the communications between the ECM and the BCM to gather information on engine speed.

Figure 12-46 Digital fuel gauge displays remaining fuel in gallons or liters. (Reprinted with the permission of Ford Motor Company)

or flashing of the fuel ISO symbol. If the warning is displayed by a bulb, usually a switch is located in the sender unit that closes the circuit. Flashing digital displays are usually controlled by the microprocessor.

▲ **WARNING:** Not all sending units used for bar graph and digital displays are the same. Some sending units used for bar graph displays increase resistance as the fuel level is decreased.

The bar graph-style gauge uses segments that represent the amount of fuel remaining in the tank (Figure 12-47). The segments divide the tank into equal levels. The display will also include the F, 1/2, and E symbols along with the ISO fuel symbol. A warning to the driver is displayed when only one bar is lit. The gauge will also alert the driver to problems in the circuit. A common method of indicating an open or short is to flash the F, 1/2, and E symbols while the gauge reads empty.

Figure 12-47 Bar graph-style of electonic instrumentation. Each segment represents a different value. (Courtesy of Chrysler Corporation).

Shop Manual
Chapter 12,
page 325

Other Digital Gauges

Most of the gauges used to display temperature, oil pressure, and charging voltage are of bar graph design. Another popular method is to use a floating pointer (Figure 12-48).

The temperature gauge will usually receive its input from an NTC thermistor. When the engine is cold, the resistance value of the thermistor is high, resulting in a low voltage input to the microprocessor. This input signal is translated into a low temperature reading on the gauge. As the engine coolant warms, the resistance value drops. At a predetermined resistance level, the microprocessor will activate an alert function to warn the driver of excessive engine temperature.

The voltmeter calculates charging voltage by comparing the voltage supplied to the instrument panel module to a reference voltage signal. The oil pressure gauge uses a piezoresistive sensor that operates like those used for conventional analog gauges.

Digital gauges perform self-tests. If a fault is found, a warning signal will be displayed to the driver. A "CO" indicates the circuit is open, a "CS" indicates the circuit is shorted. The gauge will continue to display these messages until the problem is corrected.

Digital Displays

The display can be by means of four different methods: Light emitting diodes (LEDs), liquid crystal display (LCDs), vacuum fluorescent display (VFD), and cathode ray tube (CRT).

Figure 12-48 Floating pointer indicates the value received from the sensor. (Courtesy of Chrysler Corporation)

LED Digital Displays

When first used in the instrument panel, the LED would indicate an on/off status. Chrysler used the LED in conjunction with its gauges to alert the driver of conditions requiring immediate attention. Some manufacturers are using LEDs in bar graph displays (Figure 12-49). Also, the LEDs can be combined to display alphanumeric characters. There are two common methods of using the LED for digital display: (1) seven-segment display (Figure 12-50), and (2) dot matrix display (Figure 12-51).

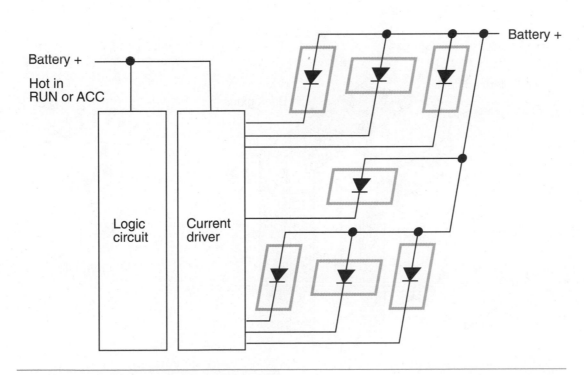

Figure 12-49 LEDs arranged to create a bar graph display.

Figure 12-50 Seven-segment display panel.

Figure 12-51 Dot matrix display panel.

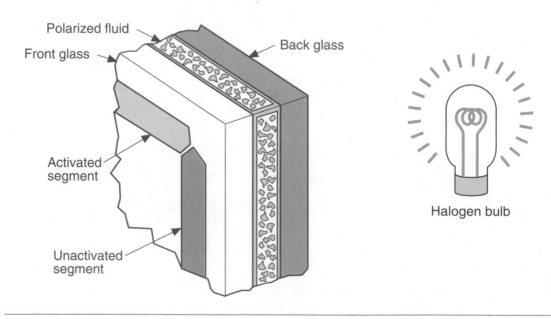

Figure 12-52 LCDs use external light through a polarized fluid.

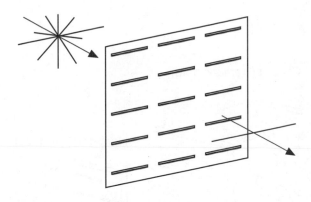

Figure 12-53 The polarizer makes the light waves vibrate in only one direction.

By activating selected segments or dots, any number or letter can be displayed. LEDs generally are designed to produce a red, green, or yellow light. They work very well in low light conditions. However, they are difficult to see in bright light. Although some manufacturers use LED readout instrument panels, their use is limited due to their comparatively high power requirements.

Liquid Crystal Displays

Liquid crystal displays (LCDs) require an external light source because they do not generate their own (Figure 12-52). The external light source can be supplied by either daylight or by an artificial light. In daylight the segments are activated from the front; the artificial light activates the LCD from the back. The artificial light can be controlled by the headlight switch or turned on whenever the ignition switch is placed in the RUN or ACC position.

The LCD construction consists of a nematic fluid that is sandwiched between two polarized glass sheets (Figure 12-54). The front polarizer is a vertical polarizer and the rear polarizer is a horizontal polarizer. The display is viewed through the vertical polarizer. The nematic fluid's molecules are arranged in such a manner that they rotate the light from the vertical polarizer 90 degrees (Figure 12-55). The light leaves the fluid in a horizontal waveform. The light continues to pass through the horizontal polarizer to the reflector. The light is then reflected back

The **nematic** fluid is a liquid crystal that has a threadlike form. It has light slots that can be rearranged by applying small amounts of voltage.

The **polarizers** make light waves vibrate in only one direction. Light is composed of waves that vibrate in several different directions. The polarizer converts the light into polarized light (Figure 12-53).

Front polarization

Front glass

Back glass

Rear polarization

Reflector

Figure 12-54 LCD construction.

Figure 12-55 The nematic fluid rotates the polarized light wave 90 degrees.

through the horizontal polarizer to the fluid. The fluid once again rotates the light wave into a vertical position and out the vertical polarizer. When light passes through the LCD in this manner, the display appears light and no pattern is seen.

When a small square wave voltage is applied to the fluid its light slots are rearranged. The fluid will no longer rotate the light waves. The light waves leave the fluid in a vertical plain and cannot pass through the horizontal polarizer to get to the reflector (Figure 12-56). Because the light cannot be reflected back, the display appears dark. Characters are displayed by controlling which segments are dark and which segments remain light (Figure 12-57).

In most instrument panels, the LCD cluster is constantly backlit with halogen lights. But a slightly different principle is used. When the segment is not activated, the light is unable to transmit through the opaque fluid and the segment appears dark (Figure 12-58). When voltage is applied to the fluid, its light slots align and allow the light to pass to the segment. The intensity of the halogen lights is controlled through pulsewidth modulation to provide the correct illumi-

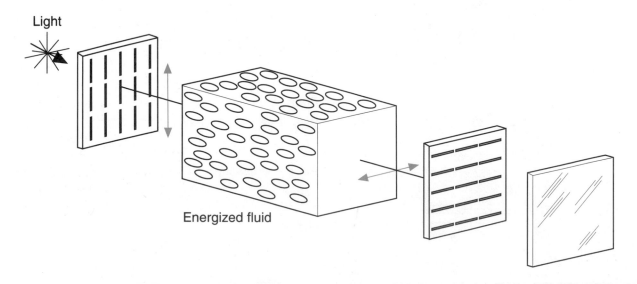

Figure 12-56 When the fluid is energized, the light wave is not rotated.

Figure 12-57 The square wave signals direct which segments will appear light and dark.

Figure 12-58 Using artificial light to display the LCD.

nation levels for the LCD under different ambient light conditions. A photocell is used to sense the amount of light intensity inside the vehicle. This information is processed by the microprocessor to determine the correct light intensity for the display. Additional control of light intensity is provided by the driver through the headlight switch rheostat.

The voltage to the fluid is provided through the polarizers that have contacts with each segment in the display. The front glass has metallized shapes where the characters will be displayed. The back glass also is metallized. The color of the display is determined by filters placed in front of the display.

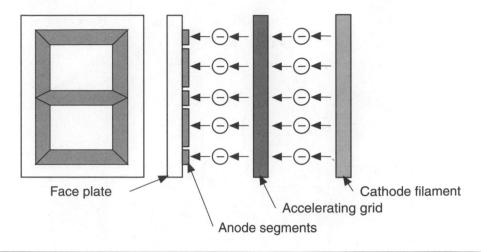

Face plate

Cathode filament

Accelerating grid

Anode segments

Figure 12-59 VFD construction.

 WARNING: LCDs operate off waveform alternating current. Do not apply DC current or the LCD will be destroyed.

Vacuum Fluorescent Displays

VFDs are the most commonly used digital display.

The vacuum fluorescent display (VFD) is constructed of a hot cathode of tungsten filaments, a grid, and a phosphorescent screen that is the anode (Figure 12-59). The components are sealed in a flat glass envelope that has been evacuated of oxygen and filled with argon or neon gas.

A constant voltage is applied to the hot cathode, which results in tungsten electrons being released from the filament wires. The grid is at a higher positive voltage than the cathode. The freed tungsten electrons are accelerated by the positive grid wires and pass through the grid to the anode. The grid ensures that the tungsten electrons will strike the anode uniformly.

The anode is at a higher positive voltage than the grid. The phosphorescent coated anode (screen) will be luminescent when the tungsten electrons strike it. The display is controlled by which segments of the screen are activated by a digital circuit. If the segment is activated, the screen will illuminate. If the segment is not activated, the electrons striking the screen have no effect on the phosphors and the screen remains off.

The segments of a VFD can be arranged in several different patterns. The most common are seven- or fourteen-segment patterns (Figure 12-60). The computer selects the sets of segments that are to emit light for the message.

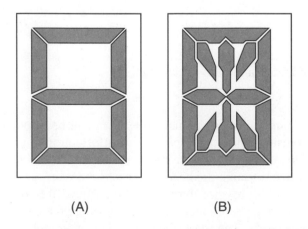

(A)   (B)

Figure 12-60 (A) Seven-segment display pattern; (B) fourteen-segment display pattern.

Resume cruise

Twilight delay `10:35` AM PM

Fasten seat belts `014739`

`55` km/h MPG

E ¼ 🔋 ¾ F
Unleaded fuel only

Low fuel

Electrical problem `0005` See diagnostic center

| | Test | Security | Brake | | 🌡 | Low washer fluid | 🛢 | | 🔋 − + | Service engine soon | Trip set | Gage |

1   10   1   11   12   2   13

Riviera

6   5   4   3   1   1

1   Air outlet
2   Graphic control center —includes radio
3   Cassette tape player
4   Glove box release
5   Deck lid release
6   Fuel access release
7   Rear defogger

8   Cruise control indicator
9   Twilight sentinel headlamp control
10   Theft deterrent system
11   Digital clock
12   Low washer fluid
13   Trip set switch

Lights
P Park
Lights off
Sentinal — Off Delay Hi
Panel lights — Lo Hi
9
Cruise
8
Hazard

Hi Wiper
Lo Wiper
Wipers off
Pulse
Push to wash
Defrost
Rear defrost
7

Climate   Summary   Radio

Off   Low   Auto   High

└ Fan ┘

Set temp   67° F   Cool ▽   Warm △

Outside   55° F   〰

Heater   Econ   Auto   Bi/Lev   Def

Gages   Diagnostic   Trip monitor

Graphic control center – Air conditioner control

Sentinal
Off   Delay   Hi

Pulse
Push   Min   Max

Panel lights
Lo   Hi

Push to wash

Electroluminescent backlit controls

Figure 12-61 CRT display. (Courtesy of General Motors Corporation)

A **cathode ray tube (CRT)** is similar to a television tube. It contains a cathode that emits electrons and an anode that attracts them. The screen will glow at the points that are hit by the electrons. Control plates dictate the direction of the electrons.

The VFD display is very bright. Most manufacturers will dim the intensity of the VFD to 75% brightness whenever the headlights are turned on. To provide sufficient brightness in the daylight, with the headlights on, the headlight switch rheostat may have an additional detent to allow bright illumination of the VFD.

CRT Displays

A cathode ray tube (CRT) display was first offered as standard equipment on the 1986 Buick Riviera (Figure 12-61). The screen of the CRT is touch sensitive. By touching the button on the screen, the menu can be changed to display different information. The menu-driven instrumentation brings up a screen with a "menu" of items. The driver can select a particular area of vehicle operation. The menu of items includes the radio, climate control, trip computer, and dash instrument information. The technician can access diagnostics through the CRT.

The CRT receives information from the BCM and ECM. It also provides inputs to the BCM and ECM in the form of driver commands to control the various functions (Figure 12-62).

Figure 12-62 The CRT receives input information from the ECM and BCM. (Courtesy of General Motors Corporation)

Figure 12-63 Electronic controlled swing needle speedometer. (Courtesy of General Motors Corporation)

Quartz Analog Instrumentation

Computer-driven quartz swing needle displays are similar in design to the air core electromagnetic gauges used in conventional analog instrument panels (Figure 12-63). A common application for this type of gauge is for the speedometer. However, it may be used for any gauge (Figure 12-64).

In most speedometer gauge systems, a permanent magnet generator sensor is installed in the transaxle or transmission. As the PM generator is rotated, it causes a small AC voltage to be induced in its coil. This AC voltage signal is sent to a buffer, then to the processing unit

The **buffer circuit** changes the AC voltage from the PM generator into a digitalized signal (Figure 12-65).

Figure 12-64 The mechanical instrument cluster receives inputs from the body and the engine controllers. (Courtesy of Chrysler Corporation)

Figure 12-65 A buffer circuit.

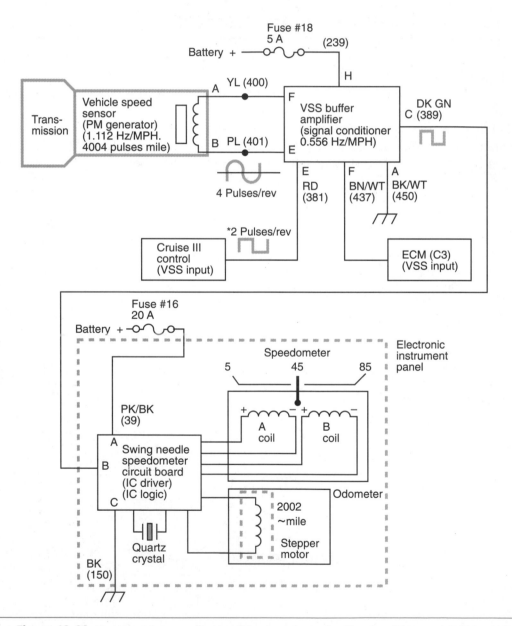

Figure 12-66 Quartz swing needle speedometer schematic. The A coil is connected to system voltage and the B coil receives a voltage that is proportional to input frequency. The magnetic armature reacts to the changing magnetic fields. (Courtesy of Chilton Book Company)

Figure 12-67 Pulse width dimming module. (Courtesy of Chrysler Corporation)

(Figure 12-66). The signal is passed to a quartz clock circuit, a gain selector circuit, and a driver circuit. The driver circuit sends voltage pulses to the coils of the gauge, the coils operate like conventional air core gauges to move the needle.

⚠ **WARNING:** The signal produced by the speed sensor can also be used by the antilock brake and the cruise control systems. If the tire size or gear ratios are changed, the operation of these systems will be affected. The speedometer must be accurately recalibrated if tires or gear ratios are changed from OE.

Digital Instrument Panel Dimming

Most conventional and computer-driven analog instrument panels use a direct input from the headlight switch rheostat to control the brightness of the display. Depending on the design and type of digital instrument panel, the display may require constant changes in its intensity so that the driver will be able to read the display under different lighting conditions.

If the vehicle is equipped with a minimum of digital displays, and an analog speedometer, the brightness level of the displays can be controlled by one input from the rheostat (Figure 12-67). In this system the body controller monitors the voltage level supplied by the headlight switch rheostat. Based on the input levels, the pulse width dimming module controls the illumination level.

Some digital instrument panel modules also use an ambient light sensor in addition to the rheostat. The ambient sensor will control the display brightness over a 35 to 1 range and the rheostat will control over a 30 to 1 range. When the headlights are turned on, the module compares the values from both inputs and determines the illumination level. When the headlights are off, the module uses only the ambient light sensor for its input.

Figure 12-68 The HUD displays various information onto the inside of the windshield. (Courtesy of General Motors Corporation)

Head-up Display

Some manufacturers have equipped selected models with a head-up display (HUD) feature. This system displays visual images onto the inside of the windshield in the driver's field of vision (Figure 12-68). With the display located in this area, drivers do not need to remove their eyes from the road to check the instrument panel. The images are projected onto the windshield from a vacuum fluorescent light source, much like a movie projector. The HUD may project speedometer, turn signal indicator, high beam indicator, and low fuel warning displays.

Voice Warning Systems

A **voice synthesizer** uses a computer-controlled phoneme generator capable of reproducing the phonemes used for basic speech. The computer puts the phonemes into the right combination to create words and sentences.

Some warning systems use a voice synthesizer to alert the driver of monitored conditions. The voice warning system can be a basic system that alerts the driver of about six conditions. Or, it may be very complex and monitor several functions.

Chrysler has a 24-function monitor with voice alert (Figure 12-69). This system supplements the warning indicators on the instrument panel and consists of the following components:

1. An alphanumeric readout panel.
2. A car graphic condition/location indicator.
3. An electronic voice alert module.

The alphanumeric readout panel provides a warning message to be displayed (Figure 12-70). The message is displayed until the condition is corrected. The car graphic indicator is a vehicle silhouette that is displayed when the ignition switch is in the RUN position (Figure 12-71). When a condition occurs that requires the driver's attention, a colored indicator will be lighted and remain on until the condition is corrected. The electronic voice alert delivers a verbal message if a new warning condition is detected. The illustration (Figure 12-72) shows the monitored conditions of this system.

Electronic monitor module

Figure 12-69 Electronic voice monitor module. (Courtesy of Chrysler Corporation)

Coolant
level low

Systems check

Figure 12-70 The readout panel displays a written message to alert the driver of problems. (Courtesy of Chrysler Corporation)

Figure 12-71 The graphic indicator lights segments to alert the driver to unsafe conditions. (Courtesy of Chrysler Corporation)

Figure 12-72 Monitored systems of the voice alert module. (Courtesy of Chrysler Corporation)

Figure 12-73 Circuit diagram of Chrysler's 24-function warning voice alert system. (Courtesy of Chrysler Corporation)

Sensors are placed throughout the vehicle to supply information to the microprocessor (Figure 12-73). Four different types of sensors supply information to the microprocessor:

1. Modules that monitor headlights, taillights, and stop lights for proper operation (Figure 12-74).

2. A thermistor that is used to monitor oil levels in the engine. When the temperature increases to a predetermined value due to lack of oil cooling, the microprocessor is sent a warning signal.

3. A voltage sensor that measures charging system output.

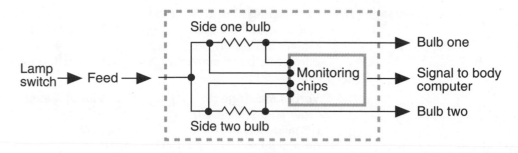

Figure 12-74 Lamp outage module detects voltage drops to determine if lamps are burned out. (Courtesy of Chrysler Corporation)

4. Normally open switches that provide ground to the microprocessor when there is a component failure or a hazardous condition. These sensors are used to monitor door ajar, brake and coolant fluid levels, oil pressure, and brake pad wear.

Additional information is supplied from an internal clock, the coolant temperature sensor, the vehicle speed sensor, and the ignition system for determining engine speed.

Some faults require more than one input to trigger the voice alert. When an unsafe or harmful condition is detected by the sensors, a warning is activated. A warning message is displayed on the readout panel and a tone sounds to alert the driver. The voice alert module delivers a verbal message by interrupting the radio (if on) and delivers the message through the radio speaker closest to the driver. Some systems use a speaker that is built into the module. The illustration (Figure 12-75) shows the verbal messages, their corresponding visual message, and the conditions that initiated the warning. Most systems provide a means of silencing the voice messages if the driver chooses.

Condition
When the driver's door is opened while the ignition switch is in the OFF, LOCK, or ACC positions, the system will monitor and, if applicable, report the following:

Verbal Message	Visual Message
"Your keys are in the ignition"	KEYS IN IGNITION
"Your headlamps are on"	EXTERIOR LAMPS ON

An intermittent chime tone will follow these messages and continue until the condition is corrected, or the door is closed.

Condition
When the ignition switch is in the ON position, the system will monitor and, if applicable, report the following:

Verbal Message (1)	Visual Message (1)
"Please close your passenger door"	PASSENGER DOOR AJAR
"Please close your driver door"	DRIVER DOOR AJAR

"Please close your rear hatch"	HATCH AJAR
"Your parking brake is on"	PARK BRAKE ENGAGED

(1) These messages are delivered when a warning condition is detected after the vehicle is in motion. When the condition is corrected, a short tone will sound to acknowledge the action.

Verbal Message (2)	Visual Message (2)
"Your engine oil pressure is critical—Engine damage may occur"	LOW OIL PRESSURE

(2) If this message is delivered when the vehicle is at cruising speeds, immediate attention is required.

If the visual message appears at idle speed, and no verbal message is given, increase the idle speed and the message should go off. If the visual message remains on, and the verbal message is also delivered, immediate attention is required.

Figure 12-75 Verbal and visual messages provided by Chrysler's 24-function warning voice alert system. (Courtesy of Chysler Corporation)

Verbal Message (3)
"Your engine temperature is above normal" . . . Followed by . . . "Your engine is overheating —prompt service is required"

Visual Message (3)
ENGINE
TEMP HIGH

(3) The first message is delivered when a sensor has determined that the engine coolant is overheating. The second message is delivered approximately 30 seconds after the first if corrective action has not been taken. Immediate attention is required.

Verbal Message (4)
"Please check your engine coolant level"

"Please check your fuel level"

"Please check your brake fluid level"

"Please check your disc brake pads"*

"Your washer fluid is low"

"Your rear washer fluid is low"

Visual Message (4)
COOLANT
LEVEL LOW

FUEL LEVEL LOW

BRAKE FLUID
LEVEL LOW

DISC BRAKE
PADS WORN

WASHER
FLUID LOW

RR WASHER
FLUID LOW

*Immediate Attention is Required! Dealer inspection of special disc brake pads is recommended.

(4) These messages are delivered when a continuous warning condition exists. Inspection is required. To clear these messages, even after the condition has been corrected, the ignition switch must be turned OFF.

Verbal Message (5)
"Please check your transmission fluid level"*
*Automatic Transaxle only

Visual Message (5)
LOW TRANS
PRESSURE*

(5) This message is delivered when a continuous warning exists while the engine is running. Immediate attention is recommended. To clear this message, even after the condition has been corrected, the ignition switch must be turned OFF.

Verbal Message (6)
"Your charging system is malfunctioning— prompt service is required"

Visual Message (6)
VOLTAGE
LOW

(6) This message is delivered when a continuous warning condition exists while the vehicle is at cruising speeds. Immediate attention is recommended. To clear this message, even after the condition has been corrected, the ignition switch must be turned OFF.

Verbal Message (7)
"Please fasten your seat belts"

Visual Message (7)
FASTEN
SEAT BELTS

(7) This message is delivered if the vehicle has been moved and the driver's seat belt is not fastened.

An intermittent chime tone will also sound for several seconds if the seat belt is not fastened.

Verbal Message (8)
"Please check your headlamp"

"Please check your brake lamp"

"Please check your tail lamp"

Visual Message (8)
HEADLAMP
OUT

BRAKE LAMP
OUT

TAIL LAMP
OUT

(8) These symptoms are constantly monitored with the lamps on or off.

If there is no warning condition to report, a short tone sounds to attract the driver's attention. The message "MONITORED SYSTEMS OK" is displayed.

Figure 12-75 (continued)

Figure 12-76 General Motor's fuel data display panel. (Courtesy of General Motors Corporation)

Figure 12-77 The deluxe driver information center provides a wide variety of information to the driver. (Courtesy of General Motors Corporation)

Travel Information Systems

Shop Manual
Chapter 12,
page 326

The travel information system can be a simple calculator that computes fuel economy, distance to empty, and remaining fuel (Figure 12-76). Other systems provide a much larger range of functions (Figure 12-77).

Fuel data centers display the amount of fuel remaining in the tank and provide additional information for the driver (Figure 12-78). By depressing the RANGE button, the body computer calculates the distance until the tank is empty by using the amount of fuel remaining and the average fuel economy. When the INST button is depressed, the fuel data center displays instantaneous fuel economy. The display is updated every 1/2 second and is computed by the body computer.

Depressing the AVG button displays average fuel economy for the total distance traveled since the reset button was last pushed. FUEL USED displays the amount of fuel that has been used since the last time this function was reset. The RESET button resets the average fuel economy and fuel used calculations. The function to be reset must be displayed on the fuel data center.

Figure 12-78 Fuel data center. (Courtesy of General Motors Corporation)

Figure 12-79 Fuel data circuit schematic. (Courtesy of General Motors Corporation)

Figure 12-80 Inputs used for the electronic vehicle information center. (Courtesy of Chrysler Corporation)

The system illustrated (Figure 12-79) uses the fuel sender unit and ignition voltage references as inputs for calculating fuel data functions. Other inputs can include speed and fuel flow sensors.

Deluxe systems may incorporate additional features such as outside temperature, compass, elapsed time, estimated time of arrival, distance to destination, day of the week, time, and average speed. The illustration (Figure 12-80) shows the inputs that are used to determine many of these functions. Fuel system calculations are determined by the sensors shown (Figure 12-81). Injector on time and vehicle speed pulses are used to determine the amount of fuel flow. Some manufacturers use a fuel flow sensor that provides pulse information to the microprocessor concerning fuel consumption (Figure 12-82).

Figure 12-81 Fuel data system inputs. The injector on time is used to calculate the rate of fuel flow. (Courtesy of Chrysler Corporation)

Figure 12-82 Some information centers use a fuel flow sensor. (Courtesy of Chrysler Corporation)

Summary

❏ Most automatic headlight dimming systems consist of a light sensitive photocell and amplifier unit, high-low beam relay, sensitivity control, dimmer switch, flash-to-pass relay, and a wiring harness.

❏ The automatic on/off with time delay has two functions: to turn on the headlights automatically when ambient light decreases to a predetermined level and to allow the headlights to remain on for a certain amount of time after the vehicle has been turned off.

❏ Fiber optics is the transmission of light through polymethylmethacrylate plastic that keeps the light rays parallel even if there are extreme bends in the plastic.

❏ The lamp outage indicator alerts the driver, through an information center on the dash or console, that a light bulb has burned out.

❏ Digital instrument clusters use digital and linear displays to notify the driver of monitored system conditions.

❏ The most common types of displays used on electronic instrument panels are light emitting diodes (LEDs), liquid crystal displays (LCDs), vacuum fluorescent displays (VFDs), and a Cathode ray tube (CRT)..

❏ Computer-driven quartz swing needle displays are similar in design to the air core electromagnetic gauges used in conventional analog instrument panels.

❏ A head-up display system displays visual images onto the inside of the windshield in the driver's field of vision.

❏ A voice synthesizer uses a computer-controlled phoneme generator that is capable of reproducing the phonemes used for basic speech.

Terms to Know

Automatic headlight dimming

Automatic on/off with time delay

Buffer circuit

Cathode ray tube (CRT)

Digital instrument clusters

Fiber optics

H-gate

Illuminated entry

Illuminated entry actuator

Instrument panel dimming

International Standards Organization (ISO)

Review Questions

Short Answer Essays

1. Describe the operation of computer-controlled concealed headlight systems.

2. List the common components of the automatic headlight system.

3. Explain the operation of body computer-controlled instrument panel illumination dimming.

4. What is the function of the sensitivity control in the automatic dimmer system?

5. What is the basic operation of the illuminated entry system?

6. Describe the operating principles of the digital speedometer.

7. Explain the operation of IC chip-type odometers.

8. Describe the operation of the electronic fuel gauge.

9. Describe the operation of quartz analog speedometers.

10. What is meant by pulse width dimming?

Fill-in-the-Blanks

1. With body computer-controlled concealed headlights, the computer receives inputs from the _____ and _____ switches.

2. The sensitivity control used with automatic dimming sets the sensitivity at which the photocell and amplifier are _____ .

3. The photocell will have _____ resistance as the ambient light level increases.

4. In some illuminated entry systems, _____ _____ signals the body computer that the courtesy lights are not required.

5. The body computer uses inputs from the _____ _____ _____ and _____ to determine the illumination level of the instrument panel lights.

6. The body computer dims the illumination lamps by using a _____ _____ _____ signal to the panel lights.

7. Digital instrument clusters use _____ and _____ displays to notify the driver of monitored system conditions.

8. Some digital instrument panel modules also use an _____ _____ sensor in addition to the rheostat.

9. Most digital fuel gauges use a fuel level sender that _____ resistance value as the fuel level decreases.

10. Computer-driven quartz swing needle displays are similar in design to the _____ _____ electromagnetic gauges used in conventional analog instrument panels.

ASE Style Review Questions

1. The sensitivity control of the automatic headlight dimming system is being discussed.
   Technician A says decreasing the sensitivity means the headlights will switch to the low beams when the approaching vehicle is farther away.
   Technician B says increasing the sensitivity means the headlights will switch to the low beams when the approaching vehicle is closer.
   Who is correct?
   A. A only
   B. B only
   C. Both A and B
   D. Neither A nor B

2. Illuminated entry is being discussed:
   Technician A says when either of the front door handles are lifted a switch in the handle will close the ground path from the actuator.
   Technician B says if the ignition switch is placed in the RUN position before the timer circuit turns off the interior lights, the timer sequence is shut off and the interior lights turn off.
   Who is correct?
   A. A only
   B. B only
   C. Both A and B
   D. Neither A nor B

3. Computer-controlled instrument panel dimming is being discussed:
   Technician A says the body computer dims the illumination lamps by varying resistance through a rheostat that is wired in series to the lights.
   Technician B says the body computer can use inputs from the panel dimming control and photocell to determine the illumination level of the instrument panel lights on certain systems.
   Who is correct?
   A. A only
   B. B only
   C. Both A and B
   D. Neither A nor B

4. Fiber optic applications are being discussed:
   Technician A says fiber optics is the transmission of light through several plastic strands that are sheathed by a polymer.
   Technician B says fiber optics are not used in automotive applications.
   Who is correct?
   A. A only
   B. B only
   C. Both A and B
   D. Neither A nor B

5. Computer-driven instrumentation is being discussed:
   Technician A says a computer-driven instrument panel uses a microprocessor to process information from various sensors and to control the gauge display.
   Technician B says some manufacturers use the body computer to perform all functions.
   Who is correct?
   A. A only
   B. B only
   C. Both A and B
   D. Neither A nor B

6. The IC chip odometer is being discussed:
   Technician A says if the chip fails, some manufacturers provide for replacement of the chip.
   Technician B says depending on the manufacturer, the new chip may be programmed to display the last odometer reading.
   Who is correct?
   A. A only
   B. B only
   C. Both A and B
   D. Neither A nor B

7. Computer-driven quartz swing needle displays are being discussed:

   Technician A says the "A" coil is connected to system voltage and the "B" coil receives a voltage that is proportional to input frequency.

   Technician B says the quartz swing needle display is similar to air core electromagnetic gauges.

   Who is correct?
   A. A only
   B. B only
   C. Both A and B
   D. Neither A nor B

8. *Technician A* says digital instrumentation displays an average of the readings received from the sensor.

   Technician B says conventional analog instrumentation is more accurate but not as decorative.

   Who is correct?
   A. A only
   B. B only
   C. Both A and B
   D. Neither A nor B

9. The microprocessor-initiated self check of the electrical instrument cluster is being discussed.

   Technician A says during the first portion of the self test all segments of the speedometer display are lit.

   Technician B says the display should not go blank during any part of the self test.

   Who is correct?
   A. A only
   B. B only
   C. Both A and B
   D. Neither A nor B

10. *Technician A* says bar graph style gauges do not provide for self tests.

    Technician B says the digital instrument panel will display "CO" to indicate the circuit is shorted.

    Who is correct?
    A. A only
    B. B only
    C. Both A and B
    D. Neither A nor B

Chassis Electronic Control Systems

Upon completion and review of this chapter, you should be able to:

❏ Explain the purpose of the automatic temperature control.

❏ Explain the purpose and operation of the control assembly in the SATC and EATC systems.

❏ List and describe the types of sensors used in SATC and EATC systems.

❏ Explain the differences in operation between semiautomatic temperature control and electronic automatic temperature control systems.

❏ Define the purpose of the cruise control system.

❏ Explain the basic operation of electromechanical cruise control systems.

❏ Explain the operating principles of the electronic cruise control system.

❏ Explain the purpose and operation of the safety switches used on electromechanical and electronic cruise control systems.

❏ Explain the purpose of passive restraint systems.

❏ Describe the basic operation of automatic seatbelts.

❏ List and explain the function of the components of the air bag module.

❏ Explain the functions of the diagnostic module used in air bag systems.

❏ Describe the operation of air bag system sensors.

❏ Explain the basic operating principles of the emergency tensioning retractor.

❏ Explain the operating principles of the memory seat feature.

❏ Describe the control concepts of electronically controlled sunroofs.

❏ Detail the operation of common antitheft systems.

❏ Explain the function of the pass-key security system.

❏ Explain the purpose and operation of automatic door lock systems.

❏ Detail the operation of the keyless entry system.

❏ Explain the operating principles of Ford's and GM's heated windshield systems.

❏ Explain the purpose of electronic shift transmissions.

❏ Explain the purpose of variable assist steering.

❏ Describe the purpose of electronic suspension systems.

❏ State the purpose of antilock braking systems.

❏ Describe the basic purpose of automatic traction control systems.

❏ Describe the purpose and configuration of vehicle sound systems.

Introduction

In this chapter you will learn the operation of the semiautomatic and automatic temperature control systems, cruise control systems, automatic passive restraint systems, and air bag systems. Today's technician will be required to service these systems. The comfort and safety of the driver and/or passengers depend on the technician properly diagnosing and repairing these systems. As with all electrical systems, the technician must have a basic understanding of the operation of these systems before attempting to perform any service.

There are many safety cautions to observe when working on air bag systems. Safe service procedures are accomplished through proper use of the service manual and by understanding the operating principles of these systems.

This chapter also discusses the many electrical accessory systems that have electronic controls added to them to provide additional features and enhancement. These accessories include memory seats, electronic sunroofs, antitheft systems, automatic door locks, keyless entry, and electronic heated windshields.

Introduction to Semiautomatic and Electronic Automatic Temperature Control

Automatic air conditioning systems operate with the same basic components as the conventional systems. The major difference is the automatic temperature control (ATC) system is capable of maintaining a preset level of comfort as selected by the driver. Sensors are used to determine the present temperatures and the system can adjust the level of heating or cooling as required.

The system uses actuators that will open and close air-blend doors to achieve the desired in-vehicle temperature. Some systems will control fan motor speeds to keep the temperature very close to that requested by the driver.

There are two types of automatic temperature control: semiautomatic temperature control (SATC) and electronic automatic temperature control (EATC). The basic difference in the two systems is in self-diagnostic capabilities. Most SATC systems do not provide for storing of trouble codes. EATC systems monitor system operation and set codes in a RAM module for diagnostic use. Other differences include actuator types and the number of sensors used.

Though the systems differ in methods of operation, they are all designed to provide in-car temperatures and humidity conditions at a preset level. The in-car humidity and temperature levels are maintained, regardless of the climate conditions outside the vehicle. The in-car humidity level is maintained at 45 to 55%.

Shop Manual
Chapter 13,
page 332

Semiautomatic Temperature Control

Basic SATC systems are not much different than manual systems. The primary difference is in the use of a programmer, electric servomotor, and/or control module to operate the actuators. The SATC system maintains a driver-selected comfort level by sensing air temperature and blend-air door positions through the programmer. The driver selects the operating mode and blower speeds manually from the control head.

Common Components

Not all systems will have all of the components described here, but most will have a combination of several of them.

Control Assembly. The control assembly used in SATC systems is similar to that used in manual systems. The main difference is the temperature control has a temperature range imprinted under it or displayed (Figure 13-1). The control assembly is located in the instrument panel and provides the means for driver input to the climate control system. The temperature control lever is a part of a sliding resistor that mechanically converts the lever setting into an electrical resistance. The driver selects operating modes (A/C, heat, defogger, and vent) and fan motor speeds through push button selection on the control assembly.

Figure 13-1 Semiautomatic temperature control assembly. (Courtesy of Chrysler Corporation)

Programmer. The push buttons of the control assembly will input a programmer that directs vacuum to actuators at the air distribution doors (except the blend-air door, which is usually controlled by a servomotor). The programmer also receives electrical input from the in-car and exterior ambient temperature sensors. Based on the inputs from the sensors and the control assembly, the programmer provides output signals to turn the compressor clutch on/off, open/close the heater water valve, and position the mode doors.

Sensors. There can be several different sensors used on the SATC system. The most common are the in-car and ambient temperature sensors.

The **control assembly** provides for driver input into the automatic temperature control microprocessor. The control assembly is also referred to as the control panel.

The **programmer** controls the blower speed, air mix doors, and vacuum motors of the SATC system. Depending on manufacturer, they are also called servo assemblies.

Most **aspirators** are tubular devices that use a venturi effect to draw air from the passenger compartment over the in-car sensor (Figure 13-2). Some manufacturers use a suction motor to draw the air over the sensor.

Figure 13-2 A typical aspirator. The main air stream creates a low pressure at the inlet of the aspirator drawing in-car air over the sensor.

Figure 13-3 The in-car sensor is a NTC thermistor located in the aspirator unit.

The in-car sensor contains a temperature sensing NTC thermistor to measure the average temperature inside the vehicle (Figure 13-3). The in-car sensor is located in the aspirator unit.

The ambient sensor is an NTC thermistor used to measure the temperature outside the vehicle (Figure 13-4). The ambient sensor is usually located behind the grill. Due to its location, and

Figure 13-4 Ambient temperature sensor.

Figure 13-5 The sunload sensor produces a signal proportional to the heat intensity of the sun's heat through the windshield.

possible influence by engine temperatures, the sensor circuit has several memory features that prevent false input.

Some systems use a sunload sensor (Figure 13-5). The sunload sensor is a photovoltaic diode that sends signals to the programmer concerning the extra generation of heat as the sun beats through the windshield. This sensor is usually located on the dash next to a speaker grill.

Electronic Automatic Temperature Control

The determining factor separating electronic automatic temperature control (EATC) systems from SATC systems is the ability for self-diagnostics. The body control module (BCM) will set trouble codes that can be accessed by the technician. In addition, the EATC system provides a continuously variable blower speed signal and readjusts interior temperature several times a second.

In addition to the sensors used in the SATC system, the EATC system may also use engine coolant temperature, vehicle speed, and throttle position sensors as inputs. The EATC system may also incorporate a cold engine lock-out switch.

There are two categories of EATC systems; BCM-controlled systems and stand-alone systems that use their own computer.

BCM-Controlled Systems

Components

Climate control is one of the primary functions of the BCM on many GM vehicles. The body computer module has central control over the EATC system. The BCM monitors all system sensors and switches, compares the data with programmed instructions, and commands the actuators to provide accurate control of the system.

The climate control panel (CCP) contains a circuit board that translates driver inputs into electrical signals (Figure 13-6). The CCP and BCM communicate with each other over a data circuit. The information sent to the CCP can be displayed by the vacuum fluorescent display.

Photovoltaic diodes are capable of producing a voltage when exposed to radiant energy.

Shop Manual
Chapter 13, page 340

Cold engine lock-out switches signal the BCM or controller to prevent blower motor operation until the air entering the passenger compartment reaches a specified temperature.

Shop Manual
Chapter 13, page 348

Figure 13-6 Climate control panel. (Courtesy of General Motors Corporation)

The BCM monitors the air conditioning system through several sensors. High side temperature is monitored through a sensor in the pressure line. By monitoring the high side temperature, the BCM is capable of making calculations that translate into pressure. The calculations are based on the pressure-temperature relationship of R-12 or R-134a. The BCM will also monitor low side pressure in the same manner through a low side temperature sensor. The BCM also receives a signal from the low pressure switch in the accumulator. The BCM will shut down the compressor clutch if system operation is not within set parameters.

The programmer uses a bidirectional motor to adjust the blend door. A potentiometer feedback signal is used by the BCM to determine blend door position. The programmer has five vacuum solenoids that control vacuum to the mode doors and heater water valves. All controls are through the BCM.

A power module controls the blower motor (Figure 13-7). The module receives blower drive signals from the BCM and amplifies them to provide variable fan blower speeds.

Operation

The BCM calculates a program number, which represents the amount of heating or cooling required to obtain the temperature set by the driver. This number is based on inputs from the control assembly (driver input), ambient temperature, and in-car temperature. Based on this number air delivery mode, fan blower speed, and blend door positioning are determined.

The **program number** zero represents maximum cooling, and 100 represents maximum heating. The program number can be observed while in the diagnostic mode.

Figure 13-7 Power module amplifies BCM signals to control the blower motor speed.

Figure 13-8 Blower control schematic of BCM-controlled EATC. (Courtesy of General Motors Corporation)

To provide the proper mix of inside air temperature entering the passenger compartment, the BCM monitors the ambient and in-car temperatures, the average low side temperature, and the coolant temperature. These inputs are combined with the program number. The BCM commands the programmer to position the blend door for the correct temperature of incoming air. The programmer feedback potentiometer is also monitored by the BCM.

Blower speed is determined by a combination of the program number and driver input temperature. The CCP will signal the BCM over data line 718 (Figure 13-8). The signal is sent

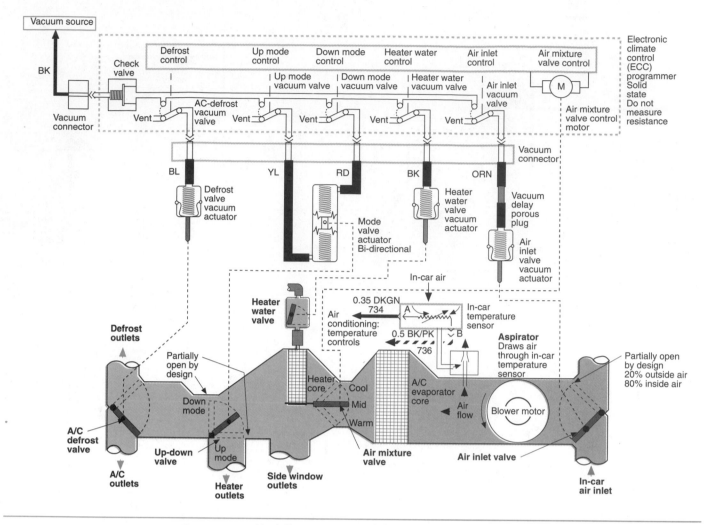

Figure 13-9 Air delivery vacuum schematic. (Courtesy of General Motors Corporation)

from the BCM to the power module from terminal A9. This signal is a constantly variable voltage proportional to blower speed. The power module will amplify the signal then apply it to the blower motor through circuit 65. The BCM monitors the blower speed through a feedback voltage from the motor on circuit 761.

Solenoid valves in the programmer control the air valves that are operated by mechanical and vacuum controls. The air-inlet, up-down, and A/C defrost valves are controlled individually (Figure 13-9). Commands from the BCM to the programmer control the operation of the solenoids.

Air conditioner compressor clutch control is performed by the engine control module (ECM) through inputs from the BCM (Figure 13-10). The ECM cycles the compressor on and off based on input signals from the high side and low side temperature sensors to the BCM. In addition, the ECM will anticipate clutch cycling and will adjust engine idle speed accordingly.

The BCM monitors system inputs and feedback signals. If these voltage signals fall outside programmed parameters, the BCM will turn on the "Service Air Cond" indicator lamp.

Figure 13-10 Air conditioning clutch controls. (Courtesy of General Motors Corporation)

Separate Computer-Controlled Systems

Several EATC systems use a separate computer for the sole purpose of climate control. The systems described here are representative examples of these types of systems.

GM Electronic Touch Climate Control

General Motors electronic touch climate control (ETCC) systems are fully automatic and regulate fan speed, air inlet, and outlet positions. The control head contains the microprocessor that will

Shop Manual
Chapter 13,
page 341

Shop Manual
Chapter 13,
page 344

Figure 13-10 (continued)

execute desired selection and remember the last selection (Figure 13-11). The control head receives inputs from ambient temperature, in-car temperature, and setting selection to determine position of the blend door and fan blower speed.

Depending on the model of vehicle the system is installed on, the mode door and water flow actuators can be controlled by either vacuum or electric servomotors (Figure 13-12). All systems use an electrically operated blend door.

Figure 13-11 Electronic touch climate control panel.

Figure 13-12 Electrically operated water valve actuator.

The control head signals the blower and A/C clutch control module to provide for clutch cycling and appropriate blower speeds (Figure 13-13). The blower motor provides up to 256 different speeds.

Ford EATC

The Ford EATC system uses a microprocessor that is built into the control assembly. The control unit controls four DC motor rotary actuators to operate each air distribution door. The sensors and inputs are the same as in previously discussed systems. The control assembly sends continuously variable voltage signals to the blower motor speed controller (BMSC). The BMSC module amplifies the signal to control motor operation. Figure 13-14 is a schematic of one EATC system used by Ford.

Shop Manual
Chapter 13,
page 344

Figure 13-13 EATC wiring schematic. (Courtesy of General Motors Corporation)

Shop Manual
Chapter 13,
page 341

Chrysler EATC

The Chrysler EATC system uses an individual computer that regulates incoming air temperature and adjusts the system as required every 7 seconds (Figure 13-15). The power-vacuum module (PVM) uses logic signals from the control assembly microprocessor to send a variable voltage signal to the blower motor. In addition, the PVM controls A/C compressor clutch and a voltage signal to the blend door actuator, and vacuum to all other actuators (Figure 13-16)

Figure 13-13 (continued)

Introduction to Electronic Cruise Control Systems

Cruise control was first introduced in the 1960s for the purpose of reducing driver fatigue. When engaged, the cruise control system sets the throttle position to maintain the desired vehicle speed.

Most cruise control systems are a combination of electrical and mechanical components. The components used depend on manufacturer and system design. However, the operating principles are similar.

Cruise control is a system that allows the vehicle to maintain a preset speed with the driver's foot off the accelerator.

Figure 13-14 Ford EATC wiring schematic. (Reprinted with the permission of Ford Motor Company)

Figure 13-15 Chrysler's EATC system components and control assembly. (Courtesy of Chrysler Corporation)

Figure 13-16 Block diagram of Chrysler EATC system. (Courtesy of Chrysler Corporation)

Upper cable & casing assembly
Vacuum release valve
Servo
Push button control switch
Electric release switch
Lower cable & casing assembly
Transducer

Figure 13-17 Components of typical electromechanical cruise control system. (Courtesy of General Motors Corporation)

Electromechanical Systems

A review of electromechanical systems is helpful when trying to understand the operation of electronic cruise control. The illustration (Figure 13-17) shows the location of the main components of the electromechanical control system. These components include:

1. Cruise control switch: The control switch is located on the turn signal stock or in the steering wheel (Figure 13-18). The switch assembly is actually a set of driver-operated switches. On most systems, the switches are ON, SET/ACCEL, COAST, and RESUME.

2. Transducer: The transducer receives vehicle speed signals through the speedometer cable. Electrical signals from the control switch, brake switch, or clutch switch are sent to the transducer. In addition, the transducer receives engine manifold vacuum. It regulates the vacuum to the servo through the electrical signals received.

Set
Resume
Coast
Accelerate

Turn signal lever

Mode control, steering wheel and on-off rocker switch, floor console

Figure 13-18 The control switch can be mounted on the turn signal stock or into the steering wheel. The switch is used to provide driver inputs for the system. (Courtesy of General Motors Corporation)

Figure 13-19 Cutaway view of the servo. Vacuum is used to compress the spring and open the throttle. (Courtesy of General Motors Corporation)

3. Servo: The servo controls throttle plate position. It is connected to the throttle plate by a rod, bead chain, or Bowden cable. The servo maintains the set speed by receiving a controlled amount of vacuum from the transducer. When vacuum is applied to the servo, the spring is compressed and the throttle plate is moved to increase speed (Figure 13-19). When the vacuum is released, the spring returns the throttle plate to reduce engine speed.

4. Safety switches: When the brake pedal is depressed, the cruise control system is disengaged through electrical and vacuum switches (Figure 13-20). The switches are usually located on the brake pedal bracket. The two switches provide a fail-safe means of assuring that the cruise control is disengaged when the brakes are applied. If one of the switches fails, the other will still be able to return vehicle speed control over to the driver. Vehicles equipped with manual transmissions may use switches on the clutch pedal to disengage the system whenever the clutch pedal is depressed.

Figure 13-20 The brake release switch and the vacuum release switch work together to disengage the cruise control switch when the brake pedal is depressed. (Courtesy of General Motors Corporation)

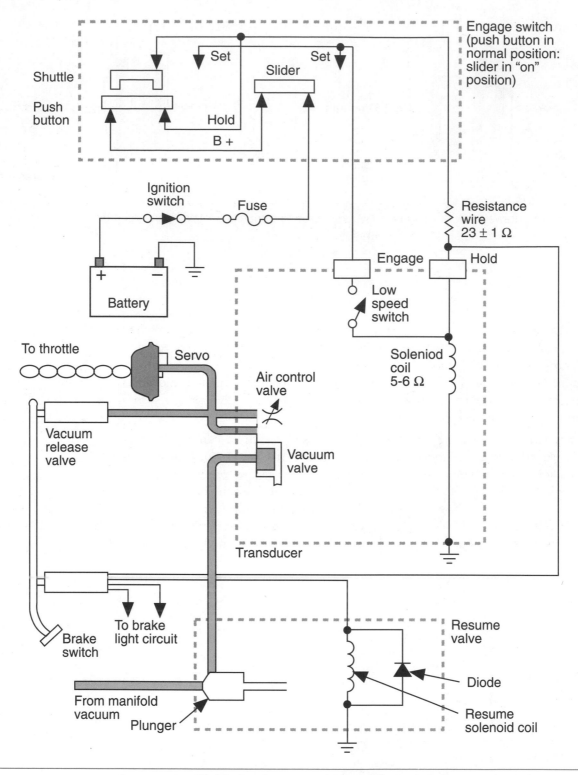

Figure 13-21 Electrical and vacuum schematic of a typical electromechanical cruise control system. (Courtesy of General Motors Corporation)

When the cruise control switch is in the "at rest" position, battery current flows through the switch to the resistance wire to the hold terminal of the transducer (Figure 13-21). Voltage to the hold terminal is too low to activate the solenoid coil because the resistor drops the voltage.

The transducer contains a rubber clutch with an operating arm. At speeds below 30 mph (48 km/h) the rubber clutch arm holds the low speed switch open. When speeds exceed 30 mph

(48 km/h), the clutch arm rotates. The rotation of the arm allows the switch to close and the system can be engaged. By pushing the momentary contact switch in the SET position, the current flow is through the engage terminal of the transducer, through the low speed switch, to the solenoid coil. The resistor is bypassed and sufficient current is applied to the solenoid to activate it. When the momentary switch is released, the current flow is returned through the hold terminal. The current applied to the solenoid coil is sufficient to hold the solenoid in the activated position.

When the solenoid is activated, the vacuum valve opens to allow engine vacuum to the servo and the brake release valve. The air control valve is a variable orifice and is the control mechanism that adjusts vacuum level to the system. At lower speed settings, the air control valve bleeds off vacuum so that less is sent to the servo. At higher set speeds, less vacuum is bled to allow for more throttle plate opening.

If the brake pedal is depressed with the cruise control system engaged, the brake switch provides an alternate path to ground and bypasses the solenoid. With the solenoid deactivated, the vacuum valve closes and returns the throttle control over to the driver. At the same time, the resume solenoid is closed and the vacuum release valve opens to release the vacuum in the system.

Electronic Cruise Control

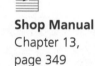

Shop Manual
Chapter 13,
page 349

The electronic cruise control system uses an electronic module to operate the actuators that control throttle position (Figure 13-22). Electronic cruise control offers more precise speed control than the electromechanical system. In addition, other benefits include:

- More frequent throttle adjustments per second.
- More consistent speed increase/decrease when using the tap-up/tap-down feature.

Figure 13-22 Block diagram of electronic cruise control system. (Courtesy of General Motors Corporation)

- Greater correction of speed variation under loads
- Rapid deceleration cut-off when deceleration rate exceeds programmed rates.
- Wheelspin cut-off when acceleration rate exceeds programmed parameters.
- System malfunction cut-off when the module determines there is a fault in the system.

Common Components

Shop Manual
Chapter 13,
page 361

Common components of the electronic cruise control system include:

1. The control module: The module can be a separate cruise control module, the engine control module, or the body control module. The operation of the systems are similar regardless of the module used.

2. The control switch: Depending on system design, the control switch contacts apply the ground circuit through resistors. Because each resistor has a different value, a different voltage is applied to the control module. In some systems the control switch will send a 12-volt signal to different terminals of the control module.

3. The brake or clutch switch.

4. Vacuum release switch.

5. Servo: The servo operates on vacuum that is controlled by supply and vent valves. These operate from controller signals to solenoids.

Depending on system design, the sensors used as inputs to the control module include the vehicle speed sensor, servo position sensor, and throttle position sensor. Other inputs are provided by the brake switch, instrument panel switch, control switch, and the park-neutral switch.

The control module receives signals from the speed sensor and the control switch. When the vehicle speed is fast enough to allow cruise control operation and the driver pushes the SET button on the control switch, an electrical signal is sent to the controller. The voltage level received by the controller is set in memory. This signal is used to create two additional signals. The two signal values are set at 1/4 mph above and below the set speed. The module uses the comparator values to change vacuum levels at the servo to maintain set vehicle speed.

Three safety modes are operated by the control module:

1. Rapid deceleration cutoff: If the module determines that deceleration rate is greater than programmed values, it will disengage the cruise control system and return operation back over to the driver.

2. Wheelspin cutoff: If the control module determines that the acceleration rate is greater than programmed values, it will disengage the system.

3. System malfunction cutoff: The module checks the operation of the switches and circuits. If it determines there is a fault, it will disable the system.

The vacuum-modulated servo is the primary actuator. Vacuum to the servo is controlled by two solenoid valves: supply and vent. The vent valve is a normally open valve and the supply valve is normally closed (Figure 13-23). The servo receives signals from the controller to operate the solenoid valves to maintain a preset throttle position.

436

Figure 13-23 Servo valve operation in electronic control system. The servo position sensor informs the controller of servo operation and position.

Principles of Operation

When the driver sends a SET signal to the controller it sets the voltage signals received from the vehicle speed sensor (VSS) into memory. It then determines the high and low comparators.

The controller energizes the supply and vent valves to allow manifold vacuum or atmospheric pressure to enter the servo. The servo uses the vacuum and pressure to move the throttle and maintain the set speed. The vehicle speed is maintained by balancing the vacuum in the servo.

If the voltage signal from the VSS drops below the low comparator value, the control module energizes the supply valve solenoid to allow more vacuum into the servo and increases the throttle opening. When the VSS signal returns to a value within the comparator levels, the supply valve solenoid is de-energized.

If the VSS signal is greater than the high comparator value, the control module de-energizes the vent solenoid valve to release vacuum in the servo. The vehicle speed is reduced until the VSS signals are between the comparator values, at which time the control module will energize the vent valve solenoid again. This constant modulation of the supply and vent valves maintains vehicle speed.

During steady cruise conditions, both valves are closed and a constant vacuum is maintained in the servo.

Passive restraints
operate
automatically with
no action required
on the part of the
driver or occupant
(Figure 13-24).

Figure 13-24 Passive automatic seatbelt system operation. (Reprinted with the permission of Ford Motor Company)

In a two-point
system the occupant
must manually lock
the lap belt.

**Inertia lock
retractors** use a
pendulum
mechanism to lock
the belt tightly
during sudden
movement
(Figure 13-26).

Passive Restraints

Federal regulations have mandated the use of automatic passive restraint systems in all vehicles sold in the United States after 1990. Two- or three-point automatic seatbelt and airbag systems are currently offered as a means of meeting this requirement.

The passive seat belt system automatically puts the shoulder and/or lap belt around the driver or occupant. The automatic seat belt system operates by means of DC motors that move the belts by means of carriers on tracks (Figure 13-25).

One end of the seat belt is attached to the carrier: the other end is connected to the inertia lock retractors. When the door is opened, the outer end of the shoulder harness moves forward (to the A-pillar) to allow for easy entry or exit (Figure 13-27). When the door is closed and the ignition switch is placed in the RUN position, the motor moves the outer end of the harness to the locked position in the B-pillar (Figure 13-28).

Figure 13-25 Passive seatbelt restraint system uses a motor to put the shoulder harness around the occupant. (Reprinted with the permission of Ford Motor Company)

Figure 13-26 Inertia lock seatbelt retractor. (Reprinted with the permission of Ford Motor Company)

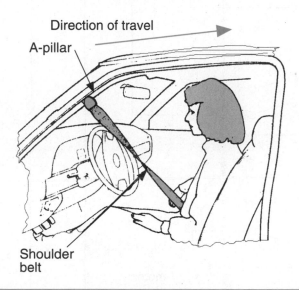

Figure 13-27 When the door is opened the motor pulls the harness to the A-pillar. (Reprinted with the permission of Ford Motor Company)

Figure 13-28 When the door is closed and the ignition switch is in the RUN position, the motor draws the harness to its lock position. (Reprinted with the permission of Ford Motor Company)

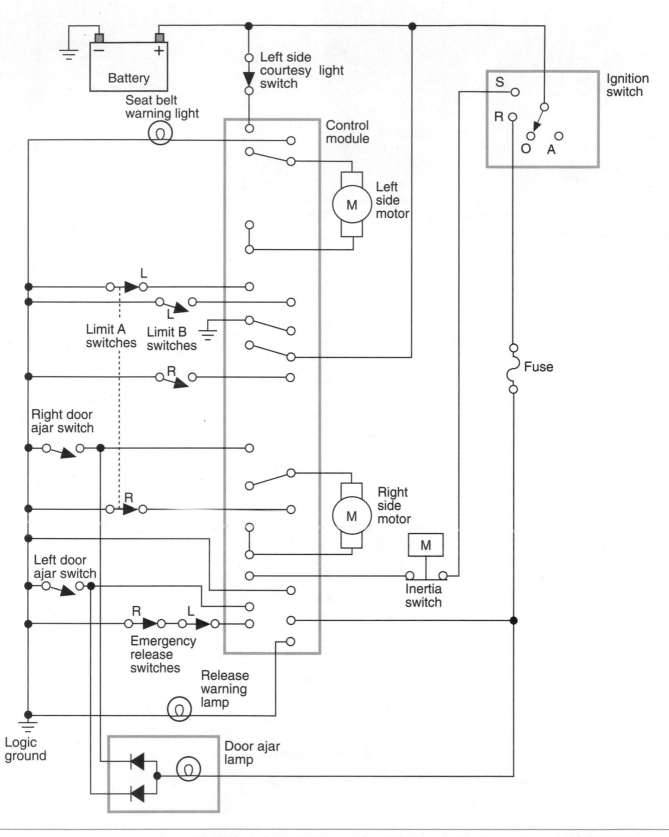

Figure 13-29 Typical circuit diagram of automatic seatbelt system using a control module.

The automatic seatbelt system uses a control module to monitor operation (Figure 13-29). The monitor receives inputs from door ajar switches, limit switches, and the emergency release switch.

The door ajar switches signal the position of the door to the module. The switch is open when the door is closed. This signal is used by the control module to activate the motor and move the harness to the lock point behind the occupant's shoulders. If the module receives a signal that the door is open, regardless of ignition switch position, it will activate the motor to move the harness to the forward position.

The limit switches inform the module of the position of the harness. When the harness is moved from the FORWARD position, the front limit switch (limit A) closes. When the harness is located in the LOCK position, the rear limit switch (limit B) opens and the module turns off the power to the motor. When the door is opened, the module reverses the power feed to the motor until the A switch is opened.

An emergency release mechanism is provided in the event that the system fails to operate. The NC emergency release switch is opened whenever the release lever is pulled. The module will turn on the warning lamp in the instrument panel and sound a chime to alert the driver. The opened switch also prevents the harness retractors from locking.

Ford incorporates the fuel pump inertia switch into the automatic seatbelt system. If the module receives a signal that the switch is open, it prevents the harness from moving to the forward position if the door opens.

The **fuel pump inertia switch** is a NC switch that will open if the vehicle is involved in an impact at speeds over 5 mph or rolls over. When the switch opens, it turns off power to the fuel pump. This is a safety feature to prevent fuel from being pumped onto the ground or hot engine components if the engine dies. The switch has to be manually reset if it is triggered (Figure 13-30).

Figure 13-30 Fuel pump inertia switch. (Reprinted with the permission of Ford Motor Company)

Airbag Systems

The need to supplement the existing restraint system during frontal collisions has led to the development of the supplemental inflatable restraint (SIR) or air bag systems (Figure 13-31). Because most air bag systems are not designed to deploy during side or rear collisions, seatbelts should always be worn in conjunction with the air bag. The air bag is a supplement and the seatbelt is the primary restraint system.

Shop Manual
Chapter 13,
page 372

Figure 13-31 Air bag sequence. (Courtesy of Chrysler Corporation)

Shop Manual
Chapter 13,
page 377

Many of the components used for driver side air bags are similar to those used in passenger side air bags. The basic operation of the two systems is the same.

The **air bag** is made of neoprene-coated nylon.

Common Components

A typical air bag system consists of sensors, a diagnostic module, a clock spring, and an air bag module. See the typical location (Figure 13-32) of the common components of the SIR system.

Air Bag Module. The air bag module is the air bag and inflator assembly packaged into a single module. This module is mounted in the center of the steering wheel (Figure 13-33).

The inflation of the air bag is through an explosive release of nitrogen gas. The igniter is an integral component of the inflator assembly. It starts a chemical reaction to inflate the air bag

Figure 13-32 Typical location of components of the air bag system. (Courtesy of Chrysler Corporation)

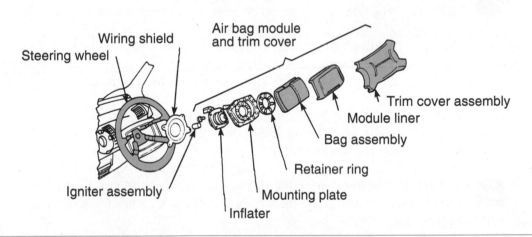

Figure 13-33 Air bag module components. (Courtesy of Chrysler Corporation)

(Figure 13-34). When current is applied to the igniter, it arcs between two pins. The spark ignites a canister of gas generating zerconic potassium perchlorate (ZPP).

The inflation assembly is composed of a solid chemical gas generator (generant) containing sodium azide and copper oxide propellant. The ZPP ignites the propellent charge. As the propellent burns, it produces nitrogen gas. The gas passes through a diffuser, where it is filtered and cooled before inflating the air bag.

> **CAUTION:** Wear gloves and eye protection when handling a deployed air bag module. Sodium hydroxide residue may remain on the bag. If this comes in contact with the skin, it can cause irritation.

The **igniter** is a combustible device that converts electric energy into thermal energy to ignite the inflator propellant.

The air bag module cannot be serviced. If it is has been deployed, or is defective, it must be replaced.

Figure 13-34 Igniter assembly.

Clock Spring. The clock spring conducts electrical signals to the module while allowing steering wheel rotation (Figure 13-35). The clock spring is located between the column and the steering wheel.

CAUTION: Whenever the air bag is deployed, the heat generated may damage the clock spring. The clock spring should be replaced whenever the air bag is deployed.

Diagnostic Module. The diagnostic module constantly monitors the readiness of the air SIR electrical system. If the module determines that there is a fault in the system, it will illuminate the indicator light. Depending on the fault, the SIR system may be disarmed until the fault is repaired.

The diagnostic module also supplies backup power to the air bag module in the event that the battery or cables are damaged during an accident. The stored charge can last for up to 10 minutes after the battery is disconnected.

CAUTION: Before servicing the air bag system, the backup power supply energy must be depleted. Disconnect the battery and isolate the cable terminal. Wait at least 5 minutes before servicing.

Figure 13-35 The clock spring provides for electrical continuity in all steering wheel positions. (Courtesy of Chrysler Corporation)

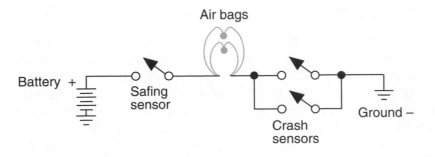

Figure 13-36 Typical sensor wiring circuit diagram.

Sensors. To prevent accidental deployment of the air bag, most systems require that at least two sensor switches be closed to deploy the air bag (Figure 13-36). A typical sensor is composed of a gold-plated ball (sensing mass) that is held in place by a magnet (Figure 13-37). At the point of sufficient force, the ball will break loose of the magnet and make contact with the electrical contacts to complete the circuit.

> ⚠️ **WARNING:** SIR system sensors must be installed with the arrow pointing to the front of the vehicle for proper operation.

The number of sensors used depends on system design. Some systems use only a single sensor and others use up to five. The name used to identify the different sensors also varies between manufacturers. Usually sensors are located in the engine and passenger compartments. The sensor in the passenger compartment determines if the collision is severe enough to inflate the air bag.

Once the two sensors are closed, the electrical circuit to the igniter is complete. The igniter starts the chemical chain reaction that produces heat. The heat causes the generant to produce nitrogen gas, which fills the air bag.

Figure 13-37 Some crash sensors hold the sensing mass by magnetic force. If the impact is severe enough to break the ball free, it will travel forward and close the electrical contacts. (Courtesy of Chrysler Corporation)

General Motors' SIR

General Motors has used several different versions of SIR systems. The version discussed here is representative of the system. Changes between models and years require that technicians follow the service manual procedures for the vehicle they are working on.

Refer to the illustration (Figure 13-38) for the location of the components used on the SIR system. The major portions of the SIR system are the deployment loop and the diagnostic energy reserve module (DERM).

The deployment loop supplies current to the inflator module in the steering wheel (Figure 13-39). The components of the deployment loop include the:

> arming sensor
>
> coil assembly
>
> inflator module
>
> discriminating sensors

The arming sensor switches power to the inflator module on the insulated side of the loop circuit. Either of the discriminating sensors can supply the ground. For the inflator module to ignite, the arming sensor and at least one discriminating sensor must close simultaneously. The complete wiring schematic of this system is illustrated (Figure 13-40).

There are two discriminating sensors used. One is located in front of the radiator, the other is part of the dual sensor located behind the instrument panel.

The DERM is designed to provide an energy reserve of 36 volts to assure deployment for a few seconds when vehicle voltage is low or lost. The DERM also maintains constant diagnostic monitoring of the electrical system. It will store a code if a fault is found and provide driver notification by illuminating the warning light. The resistor module allows the DERM to monitor the deployment loop for faults and to detect when deployment has occurred. In addition, the DERM records the SIR system status during an accident.

The sequence of events that occur during an impact of a vehicle traveling at 30 mph is as follows:

1. When an accident occurs, the arming sensor is the first to close. It will close due to sudden deceleration caused by braking, or immediately upon impact. One of the discriminating sensors will then close. The amount of time required to close the switches is within 15 milliseconds.

2. Within 40 milliseconds, the igniter module burns the propellant and generates the gas to completely fill the air bag.

3. Within 100 milliseconds, the driver's body has stopped forward movement and the air bag starts to deflate. The air bag deflates by venting the nitrogen gas through holes in the back of the bag.

4. Within 2 seconds the air bag is completely deflated.

Mercedes-Benz

The supplemental restraint system (SRS) used on some Mercedes-Benz vehicles combines the air bag with a three-point seatbelt that uses an emergency tensioning retractor (ETR). The air bag operates similar to that discussed. However, it uses only one sensor. The SRS sensor incorporates two ICs and an acceleration pickup to determine the degree and direction of impact. When the longitudinal deceleration is sufficient, the sensor sends a voltage through a bypass filter to an amplifier. The amplifier provides the voltage required to ignite the inflator module.

A voltage convertor is used to keep a constant 12 volts applied to the sensor and energy accumulator. The convertor is capable of maintaining 12 volts even though battery voltage may

---

The **arming sensor** is calibrated to close at low level velocity changes. The arming sensor is also referred to as the safing sensor.

The **discriminating sensors** are calibrated to close with velocity changes that are severe enough to warrant air bag deployment (velocity changes higher than that of the arming sensor). Discriminating sensors are also known as crash sensors.

The **dual sensor** is a combination of the arming and passenger compartment discriminating sensor.

The SRS sensor uses a mercury switch to disconnect it from the circuit during normal driving.

Figure 13-38 Component location of the GM SIR system used by Cadillac. (Courtesy of General Motors Corporation)

Figure 13-39 SIR deployment loop diagram. (Courtesy of General Motors Corporation)

Figure 13-40 General Motors SIR system wiring diagram. (Courtesy of General Motors Corporation)

Figure 13-40 (continued)

drop to as low as 4 volts. The energy accumulator operates like a capacitor to provide backup current in the event that battery voltage is totally lost.

The ETR system is installed on the passenger side. The ETR contains an igniter device that produces a high pressure gas. The gas is used to operate a pulley that pulls the seatbelt harness snugly against the passenger.

> **CAUTION:** Mercedes-Benz, Toyota, and some other manufacturers use mercury in their sensors. If these sensors require replacement, the old sensor must be treated as toxic waste material.

Shop Manual
Chapter 13,
page 379

The **memory seat** feature allows the driver to program different seat positions that can be recalled at the push of a button.

Memory Seats

The memory seat feature is an addition to the basic power seat system. Most memory seat systems share the same basic operating principles. The difference is in programming methods and number of positions that can be programmed.

The power seat system may operate in any gear position. However, the memory seat function will only operate when the transmission is in the PARK position. The purpose of the memory disable feature is to prevent accidental seat movement while the vehicle is being driven. In the PARK position, the seat memory module will receive a 12-volt signal that will enable memory operation. In any other gear selection, the 12-volt signal is removed and the memory function is disabled. This signal can come from the gear selector switch or the neutral safety switch (Figure 13-41).

In Ford's system, variable resistance sensors are used to monitor seat position instead of counting pulses.

Most systems provide for two seat positions to be stored in memory. Ford allows for three positions to be stored by pushing both position 1 and 2 buttons together. With the seat in the desired position, depressing the set memory button and moving the memory select switch to either the memory 1 or 2 position will store the seat position into the module's memory (Figure 13-42).

When the seat is moved from its memory position, the seat memory module transmits the voltage applied from the switch to the motors. The module counts the pulses produced by motor operation, and then stores the number of pulses and direction of movement in memory. When the memory switch is closed, the module will operate the seat motors until it counts down to the preset number of pulses.

The **easy exit** feature is an additional function of the memory seat that provides for easier entrance and exit of the vehicle by moving the seat all the way back and down. Some systems also move the steering wheel up and to full retract.

When the easy exit switch is closed, voltage is applied to both memory 1 and 2 inputs of the module. This signal is interrupted by the module to move the seat to its full down and full back position. As the seat moves to the easy exit position it counts the pulses and stores this information in memory.

Memory is not lost when the ignition switch is turned off. However, it is lost if the battery is disconnected. If memory is lost, the position of the seat at the time power is restored becomes set in memory for both positions.

In some systems, such as the Lincoln Continental, the easy exit feature is automatically activated when the door is opened.

Electronic Sunroof Concepts

Some manufacturers have introduced electronic control of their electric sunroofs. These systems incorporate a pair of relay circuits and a timer function into the control module. Although there are variations between manufacturers, the systems discussed here provide a study of the two basic types of systems.

Figure 13-41 The neutral safety backup switch signals the seat memory module when the transmission is in PARK. (Courtesy of General Motors Corporation)

Figure 13-42 Memory seat circuit. (Courtesy of General Motors Corporation)

Figure 13-42 (continued)

453

Figure 13-43 Toyota sunroof circuit using electronic controls.

Electronic-Controlled Toyota Sunroof

The schematics used to explain the operation of the Toyota sunroof use logic gates. If needed, refer to Chapter 11 of this manual to review the operation of the gates.

Refer to schematic (Figure 13-43) of a typical sunroof control circuit used by Toyota. The movement of the sunroof is controlled by the motor that operates a drive gear. The drive gear either pushes or pulls the connecting cable to move the sunroof.

Motor rotation is controlled by relays that are activated according to signals received from the slide, tilt, and limit switches. The limit switches are operated by a cam on the motor (Figure 13-44).

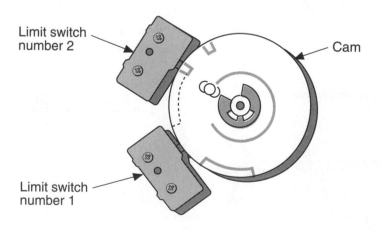

Figure 13-44 The limit switches operate off a cam on the motor.

Figure 13-45 Circuit operation when the switch is placed in the OPEN position.

The logic gates of this system operate on the principle of negative logic. When the slide switch is moved to the OPEN position, either limit switch 1 or both limit switches are closed (Figure 13-45). Limit switches 1 and 2 provide a negative side signal to the OR gate labeled F. The output from gate F is sent to gate A. Gate A is an AND gate, requiring input from gate F and the open slide switch. The output signal from gate A is used to turn on TR_2. This provides a ground path for the coil in relay 2. Battery voltage is applied to the motor through relay 2; the ground path is provided through the de-energized relay 1. Current is sent to the motor as long as the OPEN switch is depressed. If the OPEN switch is held in this position too long, a clutch in the motor disengages the motor from the drive gear.

Operation of the system during closing depends on how far the sunroof is open. If the sunroof is open more than 7.5 inches and the slide contact is moved to the CLOSE position, an input signal is sent to gate E (Figure 13-46). The other input signal required at gate E is received from the limit switches. The limit switch 1 signal passes through the OR gate G to the AND gate D. Limit switch 2 provides the second signal required by gate D. The output signal from D is the second input signal required by gate E. The output signal from E turns on TR_1. This energizes relay 1 and reverses the current flow through the motor. The motor will operate until the slide switch is opened or limit switch 2 opens.

Negative logic
defines the most negative voltage as a logical 1 in the binary code.

Figure 13-46 Circuit operation when the switch is placed in the CLOSE position and the sun roof is open more than 7.5 inches.

Figure 13-47 Circuit operation when the switch is placed in the CLOSE position and the sun roof is open less than 7.5 inches.

Figure 13-48 Circuit operation in the TILT UP position.

If the sunroof is open less than 7.5 inches and the slide switch is placed in the CLOSE position, the timer circuit is activated (Figure 13-47). The CLOSE switch signals the timer and provides an input signal to gate E. Limit switch 1 is open when the sunroof is opened less than 7.5 inches. The second input signal required by gate D is provided by the timer. The timer is activated for .5 second. This turns on TR_1 and operates the motor for .5 second, or long enough for rotation of the motor to close limit switch 1. When limit switch 1 is closed, the operation is the same as described when the sunroof is closed when it is more than 7.5 inches open.

When the tilt switch is located in the UP position, a signal is imposed on gate B (Figure 13-48). This signal is inverted by the NOT gate and is equal to the value received from the opened number 2 limit switch. The output signal from gate B turns on TR_1, which energizes relay 1 to turn on the motor. The motor clutch will disengage if the switch is held in the closed position longer than needed.

When the tilt switch is placed in the DOWN position, a signal is imposed on gate C (Figure 13-49). The second signal to gate C is received from the limit switches (both are open) through gate F. The signal from gate F is inverted by the NOT gate and is equal to that from the DOWN switch. The output signal from gate C turns on TR2 and energizes relay 2 to lower the sunroof. If the DOWN switch is held longer than necessary, limit switch 1 closes. When this switch is closed, the signals received by gate F are not opposite. This results in a mixed input to gate C and turns off the transistor.

Figure 13-49 Circuit operation during TILT DOWN.

Shop Manual
Chapter 13,
page 381

Electronically Controlled General Motors' Sunroof

See the schematic (Figure 13-50) of the sunroof system used on some GM model vehicles. The timing module uses inputs from the control switch and the limit switches to direct current flow to the motor. Depending on the inputs, the relays will be energized to rotate the motor in the proper direction. When the switch is located in the OPEN position, the open relay is

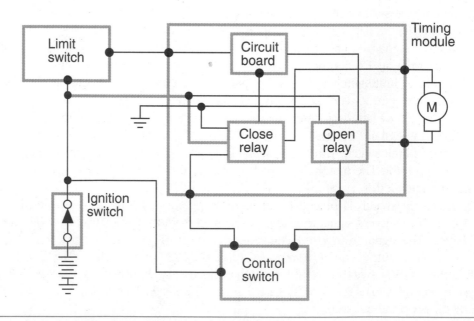

Figure 13-50 Block diagram of the GM sunroof.

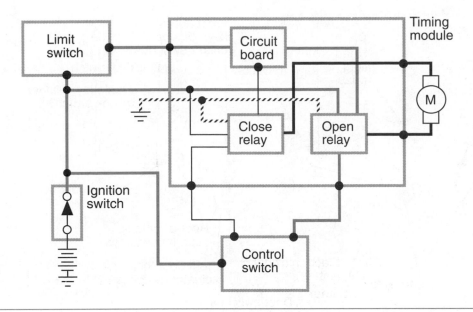

Figure 13-51 Sunroof circuit operation when the control switch is placed in the OPEN position.

energized sending current to the motor (Figure 13-51). The sunroof will continue to retract as long as the switch is held in the OPEN position. When the sunroof reaches its full open position, the limit switch will open and break the circuit to the open relay.

Placing the switch in the CLOSE position will energize the close relay (Figure 13-52). The current sent to the motor is in the opposite direction to close the sunroof. If the close switch is held until the sunroof reaches the full closed position, the limit switch will open.

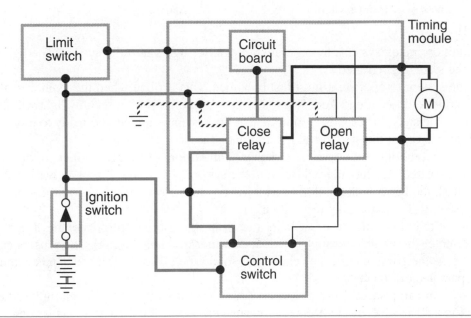

Figure 13-52 Current flow through the electronic control when the switch is placed in the CLOSE position.

Figure 13-53 Typical components of an antitheft system. (Courtesy of Mitsubishi Motor Sales of America, Inc.)

Antitheft Systems

Shop Manual
Chapter 13,
page 383

Antitheft systems are deterrent systems designed to scare off would-be thieves by sounding alarms and/or disabling the ignition system.

Arming means placing the alarm system in readiness to detect an illegal entry.

A vehicle is stolen in the United States every 26 seconds. In response to this problem, vehicle manufacturers are offering antitheft systems as optional or standard equipment. The illustration (Figure 13-53) shows many of the common components that are used in an antitheft system. These components include:

1. An electronic control module.
2. Door switches at all doors.
3. Trunk key cylinder switch.
4. Hood switch.
5. Starter inhibitor relay.
6. Horn relay.
7. Alarm.

In addition, many systems incorporate the exterior lights into the system. The lights are flashed if the system is activated.

For the system to operate, it must first be armed. This is done when the ignition switch is turned off and the doors are locked. When the driver's door is shut, a security light will illuminate for approximately 30 seconds to indicate that the system is armed and ready to function. If any other door is open, the system will not arm until it is closed.

The control module monitors the switches. If the doors or trunk are opened, or the key cylinders are rotated, the module will activate the system. The control module will sound the alarm and flash the lights until the timer circuit has counted down. At the end of the timer function, the system will automatically rearm itself.

Some systems use ultrasonic sensors that will signal the control module if someone attempts to enter the vehicle through the door or window (Figure 13-54). The sensors can be placed to sense the parameter of the vehicle and sound the alarm if someone enters within the protected parameter distance.

The system can also use current sensitive sensors that will activate the alarm if there is a change in the vehicle's electrical system. The change can occur if the courtesy lights come on or if an attempt is made to start the engine.

The following systems are provided to give you a sample of the types of antitheft systems used.

Figure 13-54 The ultrasonic sensor will trigger the alarm if someone enters the vehicle without the alarm being disarmed.

Ford Antitheft Protection System

If the system is triggered, it will sound the horn; flash the low-beam headlights, taillights, and parking lamps; and disable the ignition system. See the schematic (Figure 13-55) of the system.

The arming process is started when the ignition switch is turned off. Voltage provided to the module at terminal K is removed (Figure 13-56). When the door is opened, a voltage is applied to the courtesy lamp circuit 24 through the closed switch. This voltage energizes the inverter relay and provides a ground for module terminal J. This signal is used by the control module to provide an alternating ground at terminal D, causing the indicator lamp to blink. The flashing indicator light alerts the driver that the system is not armed. When the door lock switch is placed in the LOCK position, battery voltage is applied to terminal G of the module. The module uses this signal to apply a steady ground at terminal D, causing the indicator light to stay on continuously. When the door is closed, the door switch is opened. The opened door switch de-energizes the inverter relay coil. Terminal J is no longer grounded and the indicator light goes out after a couple of seconds.

Figure 13-55 Circuit schematic of Ford's antitheft system. (Courtesy of Chilton Book Company)

Figure 13-56 Circuit operation during the arming process. (Courtesy of Chilton Book Company)

Figure 13-57 Circuit operation when the alarm system is disarmed. (Courtesy of Chilton Book Company)

Figure 13-58 Circuit operation indicating the signal to the module when one of the doors is opened with the system armed. (Courtesy of Chilton Book Company)

To disarm the system, one of the front doors must be opened with a key or by pressing the correct code into the keyless entry keypad. Unlocking the door closes the lock cylinder switch and grounds terminal H of the module (Figure 13-57). This signal disarms the system.

Once the system is armed, if terminal J and C receive a ground signal the control module will trigger the alarm. Terminal C is grounded if the trunk tamper switch contacts close. Terminal J is grounded when the inverter relay contacts are closed. The inverter relay is controlled by the doorjamb switches. If one of the doors is opened, the switch closes and energizes the relay coil. The contacts close and ground is provided to terminal J (Figure 13-58).

When the alarm is activated, a pulsating ground is provided at module terminal F (Figure 13-59). This pulsating ground energizes and de-energizes the alarm relay. As the relay contacts open and close, a pulsating voltage is sent to the horns and exterior lights.

At the same time, the start interrupt circuit is activated. The start interrupt relay receives battery voltage from the ignition switch when it is in the START position. When the alarm is activated, the module provides a ground through terminal E, causing the relay coil to be energized. The energized relay opens the circuit to the starter system, preventing starter operation.

GM Pass-Key Antitheft System

The basic operation of the GM system is similar to that of the Ford system. An additional feature that GM offers can be used as a stand alone antitheft system or in combination with other systems. This system acts as an engine disable system, by using a pass-key arrangement. The ignition key has an electronic pellet that has a coded resistance value (Figure 13-60). Each of the different pellets used has a specific resistance value that ranges between 380 ohms and 12,300 ohms. The ignition key must be the correct cut to operate the lock and the correct electrical code to close the starter circuit.

Pass-key is derived from personal automotive security system.

Figure 13-59 The module sends a pulsating signal to the alarm relay to flash the exterior lights and sound the horn. (Courtesy of Chilton Book Company)

When the ignition key is inserted into the cylinder, the pellet makes contact with the resistor sensing contact. When the cylinder is rotated to the START position, battery voltage is sent to a decoder module. In addition, the resistance value of the key pellet is sent to the decoder module. The resistance value is compared to memory. If they match, the starter enable relay is energized. This completes the starter circuit and signals the ECM to start fuel delivery.

If the key pellet resistance does not match, the decoder will prevent starting of the engine for 2 to 4 minutes. Even if the lock cylinder is removed, the engine will not start because the start enable relay will not energize.

Figure 13-60 Basic components of the pass-key system. (Courtesy of General Motors Corporation)

Figure 13-61 Automatic door lock system utilizing the body computer. (Courtsey of Chrysler Corporation)

Automatic Door Locks

Many automobile manufacturers are incorporating automatic door locks as an additional safety and convenience system. Most systems lock the doors when the gear selector is placed in drive, the ignition switch is in RUN, and all doors are shut. Some systems will lock the doors when the gear shift selector is passed through the reverse position; others do not lock the doors unless the vehicle is moving 15 mph or faster.

The system may use the body computer to control the door lock relays (Figure 13-61), or a separate controller (Figure 13-62). The controller (or body computer) takes the place of the door lock switches for automatic operation. In order for the door lock controller to lock the doors, the following conditions must be met:

1. Ignition switch is in the RUN position.

2. Seat switch is closed by the driver.

3. All doors are closed (switches are open).

4. Gear selection is not in PARK.

5. Courtesy light switch is off.

When all of the door jam switches are open (doors closed), the ground is removed from the WHT wire to the controller (Figure 13-63). This signals the controller to enable the lock circuit. When the gear selection is moved from the PARK position, the neutral safety switch removes the power signal from the controller. The controller sends voltage through the LH seat switch to the lock relay coil. Current is sent through the motors to lock all doors.

When the gear selector is returned to the PARK position, voltage is applied through the neutral safety switch to the controller (Figure 13-64). The controller then sends power to the unlock relay coil to reverse current flow through the motors.

Shop Manual
Chapter 13,
page 388

Automatic door locks (ADL) is a passive system used to lock all doors when the required conditions are met.

Figure 13-62 Automatic door lock system that utilizes a separate control module. (Courtesy of General Motors Corporation)

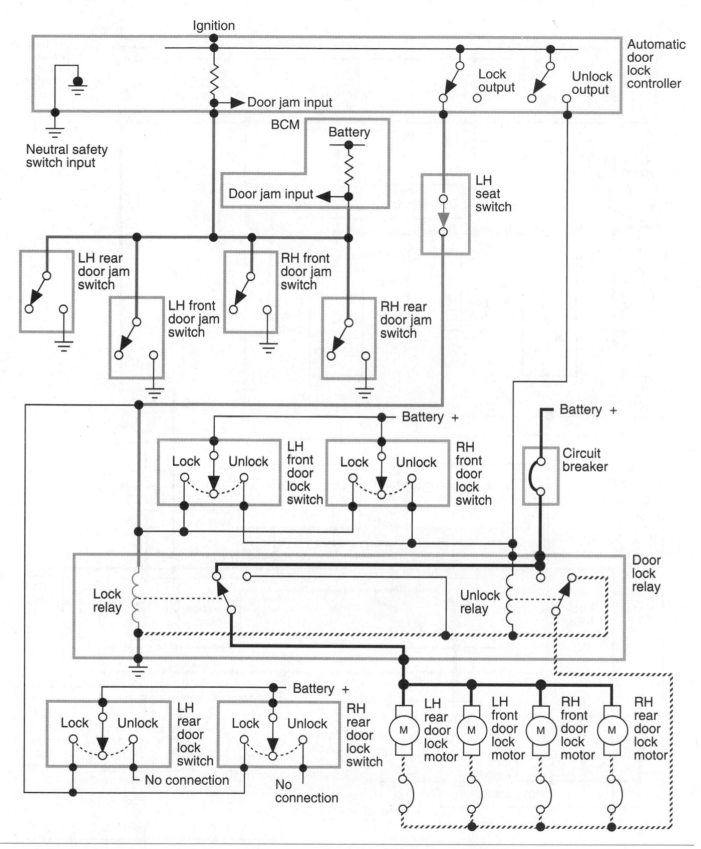

Figure 13-63 Automatic door lock system circuit schematic indicating operation during the lock procedure.

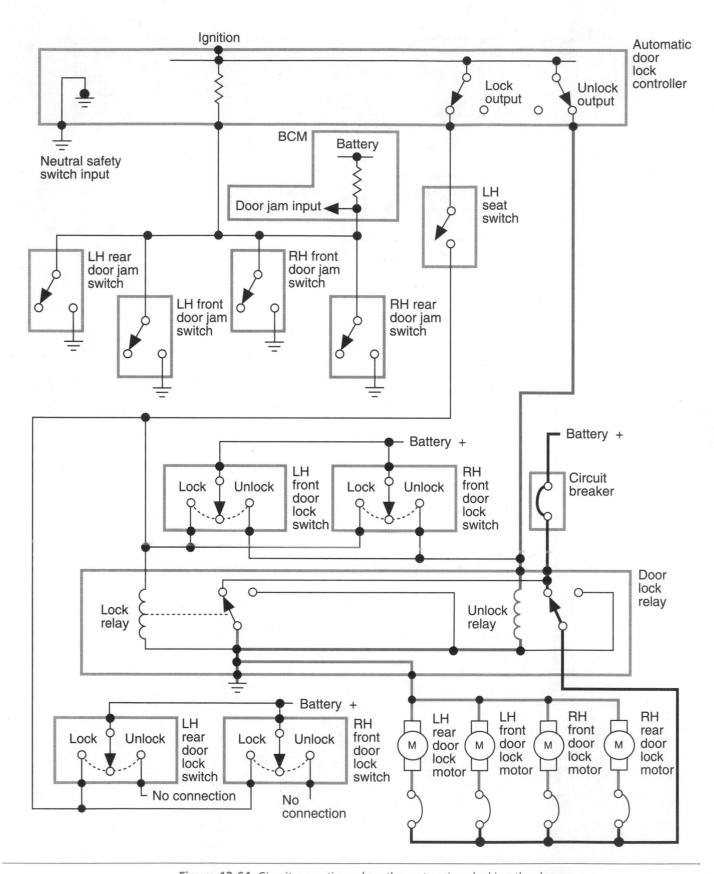

Figure 13-64 Circuit operation when the system is unlocking the doors.

Figure 13-65 Keyless entry system keypad.

Keyless Entry

The main components of the keyless entry system are the control module, a coded-button key-pad located on the driver's door, and the door lock motors.

The keypad consists of five normally open, single-pole, single-throw switches. Each switch represents two numbes: 1-2, 3-4, 5-6, 7-8, and 9-0 (Figure 13-65).

The keypad is wired into the circuit to provide input to the control module (Figure 13-66). The control module is programmed to lock the doors when the 7-8 and 9-0 switches are closed at the same time. The driver's door can be unlocked by entering a five-digit code through the keypad. The unlock code is programmed into the controller at the factory. However, the driver may enter a second code. Either code will operate the system.

Shop Manual
Chapter 13,
page 388

The **keyless entry system** allows the driver to unlock the doors or the deck lid (trunk) from outside the vehicle without the use of a key.

Ignition switch wiring to steering column

Trunk release

Keyless entry control module

Fuse panel

Keyless entry switch assembly

Seat sensor switch assembly

Deck lid latch assembly

Figure 13-66 Wiring harness and components of a typical keyless entry system. (Courtesy of Ford Motor Company)

In addition to the aforementioned functions, the keyless entry system also:

1. Unlocks all doors when the 3-4 button is pressed within 5 seconds after the five-digit code has been entered.

2. Releases the deck lid lock if the 5-6 button is pressed within 5 seconds of code entry.

3. Activates the illuminated entry system if one of the buttons is pressed.

4. Operates in conjunction with the automatic door lock system and may share the same control module.

See the schematic (Figure 13-67) of the keyless entry system used by Ford. When the 7-8 and 9-0 buttons on the keypad are pressed, the controller applies battery voltage to all motors through the lock switch (Figure 13-68).

When the five-digit code is entered, the controller closes the driver's switch to apply voltage in the opposite direction to the driver's door motor (Figure 13-69). If the driver presses the 3-4 button, the controller will apply reverse voltage to all motors to unlock the rest of the doors (Figure 13-70).

Some keyless entry systems can be operated remotely. Pressing a button on a hand-held transmitter will allow operation of the system from distances of 25 to 50 feet (Figure 13-71). When the unlock button is pressed, the driver's door unlocks and the interior lights are illuminated. If a theft deterrent system is installed on the vehicle, it is also disarmed when the unlock button is pressed. A driver exiting the vehicle can activate the door locks and arm the security system by pressing the lock button.

Shop Manual
Chapter 13,
page 393

Electronic Heated Windshield

The heated windshield system is designed to melt ice and frost from the windshield three to five times faster than conventional defroster systems (Figure 13-72). The windshield undergoes a special process during manufacturing to allow for current flow through the glass without interfering with the driver's vision.

The silver and zinc coating gives the windshield a gold tint.

There are two basic methods used to make the heated windshield:

1. Use a layer of plastic laminate that is between two layers of glass. The back of the outer layer is fused with a silver and zinc oxide coating. The coating carries the electrical current. Busbars are attached to the coating at the top and bottom of the windshield (Figure 13-73). A sensor is used to check the condition of the windshield coating. If the windshield has a crack or chip that will affect heating (Figure 13-74), the voltage drop across the resistor will indicate this condition to the control module. If the windshield is damaged, the controller will not allow heated windshield operation.

The film used on the heated windshield will block some radio or microwave signals. This may reduce the effective range of garage door openers and radar detectors.

2. Use a layer of resistive coating sprayed between the inner and outer windshield layers. The coating is transparent and does not provide any tint. A sensor is used to indicate if the coating has been damaged. If a chip or crack is not deep enough to penetrate the coating, it will not affect the system operation.

The two systems discussed here are representative of the methods used to heat the windshield.

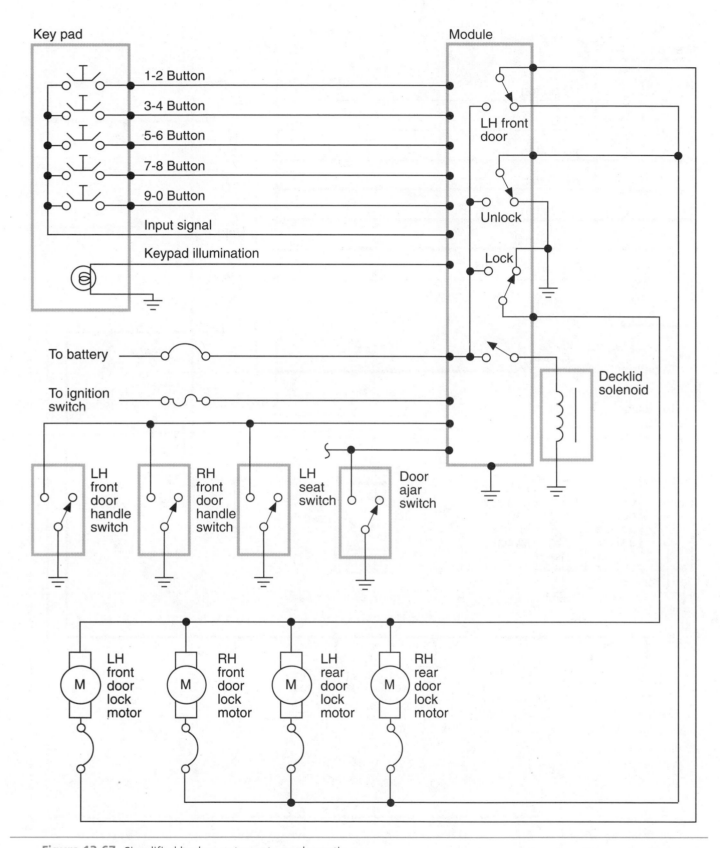

Figure 13-67 Simplified keyless entry system schematic.

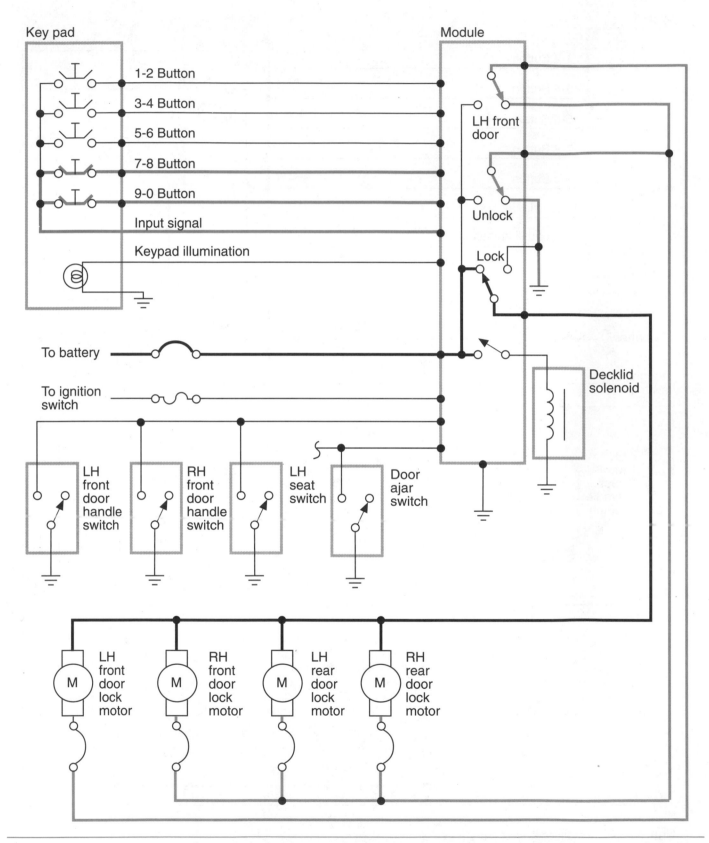

Figure 13-68 Circuit operation when the 7-8 and 9-0 buttons are pressed to lock all doors.

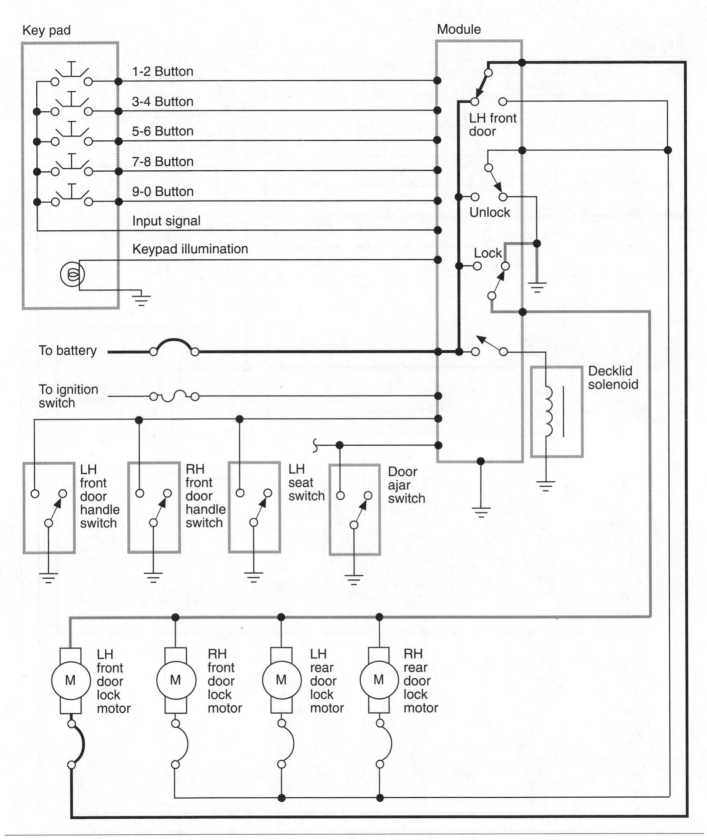

Figure 13-69 Circuit operation when the correct five-digit code is entered to unlock the driver's door.

Figure 13-70 Pressing the 3-4 button within 5 seconds of the code will unlock all doors.

Figure 13-71 Remote keyless entry system transmitter. (Courtesy of General Motors Corporation)

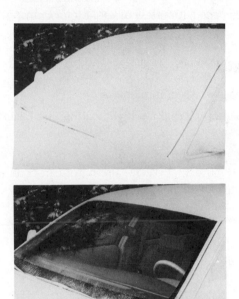

Figure 13-72 The heated windshield removes ice and frost from the windshield in just a few minutes. (Reprinted with the permission of Ford Motor Company)

Figure 13-73 The power and ground circuits are connected to the silver and zinc coating through busbars. (Reprinted with the permission of Ford Motor Company)

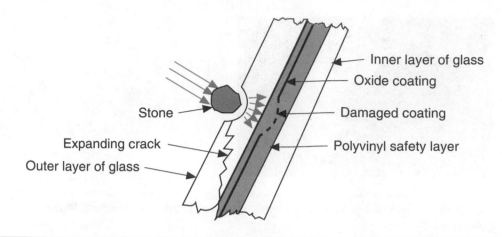

Figure 13-74 An open in the circuit can be caused by a chip or crack in the windshield. A sensor is used to prevent operation if the windshield is damaged. (Courtesy of Ford Motor Company)

Shop Manual
Chapter 13,
page 393

General Motors' Heated Windshield

General Motors' heated windshield consists of the following components:

1. The heated windshield: Contains a transparent internal resistive coating that heats when current is applied to it.

2. Special CS 144 alternator: There are three special phase terminals to provide AC power to the system's power module (Figure 13-75). The alternator can continue to supply its normal DC voltage while AC power is being supplied.

Figure 13-75 Schematic of CS 144 alternator used on vehicles equipped with heated windshields. The three terminals provide AC current to the power module.

3. The power module: Converts the AC voltage from the alternator to a higher DC voltage for use by the windshield.

4. The control module: Controls the heating cycle and provides automatic shut-down at the end of the time cycle, or if a fault is detected in the system.

5. The control switch.

See the schematic (Figure 13-76) of the GM heated windshield. When the system is activated by the driver, the control module starts its turn-on sequence. First it checks that there is more than 11.2 volts present at terminal B6. This assures there will be sufficient voltage to operate other circuits.

The second step for the control module is to check the vehicle's inside temperature. For the system to operate, the temperature must be below 65°F (18°C). Next, the controller checks the windshield sensor to see if there is any damage to the film coating.

If all of these conditions are met, the control module sends a signal to the BCM to increase the engine speed. The BCM passes the request on to the ECM. If the gear selector is in PARK or NEUTRAL, the ECM will increase the idle speed to approximately 1,400 rpm. The ECM will send a signal back to the BCM to indicate that the speed has been increased. When this feedback signal is received, the control module will turn on the power module relays. The power module will draw AC current from the alternator. The current is amplified and rectified by the power module, then sent to the windshield. Voltage at the windshield is between 50 and 90 volts.

Incorporated into the control module is a timer circuit. When the activation switch is turned on for the first time, the control module will operate the system for 3 minutes. If the switch is pressed again, at the end of the first cycle, it will result in a 1-minute cycle. If the switch is pressed while the cycle is still in operation, the system is turned off.

The BCM and ECM are used to provide certain functions when the system is activated.

Ford's Heated Windshield System

The illustration (Figure 13-77) shows the major components of the Ford heated windshield system. For the system to be activated, the engine must be running and inside temperature must be 40°F or less. When the driver activates the system the control module shuts off the voltage regulator and energizes the alternator output control relay. This switches the alternator output from the electrical system to the windshield circuit (Figure 13-78). After the switch has been completed, the control module turns on the voltage regulator to restore alternator output.

With the alternator output disconnected from the battery, battery voltage drops below 12 volts. The voltage regulator attempts to charge the battery by full fielding the alternator. Because the battery does not receive the alternator output, full field voltage reaches 30 to 70 volts. All of the full field power is sent to the windshield.

The control module will monitor the battery voltage and alternator output. It will prevent the output from increasing over 70 volts to protect the system. To prevent damage to the battery, if its voltage drops below 11 volts the control module reconnects the electrical system to the alternator.

When the system is activated, the control module sends a signal to the EEC controller to increase the idle speed to about 1,400 rpm. If the transmission is placed into a gear selection other than PARK or NEUTRAL, the EEC will return the idle speed to the normal setting.

For the system to be activated, the engine must be running.

Figure 13-76 General Motors' heated windshield schematic. (Courtesy of General Motors Corporation)

Figure 13-76 (continued)

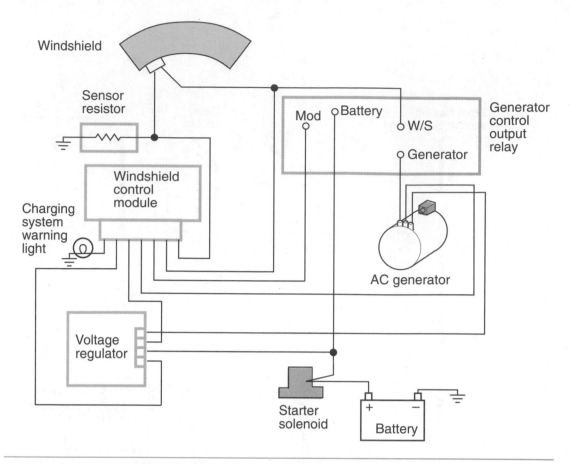

Figure 13-77 Components of Ford's heated windshield system.

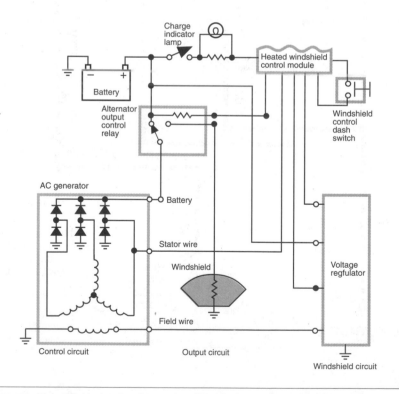

Figure 13-78 Simplified circuit schematic of Ford's heated windshield system.

Electronic Shift Transmissions

The use of solenoids and relays in controlling the operation of the engine has been expanded to include the drivetrain. Many of today's vehicles are equipped with electronic shift automatic transmissions. The control module uses several inputs to determine torque convertor clutch operation, hydraulic pressure levels, and shift points. The use of electronics within the transmission has improved shift quality and fuel economy. The Ford AXODE transaxle is discussed as an example of the principles used in electronic shift transmissions.

The AXODE transaxle is a fully automatic electronically controlled unit with a lock-up torque convertor (Figure 13-79). All major transaxle operations are controlled through the EEC-IV electronic control assembly (ECA). These functions include transaxle shifting, torque convertor clutch operation, and line pressure regulation.

The ECA receives inputs concerning throttle position, engine speed, torque convertor turbine speed, and other drivetrain operations (Figure 13-80). The ECA processes the information then controls transaxle operation through activation of five solenoids located within the valve body (Figure 13-81).

Shop Manual
Chapter 13,
page 397

AXODE is the model designation given to Ford's electronically shifted automatic transaxle with overdrive.

The **valve body** directs fluid oil under pressure to the torque convertor, servos, and clutches to control operation.

1. Torque converter
2. Piston plate clutch and damper assembly
3. Converter cover
4. Turbine
5. Impeller
6. Reactor
7. Oil pump drive shaft
8. Forward clutch
9. Low one-way clutch
10. Overdrive band
11. Direct clutch
12. Direct one-way clutch
13. Intermediate clutch
14. Reverse clutch
15. Planetary gears
16. Parking gear
17. Low/intermediate band
18. Final drive sun gear
19. Final drive planet
20. Differential assembly
21. Drive sprocket
22. Drive link assembly (chain)
23. Driven sprocket
24. Valve body
25. Oil pump

Figure 13-79 AXODE transaxle main components. (Reprinted with the permission of Ford Motor Company)

Figure 13-80 Inputs and outputs used to control transmission operation. (Reprinted with the permission of Ford Motor Company)

Figure 13-81 Output actuators and their location. (Reprinted with the permission of Ford Motor Company)

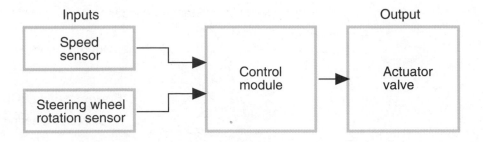

Figure 13-82 The control module receives input signals concerning vehicle speed and steering wheel rotation, then controls the actuator valve. (Reprinted with the permission of Ford Motor Company)

Speed Sensitive Steering

Most vehicles are available with some form of power steering, either as an option or as standard equipment. Conventional power steering systems provide a certain degree of assist to the driver when turning the steering wheel. The disadvantage of conventional power steering is the reduced road feel that the system offers during medium and high speeds. At these speeds it is desirable for a feeling of increased control and performance. Through the use of electronic controls, the advantages of high power assist and excellent road feel can be achieved.

Manufacturers have chosen different methods of accomplishing this task. The most common is to use a means of varying the output of the power steering pump through an electronic variable orifice (Figure 13-82). Other methods include the use of electric motor driven power steering pumps and electric rack and pinion steering (Figures 13-83 and 13-84).

Shop Manual
Chapter 13,
page 398

Figure 13-83 The first production application of electric rack and pinion steering was introduced on the Honda/Acura NSX. (Courtesy of Honda)

Steering sensor

Vehicle speed sensor

Power steering ECU

Power steering relay

Power steering box

Steering gear box

Reservoir

Vane pump

Figure 13-84 Toyota's electrohydraulic steering system has a self-contained motor in the pump (Courtesy of Toyota Motor Manufacturing, USA, Inc.)

Electronic Suspension Systems

Passive suspension systems have fixed spring rates and shock valving. Adaptive suspension systems are able to change ride characteristics by altering shock damping and ride height continuously. Active suspension systems are controlled by double acting hydraulic cylinders or solenoids (actuators) mounted at each wheel. The actuators support the vehicle's weight, instead of conventional springs or air springs.

Adaptive and active suspensions systems provide additional benefits over conventional passive suspension systems. They are able to change ride height, shock damping, and spring rates in response to changing road and driving conditions. Electronic suspension system types can vary from basic shock damping variations to a complex system of height and ride control that utilizes extensive computer programming.

Adaptive Suspension Systems

Sensors monitor vehicle speed, steering angle, ride height, brake pressure, and vehicle acceleration. They provide this information to the suspension control module. The control module then signals actuators to change shock rates in response to the changing conditions. A small actuator on top of each shock allows a variable range from firm to soft and solenoids on each air spring enable the computer to maintain constant ride height (Figure 13-85).

Depending on system design, other sensors used by the computer include G-sensors, throttle position sensors, speed sensors, roll sensors, lateral acceleration sensors, and brake switches (Figure 13-86).

Figure 13-85 Continental's air spring automatic ride control (ASARC) components. (Reprinted with the permission of Ford Motor Company)

Figure 13-86 Several sensors are used to determine the attitude of the vehicle at any given time. (Courtesy of Mitsubishi Motor Sales of America, Inc.)

Figure 13-87 Hydraulic schematic of an active suspension system.

Active Suspension Systems

There are several differences between adaptive and active suspension systems. The active system is capable of eliminating body roll and it is faster in its reaction time. The adaptive system is able to reduce body roll, but it cannot eliminate it.

Truly active suspension systems use high pressure hydraulic actuators to carry the vehicle's weight. The actuators combine the function of the shock absorber and the spring into one unit. Through control of the fluid pressure inside the actuators, ride height, body roll, damping, and spring rate can be controlled by the computer. These systems can be programmed to respond almost perfectly to all driving conditions (Figure 13-87).

The system is also able to eliminate body roll on turns by stiffening one side of the vehicle (Figure 13-88). All of these attitude control functions improve vehicle stability and increase tire traction and driver control.

Figure 13-88 System correction to eliminate body roll during a turn (left turn shown). (Courtesy of Mitsubishi Motor Sales of America, Inc.)

Labels on figure:
Modular relay
Antilock warning light
Lateral acceleration switch
Master cylinder
Booster
Control module
Wheel speed sensor (one at each wheel)
Toothed ring (one at each wheel)
Caliper (one at each wheel)
Modulator valve

Figure 13-89 Nonintegrated ABS system used on the Corvette. (Courtesy of General Motors Corporation)

Introduction to Antilock Brake Systems

The modern brake system is more than adequate to stop the vehicle under normal conditions. However, in approximately 1% of its use it will fail to stop the vehicle safely. This failure is generally the fault of drivers who allow their vehicle to enter an uncontrollable skid. Wheel lockup during braking will increase the stopping distance. A good driver knows that "pumping" the brakes during emergency stops keeps the vehicle from entering into an uncontrollable skid. A tire that is on the verge of slipping produces more friction with respect to the road than one that is locked. The antilock braking system (ABS) is designed to act in a similar manner as a driver pumping the brakes, but with much more control and at a much faster rate.

The ABS system is capable of pumping each brake up to 15 times per second. The control module can pulse the two front brakes separately and the rear brakes separately or as a pair, depending on system configuration. ABS automatically stops the vehicle in the shortest possible distance, without locking a wheel. In addition, ABS maintains directional control on almost any type of road surface or condition. Even though ABS improves vehicle braking, it cannot compensate for worn brake components, worn tires, excessive speed, or driver error.

The exact components of a system depend on manufacturer and system design. Nonintegrated ABS systems use conventional brake master cylinders with a separate hydraulic unit (Figure 13-89). Integrated ABS systems combine the brake master cylinder, hydraulic brake booster and the ABS components in a single hydraulic assembly (Figure 13-90).

Automatic Traction Control

The same technology used for ABS systems is also applied to automatic traction control. An electronic control monitor monitors the wheel speed sensors. If it determines that one of the drive wheels is spinning faster than the other, it will automatically apply the brakes to the spinning wheel. With the brake applied it requires a greater amount of torque to spin the wheel. Because a differential delivers equal torque to each drive wheel, the greater torque requirement is also transferred to the stationary or slower moving wheel. This allows the wheel that has the greatest amount of traction ability to move the vehicle.

Front wheel speed
sensor wire routing

Rear wheel speed sensor
wire routing

Sensor connection
to harness
(trunk area)

Relay
Hydraulic

Relays

Proportioner valve

Electronic brake control
module (EBCM)

Figure 13-90 Integrated ABS braking system. (Courtesy of General Motors Corporation)

Some manufacturers integrate some engine control functions into the automatic traction control system instead of or in addition to applying the brakes. If the control module senses a loss of traction, it signals the engine control module to retard the engine timing and to decrease the throttle plate position. This action will reduce the engine output in an attempt to reduce the amount of power to the drive wheels. If this action fails to reduce tire slippage, the module will cut fuel delivery to one or more engine cylinders. The reduction of engine power is to prevent overspeeding the engine.

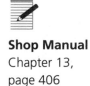

Shop Manual
Chapter 13,
page 406

Vehicle Audio Entertainment Systems

When radios were first introduced to the automotive market, they produced little more than "tinny" noise and static. Today's audio sound systems produce music and sound that rivals the best that home sound systems can produce. And with nearly the same or even greater amounts of volume or sound power!

The most common sound system configuration is the all-in-one unit more commonly called a receiver. Housed in this unit is the radio tuner, amplifier, tone controls, and unit controls for all functions. These units may also include internal capabilities such as cassette players, compact disc players, digital audiotape players, and/or graphic equalizers. Most will be electronically tuned with a display that shows all functions being accessed/controlled and digital clock functions (Figure 13-91).

Recent developments by the manufacturers have been made to take individual functions (tape, disc, equalizer, control head, tuner, amplifier, etc.) and put them in individual boxes and call them components. This would allow owners greater flexibility in selecting options to

Figure 13-91 Radios, like this one, are called receivers. They contain the basic elements of a tuner, an amplifier, and a control assembly in one housing, as well as possible functions as tape player or CD player.

Figure 13-92 Components, like those shown here, allow for a more compact and optimized mounting location(s) within the vehicle.

suit their needs and tastes (Figure 13-92). Componentizing has allowed greater dash design flexibility. Some components, such as multiple CD changers, can be remotely mounted in a trunk area for greater security.

Wiring diagrams for component systems will be more complex, (Figure 13-93). In addition to power and audio signal wires, note that some systems will have a serial data wire for microprocessor communication between components for the controlling of unit functions. Some functions are shared and integrated with factory-installed cellular phones, such as radio mute. Some systems allow remote control of functions through a control assembly mounted in the steering wheel or alternate passenger compartment location (Figure 13-94).

Figure 13-93 Schematic diagram showing the wiring hook-ups for remote-mounted components. (Reprinted with the permission of Ford Motor Company)

Hot at all times

Engine compartment fuse box

PR SND CELL PH
20 Amp

See power distribution

37 | Y
12 V
37 | Y

In-line fuse

10 Amp

720 R/Y   720 R/Y
12 V   12 V

16   4

Hot in ACC or Run

I/P fuse panel

17
10 Amp

See power distribution

296 | W/P
C440
151– 10– A8

296 | W/P

12 V (ACC/run)

5

Handset

708 | DG | 709 | W | 710 | DB | 711 | R | 712 | O | 716 | Y | 717 | T | 718 | BK

C359

708 | DG | 709 | W | 710 | DB | 711 | R | 712 | O | 716 | Y | 717 | T | 718 | BK

C413

1   6   8   11   12   18   24   23

Cellular trelephone transceiver

151– 10– F

Solid state

14   15   22   13   10   25   19   17   3

713 | BK | 714 | R | 728 | W   722 | R | 723 | BK | 724 | DG | 725 | W   0 V | 0 V | C413

694 | BK/LG   694 | BK/LG

713 | BK | 714 | R | 728 | W   722 | R | 723 | BK | 724 | DG | 725 | W

C440

See grounds

694 | BK/LG

C911   C450   Radio amplifier

Solid state

151– 10– F7

694 | BK/LG

151 10– A8

Microphone
151 12– A3

G202

Figure 13-93 (continued)

Figure 13-94 Audio system with steering wheel-mounted remote control.

491

Summary

❏ An automatic temperature control (ATC) system is capable of maintaining a preset level of comfort control as selected by the driver.

❏ There are two types of automatic temperature control: semiautomatic temperature control (SATC) and electronic automatic temperature control (EATC).

❏ The in-car sensor measures the average temperature inside the vehicle. The ambient sensor measures the temperature outside the vehicle.

❏ The sunload sensor produces a signal proportional to the heat intensity of the sun through the windshield.

❏ Cruise control is a system that allows the vehicle to maintain a preset speed with the driver's foot off the accelerator.

❏ The transducer regulates the vacuum to the servo based on the electrical signals it receives.

❏ The servo controls throttle plate position by receiving a controlled amount of vacuum from the transducer.

❏ Safety switches return control of vehicle speed to the driver when the brake pedal is depressed.

❏ The controller energizes the supply and vent valves to allow manifold vacuum to enter the servo. The servo moves the throttle to maintain the set speed. The vehicle speed is maintained by balancing the vacuum in the servo.

❏ Passive restraints operate automatically with no action required on the part of the driver or occupant.

❏ An emergency release mechanism is provided in the event that the system fails to operate.

❏ The air bag is a supplement. The seatbelt is the primary restraint system.

❏ The air bag module is composed of the air bag and inflator assembly. It is packaged in a single module and is mounted in the center of the steering wheel.

❏ The diagnostic module constantly monitors the readiness of the SIR electrical system. It supplies backup power to the air bag module in the event that the battery or cables are damaged during an accident.

❏ The memory seat feature allows the driver to program different seat positions that can be recalled at the push of a button.

❏ The easy exit feature is an additional function of the memory seat that provides for easier entrance and exit of the vehicle by moving the seat all the way back and down.

❏ Antitheft systems are deterrent systems designed to scare off would-be thieves by sounding alarms and/or disabling the ignition system.

❏ The antitheft control module monitors the switches. If the doors or trunk are opened, or the key cylinders are rotated, the module will activate the system.

❏ The pass-key system acts as an engine disable system by using an ignition key that has an electronic pellet containing a coded resistance value.

❏ Automatic door locks is a passive system used to lock all doors when the required conditions are met. Many automobile manufacturers are incorporating the system as an additional safety and convenience feature.

❏ The keyless entry system allows the driver to unlock the doors or the deck lid from outside the vehicle without the use of a key.

❏ The heated windshield system is designed to melt ice and frost from the windshield three to five times faster than conventional defroster systems.

❑ With electronically controlled transmissions, shifting, torque convertor clutch operation, and line pressure regulation are controlled through computer operation.

❑ The shift solenoids provide gear selection, based on engine controller commands, by controlling the pressure to the shift valves.

❑ In speed sensitive steering systems, steering effort is controlled based on vehicle speed and rate of steering wheel rotation.

❑ Adaptive and active suspension systems provide additional benefits over conventional passive suspension systems by varying ride height, shock damping, and spring rates in response to changing road and driving conditions.

❑ Adaptive suspension systems are able to change ride characteristics by altering shock damping and ride height continuously.

❑ Active suspension systems are controlled by double acting hydraulic cylinders or solenoids (actuators) mounted at each wheel. Instead of conventional springs or air springs, the actuators support the vehicle's weight.

❑ Nonintegrated ABS systems use conventional brake master cylinders with a separate hydraulic unit.

❑ Integrated ABS systems combine the brake master cylinder, hydraulic brake booster, and the ABS components in a single hydraulic assembly.

❑ Automatic traction control limits the amount of tire spin on slippery road conditions by applying the brakes automatically or reducing engine power automatically.

❑ Vehicle audio entertainment systems are generally only a single component (receiver). Recently manufacturers have been developing multiple components (tuner, amplifier, control head, etc.) to allow for greater flexibility.

❑ Some audio component systems utilize a serial data line to provide for communication and control of functions between those components.

Review Questions

Short Answer Essay

1. Explain the basic differences between SATC and EATC systems.

2. What is the purpose of highside and lowside temperature sensors in some EATC systems?

3. Explain the basic operating principles of the electronic cruise control system.

4. List and explain the function of the components of the air bag module.

5. List the main components of common antitheft systems.

6. What functions are controlled by the electronic shift transmission?

7. Describe the active suspension system.

8. What are the differences between passive, adaptive, and active suspensions?

9. What is the purpose of antilock braking systems?

10. Explain the difference between a radio receiver unit system and a component radio system.

Fill-in-the-Blanks

1. The ATC system uses _____ that will open and close air-blend doors to achieve the desired in-vehicle temperature.

2. The sunload sensor is a _____ diode that sends signals to the programmer concerning the extra generation of heat as the sun beats through the windshield.

3. By monitoring the high side temperature, the BCM is capable of making calculations that translate into _____ .

4. When the brake pedal is depressed, the cruise control system is disengaged through _____ and _____ switches.

5. Safe service procedures of air bag systems are accomplished through proper use of the _____ _____ and by understanding the _____ principles of these systems.

6. The _____ _____ conducts electrical signals to the module while permitting steering wheel rotation.

7. In the EVO system, steering effort is controlled based on vehicle _____ and rate of steering wheel _____ .

8. _____ suspension systems are able to change ride characteristics by altering shock damping and ride height continuously. _____ suspension systems are controlled by double acting hydraulic cylinders or solenoids mounted at each wheel.

9. Adaptive and active suspension systems provide additional benefits over conventional passive suspension systems. They are able to change _____ , shock _____ and _____ rates in response to changing road and driving conditions.

10. Radio receiver units usually contain at least the following:

    an _____ , a _____ , and function _____ .

ASE Style Review Questions

1. EATC systems are being discussed:
   Technician A says the control module or BCM will set trouble codes that can be accessed by the technician.
   Technician B says the EATC system will use fewer sensors than most SATC systems.
   Who is correct?
   A. A only
   B. B only
   C. Both A and B
   D. Neither A nor B

2. A typical electronic engine cruise control system is being discussed:
   Technician A says the system utilizes vent and supply solenoids.
   Technician B says the amount of vacuum applied to the servo is controlled by the power solenoid.
   Who is correct?
   A. A only
   B. B only
   C. Both A and B
   D. Neither A nor B

3. Electronic cruise control systems are being discussed:
   Technician A says if the voltage signal from the VSS drops below the low comparator value, the control module energizes the vent valve solenoid.
   Technician B says if the VSS signal is greater than the high comparator value, the control module energizes the vent solenoid valve.
   Who is correct?
   A. A only
   B. B only
   C. Both A and B
   D. Neither A nor B

4. Passive restraint systems are being discussed:
   Technician A says passive restraints require the manual effort of the occupant.
   Technician B says automatic seat belt systems operate by means of DC motors that move the belts by means of carriers on tracks.
   Who is correct?
   A. A only
   B. B only
   C. Both A and B
   D. Neither A nor B

5. The air bag module is being discussed:
   Technician A says the module supplies emergency current in the event battery voltage is lost.
   Technician B says the module is composed of the air bag and inflator assembly.
   Who is correct?
   A. A only
   B. B only
   C. Both A and B
   D. Neither A nor B

6. *Technician A* says the inflation assembly is composed of a solid chemical gas generator containing sodium azide and copper oxide propellent.
   Technician B says the air bag module is serviceable.
   Who is correct?
   A. A only
   B. B only
   C. Both A and B
   D. Neither A nor B

7. The keyless entry system is being discussed:
   Technician A says an additional function of the system is that the deck lid lock can be released by pressing the 5-6 button.
   Technician B says a second code can be entered into the system.
   Who is correct?
   A. A only
   B. B only
   C. Both A and B
   D. Neither A nor B

8. The heated windshield system is being discussed:
   Technician A says if the windshield has a crack or chip that will affect heating, the voltage drop across the resistor will indicate this condition to the control module.
   Technician B says if the windshield is damaged, the controller reduces the voltage to the windshield to 20 volts.
   Who is correct?
   A. A only
   B. B only
   C. Both A and B
   D. Neither A nor B

9. Electronic transmission actuators are being discussed:

Technician A says the shift solenoids regulate the amount of line pressure in the transmission.

Technician B says the electronic pressure control solenoid controls provide gear selection by controlling pressure to the shift valves.

Who is correct?

A. A only
B. B only
C. Both A and B
D. Neither A nor B

10. Automatic traction control is being discussed:

Technician A says if the electronic control monitor determines one of the drive wheels is spinning faster than the other, it will automatically apply the brakes to the spinning wheel, depending on the system.

Technician B says the module will signal the engine controller to increase power output to the drive wheels.

Who is correct?

A. A only
B. B only
C. Both A and B
D. Neither A nor B

GLOSSARY

A circuit A generator regulator circuit that uses an external grounded field circuit. In the A circuit, the regulator is on the ground side of the field coil.

Circuito A Circuito regulador del generador que utiliza un circuito inductor externo puesto a tierra. En el circuito A, el regulador se encuentra en el lado a tierra de la bobina inductora.

Active suspension systems Suspension systems that are controlled by double-acting hydraulic cylinders or solenoids (actuators) mounted at each wheel. The actuators support the vehicle's weight, instead of conventional springs or air springs.

Sistemas activos de suspensión Sistemas de suspensión controlados por cilindros hidráulicos de doble acción o por solenoides (accionadores) montados en cada rueda. Los accionadores apoyan el peso del vehículo, en vez de muelles convencionales o muelles de aire.

Actuators Devices that perform the actual work commanded by the computer. They can be in the form of a motor, relay, switch, or solenoid.

Accionadores Dispositivos que realizan el trabajo efectivo que ordena la computadora. Dichos dispositivos pueden ser un motor, un relé, un conmutador o un solenoide.

Adaptive suspension systems Suspension systems that are able to change ride characteristics by continuously altering shock damping and ride height.

Sistemas adaptadores de suspensión Sistemas de suspensión que pueden cambiar las características del viaje al alterar continuamente el amortiguamiento y la altura del viaje.

Air bag module Composed of the air bag and inflator assembly, which is packaged into a single module.

Unidad del Airbag Formada por el conjunto del Airbag y el inflador. Este conjunto se empaqueta en una sola unidad.

Air core gauge Gauge design that uses the interaction of two electromagnets and the total field effect upon a permanent magnet to cause needle movement.

Calibrador de núcleo de aire Calibrador diseñado para utilizar la interacción de dos electroimanes y el efecto inductor total sobre un imán permanente para generar el movimiento de la aguja.

Alternating current Electrical current that changes direction between positive and negative.

Corriente alterna Corriente eléctrica que recorre un circuito ya sea en dirección positiva o negativa.

Ambient temperature The temperature of the outside air.

Temperatura ambiente Temperatura del aire ambiente.

American wire gauge (AWG) System used to determine wire sizes based on the cross-sectional area of the conductor.

Calibrador americano de alambres Sistema utilizado para determinar el tamaño de los alambres, basado en el área transversal del conductor.

Ammeter A test meter used to measure current draw.

Amperímetro Instrumento de prueba utilizado para medir la intensidad de una corriente.

Amperes *See* current.

Amperios *Véase* corriente.

Analog A voltage signal that is infinitely variable or that can be changed within a given range.

Señal analógica Señal continua y variable que debe traducirse a valores numéricos discontinuos para poder ser tratada por una computadora.

Anode The positive charge electrode in a voltage cell.

Ánodo Electrodo de carga positiva de un generador de electricidad.

Antilock brakes (ABS) A brake system that automatically pulsates the brakes to prevent wheel lockup under panic stop and poor traction conditions.

Frenos antibloqueo Sistema de frenos que pulsa los frenos automáticamente para impedir el bloqueo de las ruedas en casos de emergencia y de tracción pobre.

Armature The movable component of an electric motor, which consists of a conductor wound around a laminated iron core and is used to create a magnetic field.

Armadura Pieza móvil de un motor eléctrico, compuesta de un conductor devanado sobre un núcleo de hierro laminado y que se utiliza para producir un campo magnético.

Aspirator Tubular device that uses a venturi effect to draw air from the passenger compartment over the in-car sensor. Some manufacturers use a suction motor to draw the air over the sensor.

Aspirador Dispositivo tubular que utiliza un efecto Venturi para extraer aire del compartimiento del pasajero sobre el sensor dentro del vehículo. Algunos fabricantes utilizan un motor de succión para extraer el aire sobre el sensor.

Atom The smallest part of a chemical element that still has all the characteristics of that element.

Átomo Partícula más pequeña de un elemento químico que conserva las cualidades íntegras del mismo.

Automatic headlight dimming An electronic feature that automatically switches the headlights from high beam to low beam under two different conditions: light from oncoming vehicles strikes the photocell-amplifier; or light from the taillights of a vehicle that is being passed strikes the photocell-amplifier.

Reducción automática de intensidad luminosa de los faros delanteros Característica electrónica que conmuta los faros delanteros automáticamente de luz larga a luz corta dadas las siguientes circunstancias: la luz de los vehículos que se aproximan alcanza el amplificador de fotocélula, o la luz de los faros traseros de un vehículo que se ha rebasado alcanza el amplificador de fotocélula.

Balanced atom An atom that has an equal amount of protons and electrons.

Átomo equilibrado Átomo que tiene el mismo número de protones y de electrones.

Base The center layer of a bipolar transistor.

Base Capa central de un transistor bipolar.

Battery cell The active unit of a battery.

Acumulador de batería Componente activo de una batería.

Baud rate The measure of computer data transmission speed in bits per second.

Razón de baúd Medida de la velocidad de la transmisión de datos de una computadora en bits por segundo.

B circuit A generator regulator circuit that is internally grounded. In the B circuit, the voltage regulator controls the power side of the field circuit.

Circuito B Circuito regulador del generador puesto internamente a tierra. En el circuito B, el regulador de tensión controla el lado de potencia del circuito inductor.

Bias voltage Voltage applied across a diode.

Tensión polarizadora Tensión aplicada a través de un diodo.

Bimetallic strip A metal contact wiper consisting of two different types of metals. One strip will react quicker to heat than the other, causing the strip to flex in proportion to the amount of current flow.

Banda bimetálica Contacto deslizante de metal compuesto de dos tipos de metales distintos. Una banda reaccionará más rápido al calor que la otra, haciendo que la banda se doble en proporción con la cantidad de flujo de corriente.

Binary code A series of numbers represented by 1's and 0's. Any number and word can be translated into a combination of binary 1's and 0's.

Código binario Serie de números representados por unos y ceros. Cualquier número y palabra puede traducirse en una combinación de unos y ceros binarios.

Bipolar The name used for transistors because current flows through the materials of both polarities.

Bipolar Nombre aplicado a los transistores porque la corriente fluye por conducto de materiales de ambas polaridades.

Bit A binary digit.

Bit Dígito binario.

Brushes Electrically conductive sliding contacts, usually made of copper and carbon.

Escobillas Contactos deslizantes de conduccion eléctrica, por lo general hechos de cobre y de carbono.

Bus Bar A common electrical connection to which all of the fuses in the fuse box are attached. The bus bar is connected to battery voltage.

Barra colectora Conexión eléctrica común a la que se conectan todos los fusibles de la caja de fusibles. La barra colectora se conecta a la tensión de la batería.

Buzzer An audible warning device that is used to warn the driver of possible safety hazards.

Zumbador Dispositivo audible de advertencia utilizado para prevenir al conductor de posibles riesgos a la seguridad.

Capacitance The ability of two conducting surfaces to store voltage.

Capacitancia Propiedad que permite el almacenamiento de electricidad entre dos conductores aislados entre sí.

Carbon monoxide An odorless, colorless, and toxic gas that is produced as a result of combustion.

Monóxido de carbono Gas inodoro, incoloro y tóxico producido como resultado de la combustión.

Cartridge fuses *See* maxi-fuse.

Fusibles cartucho *Véase* maxifusible.

Cathode Negatively charged electrode of a voltage cell.

Cátodo Electrodo de carga negativa de un generador de electricidad.

Choke coil Fine wire wound into a coil used to absorb oscillations in a switched circuit.

Bobina de inducción Alambre fino devanado en una bobina, utilizado para absorber oscilaciones en un circuito conmutado.

Circuit The path of electron flow consisting of the voltage source, conductors, load component, and return path to the voltage source.

Circuito Trayectoria del flujo de electrones, compuesto de la fuente de tensión, los conductores, el componente de carga y la trayectoria de regreso a la fuente de tensión.

Clock circuit A crystal that electrically vibrates when subjected to current at certain voltage levels. As a result, the chip produces very regular series of voltage pulses.

Circuito de reloj Cristal que vibra electrónicamente cuando está sujeto a una corriente a ciertos niveles de tensión. Como resultado, el fragmento produce una serie sumamente regular de impulsos de tensión.

Closed circuit A circuit that has no breaks in the path and allows current to flow.

Circuito cerrado Circuito de trayectoria ininterrumpida que permite un flujo continuo de corriente.

Cold cranking amps (CCA) Rating indicates the battery's ability to deliver a specified amount of current to start an engine at low ambient temperatures.

Amperios de arranque en frío Tasa indicativa de la capacidad de la batería para producir una cantidad específica de corriente para arrancar un motor a bajas temperaturas ambiente.

Collector The portion of a bipolar transistor that receives the majority of current carriers.

Dispositivo de toma de corriente Parte del transistor bipolar que recibe la mayoría de los portadores de corriente.

Commutator A series of conducting segments located around one end of the armature.

Conmutador Serie de segmentos conductores ubicados alrededor de un extremo de la armadura.

Computer An electronic device that stores and processes data and is capable of operating other devices.

Computadora Dispositivo electrónico que almacena y procesa datos y que es capaz de ordenar a otros dispositivos.

Condenser A capacitor made from two sheets of metal foil separated by an insulator.

Condensador Capacitador hecho de dos láminas de metal separadas por un medio aislante.

Conduction Bias voltage difference between the base and the emitter has increased to the point that the transistor is switched on. In this condition, the transistor is conducting. Output current is proportional to that of the current through the base.

Conducción La diferencia de la tensión polarizadora entre la base y el emisor ha aumentado hasta el punto que el transistor es conectado. En estas circunstancias, el transistor está conduciendo. La corriente de salida está en proporción con la de la corriente conducida en la base.

Conductor A substance that is capable of supporting the flow of electricity through it.

Conductor Sustancia capaz de conducir corriente eléctrica.

Continuity Refers to the circuit being continuous with no opens.

Continuidad Se refiere al circuito ininterrumpido, sin aberturas.

Conventional theory Electrical theory that states protons flow from a positive point to a more negative point.

Teoría convencional Teoría de electricidad la cual enuncia que los protones fluyen desde un punto positivo a un punto más negativo.

Corner lights Lamps that illuminate when the turn signals are activated. They burn steadily when the turn signal switch is in a turn position to provide additional illumination of the road in the direction of the turn.

Faros laterales Lámparas que se encienden cuando se activan las luces indicadoras para virajes. Se encienden de manera continua cuando el conmutador de las luces indicadoras para virajes está conectado para proveer iluminación adicional de la carretera hacia la dirección del viraje.

Counterelectromotive force (CEMF) An induced voltage that opposes the source voltage.

Fuerza cóntraelectromotriz Tensión inducida en oposición a la tensión fuente.

Courtesy lights Lamps that illuminate the vehicle's interior when the doors are open.

Luces interiores Lámparas que iluminan el interior del vehículo cuando las puertas están abiertas.

Covalent bonding When atoms share electrons with other atoms.

Enlace covalente Cuando los átomos comparten electrones con otros átomos.

Crystal A term used to describe a material that has a definite atom structure.

Cristal Término utilizado para describir un material que tiene una estructura atómica definida.

Current The aggregate flow of electrons through a wire. One ampere represents the movement of 6.25 billion billion electrons (or one coulomb) past one point in a conductor in one second.

Corriente Flujo combinado de electrones a través de un alambre. Un amperio representa el movimiento de 6,25 mil millones de mil millones de electrones (o un colombio) que sobrepasa un punto en un conductor en un segundo.

Cutoff When reverse-bias voltage is applied to the base leg of the transistor. In this condition, the transistor is not conducting and no current will flow.

Corte Cuando se aplica tensión polarizadora inversa a la base del transistor. En estas circunstancias, el transistor no está conduciendo y no fluirá ninguna corriente.

Darlington pair An arrangement of transistors that amplifies current by one transistor acting as a preamplifier which creates a larger base current to the second transistor.

Par Darlington Conjunto de transistores que amplifica la corriente. Un transistor actúa como preamplificador y produce una corriente base más ámplia para el segundo transistor.

d'Arsonval gauge A gauge design that uses the interaction of a permanent magnet and an electromagnet, and the total field effect to cause needle movement.

Calibrador d'Arsonval Calibrador diseñado para utilizar la interacción de un imán permanente y de un electroimán, y el efecto inductor total para generar el movimiento de la aguja.

Deep cycling Discharging the battery completely before recharging it.

Operación cíclica completa La descarga completa de la batería previo al recargo.

Delta stator A three-winding ac generator stator with the ends of each winding connected to each other.

Estátor Delta Estátor generador de corriente alterna de devanado triple, con los extremos de cada devanado conectados entre sí.

Dielectric An insulator material.

Dieléctrico Material aislante.

Digital A voltage signal is either on-off, yes-no, or high-low.

Digital Una señal de tensión está Encendida-Apagada, es Sí-No o Alta-Baja.

Dimmer switch A switch in the headlight circuit that provides the means for the driver to select either high beam or low beam operation, and to switch between the two. The dimmer switch is connected in series within the headlight circuit and controls the current path for high and low beam.

Conmutador reductor Conmutador en el circuito para faros delanteros que le permite al conductor que elegir la luz larga o la luz corta, y conmutar entre las dos. El conmutador reductor se conecta en serie dentro del circuito para faros delanteros y controla la trayectoria de la corriente para la luz larga y la luz corta.

Diode An electrical one-way check valve that will allow current to flow in one direction only.

Diodo Válvula eléctrica de retención, de una vía, que permite que la corriente fluya en una sola dirección.

Diode rectifier bridge A series of diodes that are used to provide a reasonably constant dc voltage to the vehicle's electrical system and battery.

Puente rectificador de diodo Serie de diodos utilizados para proveerles una tensión de corriente continua bastante constante al sistema eléctrico y a la batería del vehículo.

Diode trio Used by some manufacturers to rectify the stator of an ac generator current so that it can be used to create the magnetic field in the field coil of the rotor.

Trío de diodos Utilizado por algunos fabricantes para rectificar el estátor de la corriente de un generador de corriente alterna y poder así utilizarlo para crear el campo magnético en la bobina inductora del rotor.

Direct current (dc) Electric current that flows in one direction.

Corriente continua Corriente eléctrica que fluye en una dirección.

Discrete devices Electrical components that are made separately and have wire leads for connections to an integrated circuit.

Dispositivos discretos Componentes eléctricos hechos uno a uno; tienen conductores de alambre para hacer conexiones a un circuito integrado.

Doping The addition of another element with three or five valence electrons to a pure semiconductor.

Impurificación La adición de otro elemento con tres o cinco electrones de valencia a un semiconductor puro.

Double filament lamp A lamp designed to execute more than one function. It can be used in the stoplight circuit, taillight circuit, and the turn signal circuit combined.

Lámpara con filamento doble Lámpara diseñada para llevar a cabo más de una función. Puede utilizarse en una combinación de los circuitos de faros de freno, de faros traseros y de luces indicadoras para virajes.

Drain The portion of a field-effect transistor that receives the holes or electrons.

Drenador Parte de un transistor de efecto de campo que recibe los agujeros o electrones.

Duty cycle The percentage of on time to total cycle time.

Ciclo de trabajo Porcentaje del trabajo efectivo a tiempo total del ciclo.

Eddy currents Small induced currents.

Corriente de Foucault Pequeñas corrientes inducidas.

Electrical load The working device of the circuit.

Carga eléctrica Dispositivo de trabajo del circuito.

Electrically Erasable PROM (EEPROM) Memory chip that allows for electrically changing the information one bit at a time.

Capacidad de borrado electrónico PROM Fragmento de memoria que permite el cambio eléctrico de la información un bit a la vez.

Electrochemical The chemical action of two dissimilar materials in a chemical solution.

Electroquímico Acción química de dos materiales distintos en una solución química.

Electrolyte A solution of 64% water and 36% sulfuric acid.

Electrolito Solución de un 64% de agua y un 36% de ácido sulfúrico.

Electromagnetic gauge Gauge that produces needle movement by magnetic forces.

Calibrador electromagnético Calibrador que genera el movimiento de la aguja mediante fuerzas magnéticas.

Electromagnetic induction The production of voltage and current within a conductor as a result of relative motion within a magnetic field.

Inducción electromagnética Producción de tensión y de corriente dentro de un conductor como resultado del movimiento relativo dentro de un campo magnético.

Electromagnetic interference (EMI) An undesirable creation of electromagnetism whenever current is switched on and off.

Interferencia electromagnética Fenómeno de electromagnetismo no deseable que resulta cuando se conecta y se desconecta la corriente.

Electromagnetism A form of magnetism that occurs when current flows through a conductor.

Electromagnetismo Forma de magnetismo que ocurre cuando la corriente fluye a través de un conductor.

Electromotive force (EMF) *See* voltage.

Fuerza electromotriz *Véase* tensión.

Electron Negative-charged particles of an atom.

Electrón Partículas de carga negativa de un átomo.

Electron theory Defines electrical movement as from negative to positive.

Teoría del electrón Define el movimiento eléctrico como el movimiento de lo negativo a lo positivo.

Electrostatic field   The field that is between the two oppositely charged plates.

Campo electrostático   Campo que se encuentra entre las placas de carga opuesta.

Emitter   The outer layer of the transistor, which supplies the majority of current carriers.

Emisor   Capa exterior del transistor que suministra la mayor parte de los portadores de corriente.

Equivalent series load (equivalent resistance)   The total resistance of a parallel circuit, which is equivalent to the resistance of a single load in series with the voltage source.

Carga en serie equivalente (resistencia equivalente)   Resistencia total de un circuito en paralelo, equivalente a la resistencia de una sola carga en serie con la fuente de tensión.

Erasable PROM (EPROM)   Similar to PROM except that its contents can be erased to allow for new data to be installed. A piece of Mylar tape covers a window. If the tape is removed, the microcircuit is exposed to ultraviolet light and erases its memory.

Capacidad de borrado PROM   Parecido al PROM, pero su contenido puede borrarse para permitir la instalación de nuevos datos. Un trozo de cinta Mylar cubre una ventana; si se remueve la cinta, el microcircuito queda expuesto a la luz ultravioleta y borra la memoria.

Excitation current   Current that magnetically excites the field circuit of the ac generator.

Corriente de excitación   Corriente que excita magnéticamente al circuito inductor del generador de corriente alterna.

Feedback   1. Data concerning the effects of the computer's commands are fed back to the computer as an input signal. Used to determine if the desired result has been achieved. 2. A condition that can occur when electricity seeks a path of lower resistance, but the alternate path operates a component other than that intended. Feedback can be classified as a short.

Realimentación   1. Datos referentes a los efectos de las órdenes de la computadora se suministran a la misma como señal de entrada. La realimentación se utiliza para determinar si se ha logrado el resultado deseado. 2. Condición que puede ocurrir cuando la electricidad busca una trayectoria de menos resistencia, pero la trayectoria alterna opera otro componente que aquel deseado. La realimentación puede clasificarse como un cortocircuito.

Fiber optics   A medium of transmitting for the transmission of light through polymethylmethacrylate plastic that keeps the light rays parallel even if there are extreme bends in the plastic.

Transmisión por fibra óptica   Técnica de transmisión de luz por medio de un plástico de polimetacrilato de metilo que mantiene los rayos de luz paralelos aunque el plástico esté sumamente torcido.

Field-effect transistor (FET)   A unipolar transistor in which current flow is controlled by voltage in a capacitance field.

Transistor de efecto de campo   Transistor unipolar en el cual la tensión en un campo de capacitancia controla el flujo de corriente.

Floor jack   A portable hydraulic tool used to raise and lower a vehicle.

Gato de pie   Herramienta hidráulica portátil utilizada para levantar y bajar un vehículo.

Flux density   The number of flux lines per square centimeter.

Densidad de flujo   Número de líneas de flujo por centímetro cuadrado.

Flux lines   Magnetic lines of force.

Líneas de flujo   Líneas de fuerza magnética.

Forward bias   A positive voltage that is applied to the P-type material and negative voltage to the N-type material of a semiconductor.

Polarización directa   Tensión positiva aplicada al material P y tensión negativa aplicada al material N de un semiconductor.

Full field   Maximum ac generator output.

Campo completo   Salida máxima de un generador de corriente alterna.

Fuse   A replaceable circuit protection device that will melt should the current passing through it exceed its rating.

Fusible   Dispositivo reemplazable de protección del circuito que se fundirá si la corriente que fluye por el mismo excede su valor determinado.

Fuse box   A term used to indicate the central location of the fuses contained in a single holding fixture.

Caja de fusibles   Término utilizado para indicar la ubicación central de los fusibles contenidos en un solo elemento permanente.

Fusible link   A wire made of meltable material with a special heat-resistant insulation. When there is an overload in the circuit, the link melts and opens the circuit.

Cartucho de fusible   Alambre hecho de material fusible con aislamiento especial resistente al calor. Cuando ocurre una sobrecarga en el circuito, el cartucho se funde y abre el circuito.

Gain   The ratio of amplification in an electronic device.

Ganancia   Razón de amplificación en un dispositivo electrónico.

Ganged   Refers to a type of switch in which all wipers of the switch move together.

Acoplado en tándem   Se refiere a un tipo de conmutador en el cual todos los contactos deslizantes del mismo se mueven juntos.

Gate   The portion of a field-effect transistor that controls the capacitive field and current flow.

Compuerta   Parte de un transistor de efecto de campo que controla el campo capacitivo y el flujo de corriente.

Gauge   1. A device that displays the measurement of a monitored system by the use of a needle or pointer that moves along a calibrated scale. 2. The number that is assigned to a wire to indicate its size. The larger the number, the smaller the diameter of the conductor.

Calibrador   1. Dispositivo que muestra la medida de un sistema regulado por medio de una aguja o indicador que se mueve a través de una escala calibrada. 2. El número asignado a un alambre indica su tamaño. Mientras mayor sea el número, más pequeño será el diámetro del conductor.

Ground   The common negative connection of the electrical system. It is the point of lowest voltage.

Tierra   Conexión negativa común del sistema eléctrico. Es el punto de tensión más baja.

Grounded circuit   An electrical defect that allows current to return to ground before it has reached the intended load component.

Circuito puesto a tierra   Falla eléctrica que permite el regreso de corriente a tierra antes de alcanzar el componente de carga deseado.

Ground side   The portion of the circuit that is from the load component to the negative side of the source.

Lado a tierra   Parte del circuito que va del componente de carga al lado negativo de la fuente.

Half-wave rectification   Rectification of one-half of an ac voltage.

Rectificación de media onda   Rectificación en la que la corriente fluye únicamente durante semiciclos alternados.

Hall-effect switch   A sensor that operates on the principle that if a current is allowed to flow through thin conducting material being exposed to a magnetic field, another voltage is produced.

Conmutador de efecto Hall   Sensor que funciona basado en el principio de que si se permite el flujo de corriente a través de un material conductor delgado que ha sido expuesto a un campo magnético, se produce otra tensión.

Halogen   The term used to identify a group of chemically related nonmetallic elements. These elements include chlorine, fluorine, and iodine.

Halógeno   Término utilizado para identificar un grupo de elementos no metálicos relacionados químicamente. Dichos elementos incluyen el cloro, el flúor y el yodo.

Hand tools Tools that use only the force generated from the body to operate. They multiply the force received through leverage to accomplish the work.

Herramientas manuales Herramientas que para funcionar sólo necesitan la fuerza generada por el cuerpo. Para llevar a cabo el trabajo, las herramientas multiplican la fuerza que reciben por medio de la palancada.

Heat sink An object that absorbs and dissipates heat from another object.

Dispersador térmico Objeto que absorbe y disipa el calor de otro objeto.

H-gate A set of four transistors that can reverse current.

Compuerta H Juego de cuatro transistores que pueden invertir la corriente.

Hoist A lift that is used to raise the entire vehicle.

Elevador Montacargas utilizado para elevar el vehículo en su totalidad.

Hole The absence of an electron in an element's atom. These holes are said to be positively charged since they have a tendency to attract free electrons into the hole.

Agujero Ausencia de un electrón en el átomo de un elemento. Se dice que dichos agujeros tienen una carga positiva puesto que tienden a atraer electrones libres hacia el agujero.

Hydrometer A test instrument used to check the specific gravity of the electrolyte to determine the battery's state of charge.

Hidrómetro Instrumento de prueba utilizado para verificar la gravedad específica del electrolito y así determinar el estado de la carga de la batería.

Incandescence The process of changing energy forms to produce light.

Incandescencia Proceso a través del cual se cambian las formas de energía para producir luz.

Induced voltage Voltage that is produced in a conductor as a result of relative motion within magnetic flux lines.

Tensión inducida Tensión producida en un conductor como resultado del movimiento relativo dentro de líneas de flujo magnético.

Induction The magnetic process of producing a current flow in a wire without any actual contact to the wire. To induce 1 volt, 100 million magnetic lines of force must be cut per second.

Inducción Proceso magnético a través del cual se produce un flujo de corriente en un alambre sin contacto real alguno con el alambre. Para inducir 1 voltio, deben producirse 100 millones de líneas de fuerza magnética por segundo.

Inertia engagement A type of starter motor that uses rotating inertia to engage the drive pinion with the engine flywheel.

Conexión por inercia Tipo de motor de arranque que utiliza inercia giratoria para engranar el piñón de mando con el volante de la máquina.

Instrument voltage regulator (IVR) Provides a constant voltage to the gauge, regardless of the voltage output of the charging system.

Instrumento regulador de tensión Le provee tensión constante al calibrador, sin importar cual sea la salida de tensión del sistema de carga.

Insulated side The portion of the circuit from the positive side of the source to the load component.

Lado aislado Parte del circuito que va del lado positivo de la fuente al componente de carga.

Insulator A substance that is not capable of supporting the flow of electricity.

Aislador Sustancia que no es capaz de soportar el flujo de electricidad.

Integrated circuit (IC chip) A complex circuit of thousands of transistors, diodes, resistors, capacitors, and other electronic devices that are formed onto a small silicon chip. As many as 30,000 transistors can be placed on a chip that is 1/4 inch (6.35 mm) square.

Circuito integrado (Fragmento CI) Circuito complejo de miles de transistores, diodos, resistores, condensadores, y otros dispositivos electrónicos formados en un fragmento pequeño de silicio. En un fragmento de 1/4 de pulgada (6,35 mm) cuadrada, pueden colocarse hasta 30.000 transistores.

Interface Used to protect the computer from excessive voltage levels and to translate input and output signals.

Interfase Utilizada para proteger la computadora de niveles excesivos de tensión y traducir señales de entrada y salida.

Ion An atom or group of atoms that has an electrical charge.

Ion Átomo o grupo de átomos que poseen una carga eléctrica.

Jack stands Support devices used to hold the vehicle off the floor after it has been raised by the floor jack.

Soportes de gato Dispositivos de soporte utilizados para sostener el vehículo sobre el suelo después de haber sido levantado con el gato de pie.

Lamp A device that produces light as a result of current flow through a filament. The filament is enclosed within a glass envelope and is a type of resistance wire that is generally made from tungsten.

Lámpara Dispositivo que produce luz como resultado del flujo de corriente a través de un filamento. El filamento es un tipo de alambre de resistencia hecho por lo general de tungsteno, que es encerrado dentro de una bombilla.

Lamp outage module A current-measuring sensor that contains a set of resistors, wired in series with the power supply to the headlights, taillights, and stop lights. If the sensor indicates that a lamp is burned out, the module will alert the driver.

Unidad de avería de la lámpara Sensor para medir corriente que incluye un juego de resistores, alambrado en serie con la fuente de alimentación a los faros delanteros, traseros y a las luces de freno. Si el sensor indica que se ha apagado una lámpara, la unidad le avisará al conductor.

Light-emitting diode (LED) A gallium-arsenide diode that converts the energy developed when holes and electrons collide during normal diode operation into light.

Diodo emisor de luz Diodo semiconductor de galio y arseniuro que convierte en luz la energía producida por la colisión de agujeros y electrones durante el funcionamiento normal del diodo.

Linearity Refers to the sensor signal being as constantly proportional to the measured value as possible. It is an expression of the sensor's accuracy.

Linealidad Significa que la variación del valor de una magnitud es lo más proporcional posible a la variación del valor de otra magnitud. Expresa la precisión del sensor.

Liquid crystal display (LCD) A display that sandwiches electrodes and polarized fluid between layers of glass. When voltage is applied to the electrodes, the light slots of the fluid are rearranged to allow light to pass through.

Visualizador de cristal líquido Visualizador digital que consta de dos láminas de vidrio selladas, entre las cuales se encuentran los electrodos y el fluido polarizado. Cuando se aplica tensión a los electrodos, se rompe la disposición de las moléculas para permitir la formación de caracteres visibles.

Logic gates Electronic circuits that act as gates to output voltage signals depending on different combinations of input signals.

Compuertas lógicas Circuitos electrónicos que gobiernan señales de tensión de salida, dependiendo de las diferentes combinaciones de señales de entrada.

Magnetic field The area surrounding a magnet where energy is exerted due to the atoms aligning in the material.

Campo magnético Espacio que rodea un imán donde se emplea la energía debido a la alineación de los átomos en el material.

Magnetic flux density The concentration of the magnetic lines of force.

Densidad de flujo magnético Número de líneas de fuerza magnética.

Magnetic pulse generator Sensor that uses the principle of magnetic induction to produce a voltage signal. Magnetic pulse generators are commonly used to send data to the computer concerning the speed of the monitored component.

Generador de impulsos magnéticos Sensor que funciona según el principio de inducción magnética para producir una señal de tensión. Los generadores de impulsos magnéticos se utilizan comúnmente para transmitir datos a la computadora relacionados a la velocidad del componente regulado.

Magnetism An energy form resulting from atoms aligning within certain materials, giving the materials the ability to attract other metals.

Magnetismo Forma de energía que resulta de la alineación de átomos dentro de ciertos materiales y que le da a éstos la capacidad de atraer otros metales.

Maxi-fuse A circuit protection device that looks similar to a blade-type fuse except that it is larger and has a higher amperage capacity. Maxi-fuses are used because they are less likely to cause an underhood fire when there is an overload in the circuit. If the fusible link burned in two, it is possible that the "hot" side of the fuse could come into contact with the vehicle frame and the wire could catch on fire.

Maxifusible Dispositivo de protección del circuito parecido a un fusible de tipo de cuchilla, pero más grande y con mayor capacidad de amperaje. Se utilizan maxifusibles porque existen menos probabilidades de que ocasionen un incendio debajo de la capota cuando ocurra una sobrecarga en el circuito. Si el cartucho de fusible se quemase en dos partes, es posible que el lado "cargado" del fusible entre en contacto con el armazón del vehículo y que el alambre se encienda.

Momentary contact A switch type that operates only when held in position.

Contacto momentáneo Tipo de conmutador que funciona solamente cuando se mantiene en su posición.

Multiplexing A means of transmitting information between computers. It is a system in which electrical signals are transmitted by a peripheral serial bus instead of conventional wires, allowing several devices to share signals on a common conductor.

Multiplexaje Medio de transmitir información entre computadoras. Es un sistema en el cual las señales eléctricas son transmitidas por una colectora periférica en serie en vez de por líneas convencionales. Esto permite que varios dispositivos compartan señales en un conductor común.

Mutual induction A desirable induction.

Inducción mutua Inducción deseable.

Negative logic Defines the most negative voltage as a logical 1 in the binary code.

Lógica negativa Define la tensión más negativa como un 1 lógico en el código binario.

Negative temperature coefficient (NTC) thermistors Thermistors that reduce their resistance as the temperature increases.

Termistores con coeficiente negativo de temperatura Termistores que disminuyen su resistencia según aumenta la temperatura.

Neutral atom *See* balanced atom.

Átomo neutro *Véase* átomo equilibrado.

Neutral junction The center connection to which the common ends of a Y-type stator winding are connected.

Empalme neutro Conexión central a la cual se conectan los extremos comunes de un devanado del estátor de tipo Y.

Neutrons Particles of an atom that have no charge.

Neutrones Partículas de un átomo desprovistas de carga.

Nonvolatile RAM RAM memory that will retain its memory if battery voltage is disconnected. NVRAM is a combination of RAM and EEPROM into the same chip. During normal operation, data is written to and read from the RAM portion of the chip. If the power is removed from the chip, or at programmed timed intervals, the data is transferred from RAM to the EEPROM portion of the chip. When the power is restored to the chip, the EEPROM will write the data back to the RAM.

Memoria de acceso aleatorio no volátil [NV RAM] Memoria de acceso aleatorio (RAM) que retiene su memoria si se desconecta la carga de la batería. La NV RAM es una combinación de RAM y EEPROM en el mismo fragmento. Durante el funcionamiento normal, los datos se escriben en y se leen de la parte RAM del fragmento. Si se remueve la alimentación del fragmento, o si se remueve ésta a intervalos programados, se transfieren los datos de la RAM a la parte del EEPROM del fragmento. Cuando se restaura la alimentación en el fragmento, el EEPROM volverá a escribir los datos en la RAM.

Normally closed (NC) switch A switch designation denoting that the contacts are closed until acted upon by an outside force.

Conmutador normalmente cerrado Nombre aplicado a un conmutador cuyos contactos permanecerán cerrados hasta que sean accionados por una fuerza exterior.

Normally open (NO) switch A switch designation denoting that the contacts are open until acted upon by an outside force.

Conmutador normalmente abierto Nombre aplicado a un conmutador cuyos contactos permanecerán abiertos hasta que sean accionados por una fuerza exterior.

N-type material When there are free electrons, the material is called an N-type material. The N means negative and indicates that it is the negative side of the circuit that pushes electrons through the semiconductor and the positive side that attracts the free electrons.

Material tipo N Al material se le llama material tipo N cuando hay electrones libres. La N significa negativo e indica que el lado negativo del circuito empuja los electrones a través del semiconductor y el lado positivo atrae los electrones libres.

Nucleus The core of an atom that contains the protons and neutrons.

Núcleo Parte central de un átomo que contiene los protones y los neutrones.

Occupational safety glasses Eye protection that is designed with special high-impact lens and frames, and provides for side protection.

Gafas de protección para el trabajo Gafas diseñadas con cristales y monturas especiales resistentes y provistas de protección lateral.

Odometer A mechanical counter in the speedometer unit indicating total miles accumulated on the vehicle.

Odómetro Aparato mecánico en la unidad del velocímetro con el que se cuentan las millas totales recorridas por el vehículo.

Ohm Unit of measure for resistance. One ohm is the resistance of a conductor such that a constant current of 1 ampere in it produces a voltage of 1 volt between its ends.

Ohmio Unidad de resistencia eléctrica. Un ohmio es la resistencia de un conductor si una corriente constante de 1 amperio en el conductor produce una tensión de 1 voltio entre los dos extremos.

Ohmmeter A test meter used to measure resistance and continuity in a circuit.

Ohmiómetro Instrumento de prueba utilizado para medir la resistencia y la continuidad en un circuito.

Ohm's law Defines the relationship between current, voltage, and resistance.

Ley de Ohm Define la relación entre la corriente, la tensión y la resistencia.

Open circuit A term used to indicate that current flow is stopped. By opening the circuit, the path for electron flow is broken.

Circuito abierto Término utilizado para indicar que el flujo de corriente ha sido detenido. Al abrirse el circuito, se interrumpe la trayectoria para el flujo de electrones.

Oscillate Fast back and forth movement.
Oscilar Moverse rápidamente de atrás para adelante.

Overload Excess current flow in a circuit.
Sobrecarga Flujo de corriente superior a la que tiene asignada un circuito.

Parallel circuit A circuit that provides two or more paths for electricity to flow.
Circuito en paralelo Circuito que provee dos o más trayectorias para que circule la electricidad.

Parasitic loads Electrical loads that are still present when the ignition switch is in the OFF position.
Cargas parásitas Cargas eléctricas que todavía se encuentran presente cuando el botón conmutador de encendido está en la posición OFF.

Park switch Contact points located inside the wiper motor assembly that supply current to the motor after the wiper control switch has been turned to the PARK position. This allows the motor to continue operating until the wipers have reached their PARK position.
Conmutador PARK Puntos de contacto ubicados dentro del conjunto del motor del frotador que le suministran corriente al motor después de que el conmutador para el control de los frotadores haya sido colocado en la posición PARK. Esto permite que el motor continue su funcionamiento hasta que los frotadores hayan alcanzado la posición original.

Passive suspension systems Use fixed spring rates and shock valving.
Sistemas pasivos de suspensión Utilizan elasticidad de muelle constante y dotación con válvulas amortigadoras.

Permeability Term used to indicate the magnetic conductivity of a substance compared with the conductivity of air. The greater the permeability, the greater the magnetic conductivity and the easier a substance can be magnetized.
Permeabilidad Término utilizado para indicar la aptitud de una sustancia en relación con la del aire, de dar paso a las líneas de fuerza magnética. Mientras mayor sea la permeabilidad, mayor será la conductividad magnética y más fácilmente se comunicará a un cuerpo propiedades magnéticas.

Photocell A variable resistor that uses light to change resistance.
Fotocélula Resistor variable que utiliza luz para cambiar la resistencia.

Phototransistor A transistor that is sensitive to light.
Fototransistor Transistor sensible a la luz.

Photovoltaic diodes Diodes capable of producing a voltage when exposed to radiant energy.
Diodos fotovoltaicos Diodos capaces de generar una tensión cuando se encuentran expuestos a la energía de radiación.

Pickup coil The stationary component of the magnetic pulse generator consisting of a weak permanent magnet that has fine wire wound around it. As the timing disc rotates in front of it, the changes of magnetic lines of force generate a small voltage signal in the coil.
Bobina captadora Componente fijo del generador de impulsos magnéticos compuesta de un imán permanente débil devanado con alambre fino. Mientras gira el disco sincronizador enfrente de él, los cambios de las líneas de fuerza magnética generan una pequeña señal de tensión en la bobina.

Piezoelectricity Voltage produced by the application of pressure to certain crystals.
Piezoelectricidad Generación de polarización eléctrica en ciertos cristales a consecuencia de la aplicación de tensiones mecánicas.

Piezoresistive sensor A sensor that is sensitive to pressure changes.
Sensor piezoresistivo Sensor susceptible a los cambios de presión.

P-material Silicon or germanium that is doped with boron or gallium to create a shortage of electrons.
Material-P Boro o galio añadidos al silicio o al germanio para crear una insuficiencia de electrones.

Pneumatic tools Power tools that are powered by compressed air.
Herrimientas neumáticas Herramientas mecánicas accionadas por aire comprimido.

PN junction The point at which two opposite kinds of semiconductor materials are joined together.
Unión pn Zona de unión en la que se conectan dos tipos opuestos de materiales semiconductores.

Pole shoes The components of an electric motor that are made of high-magnetic permeability material to help concentrate and direct the lines of force in the field assembly.
Expansión polar Componentes de un motor eléctrico hechos de material magnético de gran permeabilidad para ayudar a concentrar y dirigir las líneas de fuerza en el conjunto inductor.

Positive temperature coefficient (PTC) thermistors Thermistors that increase their resistance as the temperature increases.
Termistores con coeficiente positivo de temperatura Termistores que aumentan su resistencia según aumenta la temperatura.

Potentiometer A variable resistor that acts as a circuit divider to provide accurate voltage drop readings proportional to movement.
Potenciómetro Resistor variable que actúa como un divisor de circuito para obtener lecturas de perdidas de tensión precisas en proporcion con el movimiento.

Power tools Tools that use forces other than those generated from the body. They can use compressed air, electricity, or hydraulic pressure to generate and multiply force.
Herramientas mecánicas Herramientas que utilizan fuerzas distintas a las generadas por el cuerpo. Dichas fuerzas pueden ser el aire comprimido, la electricidad, o la presión hidráulica para generar y multiplicar la fuerza.

Primary wiring Conductors that carry low voltage and current. The insulation of primary wires is usually thin.
Hilos primarios Hilos conductores de tensión y corriente bajas. El aislamiento de hilos primarios es normalmente delgado.

Program A set of instructions that the computer must follow to achieve desired results.
Programa Conjunto de instrucciones que la computadora debe seguir para lograr los resultados deseados.

PROM (programmable read only memory) Memory chip that contains specific data that pertains to the exact vehicle in which the computer is installed. This information may be used to inform the CPU of the accessories that are equipped on the vehicle.
PROM (memoria de sólo lectura programable) Fragmento de memoria que contiene datos específicos referentes al vehículo particular en el que se instala la computadora. Esta información puede utilizarse para informar a la UCP sobre los accesorios de los cuales el vehículo está dotado.

Protection device Circuit protector that is designed to "turn off" the system that it protects. This is done by creating an open to prevent a complete circuit.
Dispositivo de protección Protector de circuito diseñado para "desconectar" el sistema al que provee protección. Esto se hace abriendo el circuito para impedir un circuito completo.

Proton Positively charged particles contained in the nucleus of an atom.
Protón Partículas con carga positiva que se encuentran en el núcleo de todo átomo.

Prove-out circuit A function of the ignition switch that completes the warning light circuit to ground through the ignition switch when it is in the START position. The warning light will be on during engine cranking to indicate to the driver that the bulb is working properly.
Circuito de prueba Función del botón conmutador de encendido que completa el circuito de la luz de aviso para que se ponga a tierra a través del botón conmutador de encendido cuando éste se encuentra en la posición START. La luz de aviso se encenderá durante el

arranque del motor para avisarle al conductor que la bombilla funciona correctamente.

Pulse width   The length of time in milliseconds that an actuator is energized.

Duración de impulsos   Espacio de tiempo en milisegundos en el que se excita un accionador.

Pulse width modulation   On/off cycling of a component. The period of time for each cycle does not change, only the amount of on time in each cycle changes.

Modulación de duración de impulsos   Modulación de impulsos de un componente. El espacio de tiempo de cada ciclo no varía; lo que varía es la cantidad de trabajo efectivo de cada ciclo.

Radiofrequency interference (RFI)   Radio and television interference caused by electromagnetic energy.

Interferencia de frecuencia radioeléctrica   Interferencia en la radio y en la televisión producida por energía electromagnética.

RAM (random access memory)   Stores temporary information that can be read from or written to by the CPU. RAM can be designed as volatile or nonvolatile.

RAM (memoria de acceso aleatorio)   Almacena datos temporales que la UCP puede leer o escribir. La RAM puede ser volátil o no volátil.

Rectification   The converting of ac current to dc current.

Rectificación   Proceso a través del cual la corriente alterna es transformada en una corriente continua.

Relay   A device that uses low current to control a high-current circuit. Low current is used to energize the electromagnetic coil, while high current is able to pass over the relay contacts.

Relé   Dispositivo que utiliza corriente baja para controlar un circuito de corriente alta. La corriente baja se utiliza para excitar la bobina electromagnética, mientras que la corriente alta puede transmitirse a través de los contactos del relé.

Reluctance   A term used to indicate a material's resistance to the passage of flux lines.

Reluctancia   Término utilizado para señalar la resistencia ofrecida por un circuito al paso del flujo magnético.

Reserve-capacity rating   An indicator, in minutes, of how long the vehicle can be driven, with the headlights on, if the charging system should fail. The reserve-capacity rating is determined by the length of time, in minutes, that a fully charged battery can be discharged at 25 amperes before battery cell voltage drops below 1.75 volts per cell.

Clasificación de capacidad en reserva   Indicación, en minutos, de cuánto tiempo un vehículo puede continuar siendo conducido, con los faros delanteros encendidos, en caso de que ocurriese una falla en el sistema de carga. La clasificación de capacidad en reserva se determina por el espacio de tiempo, en minutos, en el que una batería completamente cargada puede descargarse a 25 amperios antes de que la tensión del acumulador de la batería disminuya a un nivel inferior de 1,75 amperios por acumulador.

Resistance   Opposition to current flow.

Resistencia   Oposición que presenta un conductor al paso de la corriente eléctrica.

Reversed-bias   A positive voltage is applied to the N-type material and negative voltage is applied to the P-type material of a semiconductor.

Polarización inversa   Tensión positiva aplicada al material N y tensión negativa aplicada al material P de un semiconductor.

Rheostat   A two-terminal variable resistor used to regulate the strength of an electrical current.

Reóstato   Resistor variable de dos bornes utilizado para regular la resistencia de una corriente eléctrica.

ROM (read only memory)   Memory chip that stores permanent information. This information is used to instruct the computer on what to do in response to input data. The CPU reads the information contained in ROM, but it cannot write to it or change it.

ROM (memoria de sólo lectura)   Fragmento de memoria que almacena datos en forma permanente. Dichos datos se utilizan para darle instrucciones a la computadora sobre cómo dirigir la ejecución de una operación de entrada. La UCP lee los datos que contiene la ROM, pero no puede escribir en ella o puede cambiarla.

Rotor   The component of the ac generator that is rotated by the drive belt and creates the rotating magnetic field of the ac generator.

Rotor   Parte rotativa del generador de corriente alterna accionada por la correa de transmisión y que produce el campo magnético rotativo del generador de corriente alterna.

Safety goggles   Eye protection device that fits against the face and forehead to seal off the eyes from outside elements.

Gafas de seguridad   Dispositivo protector que se coloca delante de los ojos para preservarlos de elementos extraños.

Safety stands   *See* Jack stands.

Soportes de seguridad   *Véase* soportes de gato.

Saturation   1. The point at which the magnetic strength eventually levels off, and where an additional increase of the magnetizing force current no longer increases the magnetic field strength. 2. The point where forward-bias voltage to the base leg is at a maximum. With bias voltage at the high limits, output current is also at its maximum.

Saturación   1. Máxima potencia posible de un campo magnético, donde un aumento adicional de la corriente de fuerza magnética no logra aumentar la potencia del campo magnético. 2. La tensión de polarización directa a la base está en su máximo. Ya que polarización directa ha alcanzado su límite máximo, la corriente de salida también alcanza éste.

Sealed-beam headlight   A self-contained glass unit that consists of a filament, an inner reflector, and an outer glass lens.

Faro delantero sellado   Unidad de vidrio que contiene un filamento, un reflector interior y una lente exterior de vidrio.

Secondary wiring   Conductors, such as battery cables and ignition spark plug wires, that are used to carry high voltage or high current. Secondary wires have extra thick insulation.

Hilos secundarios   Conductores, tales como cables de batería e hilos de bujías del encendido, utilizados para transmitir tensión o corriente alta. Los hilos secundarios poseen un aislamiento sumamente grueso.

Semiconductor   An element that is neither a conductor nor an insulator. Semiconductors are materials that conduct electric current under certain conditions, yet will not conduct under other conditions.

Semiconductor   Elemento que no es ni conductor ni aislante. Los semiconductores son materiales que transmiten corriente eléctrica bajo ciertas circunstancias, pero no la transmiten bajo otras.

Sender unit   The sensor for the gauge. It is a variable resistor that changes resistance values with changing monitored conditions.

Unidad emisora   Sensor para el calibrador. Es un resistor variable que cambia los valores de resistencia según cambian las condiciones reguladas.

Sensor   Any device that provides an input to the computer.

Sensor   Cualquier dispositivo que le transmite información a la computadora.

Series circuit   A circuit that provides a single path for current flow from the electrical source through all the circuit's components, and back to the source.

Circuito en serie   Circuito que provee una trayectoria única para el flujo de corriente de la fuente eléctrica a través de todos los componentes del circuito, y de nuevo hacia la fuente.

Series-parallel circuit   A circuit that has some loads in series and some in parallel.

Circuito en series paralelas   Circuito que tiene unas cargas en serie y otras en paralelo.

Servomotor   An electrical motor that produces rotation of less than a full turn. A feedback mechanism is used to position itself to the exact degree of rotation required.

Servomotor   Motor eléctrico que genera rotación de menos de una revolución completa. Utiliza un mecanismo de realimentación para ubicarse al grado exacto de la rotación requerida.

Shell   The electron orbit around the nucleus of an atom.

Corteza   Órbita de electrones alrededor del núcleo del átomo.

Short   An electrical fault that allows for electrical current to bypass its normal path.

Cortocircuito   Falla eléctrica que permite que la corriente eléctrica se desvíe de su trayectoria normal.

Shunt circuits   The branches of the parallel circuit.

Circuitos en derivación   Las ramas del circuito en paralelo.

Shutter wheel   A metal wheel consisting of a series of alternating windows and vanes. It creates a magnetic shunt that changes the strength of the magnetic field from the permanent magnet of the Hall-effect switch or magnetic pulse generator.

Rueda obturadora   Rueda metálica compuesta de una serie de ventanas y aspas alternas. Genera una derivación magnética que cambia la potencia del campo magnético, del imán permanente del conmutador de efecto Hall o del generador de impulsos magnéticos.

Solenoid   An electromagnetic device that uses movement of a plunger to exert a pulling or holding force.

Solenoide   Dispositivo electromagnético que utiliza el movimiento de un pulsador para ejercer una fuerza de arrastre o de retención.

Source   The portion of a field-effect transistor that supplies the current-carrying holes or electrons.

Fuente   Terminal de un transistor de efecto de campo que provee los agujeros o electrones portadores de corriente.

Specific gravity   The weight of a given volume of a liquid divided by the weight of an equal volume of water.

Gravedad específica   El peso de un volumen dado de líquido dividido por el peso de un volumen igual de agua.

Speedometer   An instrument panel gauge that indicates the speed of the vehicle.

Velocímetro   Calibrador en el panel de instrumentos que marca la velocidad del vehículo.

Starter drive   The part of the starter motor that engages the armature to the engine flywheel ring gear.

Transmisión de arranque   Parte del motor de arranque que engrana la armadura a la corona del volante de la máquina.

State of charge   The condition of a battery's electrolyte and plate materials at any given time.

Estado de carga   Condición del electrolito y de los materiales de la placa de una batería en cualquier momento dado.

Static electricity   Electricity that is not in motion.

Electricidad estática   Electricidad que no está en movimiento.

Stator   The stationary coil of the ac generator where current is produced.

Estátor   Bobina fija del generador de corriente alterna donde se genera corriente.

Stepped resistor   A resistor that has two or more fixed resistor values.

Resistor de secciones escalonadas   Resistor que tiene dos o más valores de resistencia fija.

Stepper motor   An electrical motor that contains a permanent magnet armature with two or four field coils. Can be used to move the controlled device to whatever location is desired. By applying voltage pulses to selected coils of the motor, the armature will turn a specific number of degrees. When the same voltage pulses are applied to the opposite coils, the armature will rotate the same number of degrees in the opposite direction.

Motor paso a paso   Motor eléctrico que contiene una armadura magnética fija con dos o cuatro bobinas inductoras. Puede utilizarse para mover el dispositivo regulado a cualquier lugar deseado. Al aplicárseles impulsos de tensión a ciertas bobinas del motor, la armadura girará un número específico de grados. Cuando estos mismos impulsos de tensión se aplican a las bobinas opuestas, la armadura girará el mismo número de grados en la dirección opuesta.

Tachometer   An instrument that measures the speed of the engine in revolutions per minute (rpm).

Tacómetro   Instrumento que mide la velocidad del motor en revoluciones por minuto (rpm).

Thermistor   A solid-state variable resistor made from a semiconductor material that changes resistance in relation to temperature changes.

Termistor   Resistor variable de estado sólido hecho de un material semiconductor que cambia su resistencia en relación con los cambios de temperatura.

Three-coil gauge   A gauge design that uses the interaction of three electromagnets and the total field effect upon a permanent magnet to cause needle movement.

Calibrador de tres bobinas   Calibrador diseñado para utilizar la interacción de tres electroimanes y el efecto inductor total sobre un imán permanente para producir el movimiento de la aguja.

Throw   Term used in reference to electrical switches or relays referring to the number of output circuits from the switch.

Posición activa   Término utilizado para conmutadores o relés eléctricos en relación con el número de circuitos de salida del conmutador.

Thyristor   A semiconductor switching device composed of alternating N and P layers. It can also be used to rectify current from ac to dc.

Tiristor   Dispositivo de conmutación del semiconductor compuesto de capas alternas de N y P. Puede utilizarse también para rectificar la corriente de corriente alterna a corriente continua.

Transducer   A device that changes energy from one form into another.

Transductor   Dispositivo que cambia la energía de una forma a otra.

Transistor   A three-layer semiconductor used as a very fast switching device.

Transistor   Semiconductor de tres capas utilizado como dispositivo de conmutación sumamente rápido.

Two-coil gauge   A gauge design that uses the interaction of two electromagnets and the total field effect upon an armature to cause needle movement.

Calibrador de dos bobinas   Calibrador diseñado para utilizar la interacción de dos electroimanes y el efecto inductor total sobre una armadura para generar el movimiento de la aguja.

Vacuum distribution valve   A valve used in vacuum-controlled concealed headlight systems. It controls the direction of vacuum to various vacuum motors or to vent.

Válvula de distribución al vacío   Válvula utilizada en el sistema de faros delanteros ocultos controlado al vacío. Regula la dirección del vacío a varios motores al vacío o sirve para dar salida del sistema.

Vacuum fluorescent display (VFD)   A display type that uses anode segments coated with phosphor and bombarded with tungsten electrons to cause the segments to glow.

Visualización de fluorescencia al vacío   Tipo de visualización que utiliza segmentos ánodos cubiertos de fósforo y bombardeados de electrones de tungsteno para producir la luminiscencia de los segmentos.

Valence ring   The outermost orbit of the atom.

Anillo de valencia   Órbita más exterior del átomo.

Variable resistor   A resistor that provides for an infinite number of resistance values within a range.

Resistor variable   Resistor que provee un número infinito de valores de resistencia dentro de un margen.

Volatile RAM   RAM memory that is erased when it is disconnected from its power source. Also known as Keep Alive Memory.

RAM volátil   Memoria RAM cuyos datos se perderán cuando se la desconecta de la fuente de alimentación. Conocida también como memoria de entretenimiento.

Volt   The unit used to measure the amount of electrical force.

Voltio   Unidad práctica de tensión para medir la cantidad de fuerza eléctrica.

Voltage   The difference or potential that indicates an excess of electrons at the end of the circuit the farthest from the electromotive force. It is the electrical pressure that causes electrons to move through a circuit. One volt is the amount of pressure required to move one amp of current through one ohm of resistance.

Tensión   Diferencia o potencial que indica un exceso de electrones al punto del circuito que se encuentra más alejado de la fuerza electromotriz. La presión eléctrica genera el movimiento de electrones a través de un circuito. Un voltio equivale a la cantidad de presión requerida para mover un amperio de corriente a través de un ohmio de resistencia.

Voltage drop   A resistance in the circuit that reduces the electrical pressure available after the resistance. The resistance can be either the load component, the conductors, any connections, or unwanted resistance.

Caída de tensión   Resistencia en el circuito que disminuye la presión eléctrica disponible después de la resistencia. La resistencia puede ser el componente de carga, los conductores, cualquier conexión o resistencia no deseada.

Voltage regulator   Used to control the output voltage of the ac generator, based on charging system demands, by controlling field current.

Regulador de tensión   Dispositivo cuya función es mantener la tensión de salida del generador de corriente alterna, de acuerdo a las variaciones en la corriente de carga, controlando la corriente inductora.

Voltmeter   A test meter used to read the pressure behind the flow of electrons.

Voltímetro   Instrumento de prueba utilizado para medir la presión del flujo de electrones.

Wake-up signal   An input signal used to notify the body computer that an engine start and operation of accessories is going to be initiated soon. This signal is used to warm up the circuits that will be processing information.

Señal despertadora   Señal de entrada para avisarle a la computadora del vehículo que el arranque del motor y el funcionamiento de los accesorios se iniciarán dentro de poco. Dicha señal se utiliza para calentar los circuitos que procesarán los datos.

Warning light   A lamp that is illuminated to warn the driver of a possible problem or hazardous condition.

Luz de aviso   Lámpara que se enciende para avisarle al conductor sobre posibles problemas o condiciones peligrosas.

Watt   The unit of measure of electrical power, which is the equivalent of horsepower. One horsepower is equal to 746 watts.

Watio   Unidad de potencia eléctrica, equivalente a un caballo de vapor. 746 watios equivalen a un caballo de vapor (CV).

Wattage   A measure of the total electrical work being performed per unit of time.

Vataje   Medida del trabajo eléctrico total realizado por unidad de tiempo.

Wheatstone bridge   A series-parallel arrangement of resistors between an input terminal and ground.

Puente de Wheatstone   Conjunto de resistores en series paralelas entre un borne de entrada y tierra.

Wiring diagram   An electrical schematic that shows a representation of actual electrical or electronic components and the wiring of the vehicle's electrical systems.

Esquema de conexciones   Esquema en el que se muestran las conexiones internas de los componentes eléctricos o electrónicos reales y las de los sistemas eléctricos del vehículo.

Wiring harness   A group of wires enclosed in a conduit and routed to specific areas of the vehicle.

Cableado preformado   Conjunto de alambres envueltos en un conducto y dirigidos hacia áreas específicas del vehículo.

Y-type stator   A three-winding ac generator that has one end of each winding connected at the neutral junction.

Estátor de tipo Y   Generador de corriente alterna de devanado triple; un extremo de cada devanado se conecta al empalme neutro.

Zener diode   A diode that allows reverse current to flow above a set voltage limit.

Diodo Zener   Diodo que permite que el flujo de corriente en dirección inversa sobrepase el límite de tensión determinado.

Zener voltage   The voltage that is reached when a diode conducts in reverse direction.

Tensión de Zener   Tensión alcanzada cuando un diodo conduce en una dirección inversa.

INDEX

Note: Page numbers in **BOLD type** reference non-text material.

Exclusive-OR gate, 335
Exterior lights, 154
External grounded field circuit, **252**
Eye, protection, 2–5

Face shield, **3**
Farads, defined, **26**
Feedback
    defined, **177**
    signals, 349
FET transistors, 67–68
Fiber optics, 376–77
Field
    coils, 209–10
    currents, charging system regulation and, 252–53
    effect transistor, 67–68
    relay, **254**
Fire extinguishers, 9–10
Fires, 9
    classes of, **10**
Flash to pass, 153
    circuit, **155**
Flasher, turn signal, **166**
Flip-flop circuits, RS/clocked RS, 336, **337**
Floor jack
    described, **6**
    safety with, 6–7
Flux density
    magnetic
        concentrating, 42, **43**
        described, **39**
        increasing, 42
Ford
    AC generators and, 269–70
    antitheft systems, 461–63
    electronic touch climate control, 427, **430**
    heated windshield, 477
        schematic, **480**
Forward bias, defined, **61**
Fuel
    data center, 409
        circuit for, **410**
        system inputs, **412**
    gauges, digital instrumentation of, 390–91
    level sending unit, 196
    pump, inertia switch, **441**
Full field current, **257**
Full wave rectification, **242**
Fuse box, described, **50**
Fuses, 49–50
    described, **50**
Fusible links, 50, 52

Ganged
    defined, **55**
    switch, 55
Gassing, defined, **121**

Gauges
    air core, 194
    bimetallic, 189–90
    d'Arsonval, 190–91
    defined, **188**
    electromagnetic, 190–94
    instrument voltage regulator, 188–89
        described, **189**
    sending units, 195–96
    three-coil, 191–93
    two-coil, 193–94
Gear reduction starters, 223–24
General Motors
    AC generators and, 268
    air bag system, 446
        component location, **447**
        deployment loop, **447**
        wiring diagram, **448–49**
    antitheft systems, 463–64
    electronic touch climate control, 425–27
    heated windshield, 476–77
        schematic, **478–79**
    sunroof, 458–59
    Twilight Sentinel System, 370, **371**
Generators
    AC, 235–44
        brushes, 237–38
        brushless, 273
        currents, 246–47
        diode rectifier bridge, 240–44
        housing/cooling fan, 245–46
        operation overview, 247–51
        rotors, 235–37
        stators, 238–40
    DC, 234
    magnetic pulse, 344–46
    permanent magnet, **344**
Germanium, crystal structure, **38**
Glasses, safety, **2**
Goggles, safety, **3**
Grids
    battery, 117
    growth of, **122, 123**
Ground circuit, **81, 82**
    described, **22**

H-gate, described, 387
Half field current, **257**
Half-wave rectification, **241**
Hall-effect switches, 347–48
Halogen headlights, 139–40
Hand tools
    described, **5**
    safety with, 5
Harness, wiring, 96–97
Hazard warning system, **166**
    current flow in, **168**